FOURTH EDITION

D1119109

02/07
27.50

The
Promotable
WOMAN

Norma Carr-Ruffino, Ph.D.

CAREER
PRESS
Franklin Lakes, NJ

THE PROMOTABLE WOMAN, 4TH EDITION
TYPESET BY EILEEN DOW MUNSON
Cover design by Cheryl Cohan Finbow
Printed in the U.S.A. by Book-mart Press

To order this title, please call toll-free 1-800-CAREER-1 (NJ and Canada: 201-848-0310) to order using VISA or MasterCard, or for further information on books from Career Press.

The Career Press, Inc., 3 Tice Road, PO Box 687,
Franklin Lakes, NJ 07417
www.careerpress.com

Library of Congress Cataloging-in-Publication Data

Carr-Ruffino, Norma.
    The Promotable woman / by Norma Carr-Ruffino.--4th ed.
        p. cm.
    Includes index.
    ISBN 1-56414-776-2 (paper)
        1. Women executives. 2. Executive ability. 3. Management. 4. Women employees--Promotions.
        I. Title.

HD6054.3.C37 2005
658.4'09'082--dc22

2004054482

Contents

How This Book Can Change Your Life

If you're a woman who works, you know that managing a career and getting ahead is different for you than it is for your male coworkers. For one thing, the corporate culture where you work is likely to reflect male values and workstyles. Most of the role models at the top are likely to be men. Most people in our culture expect that men will have careers, be the main providers for their families, and aspire to leadership positions. They expect that women will take primary responsibility for housework and childcare. These traditional expectations mean that you, as a career woman, face challenges and opportunities that are different from those of career men.

Overcoming old obstacles. Career women were rare before the 1970s, and the cultural beliefs that kept them at home or in menial-level jobs are still around, creating obstacles to career success. The greatest obstacles are old stereotypes about women's suitability for the business world, their level of career commitment, their emotional stability, their ability to gain acceptance in high positions, and their decision-making ability—in general, their credibility as effective leaders and professionals. It's bad enough when people in your workplace hold these stereotypes, but it's worse when you hold them yourself. And when you're unaware that you hold them, it can be disastrous.

This book can change your life if you're ready to recognize your self-limiting beliefs and replace them with self-empowering beliefs—and if you're ready to gain power and credibility in today's corporate cultures. In this book, you'll learn how to do that, as well as how to create your own success by identifying the type of life and career you want and using powerful strategies and techniques for achieving it. You'll master strategies for overcoming role conflict and the heavy demands placed upon you as a working wife or mother by learning to balance multiple priorities and to minimize stress. You'll learn how to process your emotions so that they become a power source rather than a liability. And you'll master strategies for speaking up in a man's world while retaining the best of your feminine leadership style.

Seeing new opportunities for women. As you grew up, you were probably rewarded when you let go of your ego and status concerns and focused on building close personal relationships, accepting people's odd ways, intuitively tuning in to people, and bringing people together in cooperative efforts. Meanwhile, the boys you knew were being rewarded for competing effectively, building status and credibility among the other boys, and guarding that status. Competition and status are the name of the game in traditional organizations, so men's socialization has always been a career advantage in these arenas.

During the 1990s, many business leaders began to recognize that an increasingly high-tech workplace and global marketplace called for a high-personal-touch leadership style, a style that tends to come naturally to most women. In more and more organizations, this leadership style is exactly what's needed to inspire and motivate today's well-educated, technically savvy employees. This facilitative style is what effective teams need as they become more self-managing and innovative. If you develop high-tech skills and build upon them—and if you combine this with a people-focused leadership style—you offer an unbeatable combination to any forward-thinking organization. That's your woman's advantage; in this book, you'll learn how to use it most effectively.

Creating a better world. This book is intended to help you grow personally and professionally. When you build your reputation as an effective leader and professional person, you also build the reputation of career women in general. I urge you to share with other women the knowledge and awareness you gain through this exciting process of growth and development. As we support one another, we not only help ourselves, we also increase the level of acceptance for women in leadership roles; we open a little wider the doors of opportunity for all types of people who in the past were considered unsuitable for such roles. This mutual support and self-effort can also help build a stronger democratic society and create a better world for women *and* men everywhere. As Margaret Mead said, "Never doubt that a small group of thoughtful, committed citizens can change the world. Indeed, it is the only thing that ever has."

Giving thanks. I'm especially grateful to the many people who helped to define and shape this book, including:

> The editors and reviewers who queried and suggested.

> The participants who attended my seminars throughout the United States and my courses at San Francisco State University—who told me what they needed more of and less of.

> The graduate research assistants who poked through library stacks and surfed the Internet to bring my files up to date.

Many of these women have shared with me the ways in which these materials have changed their lives. Our goal is to create a book that will help you change yours.

Dedicating: Finally, I want to thank my family and to dedicate this book to

Fredo
and to the women in my family:
Andrea, Ava, Bobbie, Elisha,
Lauren, Meghan, Natalie, and Vickie Smith,
Erica Carr Black, Frances Carr,
and Linda Ruffino Benvenuto

—Norma Carr-Ruffino, Ph.D.

Maximize Your Innate People Skills and Creativity

All acts performed in the world begin in the imagination.
—Barbara Grizzuti Harrison

The ever-changing business world has survived the dot-com bust and has become more interconnected than ever. Wired, "internetted," webbed, computerized, high-tech, service-oriented, knowledge-based, and globally connected—the typical business today bears little resemblance to the traditional hierarchies of the past.

Such dramatic change breaks up old male-only enclaves and opens doors to anyone who can help leaders figure out how to capitalize on the opportunities and fend off the threats. It offers exciting opportunities for women who learn to maximize their innate advantages, which include their:

▶ People-orientation.
▶ Drive to connect and build relationships.
▶ Emotional Intelligence based on empathy and compassion.
▶ Intuitive Intelligence that receives information from many "non-rational" sources.
▶ Creative Intelligence, based on these skills, which can fuel vital business innovations.

When you integrate these innate advantages into leadership, entrepreneurial, and management skills, you can find exciting career niches in the emerging new business paradigms.

Before exploring some specific ways that women use to thrive in this changing business scenario, see how your own beliefs fit in.

How does women's leadership style fit in today's business world?

1. Are demands for innovation in business best fulfilled by women's typical traits and style? Or by men's?
2. Do employees who are well-educated and independent work best with the leadership styles most typical of women? Or of men?
3. Do people perceive women as more dependable and honest than men in business dealings?

Rapid technological change offers you the greatest opportunity if you learn how to take the lead in successfully anticipating cultural, marketplace, and technological paradigm shifts. Change also offers you opportunities to take such actions as creating innovative teams that build insightful scenarios of the future and anticipate the opportunities such scenarios offer the company. Change provides chances for you to become entrepreneurial and innovative enough to create business ventures that fill customer needs.

Today's leaders must rely on their intuitive insights, knowledge of the trends, and skills at scanning, visioning, and motivating people. This means your natural woman's ways of leading can boost your chances of career success. It also means that you, as a woman, have wide-open career opportunities—as never before. Companies are looking for the right combination of skills and advantages. If you have the marketplace skills to produce needed results—and you're willing to use them—you can be wildly successful in today's workplace. Not only that, but being a woman is actually becoming a workplace advantage for reasons like these:

▶ As newcomers to the halls of business power, women bring a fresh perspective that can help companies identify shifting paradigms and adjust their priorities accordingly.

▶ Women's participative, supportive ways of leading are the ways needed in a workplace of well-educated technical and professional employees.

▶ Women's openness to inner creativity and intuitive insights allow them to become prolific in the creative problem-solving that's so important for creating and cashing in on paradigm shifts.

▶ As customers, suppliers, employees, and other stakeholders in the company's operation become more diverse, corporate leaders must also be diverse in order to fully understand these stakeholders and meet their needs and wants. Women not only understand women's issues, needs, and wants, they're also likely to understand diversity issues and to empathize readily with all types of people.

You can adopt several major strategies to make the most of your woman's advantage in these new scenarios.

▶ First, understand how women's leadership methods differ from men's and where your advantage may lie.

▶ Second, learn to recognize paradigm patterns. This will increase your chances of leading the way to new paradigms, entrepreneuring new business ventures within and between paradigms, and managing in ways that enhance current paradigms.

▶ Third, understand those major cultural and marketplace paradigm shifts that most affect you as a woman.

▶ Fourth, build upon those ways of leading that come most naturally to you as a woman.

▶ Fifth, understand the major technological paradigm shifts that are occurring.

▶ Sixth, take a leadership role in technological change.

Ann Fudge, CEO of Young & Rubicam, exemplifies many of the trademarks of women's typical leadership style.

Ann Fudge,
CEO of Young & Rubicam

In 2001 Ann Fudge quit her 25-year stint with Kraft Foods, even though she was running a $5 billion division, to take an indefinite sabbatical leave from the world of work. She said that she simply wanted the time to live a fuller life—bicycling in foreign countries, enjoying her weekend home, practicing yoga, and working through books such as *The Artist's Way* to develop creativity. A great release, but few executives are able to return after such a break.

Ann has a life history of breaking with tradition, both as an African American and as an executive woman. While working on her management degree at Simmons College (1973), she married and had a child. While earning a Harvard MBA (1977), she had her second child.

In early 2003 Ann got an offer to return to the executive suite as chairman and CEO of Young & Rubicam Brands and of Y&R, its ad agency. The caller was looking for someone with Ann's people skills and intuitive sense of the market. She was tempted, thinking, "Here's a chance for me to make a real difference in a hurry." She could imagine turning the company from an insular idea factory bogged down in its own turf battles into a client-focused, effective operation. Her vision: A collaborative family of independent businesses working together to diagnose and solve customers' problems

So in 2003 Ann Fudge returned. She faced many challenges. Neglect, executive greed, and a messy merger had resulted in the loss of key accounts, such as Burger King. Billings had fallen from $3.4 billion in 1998, to about $1 billion by 2003. The various divisions of the group rarely collaborated, and many employees were bitter.

Some colleagues admire her vision, intelligence, and warmth, saying she's a breath of fresh air. Others express worry about whether someone who spent two years just hanging out has the 24/7 drive and fire in the belly needed for success at this level. Yet 15-hour days are not rare for her as she travels the world to personally visit people in all the Y&R offices. In the first year she reorganized top staff to make them directly responsible for all their clients' needs and moved to cut costs. She is pushing to gain more business in specific areas—relying on better serving existing clients more than drumming up new ones.

Ann launched an initiative she calls FIT—for focus, innovation, and teamwork—which aims to simplify processes in the ad industry. It's based on the concept of Lean Six Sigma, first developed for manufacturing firms and later adapted to service firms. This approach integrates the production efficiencies of the "lean enterprise" with the cost and quality tools of Six Sigma. Key aspects revolve around how a firm learns to DMAIC; that is, define, measure, analyze, improve, and control its processes. Noting that the approach boosted productivity at Kraft, she says it will free up time for more creativity at Y&R.

Strategy #1

Access Your Innovative Advantage

As a woman, you finally have more advantages than barriers in this hot new arena—if you know how to leverage your innate intelligences into innovative skills. You're advantaged because the culture has given you more freedom and encouragement to express your emotions and to act on your intuition—to use the entire range of your intelligences.

Everyone wants to become more creative—to develop innovative skills, but how?

Why Innovative Skills? Why Now?

Our competitive global marketplace is far more complex and chaotic than anything we humans have ever experienced. And Internet connections have accelerated this complexity, creating a New Net Economy. The infotech marketplace has changed the rules of doing business. It's changed the way we think about the most valuable assets of a business, and even how we view the business itself—as an idea factory. All this means that we've brought about the Innovation Age—a time when innovative skills are seen as a firm's most valuable asset.

Complexity, Chaos, and Innovation

Now is the perfect time to be a creative person because this is the age of complexity thinking, which means thriving on chaos by relaxing and allowing new meaningful patterns to emerge in your mind. Key elements of the New Economy include continually-evolving technological change, lightning-fast global communication, and a constantly-shifting global marketplace. These elements obviously create more chaos than we experienced in the old industrialized economy.

To become a complexity thinker, your first goal is to become comfortable with a certain level of chaos. Just allow it; let it be. Your next goal is to detect patterns emerging from this chaos. Ask yourself, *Which of these patterns points to a new opportunity for me or my company?* Ultimately, you're looking for clues to the Next New Thing—as well as the problems such change can bring. You need to know when and where to bring order to the emerging patterns and how to harness them for your own purposes. That means recognizing what paradigm you're in, when it is about to shift.

Infotech Networks

The New Economy is a networked economy that lets you make your career niche a more innovative one. This economy not only demands that you be more innovative, it richly rewards you when you come through. You can tap into the wealth of information available through the Internet (infotech) to help you clear your mind, to find the space for more communication, and to hurdle barriers to dreaming up new ideas. Infotech is allowing all businesses—even manufacturing firms—to become idea factories.

We've still got to have factories, but we must change their focus from mass production to continuous creativity. All companies must come to see themselves more or less as idea factories. They must apply the principle of interdependency.

Our mindset is shifting from a mechanical, observer-observed separateness to a wholistic, interdependent connectedness. Competition is more about exploiting an aspect of interdependency, of being part of an ecological whole, than about beating out another company. Mastery is about moving from an abstract intellectual understanding of something to an understanding that's cellular, integrated into your worldview.

We have computer networks and related technology that lets us play with ideas without the former limitations of time and space. We can preserve our creative energy while we vastly expand our creative choices.

The global marketplace endlessly demands the imaginative, the new, the experimental, the faster, the better, and the cheaper. The high level of market competition in that world puts a premium on Creative Intelligence and innovative skills—and as a woman you have an innate advantage that you can build upon.

Creative Intelligence: Using All Your Brainpower

You are almost certainly more intelligent than you think you are. That's because you have many types of intelligence—categorized here into seven types—and about 90 percent of your intelligence has little to do with typical cultural ideas about what intelligence is.

Intelligence experts are learning ways to boost overall intelligence—especially Creative Intelligence—by recognizing the various types of intelligence that we humans actually have access to. One powerful approach is to work with seven intelligences that stem from your three brains. You can easily become aware of each type of intelligence when it's in action. You can use some simple techniques for boosting each type of intelligence—and increase your *smarts* throughout your life. Finally, you can practice using each intelligence as you recognize new opportunities and devise new ways to respond to them—and when you generate creative solutions to problems. You can gain skill at weaving together the intelligences you've expanded in ways that produce new ideas and innovations.

You learn how to move beyond the self-limiting patterns and boundaries of your Basic Intelligence, and how to harness the energies of your Motivational and Emotional Intelligences. You can link these powerful lower-level intelligences to your higher-level intelligences, such as intuition. This is how you build your Creative Intelligence and innovative skills.

You can use strategies for recognizing the various types of thinking processes—from rational, logical linear thinking to associative, connective, relationship thinking to sensory thinking that uses your five senses to bring the outside in (visual seeing) and to bring the inside out (imagining, visualizing). You can and do link all these intelligences to your Intuitive Intelligence, which is your connection to the universal Web of Life. You can use your intuition in ways that provide feedback, so you begin to trust your intuitive hits. This weaving together of all the threads of your brainpower equals Creative Intelligence.

This Creative Intelligence model will help you use more of your brainpower—as you become more creative in the way you view reality and function within it, and as you develop the innovative skills you apply to opportunities and problems around you.

PEOPLE USE ONLY ABOUT

10 PERCENT OF THEIR BRAINPOWER.

Intelligence experts have been saying this for decades. Have you ever wondered why we use so little of our brainpower? Most experts now believe it's because of Western culture's love affair with the straight line. In science, academia, and business we have been so caught up in the rational, logical, step-by-step analytical approach, separating ourselves, the observers, from what we're observing, that we've ignored our other types of intelligence. Now we're beginning to see Rational Intelligence as only one of at least seven types of human intelligence. When you do this, you free yourself to use much more of that precious brainpower—and to become much more creative.

As a woman, you already know how to move beyond Rational Intelligence because you regularly use your other intelligences. The advantage is this: When you need creative ideas, you have a whole array of creative resources to pull from. You can learn how your seven innate intelligences feed into the creative process, and how to continually expand those intelligences that make up Creative Intelligence. Then you'll have a set of skills for responding to new opportunities and problems that crop up. You can respond in ways that lead to innovation.

3 Brains = 7 Intelligences

You actually have three brains: the neocortex connected with your thinking processes, the limbic brain connected with your emotional processes, and the basic pattern-parameter brain connected with your instinctual and routine behavior, as symbolically depicted in Snapshot #1. These are related to your seven types of intelligence as follows:

- ▶ Basic Pattern-Parameter—Intelligence concentrated at the base of the brain.
- ▶ Emotional and Motivational—Two intelligences concentrated in the inner midbrain.
- ▶ Rational—Intelligence concentrated in the left neocortex or large forebrain.
- ▶ Associative, Sensory, and Intuitive—Three powerful intelligences concentrated in the right neocortex.

The words *concentrated in* imply that the intelligences are not restricted to a certain part of the body. In fact, research indicates that every cell in your body is highly intelligent, and that *molecules of emotion* travel throughout your body and are an aspect of Emotional Intelligence.

Behavioral Pattern-Parameter Intelligences of the Basic Brain (Doing)

The basic brain consists of your brain stem and spinal cord. It's sometimes called the reptilian brain because it's been in the evolutionary chain the longest of the three brains, and reptiles have this type of brain. Elaine de Beauport, whose research-based book *The Three Faces of Mind* [1996] won a Hoover Book Award, found that three major intelligences stem from this brain: Basic, Pattern, and Parameter Intelligences, which we will combine for discussion purposes. These intelligences are crucial for removing personal blocks to creativity; for example, rigid habit patterns, limits or boundaries you place on yourself, and denial of dreams. But in general, Basic Pattern-Parameter Intelligences are less directly connected to creativity than the other intelligences.

Basic Pattern-Parameter Intelligence focuses on what you instinctively move toward and move away from—those people, situations, and things you tend to seek out and embrace, and those that you avoid. These movements become your habits, routines, and little rituals, and developing this intelligence requires that you recognize your habit patterns and those of others. Most of these patterns are deeply ingrained in your culture and family. They're based on what you were taught and what you decided about life. Some patterns are necessary and helpful in your current life. Other patterns form barriers to creativity and innovation and tend to sabotage your efforts to develop new skills and to change your life.

Parameter Intelligence refers to limits or boundaries. Your basic-brain movements, toward things and away from things, all take place within specific boundaries and limits—your own, those of others, those of organizations. They're related to your territory, your comfort zone, and to the concept of paradigms and paradigm shifts—rules and boundaries for succeeding in a particular situation or paradigm and moving beyond these limits to create new paradigms. You boost your Parameter Intelligence by recognizing unnecessary and limiting boundaries, rules, and paradigms—your own and others.

Emotional Intelligences of the Midbrain (Feeling)

All mammals have a limbic brain. It's sometimes called the middle brain because it lies under the neocortex and above the brain stem. One of its major function is producing the emotions we need in order to conceive and nurture our young and to relate together in groups in order to raise them.

Emotional Intelligence is your awareness, expression, and management of your emotions, your feelings, and your moods. It allows you to tune into the feelings and moods of other people; therefore, it is the key to developing your people skills, which are built upon empathy and compassion. It includes how you are affected by people, things, or situations, as well as how you affect or influence them.

Motivational Intelligence refers to what turns you on in life, what you want or desire, what you feel passionately about. It's built upon self-awareness—knowing what you like to do and are good at, seeing how this ties in with your purpose in life and why you're here, and finding your niche in the workplace where you can achieve this purpose or life mission. It's the drive to fully develop and express yourself creatively.

Right-Brain/Left-Brain Intelligences of the Neocortex (Thinking)

Your neocortex is made up of two distinct halves, often called the left brain and the right brain. Rational Intelligence is a function of your left brain, and your right brain is the seat of three intelligences: Associative, Sensory, and Intuitive.

Rational Intelligence is seated in the left neocortex. It's sometimes called left-brain thinking. You use it to study how the parts of things work and fit together into a whole, with a special focus on the parts. You use it when you focus on step-by-step reasoning, cause-and-effect logic, and how things occur over time. This is virtually the only intelligence that has traditionally been respected and nurtured in Western academia, science, and business. The part of the brain, perhaps 10 percent, that most educated adults use most often is the rational left brain.

The right neocortex, where you do *right-brain thinking*, provides you with three major types of intelligence. This type of thinking is simultaneous, spatial, associative, whole-to-parts with more focus on the whole, and timeless.

Associative Intelligence is what you use when you focus on relationships between things—how things are alike or different.

Sensory Intelligence occurs when you use your senses—when you see, hear, smell, taste, and feel your body moving kinesthetically in space. It's related to visualizing things, drawing them, expressing them musically, dancing, doing sports, cooking creatively, etc.

Intuitive Intelligence is your higher-level inner knowing. It bypasses or aids the step-by-step, sequential-time, cause-effect ways of learning and goes directly to more wholistic, timeless experiences. In a sense, all life over all time may be felt as having a wholeness and a connection that are timeless. We're learning more about how we are all energetically connected and how we can naturally tune in to other persons, their feelings, and their life situations.

Now that creativity in the workplace is such a hot skill, moving beyond Rational Intelligence is becoming respectable. Although it will always be essential, Rational Intelligence is only a small slice of the intelligence pie.

Accessing Your Creative Intelligence

Your Creative Intelligence is the result of using all seven of your intelligences at the appropriate times and in the best combinations and interactions, as suggested in Snapshot #1. The best way to access and integrate all of them is to spend more and more time totally present in the Now, and to develop the art of complete acceptance of What-Is in each present moment.

Snapshot #1: Creative Intelligence Model

Creative Intelligence = 7 Intelligences

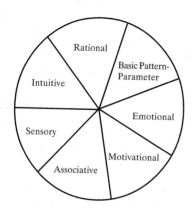

Boosting Each Intelligence
1. Identifying your own myths and blocks.
2. Recognizing this intelligence at work.
3. Boosting this intelligence.
4. Learning creative techniques based on it.
5. Applying creative techniques to situations.

Note: The pie and its segments are a theoretical model, and the proportions are approximate and symbolic because the exact proportion that each intelligence plays in creativity cannot be pinpointed

This Total Presence empowers you to use your Creative Intelligence as a synergistic process that integrates all your intelligences. This results in a brilliance that's greater than the sum of the parts—and it's sometimes called the *flow factor*.

How All Your Intelligences Work Together

In your daily life, your three brains, with their various types of intelligence, work together to help you protect yourself and to learn, grow, and create. You rarely, say, use only your Basic Intelligence of moving toward and moving away from something, or just your Pattern Intelligence of following old imprinted habits. Usually these basic experiences are accompanied by some type of emotion, ranging from very mild to intense. And these emotions fuel your motivation to take action. They also help you to remember and to learn, because the more emotional the experience, the more vivid it is in your memory.

From visioning to intuiting. When you have a vision of something new that you want to create or achieve, it's probably based on some similar pattern or type of thing that you have already experienced. You associate this old experience with a new vision that goes beyond the old parameters and patterns. Often you tap your intuition for inspiration about what to create next in your life and for guidance on how to respond to life's challenges and opportunities. Intuitive messages may come to you through your dreams via the basic brain, through your feelings via the emotional brain, and through your senses, associations, and thoughts via the neocortex.

Complex learning. You learn, or gain intelligence, through all three brains. For example, using your basic brain, you learn primarily by trial-and-error experiences and by imitating role models. Using your emotional brain, you learn through your feeling responses to various experiences. They provide a charge that motivates you toward or away from such experiences. Using your neocortex, you learn by analyzing, planning, and evaluating in a rational way. You learn by associating one thing to another—comparing, contrasting, and studying relationships. You learn through your senses—seeing, hearing, smelling, tasting, and touching things in the physical world. You also learn by tuning into messages from your intuition—which puts together all the other learning. Your intuition also brings in information from the interconnected Web of Life at all three levels of consciousness: subconscious, conscious, and superconscious.

Innovative skills. In today's job market, you boost your value by boosting your ability to use all your intelligences to respond creatively to today's rapidly changing problems and opportunities. Many of these problem-opportunities are taken on by teams of people. Therefore, learning how to function creatively within a team, how to lead team innovation, and how to apply creative group techniques are crucial skills.

You need all your intelligences to recognize paradigm problems and opportunities and to take the lead in creating paradigm shifts and responding to them. You'll learn how to step back and see the big picture so you can ignite the changes your organization needs. You can take a lead role in recognizing which problem-solutions can leverage a paradigm shift. You can identify opportunities that the most recent Next New Thing has opened up. And you can help develop innovative responses to the ever-emerging marketplace.

Strategy #2

Understand Women's Leadership Profile

Patterns that are typical of women leaders have been identified by Judith Rosener, Sally Helgesen, and other published researchers. They include a gentler use of power and a greater interest in empowering others, a more democratic approach with greater sharing and participation, more information and communication in general, more focus on long-range results, and a greater concern and interest in the individuals they lead.

Power and empowerment. Women are much more likely than men to use leadership power based on charisma, work record, and contacts rather than organizational position power. They rarely use coercion, while men's use of power is more likely to be coercive. Women are more interested in empowering others.

Participation and equality. Women are more willing to share information with employees and to deal with them as equals. They have a more inclusive style—including everyone in the *inner circle*—a key factor in meeting the needs and desires of diverse employees. Most women seldom or never give orders, preferring instead to foster employees' participation in decision-making. Women don't see their position in the organization as a platform for influence. Instead, they operate from their personal base of influence, their relationships with employees, and their expertise with the work.

Employee-involved, team-based leadership. Women achieve a high degree of employee involvement that results in a team-based leadership style. They focus more on participation and employee involvement as a basis for team management. The quality of the interpersonal relationships they build is based on mutual trust and respect—and they foster mutual trust and respect with and among employees. These relationships are not adversarial nor superior-subordinate in nature, so moving to self-managing teams is a natural for women leaders. Sharing common goals and wanting to grow together is important to them.

Rich communication. Women leaders tend to be more effective communicators than their male colleagues. They view good communication with employees as very important. This includes being open, willing to talk things out, and being eager to discuss situations that need clarification.

Entrepreneurial vision. Women leaders tend to take a long-range view of the future and encourage employees to share that vision. Women's leadership style serves as a motivating force to achieve the organization's mission.

A people focus. Sally Helgesen's study of women's workstyles indicates that women pay more attention to people and relationships than their male colleagues, as explained in her book *The Female Advantage*. A study of male leaders' activities done by Henry Mintzberg, author of *The Nature of Managerial Work*, is used for comparison purposes in Snapshot #2.

Snapshot #2: Comparison of Male and Female Managers

Mintzberg's study of male managers	Helgesen's study of female managers
Men worked at an unrelenting pace, with no breaks in activity during the day.	Women worked at a steady pace, with small breaks.
Men's days were characterized by interruption, discontinuity, and fragmentation.	Women viewed unscheduled tasks and encounters as a chance to be accessible to team members, to be involved, responsible, caring, and helpful.
Men spared little time for activities not directly related to their work.	Women made time for activities not directly related to work; for example, family life had greater priority.
Men showed a preference for live action encounters.	Women preferred live action encounters, but scheduled time to attend to mail.
Men lacked time for reflection.	Women focused on the ecology of leadership, finding time for reflection, and keeping the long term in focus, as well as relating decisions to their larger effect upon families, education, environment, and even world peace.
Men maintained a complex network of relationships with people outside the organization.	Women maintained a complex network of relationships with people outside the organization.
Men identified themselves with their jobs.	Women identified themselves as complex and multifaceted.
Men had difficulty sharing information.	Women scheduled time for sharing information.

Strategy #3
Understand Cultural Shifts That Affect Women

The major shifts to a global marketplace and computer-related technology are bringing about new opportunities for "outsiders," and these are two of the marketplace and cultural paradigm shifts that profoundly affect your opportunities as a woman. A third major shift is the resulting new corporate cultures with increasingly diverse, empowered employees who work best with a leadership style that's natural to most women. A fourth shift is toward more flexible corporate structures that reflect the typical woman's worldview: a web of personal connections.

Cultural Shift #1: New Opportunities in the Global Marketplace

The most dramatic change in recent years is the omnipresence of a global marketplace that has created intense competition for all corporations and unprecedented opportunities for women.

▶ Most companies are doing business in other countries.

▶ All companies are competing to provide ever-higher-quality products and prices at ever-lower costs.

▶ As a result, companies are outsourcing more work, creating opportunities for suppliers, distributors, deal-makers, consultants, and professionals.

▶ Most company and job growth is in high-tech markets and services, not manufacturing.

▶ People, companies, and whole societies are growing in technical and psychological knowledge.

▶ Fewer traditional barriers exist for women and minorities to become full participants. Change shakes up the status quo and creates openings.

New opportunities for "outsiders." Virtually all large companies are now multinational, as are many small and medium ones. Companies must become increasingly adept at identifying market niches, adopting innovative approaches, and offering top-quality products and services. Such major shakeups of the status quo always open doors of opportunity to newcomers and outsiders, including talented women.

Doors are opening in situations where people are tired of the unethical deals and money-grubbing of male executives. To most people, women represent a *fresh face* without the backroom connections and long years of deal-making that male executives are saddled with. For example, people's concerns about the growing power and declining ethical accountability of multinational corporations translate into a new respect for ethical decision-makers. Several recent surveys indicate that people believe women can bring special talents to dealing with and cleaning up scandals caused by greed and manipulation. People tend to trust women's ethical standards and level of honesty—both in business and in politics.

New opportunities for women leaders. Savvy corporations are competing for people who can produce and perform in rapidly changing, highly competitive markets. In the 1980s, talented women advanced faster in rapidly growing high-tech companies than in traditional ones, and this trend continues.

The United States has taken the lead in the global economy, and women's leadership is making a critical difference. Women are starting small businesses at twice the rate of men and own one-third of U.S. businesses. Many women entrepreneurs—as well as women working for large corporations—are doing business with other countries. Such women usually do well in global trade, even in countries where women are rarely allowed to take leadership roles in business, such as Asia. Nancy Adler found in her research that although a culture may frown on its own women going into business, foreign women are often viewed differently.

As a woman, you have a distinct advantage in working with the new employees entering the workplace—we'll discuss more about this later. You can build on your personal brand of people skills to exercise leadership in the new corporate cultures that are emerging in response to global competition and new employee expectations. Keep these suggestions in mind:

▸ Keep on keeping up. Ask. Listen. Learn. Make up your mind to be a lifelong learner. Success at work demands huge growth—even after you pay your dues—in order to learn new approaches, skills, and techniques. A turbulent environment offers many opportunities for growth *if* you're willing to take some risks and to reflect honestly on your experiences.

▸ Know how to bring in money. Be entrepreneurial—either within a firm you work for or by starting your own small business. Increasingly, success is going to the small and entrepreneurial, not the big and bureaucratic.

▸ Build your leadership skills as well as your managerial and entrepreneurial skills. Success in today's organizations increasingly requires all three, even at entry levels.

▸ Be unconventional. Scan the horizon for innovative approaches and capitalize on the opportunities available in this fast-moving, competitive business environment, while also watching out for hazards that change always brings.

▸ Be an able competitor. Set high standards for what you produce and the way you produce it. Move into a career path and a job where you can set goals that are important to you, goals that you have a strong desire to achieve.

▸ Join firms and teams that keep up with the competition and value high standards and continual learning—a place where you can grow and gain self-confidence in competitive situations.

▸ Seek a nonlinear career path so you can learn more, with positions that stretch you, bosses who will encourage your growth, and environments that allow for experimentation and innovation.

▸ If you want to start your own business, consider providing what the new slimmed-down big corporations need, such as supplies, products, consulting services, or other services—or distributing big businesses' products.

▸ Scan the horizon for problems and needs created by changes in the marketplace and workplace. Visionaries who scan the horizon are trend-watchers. Small seedling shifts pop up all the time, but 99 percent of business-watchers can't see them. Astute leaders continually read articles, books, and newsletters written by people who do nothing but identify and evaluate trends—authors such as John Naisbitt and Faith Popcorn.

Cultural Shift #2: New Corporate Cultures That Need Women's Leadership Ways

A paradigm shift that started in the 1980s and is stronger than ever today: Companies continue to decentralize authority and decision-making, moving it down, even to the work-team level. This has led to related shifts that are causing corporate cultures to change dramatically and rapidly in some of the following ways.

▶ Self-directed work teams increasingly make most of the decisions that affect their work. They increasingly network with other teams, persons, and outside resource people to accomplish their work.

▶ Creative and empowered employees are in. On the way out are employees with a few limited skills in doing the same old grind, doing it as they're told.

▶ More women are available who have the education, experience, and career vision, and who are ready to accept the challenges and demands of new responsibilities.

▶ Successful leaders are finding ways to empower team members and are moving away from traditional control-oriented management styles.

A picture of this shift is shown in Snapshot #3, comparing the old and the new workforce, company focus, and structures.

Snapshot #3: Corporate Cultures—Old and New

	Traditional Organization	Leading-Edge Organization
Workforce	• Expendable. • Needs few skills. • Narrow job definition.	• A resource to be developed. • Needs many skills. • Jobs with flexible scope; encouraged to develop more skills.
Focus	• We-they relationship. • Homogeneous. • Specialization. • Driven by technology. • Change is the exception.	• Partnership. • Diverse. • Applying special knowledge to larger problems. • Driven by customers' needs. • Change is the rule.
Structure	• Hierarchical. • Teams formed as needed.	• Flatter organizational structure. • Teams structured into organization, used to create synergy, and take over some or all of managers' work.

New employee profiles call for women's leadership ways. People in the workplace are changing. Those entering the workplace today tend to have certain traits and expectations that women relate to and can harness in creating dynamic, innovative, self-directed work teams. It's becoming more likely that the employees in your workplace:

▶ Can think critically, plan strategically, and adapt to change. They're better educated, more highly skilled, and more creative than in the past.

▶ Understand that neither the government nor the corporation can be depended on to take care of them and that their security lies in the skills and attributes they can take to their next jobs.

▶ Are mobile. They will probably change careers three times, according to the Labor Department; five times, according to most career consultants. And within each career, a person may change companies several times.

▶ Insist on balancing the top priorities of career, family, and personal interests. In the 1980s, it was mainly women who operated from these values. Nowadays, both men and women of the new generation tend to insist on balanced priorities.

▶ Perform mental tasks. They're paid for their knowledge more than for manual labor. More and more, work is what goes on inside workers' heads. It's how they communicate, what they write, and what they say in meetings. Mental tasks can't be supervised in the same way manual tasks are supervised.

▶ Function better within self-directed teams rather than traditional control-oriented, top-down management. They'll seek escape from hierarchical cultures.

▶ Are more likely to be women and minorities than in the past.

Women's leadership ways fit this employee profile.

Diverse employees need women's leadership ways. A shift that's profoundly affecting everyone in the workplace is the increasing diversity of employees who are moving into technical, professional, and managerial positions. We increasingly see people from many cultures and lifestyles—as well as more and more women—in positions of power and influence. These trends are startling because we still think of the American business culture as primarily a Euro-American (Caucasian) male culture. And it is, because in 2003:

▶ 95 percent of top managers were Euro-American men.

▶ 85 percent of U.S. Congressmen, who make laws affecting the workplace, were Euro-American men.

Meanwhile, according to the U.S. Labor Department and Census Bureau, in 2000:

▶ 63 percent of the workforce consisted of women and minorities (33 percent Euro-American women, and 30 percent minority men and women).

▶ 37 percent of the workforce consisted of Euro-American men, and 25 percent of them were classified as either over-65, gay, disabled, or obese.

▶ Only about 28 percent of the workforce, therefore, consisted of Euro-American men who did *not* fall into one of these diversity categories.

And diversity is increasing. Ever since the 1990s:

▶ 15 percent of new employees entering the workforce are Euro-American men.

▶ 85 percent are women and minorities.

As a woman, you have an advantage in working with talented employees from diverse groups because:

▶ You have direct experience in dealing with stereotypes and self-limiting beliefs rooted in the socialization process.

▶ You're likely to know what it's like to feel excluded, and you understand how to include people.

▶ You're likely to be a quick study in gaining diversity skills.

The largest group among the new workers is working mothers. As a woman, and perhaps a mother, you're in a position to understand and empathize with the needs and desires of working mothers. Despite the huge increase in working mothers, still only about 10 percent of organizations with 10 or more employees provide any direct childcare benefits, such as day care or financial assistance. Most provide inadequate maternity leave provisions.

Leadership styles that work. When we look at what companies need from their leaders these days, we can see that women's ways fit those needs quite well. Companies need leaders who:

▶ Use more flexible ways of viewing and identifying managerial talent.

▶ Achieve fast-paced information exchange.

▶ Have a broad vision and a diverse portfolio of skills.

▶ Think creatively and contribute to needed innovation.

▶ Have an ecological mentality, stressing the interrelatedness of all things.

▶ Reconcile a concern for bottom-line results with a concern for people (leaders who focus on both the ends and the means).

▶ Are skilled at both planning and problem-solving.

▶ Have rich people skills, including communication, team facilitation, negotiation, and conflict resolution.

This profile fits women's leadership style and is opening more doors for women.

Cultural Shift #3: New Corporate Structures That Reflect Women's Ways

The structure of companies is changing to reflect how people interact within the company and with outside players. The new structure resembles a web, with rich communication lines among many players, little hierarchy, and less formality. Georgetown University linguistics professor Deborah Tannen's research on women's and men's communication patterns and worldviews indicates that women relate in ways best symbolized by the web. In contrast, men relate in more hierarchical ways, symbolized by the pyramid that is typical of yesterday's organizations. Today's web structure reflects a more feminine way of relating to people.

As a result of structural changes, companies need leaders who function well with less chain of command, more democratic systems and structure—webs, not pyramids. This style comes naturally to most women.

Strategy #4

Build Upon Your Woman's Ways of Leading

How can you tie into these cultural and marketplace paradigm shifts to create a wildly successful career? Begin by understanding that in a traditional business culture based on the military model, with its authoritarian values and rigid hierarchy, men's traditional management style works best. But as more and more organizations move away from this model to a more open, informal, democratic model, women can be equally capable of inspiring commitment and bringing out the best in people. In fact, according to John Naisbitt, author of *Megatrends*, being raised a man is no longer an advantage. Women, who don't need to unlearn old authoritarian behavior, actually have a people-skills edge. You need to become aware of your own strengths and weaknesses and carefully match them with the available opportunities. Keeping in mind that we all have both feminine and masculine traits, you can build upon your already-existing feminine strengths and develop appropriate masculine strengths for balance.

As you build upon your woman's ways of leading, focus especially on your tendencies to empower people, to use a facilitative leadership style, to treat people with empathy and sensitivity, and to confirm people's belief in women's integrity by consistently acting in ways that build trust.

Leadership Skill #1: Empower People

Build upon your desire to empower people. This may be the most important step you can take to fit into today's organizational cultures—because an underlying theme of all the current paradigm shifts is the individual. Although people are working together in more dynamic ways, organizational power increasingly comes from the power of individuals working together in teams. Most women are socialized to win commitment from people rather than to autocratically give orders and apply controls. Women tend to adapt more naturally to the role of teacher/facilitator/coach than to the role of director/overseer. Most women have historically been trained to subordinate their own success and focus on helping others, such as husbands and children, to achieve success. It seems natural to them to focus more on team success than personal glory.

Remember, it's okay to place more importance on sharing power with all members of the organization than on keeping the power for yourself. When you share power, you empower others to achieve the visions you've shared. Your tendencies to care about others, to want to personally connect with them, to communicate with them, and to share information with them can help you in your efforts to empower people.

Leadership Skill #2: Use a Facilitative Leadership Style

At last, U.S. business is learning that people support what they help create, and that everyday operational decisions are best made at the levels where they will be carried out. However, top-down leadership and communication is still the rule in many U.S. organizations. Modern managers may encourage employees to ask questions, state opinions, and share information, but they seldom ask employees to make plans, solve problems, make decisions, create new procedures, or find out what went wrong. Because many companies have been forced by global competition to flatten their hierarchies, middle management has thinned out and teams are taking on many management responsibilities. Managers have moved from using a traditional, directive style to an updated consultative style to, more recently, a facilitative team leader style, as shown in Snapshot #4 on page 25.

The companies that are thriving and surviving in this global competition are structuring themselves to make optimal use of business development teams. These teams may search out and find new opportunities to add value and meet customer needs and wants. They may improvise and innovate to fill such needs, and they implement their plans to deliver timely products or services at competitive prices. These new developments call for greater self-management by work teams and for leaders who know how to facilitate the opportunity-seeking, problem-solving, decision-making, goal-setting, and development of work procedures that such teams do. So relax and rely more on your one-on-one people skills than on any position power within the hierarchy that you may have.

Leadership Skill #3: Access Your Empathy and Sensitivity

You've either been through the fire of struggling to balance a career, a family, and personal interests, or you can picture yourself in this situation. This gives you a personal sense of the ways in which the workplace must be made flexible enough to attract and retain highly qualified women and minorities. Here's an overview of ways to build on your feminine strengths to boost your career success:

Be democratic. Aim to be a democratic but demanding facilitator of change rather than a parent figure. Build on your tendency to respect people and to encourage self-management, self-directed teams, and entrepreneurial units, such as business development teams. Inspire commitment from your team members by operating consistently from fair, honest principles and by creating an environment where everyone is included, and everyone has a chance to shine and grow. Women tend to prefer informality at work, so use informal processes in order to achieve rapidly changing goals.

Provide nurturing, support, and challenge. See your greatest role as helping people succeed, learn, and grow. Constantly challenge your people to learn new skills, and support them in doing so. Encourage today's better-educated workers to be more entrepreneurial, self-managing, and oriented toward lifelong learning. Focus on helping people learn a variety of tasks (cross-training) and meet ever-changing performance goals geared to their individual strengths and interests as well as to organizational needs. This is more powerful than the old focus on formal job titles and descriptions.

Support working mothers' needs. As a woman, you can certainly understand working mothers' major concerns, which center around the flexibility they need to balance their home and job responsibilities. Use your influence to provide flexible job arrangements, such as flextime, part-time, job-sharing, contract work, and home offices.

Work toward providing flexible benefits, such as day care, maternity leave, and family medical leave. Women typically take major responsibility for care of elderly family members. You can support working women in these crucial efforts.

Develop diverse employees. Build on your understanding of being stereotyped, being considered a second-class citizen, and being treated as an outsider to business power—to empathize with diverse employees, to meet their needs, and to help them make a contribution.

important page

Snapshot #4: Evolution of Leadership Styles   ✗ *best*

Traditional Manager *Directive*	Updated Manager *Consultative*	Team Leader *Facilitative*
Sets goals. Solves problems. Decides. Tells. Directs others. Uses authority to get things done. Cracks the whip, threatens. Structured.	Consults in goal-setting. Good problem-solver. Consults, then decides. Sells. Delegates. Motivates others to get things done. Coaches, teaches. More open, friendly.	Shares in goal-setting. Helps teams solve problems. Shares in decision-making. Asks questions, listens. Directs the team process. Empowers others to get things done. Develops team, inspires. Flexible.
Message to employees: *Don't think, keep quiet, cater to me.* Favoritism, pets. Little or no feedback. Unskilled at the work. No counseling.	*I'm receptive to your ideas.* More participative environment. Performance evaluations. Pitches in when needed. Performance counseling.	*You do it; I'll support you.* Models what's expected, supports, sustains. Frequent performance feedback. Resource for team efforts. Supports team, helps with team's struggles.
Communication skills: One-way, top-down, poor communications. Few people skills. Knows all answers. Tight control, task-oriented. Little contact with other departments, functions. Gets special privileges. Quantity above quality.	Two-way communication. Better people skills. Encourages people to share ideas. Tight control, people-oriented. More contact with other departments. Gets ahead by knowing people. More conscious of quality.	Rich, skilled communication. Encourages team to high performance. Can rely on others' expertise. Team control, team-oriented. Gets resources for team needs. Egalitarian. Leads Total Quality Management (TQM).
Focus: Bosses' expectations. Homogeneous groups. Takes credit for the work.	Boss/worker. Others adapt to group. Shares credit.	Team needs in context of firm's needs. Two-way adaptation, flexible team culture. Gives credit to team.
Resolution strategy: Win/lose.	Compromise.	Win/win, consensus.

Access your understanding and instincts to find ways to meet their needs, help them succeed, inspire their commitment, and elicit their enthusiasm for making solid, innovative contributions.

Leadership Skill #4: Build Trust Through Honesty and Integrity

Most people are fed up with greedy, dishonest leaders and tend to trust women leaders more than men, according to John Naisbitt's research. Women can validate this trust by consistently rising to the occasion.

Let your decisions demonstrate your integrity. First identify your values and principles—where you draw the line on various issues. Then be sure your decisions align with those values and principles. People will begin to notice, and you'll become a positive role model. Follow successful strategies for dealing with tough ethical decisions.

- ▶ Learn to see an ethical dilemma coming.
- ▶ Recognize that there is a dilemma.
- ▶ Realize the choices available—the range of responsible options.
- ▶ Think ahead and practice your responses.

Answer the tough ethical questions. Establish and stay in touch with your ethical principles and boundaries—know where you draw the line. In a volatile world, it's easy to lose touch with your moral boundaries, especially when big money is at stake. Start observing the ethical issues that others face—in your office, in news stories, in books. Ask yourself the following questions when you face a tough decision:

- ▶ Is it legal? Will any policies, regulations, or rules be violated? Is the proposed action consistent with past practice?
- ▶ Does the situation require that I lie about the process or the results?
- ▶ Do I consider this an unusual situation that demands an unusual response?
- ▶ Am I acting fairly? Would I want to be treated in this way?
- ▶ Will I have to hide or keep my actions secret? Has someone warned me not to disclose my actions to anyone?
- ▶ Would I be able to discuss the proposed situation or action with my immediate supervisor? The president of the company? My family? The company's clients?
- ▶ How would I feel if the details of this situation appeared in the media?
- ▶ If a close friend took this action, how would I feel?
- ▶ How do I feel about this? Am I feeling unusually anxious? Fearful? Does my conscience bother me?

With practice, ethical decision-making becomes easier and more consistent.

Inspire loyalty. It's more difficult to inspire loyalty in these downsizing days, but the best leaders earn personal loyalty by acting in ways that inspire it. If you're like many women, you've had to earn respect and loyalty every step of the way in your career. Therefore, you understand this unwritten rule. Be ready to apply it by keeping your promises, always, and applying the other ethical principles that form your bottom-line action boundaries.

Strategy #5

What is a paradigm

Recognize Paradigm Patterns

How does *your* leadership style fit the typical woman's profile? Once you recognize the traits and skills you have to offer, you can match them to the needs of new corporate cultures and structures that are emerging. A powerful skill in this rapidly changing business environment is the skill of recognizing paradigm patterns and cycles. This skill can help you in matching your profile to the opportunities that are opening up. Such savvy also allows you to survive and thrive during paradigm shifts.

Paradigm Skill #1: Know How to Identify a Paradigm

A paradigm is a mental model of how something works. According to Joel Barker, author of *Future Edge,* to be considered a paradigm, the model must include three factors:

1. **A set of rules** that
2. **establishes or defines the boundaries of the model** and
3. **tells you how to behave inside the boundaries in order to succeed**.

People who adopt a particular paradigm measure success by the ability to solve problems within it.

Think of a culture, society, worldview, organization, or business as a forest. Each paradigm is a tree in the forest. For example, a business will have management paradigms, sales paradigms, human resources paradigms, and recruitment paradigms. We're defining a paradigm as a mental model, but it is also seen by various people as a theory, an ideology, a mind-set, a frame of reference, a method, a protocol, common sense, consensus reality, or conventional wisdom. A paradigm can also be a set of beliefs, principles, standards, routines, assumptions, conventions, patterns, habits, traditions, customs, prejudices, or rituals. The forest of paradigms we find in a business, a culture, or a worldview are interdependent, so you never change just one paradigm. When you change one, it affects all the others, so they too must shift to some degree—from very slightly, to dramatically.

director — consultant - facilitator

Paradigm Skill #2: Recognize Paradigm Cycles and Shifts

A paradigm shift is a change from the current model to a new model, with a new set of rules and boundaries. It's a new game that requires different behavior in order to succeed. For example, when women started moving into power positions 20 or 30 years ago, there was a major paradigm shift that affected business, marriage, family, child rearing, education, courtship, and perhaps most of the trees in our cultural forest. The mental model of what it means to be a good wife, mother, husband, father all began to shift. People are still trying to figure out all the new rules and boundaries.

To identify where paradigm shifts are likely to occur, notice where people are trying to change the rules; that's the earliest sign of significant change possibilities. When the rules change, the whole world can change.

When do the rules change—when do new paradigms appear? Usually, it's when someone figures out how to solve one or more major problems that cannot be solved using the rules and boundaries of the old paradigm. In effect, someone figures out how to do something better, something important that needs to be improved, and enough people jump on the bandwagon to make a shift occur. Often it's when someone solves a problem in a new way—not using the old rules. Such explorers often think this new way could be a model for solving a wide range of similar problems. Let's look at typical phases of a new paradigm.

Phase 1: Beginning of new paradigm. Progress in solving multiple problems by using the new paradigm is slow. Discovering the boundaries and rules of a new paradigm is usually a slow and tricky process.

Phase 2: Becoming established. Boundaries and rules are becoming well-established. The rate of problem-solving rapidly increases. This is the phase of great money-making opportunities—when whole new industries may develop.

Phase 3: Well-established. The rate of problem-solving slows down because simpler problems have been solved and what's left are the hard nuts that may require a new paradigm to crack. The players put them aside, usually with the intent of getting back to them sooner or later, typically because of the lack of some technology or tool, or the inability to use the paradigm in sophisticated ways. Later the players become better at what they do and solve more of the hard nuts, but usually a small subset of problems is left unsolved. What's needed is a paradigm shift in order to solve them. Sooner or later, every paradigm begins to develop a very special set of problems that everyone in the field wants to know how to solve, and no one even knows how to begin.

Paradigm Skill #3: Access the Continual Paradigm-Shift Process

During Phase 1, the new paradigm is usually in competition with other paradigms that are being developed to solve the problem. The paradigm that can survive to the beginning of Phase 2 will almost always win—even if other paradigms would be better in the long run. If the paradigm explorers face artificial barriers—such as government regulation, a distorted marketplace, or big companies that crush competition—then competing paradigms may not show up until Phase 3. However, it's most likely that a competing paradigm will appear and be accepted late in Phase 2 because there will be enough unsolved problems to trigger the search. The need is felt. Here's the usual process in more detail:

Phase 3 of an old paradigm:
▶ The established paradigm begins to be less effective.
▶ People in the field who are affected begin to lose trust in the old rules.
▶ Turbulence and a sense of crisis grow as trust is reduced.

Phase 1 of a new paradigm:
▶ Visionaries and explorers step forward to propose their solutions, which may actually be old ideas whose time has come.
▶ Turbulence and crisis increase even more as paradigm conflict becomes obvious.
▶ People in the field become upset and demand clear solutions.

▸ People begin to believe that one of the proposed new paradigms can solve a small set of significant problems that the old paradigm cannot.

▸ Pioneers take the lead to accept the new paradigm based on intuition that it will work.

Phase 2 of a new paradigm:

▸ As support and funding grow, the new paradigm picks up momentum.

▸ Turbulence and crisis decrease as the new paradigm starts solving the problems; people in the field have a new, more successful way to deal with the world.

▸ You will have significant competitive advantage if you can anticipate shifts and become a pioneer in adopting a new paradigm that allows you to lead people out of the turbulence and crisis such shifts create. You can take the lead in making your company a pioneer, giving it a competitive advantage.

Strategy #6
Take a Leadership Role in Technological Change

To take a leadership role in the midst of these technological shifts, begin by using your knowledge of paradigms to boost your career success, learning to recognize opportunities and barriers so you can stay a step ahead of shifting paradigms. Recognize what runs the new economy and the Net-oriented businesses that are being created by the new technology. Use a Net-oriented leadership style to integrate people into teams and networks, harness innovation in "now time," and focus on lifelong learning and knowledge, being sure to include people from diverse groups.

Tech Skill #1: Use Paradigm Savvy to Boost Leadership Success

Recognizing paradigms helps you know when it's time to focus on your management skills, your entrepreneurial skills, and your leadership skills.

Manage better. You manage within a paradigm by applying the mission, strategies, tactics, techniques, goals, systems, procedures, and guiding principles—what we're loosely calling the rules. A manager's job is paradigm enhancement—taking the rules and making them better. This is what most executives and managers in most corporations spend about 90 percent of their work time doing.

Lead better. You lead when you take the risk of leaving one paradigm while it's still successful, and going to a new unproved paradigm. You use your intuitive judgment, assess the risk, and if you decide it's time to shift, you convey your vision of the new paradigm to employees. You inspire them to follow that vision and bring it about. That's what good leaders and entrepreneurs do with the other 10 percent of their work time. And these tend to be women's ways of leading. Because of the increasingly rapid rate of paradigm shifts, you need to be good at that as well as paradigm enhancement in order to succeed in today's marketplace and workplace.

write this down

The old leadership style was to create a vision and sell it down to others, using a brilliant, take-charge, rally-the-troops approach. This style won't work any more. The new enterprise sees the leader as a collective, networked, virtual workforce with power flowing from a jointly created and shared vision. Leadership is preferably not embodied in one person, but in a collective body. Vision is achieved and transmitted collectively.

Infotech creates within an organization whole networks of human intelligence and new knowledge power as people work to transform both the enterprise and themselves. It's collective leadership. Net-oriented leadership begins in teams through the collective action of people working to create new visions or solve problems. Of course, there must still be a CEO. If the CEO encourages Net-oriented leadership, the networked teams can take the leap into the transformation process and keep obsoleting, then recreating, themselves.

Leadership can and will be achieved virtually on computer networks—more and more. Human intelligence can be networked, and this network has far greater capacity for pervasive vision and collective action than does the lone leader at the top. As people online share their verbal ideas and their facial expressions, body language, designs, notes, drawings, and tools, the potential for collective thinking and action expands across the company and beyond. Bottom line: Get on the Net!

There's a chicken-egg relationship between being informed and participating in the world. According to John Seely Brown, participant at the 1993 Aspen Institute conference on telecommunications policy, you can't really be informed unless you participate—and you can't really meaningfully participate unless you're informed. It's engagement through being, and information technology is the essential tool. If you want to, you can be a leader in the transformation.

Map the future. To take the lead, you must break free from the past—from the old technology legacy. How? With your team, create a model of the future and of how your business must look in order to succeed in that future. Map that to the technology you now have. Do a gap analysis between where you are and where you need to go. Build a set of migration scenarios and plans for getting there so your team can invest their time and energy in moving toward the new business model. Increasingly, the tools you need for doing this will be available on the Net and won't have to be constructed internally by your company.

Lead transformation. These rapidly changing paradigms call for people who can take the lead in transforming the organization. Transformation doesn't mean just adapting here and there—it means becoming a whole new organization, over and over again as times change. This new kind of leader is one who:

▶ Has the curiosity and confidence to lead people into new paradigms.

▶ Can balance the need for business growth and profit with the needs of employees, customers, and society for privacy, fairness, and a share in the wealth they create.

▶ Has the vision to think socially, the courage to act, and the strength to lead their people over and around barriers.

Reward paradigm-shift behavior. If you're not willing to seriously listen to employees' ideas on how to do something better, you're sending the message that people must stay within the prevailing paradigm. Invite people to step outside the boundaries and find new ways to solve old problems. The more actively you search for new paradigms yourself—and talk about that search—the more likely your team members are to search *with* you and *for* you. Two basic things can happen when you step outside the boundaries of your current paradigm:

1. You find ways to apply the prevailing paradigm rules in a new, uncharted area—you do what your company knows how to do, but you do it in a new arena.

2. You find a new domain that will require a new paradigm to solve the problems in it.

In the first instance, you use the old paradigm, but you move out the boundaries. For example, you find a new type of customer with problems that can be solved with your current paradigm—moving out your customer boundary line. In the second instance, you attack problems that cannot be solved with your current paradigm. Perhaps your current customers have such problems. They're open to allowing your company to solve them, but you must find a new paradigm in order to do so.

Allow and reward cross-talk between people from different departments or divisions. They need to understand one another's problems. People will begin making connections in their minds about how to use some rule or tool in their own paradigm to help their peer solve a problem in another division. They'll begin connecting what a colleague has explained with a possible solution to their own problem. Keep an open mind and be constantly alert for the possibility of connecting two, three, or more ideas.

Reduce paradigm-shift risks. Encourage people to find innovative new solutions to problems by reducing the risks they face when they propose new boundaries, rules, and paradigms. For example, create an Innovation Committee that periodically holds Explore-New-Ideas Sessions. If the committee believes the ideas might work, they and the proposer carry the idea to top management. If not, the idea might go anonymously into an idea pool where ideas are reviewed periodically for possible connections and combinations. The agreement that the committee makes is to never make a person or an idea wrong, to never ridicule, and to always value and appreciate the proposers' effort. The idea is to build trust, encourage creativity, and reduce the risk of being wrong.

Tech Skill #2: Identify Paradigm-Shift Opportunities and Barriers

How can you identify problems that need a new paradigm in your field? Ask yourself, *What are the problems all my peers want to solve and don't have the slightest idea how?* Write them down. Then ask yourself, *Which phase am I functioning in? Who's likely to support and resist my change ideas?*

▶ Are you an explorer, a leader, starting to develop a new way of solving the problems—in Phase 1? Or are you dealing with problems that are subtle, sophisticated, expensive, and intensive—in Phase 3—moving toward a new Phase 1?

▶ Are you a pioneer, a leader, or an entrepreneur who is willing to take a chance on a new paradigm being developed by an explorer—early in Phase 2?

▶ Are you a settler, a manager, solving problems with efficiency and effectiveness—later in Phase 2?

▶ Or, heaven forbid, are you a resister to major change that would move people out of the phase you're comfortable with?

Explorers start with the unsolved problems in Phase 3 and see that they must be solved outside the current paradigm, which moves them into Phase 1 of a new paradigm. Where is this explorer likely to come from? Usually it's an outsider, someone who really doesn't understand the prevailing paradigm in all its subtleties—or at all. It may be someone who's new to the field and isn't stuck in its accepted beliefs. It may be a loner who's been working at the fringes of the field and knows it, but isn't boxed in by the rules. It may be a tinkerer who gets in there himself to work on a problem that's in the way.

Pioneers buy into explorers' thinking. They bring in the needed brainpower, muscle power, time, effort, and money to create the critical mass that drives the new paradigm into Phase 2. Both explorers and pioneers follow their intuition, their hearts, and their feelings, and they both take the risk of backing a new paradigm.

Settlers enter later in Phase 2; therefore, they take much smaller risks.

Resisters cling to the status quo because it worked for them, and they are not willing to take the risks and make the changes necessary for success in the new paradigm. When a paradigm shifts, everyone functioning within it goes back to zero. Your expertise in solving the old problems with the old rules is not worth much except for the basic skills you can transfer, such as basic problem-solving, decision-making, people skills, etc. For example, directive managers, who tell employees what to do and when to do it, find themselves irrelevant when workers are reorganized into self-managing teams. When you ask someone to change their paradigm, you're asking them to give up their investment in the status quo and the rewards it provides them. Resisters are usually the corporate insiders who have much to lose from major change, but corporate outsiders have nothing invested and everything to gain.

These are the typical forces that block and drive paradigm shifts.

Tech Skill #3: Thrive in All the Phases

North American business usually takes the lead in exploring and discovering new paradigms, breaking out of an old Phase 3 into a new Phase 1. But Japanese business has often taken the lead in pioneering, getting in early in Phase 2 and staying the course—whether it's computer chips, VCRs, or TQM. Continuous improvement is part of TQM, a paradigm discovered in the United States but perfected in Japan. The goal of continuous improvement is to find a way every day to get just one-tenth of 1 percent improvement in what you make or do. Over a work year of 240 days, that's a 24 percent improvement. If you use continuous improvement from the beginning of Phase 2, you solve more of the problems of the paradigm more quickly. This can give you an enormous competitive advantage over anyone who gets into the new paradigm after you. For example, the Sony

Walkman added auto reverse, bass and treble controls, special smaller headphones, shock resistance, water resistance, electronic radio tuning, smaller size, rechargeable batteries, still smaller size, Dolby, and an alarm clock.

Paradigm pioneers who practice continuous improvement never give an even break to the settlers who come later in Phase 2. The pioneers can always be a step ahead to make their product more irresistible to the buying public. And every day a settler delays getting into the market, the less of the market is left for them and the more it costs to enter and compete with the trailblazers. For pioneers, it's not first-in/big risk, but first-in/big potential advantage.

Avoid Paradigm Blindness

What we perceive is dramatically determined by our paradigms. What may be perfectly visible and perfectly obvious to persons with one paradigm may be quite literally invisible to persons with a different paradigm. In other words, it's possible that you will not be able to see data that's right before your eyes if it doesn't fit into your paradigm. In fact, all the senses have paradigm filters, so you can listen but not hear, touch but not feel, and sniff but not smell. You see best what you're supposed to see or expect to see. You see poorly, if at all, the data that does not fit into your paradigm.

Most of us have heard the story of 17th-century European explorers who anchored their sailing ships in New World ports and rowed in to meet the natives. When the explorers pointed out their ship to the natives, they couldn't see the vessel—huge by their standards—sitting far out on the horizon. This was because it was simply not within their experience or mind-set. They couldn't pick it out from the haze, the waves, the clouds, the rest of the environment.

Paradigms define what's important and what's not. You ignore or eliminate input that's unnecessary, or alter it to fit your expectations. You can also create needed data that doesn't exist and totally believe that it's real. To see the future more clearly, put aside the certainties of your paradigms and examine the fringes for the people who are changing the rules and boundaries.

Stay a Step Ahead of Shifting Paradigms

In your leadership role, you can identify the possibility of a paradigm shift in your field by asking yourself:

▶ What really needs to be done but is impossible to do, but if it could be done, would fundamentally change my field?

▶ What problem really needs to be solved, but no one has been able to solve it, and if they did, would fundamentally change the field?

Ask the questions often, of everyone, and listen to the answers. It will keep you in touch with that strange space on the other side of your boundaries where you could be put back to zero. Your best job insurance is to know what your prevailing paradigm is and how it might change. You can't stop the process but you can learn to solve the problems the paradigm addresses. If you can spot the signs of change early—know what the changes are—you can take part in the paradigm shift. Perhaps you will even become an explorer or pioneer. This will help guarantee that you're a part of it.

gov't vs cctsa

To help you understand the concept of paradigms and paradigm shifts, review the following examples of recent paradigm shifts. Think about how they are changing, or will change, the rules of the game in your workplace—as well as the boundaries or limits of action and the behaviors people need in order to succeed.

Tech Skill #4: Integrate People Into Teams and Networks

The Net-oriented organization is a vast web of relationships from all levels and business functions. The boundaries inside and outside are ever-changing and penetrable. Small companies can band together to act like large ones, achieving large-company massive buying power and access to money and other resources. Larger companies are breaking down into smaller clusters so that they can achieve the advantages typical of small companies—agility, autonomy, and flexibility. They can retain the resources of the large parent corporation without being burdened by its old, deadening bureaucracies. Integrating people into teams that network with others has become a way to create wealth.

The virtual corporation is a business where much of the work, meeting, and communication take place on computer screens, fax machines, car phones, voice mail, and video conferences. Work teams may include company specialists, independent contractors, suppliers, customers, and investors. They may be scattered around the globe, change from month to month and never meet face to face, or they may be self-managing teams that meet every day. They may work together to develop the plans, set the standards, identify and solve the problems, make the decisions, and provide the products and services. In any case, the degree of success or failure depends heavily on people's relationships with one another.

The Net-oriented enterprise, according to high-tech expert Don Tapscott, will be a far-reaching extension of the virtual corporation because it will access external business partners and constantly reconfigure its business relationships, perhaps with a dramatic increase in outsourcing. It will act like the Internet—participative and synergistic. The overall economy will act the same way. Already, walls are coming down between manufacturers, suppliers, customers, and even competitors. We're seeing Net-oriented business, government, learning, and healthcare, as well as other segments. The major utility of the 21st century is the information infrastructure—the broadband highway of fiber optics.

Customers as team members will become commonplace. Television viewers or Internet users, for example, can become producers of the product or service they get. For example, they could highlight the top 10 topics they're interested in and specify the preferred news sources, talk shows, and graphic styles they want in their custom news report. Consumers become coproducers when they create and send messages to colleagues, contribute to bulletin board discussion groups, select the ending of movies, walk through virtual homes, or test-drive virtual cars.

With the new computer capabilities, organizations can do more than just consume information and technology. They can begin to produce infotech. For example, automobile manufacturers can do more than just assemble cars. They can produce on the Net the infomercials, driver navigational tools, and other services that customers need or want.

Tech Skill #5: Harness Innovation in "Now Time"

The new economy is an innovation-based economy. Leading-edge companies know they must make their own products obsolete before someone else does. Most large U.S. companies introduce more than one new product a day. In 1995, Sony introduced 5,000 new products. Microsoft executive Kim Drew says, "No matter how good your product, you're only 18 months away from failure." Products come and go more rapidly all the time. The average time to create and manufacture a new product has dropped from 2,500-person days per product, to three hours. About 90 percent of Miller's beer revenues come from beers that didn't exist 24 months ago.

Companies must also obsolete their own businesses—creating a new type of business with new relationships before a competitor does. Toyota's theory is to reinvent their company proactively in order to ride the wave of change.

Do it now and then immediately work on doing it better. This is a key driver and variable in the economic activity and business success of the new organization. In the past, such inventions as cameras and copy machines provided revenues for decades. Today, consumer electronic products have a typical product life of two months. *Just-in-time* applies to everything from when goods are received from suppliers, to when products are shipped to customers.

Human imagination is the main source of value in this high-tech world. The company's major challenge is to create a climate—usually a small-firm climate—in which innovation is valued, encouraged, and rewarded.

With the fast pace of change and complexity of markets, customers often don't know what's possible and what to ask for. Business leaders must innovate beyond what their customers can imagine. They must understand the needs of their customers. They must thoroughly understand what's possible with the emerging technologies, then provide products and services that surprise and delight customers. To accomplish this, leaders must establish an organizational climate where risk-taking is rewarded and creativity can blossom.

Tech Skill #6: Focus on Knowledge and Lifelong Learning

The key to an organization's success in this new economy lies in the knowledge and creative genius of the product strategists, developers, and marketers. What counts is a company's ability to attract, retain, and continually grow the capabilities of knowledge workers and provide the environment for innovation and creativity. Lifelong organizational learning becomes the only sustainable competitive advantage a company can create.

Team Collaboration. If a picture is worth a thousand words, the right multimedia document accessed at the right time is worth a thousand pictures. E-mail is just the beginning of a whole new way of human collaboration. Product planners working as a team may be scattered in various locations—home, hotel room, office.

Knowledge Value. The costs of information and coordination are dropping. More than ever, we're able to create wealth by adding knowledge to each product at every step. Theoretically, all a person needs in order to succeed in today's economy is a good brain, a telephone, a modem, and a personal computer. But in practice most knowledge workers also need motivation and trustful team relationships to be effective. Knowledge workers are the owners of this new means of production, and they're better positioned than any work group in history to share in the wealth.

Working-Learning. Effective leaders in effective business organizations will understand what makes today's knowledge workers tick and how to keep them motivated in the Net-oriented firm. To begin with, businesses must provide more and more of the learning, relying less on schools. Two reason are that working and learning are becoming the same activity for most people, and knowledge is such an important part of production. Products and services designed to help people learn are badly needed, and there are vast, growing opportunities for those who can deliver them. Self-paced interactive learning delivered through computer disks is just one of the new learning technologies that's meeting employees' needs for continual learning.

Lifelong Learning. On the other hand, individual employees also must take responsibility for lifelong learning. The entrepreneurial process creates the environment in which people can take the initiative and gives the structure necessary for people to do so. Leaders are responsible for building organizations in which people can continually expand their capacities to understand complexity, clarify vision, improve their shared mental models—organizations where people can take responsibility for their learning.

Women's Challenges and Opportunities. As a woman in the midst of these paradigm shifts, you are faced with greater opportunities and challenges than have ever been faced by women in the work world. You have the opportunity to take the lead in creating the world of tomorrow. We know that good leaders don't just wait for the future to happen; they help create it. Together, people's values, aspirations, and growing expectations will shape and drive the transformation of our businesses and our world. And by networking on intranets and the Internet, we can do it consciously. Leadership in the new organization is your personal opportunity and responsibility to bring women's ways of leading into the business world. It's your opportunity to create a career that makes the positive contribution you want to make. You can take control of your destiny and help create humanity's destiny.

Skill Builders

Skill Builder #1: What Paradigms Define Your Success?

Purpose: To develop skill in recognizing paradigms and paradigm shifts.

1. In your area of expertise, what needs to be done differently but can't be done differently, and if it were, would fundamentally change the way people play the game and do their work?
2. What problem in your area or field needs to be solved but hasn't been, and if it were, would fundamentally change the game?
3. How would you describe the paradigm(s) you uncovered in your answers to Questions 1 and 2?
4. What are the rules of the game?

5. What are the boundaries or limits of the game?
6. What are the success behaviors they define?
7. What can you do you to enhance the current paradigm? What are your ideas for solving a problem or doing something so differently it would create new rules and boundaries?

Skill Builder #2: Overcome Fear of Success

Purpose: To identify fears that can block or limit your ability to achieve your goals, including conscious fears and hidden fears.

Is it possible that you have hidden reservations about achieving a successful career? Could it be that you actually fear some aspects of success? Such fears can result in self-sabotage of career goals. The best way to overcome them is to uncover them and then establish new beliefs about success. Statements #1 through #4 of this Skill Builder are designed to help you further identify success fears and their sources. Statements #5 through #7 are designed to help you establish new beliefs about success.

Step 1: For each of the following statements, beginning with Statement #1 and following through in sequence, do the following:

➡ Read the statements.
➡ Close your eyes, breathe deeply, and relax.
➡ Focus on the statement; don't analyze it or try to figure out what the *best response* should be.
➡ Notice what comes up, what spontaneously occurs to you.
➡ Open your eyes and finish the statement by writing your responses in approximately the sequence in which they occurred to you.

Statements:
1. I want to reach my career goals, but....
2. To achieve my career goals, I might have to give up....
3. Maybe I don't really deserve to succeed because....
4. Some *don't-deserve* or warning messages my parents or others gave me are....
5. I can handle abundant success because....
6. My top three priorities are....
7. I deserve abundant success because....

Step 2: Summarize your responses to Statements #5, #6, and #7. Write each on a separate index card. Each week, select a different card and place it where you'll see it several times a day. Become your own best supporter. Repeat one of these positive affirmations at least once a day.

Skill Builder #3: Learn to Manage Fear

Purpose: To name your fears, uncover hidden fears, to get at *root* fears.

Step 1: Name your fears. List any and all fears that come to your mind.

Step 2: Find the most powerful fears. Rank the fears you listed according to the power you think they have over you to block your willingness to set goals and to achieve them.

Step 3: Find root fears. For your most intense or frequent fear ask, *Why do I experience fear in this type of situation? What am I really afraid will happen?* Write your answer next to the fear statement. Then ask yourself again why you are afraid, and write down your answer. Keep asking yourself the same question until you feel you've discovered the root of the fear, the ultimate consequence you're really afraid of.

Step 4: Deal with the worst that could happen. Deal directly with the ultimate consequences you uncovered in Step 3.

➡ Ask yourself, *What are the worst things that can happen in this situation?* Imagine all the consequences. List them here.

➡ Close your eyes and let your imagination run rampant; fully experience the fear and any other emotions that come in as you imagine these *awful* consequences occurring.

➡ When your emotions have run their course, allow them to be lifted. Allow yourself to breathe deeply, relax, and let go. Be aware that you're letting go of the desperate need to avoid such terrible consequences.

➡ See yourself handling them comfortably. (You may have to spend days or even weeks getting to the point where you can honestly say, *I can handle those consequences; it wouldn't be the end of the world. I could move up and out from there.*)

Step 5: See the self-sabotage. Ask yourself, *What goals was this fear blocking my wholehearted commitment to?* List them here. Next, picture yourself moving toward each goal with the relaxed intention of achieving it. Whenever you think about this goal, relax and focus on achieving it, free of fear. If fear or fear-related feelings do come up, repeat Step #3 and #4.

Step 6: Handle fears one at a time. Repeat Steps #3 through #5 for your other major fears, one fear at a time.

2

Boost Your Power Image

Women and girls have to own a part of the system—stocks, bonds, a business—if we aren't going to be owned by it.
                        —Joline Godfrey, business executive

In order to access power in the new corporate cultures, you'll probably have to overcome some external organizational barriers as well as some internal barriers, such as self-limiting beliefs. You must understand power and how to use it, as well as ways of gaining credibility and power in today's organizations. Before you delve into the basics of corporate power, think about your current beliefs about it.

What about women and corporate power?

1. Is the typical woman's greatest barrier to corporate power the company's male business culture or her own self-limiting beliefs?
2. Are corporate cultures based primarily on the leaders' beliefs and values or the rules and procedures for getting things done?
3. Are strong corporate cultures more effective than weak ones in the new workplace?
4. Are staff positions usually more powerful than line positions?

We'll look at the power image of Carly Fiorina, CEO of Hewlett-Packard, who has been very successful in gaining credibility in organizations. But first, assess your own power profile by completing the following Self-Awareness Activity.

Self-Awareness Activity #1: What's Your Power Profile?

To raise your awareness of your beliefs about power, complete the following steps:

Step 1: In response to each of the following five statements, write the first thoughts and feelings that occur to you. Don't try to analyze what your response *should* be; your first reaction is the most valuable for this exercise.

1. *Power.* When I think of power, I think of....
2. *Powerless.* Some situations in which I have felt powerless are....
3. *Powerful.* Some situations in which I have felt powerful are....
4. *Power drains.* Some typical behaviors that drain away a woman's professional power image (make her appear less powerful) are....
5. *Power boosts.* Some typical behaviors that boost a woman's professional power image (make her appear more powerful) are....

Step 2: Compare your responses to Statement #2 to those for Statement #3. How can you eliminate or minimize situations in which you feel powerless? How can you increase the situations in which you feel powerful?

Step 3: Compare your responses to Statements #4 and #5. How can you eliminate or minimize your power drains? How can you expand or increase your power boosts?

Many women associate negative feelings and thoughts with the concept of power and are somewhat uncomfortable with the idea of assuming and using power. This attitude contrasts vividly with the typical male attitude. Most men assume that they will be expected to wield power in many capacities throughout their lives and tend to be comfortable with the idea. But what is power?

> **POWER IS THE ABILITY TO MAKE THINGS HAPPEN,**
> **TO INFLUENCE PEOPLE AND EVENTS.**

effective leader

Implied in this definition is the ability to influence yourself—that is, to direct your own life and to command your inner resources. Effective leaders are comfortable with using power. Consider the idea that power itself is neither good nor bad. How you use power and how its use affects other people is what counts. If you're uncomfortable with the idea of wielding power, this thought may help: Wherever you find groups of people, you find leaders—people who have and use power. If you have leadership qualities, the leader might as well be you. In fact, you may be able to use power in a more positive way.

Strategy #1

Overcome Self-Limiting Barriers

Most of the barriers that limit women's career options stem from traditions of the past. Such traditions can affect your career in two basic ways:

1. **Your self-image:** How you picture yourself and, therefore, the roles and behaviors you're comfortable with.
2. **Others' stereotypes:** What others expect of you—their preconceived notions of women's abilities, traits, strengths, and weaknesses, and their resulting beliefs and expectations about proper behaviors and roles.

Once you become aware of your self-limiting beliefs, you're free to start replacing them with beliefs that empower you. As you move into your power, you'll see how you can create your roles by functioning outside others' limiting beliefs and stereotypes and by developing both your feminine and masculine strengths.

Personal Skill #1: Replace Your Self-Limiting Beliefs

For the past 20 years, women in the United States have filled two-thirds of new jobs, and will continue to do so well into the next century. Women dominate the information society as workers, professionals, and entrepreneurs. If you're 35 years old or more, you probably set your career goals in the days when women were a minority in the workforce. You probably set them too low and may be holding yourself back.

Carly Fiorina, CEO of Hewlett-Packard

When Carly Fiorina became president and CEO of Hewlett-Packard Development Company, L.P. (HP) in 1999, she was the first woman in history to work her way up through the ranks to become head of a company of this size and stature. HP, a leading global provider of computers and computer-related products, is one of the 30 "blue-chip" companies that makes up the Dow Jones Index. In 2003, it had close to $50 billion in annual revenue and was ranked 13 on the *Fortune* 500 list.

Carly was already crowned the most powerful woman in American business by *Fortune* magazine before joining HP, the world's second largest computer-maker. She moved around a lot as a kid and spent time at high schools in England, Ghana, and the United States. She graduated with honors from Stanford, where she studied medieval history and philosophy, and then went on to law school at UCLA. After two weeks, she knew that following her dad's footsteps into law would not make her happy, and she dropped out. Breaking the news to her dad (a federal court judge) was one of the hardest things she's ever had to do, she said. However, she went on to get master's degrees in business from the University of Maryland and MIT.

In 1980, at age 25, she landed an entry-level job with AT&T, and steadily rose through the ranks until she became president of a spinoff company, Lucent Technologies, Inc. She successfully guided Lucent out from the shadow of AT&T and through an IPO worth $3 billion in 1996. Since then, she's done nothing to weaken her foothold as a major player in American big business.

Taking over at HP, however, meant that Carly was breaking new ground into previously male-only territory. Onlookers wondered if she could muster her "charismatic salesmanship, earthy wit, and iron will" to rescue a $40 billion company from a painful period of decline. If she made the wrong decisions, she could wipe out HP, a fabled institution whose founders helped create Silicon Valley. She responded by making a perilous bid to remake HP with a record-shattering $20 billion acquisition of Compaq Computer, a major competitor. The takeover became a compelling drama that was followed by the general public as well as the business world. Her later description of this most dangerous year of her life: "perfect enough."

Carly somehow finds time to serve on the board of PowerUp, a coalition of businesses, nonprofits, and the government with the goal of providing underserved children access to technology.

Stereotyped beliefs can lead to feminine attitudes and actions that may be quite appropriate in some situations, but frequently self-defeating in business situations. Do you have some of the self-limiting beliefs typical of women in our culture? If so, they'll probably create a career barrier for you at some time. Find out by completing Self-Awareness Activity #2.

Self-Awareness Activity #2: Do You Have Self-Limiting Beliefs?

Purpose: To identify possible self-limiting beliefs that are typical of women in our culture, indicate whether you agree or disagree with the following statements by placing the appropriate number to the left of each statement, as follows:

    5 = Yes, nearly always   4 = Usually or frequently   3 = Sometimes

    2 = Not often   1 = Rarely or never

____ 1. I don't talk about my career goals and ambitions when I'm on the job.

____ 2. I don't brag or toot my own horn. I let others find out about my abilities and achievements rather than talk about them myself.

____ 3. I'm uncomfortable with being the center of attention. I function better out of the limelight.

____ 4. I'm not very good with numbers.

____ 5. I don't think of myself as a problem-solver.

____ 6. Making decisions is troublesome for me.

____ 7. Maybe I'll learn to use the computer some day.

____ 8. Office politics is dirty politics.

____ 9. Power corrupts, and absolute power leads to absolute corruption.

____ 10. I just focus on my job and my business. I don't get involved in goings-on outside the company or matters inside the company that don't directly affect me.

____ 11. When my coworker gets bossy, I'd rather go along than cause a scene.

____ 12. When my manager jumps on my case, I usually feel he doesn't like me because I didn't do what he expected.

____ 13. Starting your own business is too risky.

____ 14. The way to succeed in today's business world is to develop your business skills.

____ 15. Men don't like women who are too smart or too successful.

Self-awareness follow-up: See the answer key on page 74 to interpret your results; then read the following six typical self-limiting beliefs of women, identify your own self-limiting beliefs, and rewrite them as empowering beliefs.

Self-limiting beliefs are your internal barriers to achieving the career success you want, and they're related to what you've learned about how women should be in our culture. Now let's look at some specific self-limiting beliefs reflected in the questions you answered in Self-Awareness Activity #2.

1. A tendency to suppress or hide ambitions and goals, to wait to be asked, to expect those in command to notice and acknowledge your potential and achievements, and to direct your career progress. This is related to keeping quiet about your abilities and achievements, even in a business setting with people who need to know about them. This is also related to avoiding the spotlight or taking action that will result in your gaining visibility within the organization.

2. A lack of confidence in your ability to handle financial matters, projects requiring math or technical skills, situations requiring astute problem-solving and decision-making abilities.

3. The desire to avoid office politics, the gaining and effective use of power. This is related to traditional beliefs that women should not get too involved in the organization's role in the industry, its inner workings, sources of power, and career paths.

4. A tendency to capitulate quickly to the wishes of others, especially men, when they attempt to dominate—a lack of assertiveness.

5. A tendency to personalize events, criticism, and messages of others, to react emotionally, and to act out such reactions. These may lead to more focus on self-development than on working as part of a team to meet organizational goals (and in the process some personal goals) and on developing an organizational power base.

6. A tendency to react to risky situations by focusing on the possible loss or danger involved rather than realistically assessing the probable gains and losses. This is related to a tendency (conscious or subconscious) to fear success in the business world.

You should now be ready to identify your own self-limiting beliefs and to rewrite them as empowering beliefs.

Personal Skill #2: Resolve Your Conflicting Beliefs

Role conflict is a common problem for career women. Skill Builders #1 and #2 in Chapter 1 gave you a chance to get in touch with beliefs that often underlie role conflict. What did you find out about yourself? Both men and women are sometimes afflicted with fear of failure—fear that if they let people know they're trying to achieve a particular goal and actually go for it, they'll be humiliated and perhaps rejected if they don't succeed. The fear of success is generally a woman's problem and is based mainly on the belief that if she becomes a successful career woman, she won't be viewed as desirable. University of Michigan professor Matina Horner has done research on the fear of success and has found that up to 65 percent of women experience some fear of success, compared with only 10 percent of men.

Women's fearful reactions can range in intensity from disturbing to terrifying. Women's desire for close relationships is normally more primary than men's, and attracting and holding a man has traditionally been extremely important to most women. And because having a career was neither expected nor condoned, when career goals enter the picture, conflict frequently occurs. If you experience fear of success due to conflicting goals and roles, it's probably mostly subconscious and can take several forms, including:

▸ **Mild to severe paralysis.** You allow your career to lie stagnant between the two conflicting needs—to succeed and to attract or hold a man.

▸ **Self-sabotage.** You manage somehow to take actions and make moves or decisions that undermine your career goals.

▸ **Energy drain**. You use much emotional energy in trying to repress parts of your personality that you subconsciously believe are unacceptable, threatening, or otherwise frightening to men. This drains away energy you need to achieve your goals.

Recognize the Cinderella complex. One form of fear of success is called the Cinderella complex by researcher Colette Dowling. Cinderellas sabotage their careers because they fear they'll become so independent, and perhaps aggressive, that they won't appeal to Prince Charming when he comes along. Their expectations, fears, and resulting self-sabotage are all going on at the subconscious level, and so they move toward disaster as sleepwalkers. Deep down, Cinderella fervently hopes the Prince will come along, sweep her off her feet, and make her happy ever after. The belief is, *I don't have the personal power to create my own happiness and my own life—either as a powerful single woman or with the right man as a power couple.*

Do you have just a touch of Cinderella somewhere inside? Is some little part of you really waiting for Prince Charming to come along and make you happy forever after? It's important to identify such fantasies and decide if you need to replace them with more realistic goals that allow you to step into your own power. After all, Cinderella was a victim who needed rescuing—hardly a role compatible with that of a successful career woman.

Break out of old patterns. Are you willing to build a satisfying life on your own? Are you willing to hold out for a partner who has a deep inner confidence in his own manhood and competence, one who prefers to relate to a woman on an equal basis? Men who operate at this level won't resent your accomplishments or try to dominate you. This approach to close relationships can free you to grow and develop and to advance toward all your goals with support instead of sabotage. It allows you to be open and direct about your abilities and achievements in your dealings with men. In turn, you can gladly let those men who are threatened by your competence move on, rather than clutter up your life with problem relationships.

Many women reach adulthood with a number of self-limiting beliefs and resulting fears that they picked up from their families and the people in their communities. These beliefs are also absorbed from the culture-at-large through the books and newspapers we read and the television programs we watch. Such beliefs are usually based on what we perceive as the expectations of others about how we probably are and how we should behave. The fact that others' expectations of appropriate behavior for leaders often conflict with their ideas of appropriate feminine behavior creates problems for many women.

Strategy #2
Play Outside Others' Beliefs and Stereotypes

Women of all ethnicities and lifestyles must deal with cultural stereotypes about women's typical traits. According to the 1995 Glass Ceiling Commission, the following stereotyped beliefs about women in business create the greatest barriers:

▶ Women don't want to work.

▶ Women aren't as committed to careers as men.

▶ Women aren't tough enough to fill some positions.

▶ Women can't or won't work long or unusual hours—or relocate.

▶ Women can't or won't make tough decisions.

- Women are too emotional.
- Women are too passive, too aggressive, or not aggressive enough.
- Women can't crunch numbers.

Don't let others' stereotyped expectations seduce you into behaving just as they expect you to, if it means you won't be acting naturally. Break out of the expectations box so you can develop alternative ways of being—along with the skills and strategies that you decide are most effective for career success.

The best way to break out of gender stereotypes is to create the image of a person who simply doesn't fit into any of the usual molds—you have plenty of the strengths normally attributed to women as well as those attributed to men. By being your own unique person, you can overcome general stereotypes about women's roles and skills, as well as specific stereotypes about the *woman boss*. You can also challenge the myth that women are not as well-qualified as men for leadership roles.

Breakout Skill #1: Build Both Feminine and Masculine Strengths

As you grew up, the stereotyped expectations of others exerted a powerful influence in your life. This socialization process molded much of your behavior as a child because you got payoffs—admiration, approval, and other good things—for acting in the expected ways. By now, you've probably forgotten how the process occurred, and you've internalized many of those expectations as your own beliefs about proper behavior. Now it's time to bring them up to your awareness, reexamine them, and decide which ones to keep and which ones to toss.

Perhaps your community, family, or personal beliefs about appropriate behavior for women differ from those of the culture-at-large, so you have fewer self-limiting beliefs than most women. Still, operating on your own terms can be difficult because your coworkers and managers may be caught up in the typical cultural expectations shown in Snapshot #1.

Snapshot #1: Traditional Gender Traits, According to Men and Women Managers

Masculine	Gender Neutral	Feminine
assertive	adaptive	gentle, nurturing
independent	tactful	understanding
analytical	sincere	compassionate
competitive	committed	sensitive
dominant	innovative	emotional
autocratic	inspired	sentimental
aggressive	reliable	submissive
tough	systematic	dependent
	effective	excitable

In a recent survey, Alice Sargent, author of *Androgynous Manager*, found that successful men and women executives described themselves as having an equal mix of traits they considered feminine and masculine. Do you need to develop strengths you've neglected because they weren't typically expected of women in your community? Identify some typical male strengths that you want to enhance by reviewing Snapshot #2 on page 47, and circling strengths you want to develop.

Notice that the masculine traits are also the traits traditionally expected of successful leaders in our culture. But new corporate cultures, which are adapting to new types of employees, are valuing the feminine traits too. Especially valuable are understanding, compassion, sensitivity, and nurturing—in the sense of supporting worker growth and achievement. When these traits are translated into relating well with coworkers and others, and establishing effective two-way communication with them, they provide a distinct advantage for women.

If you work in a community or organization that holds onto traditional expectations of feminine behavior, you must perform a balancing act to succeed. You must convey a professional image that's usually identified with masculine traits, while still retaining the best aspects of your femininity. It takes skill, but numerous women have managed it and have won over the people they need as a support base for their success. They've done it by building on their present strengths, adapting these strengths to business settings, and developing some of the traits typical of effective male managers.

Which of the traits and skills shown in Snapshot #2 are part of your repertoire? Like most traits and skills, they can be either a strength or a liability, depending on the situation and how you use them. How can you build on these special skills in your leadership role? How can you adapt them to the rules of the business game so they create opportunities rather than barriers?

Breakout Skill #2: Overcome Typical Female Stereotypes and Traps

When you become aware of the stereotyped roles and activities typically assigned to women in our culture, you can avoid common traps created by such stereotypes.

Stereotyped Roles

Perhaps the largest problem women managers face stems from gender-role stereotyping. Most men you'll encounter will probably try to place you in some category they are familiar with, typically one of the following four:

Mom. Men may look to you as a mother-figure to provide nurturing. If you accept the nurturer role, you'll probably find yourself being the nurturer at times, and the critic at others. These two modes fit the mom role, and it's the critical mode that usually causes trouble. Most men remember too vividly being bossed around by mom, and they're not ready to allow another woman to do it.

Daughter or kid sister. The most typical male-female relationship, however, is man as parent, woman as child. If you fall into that lesser role, you'll get the payoff of being protected, but you'll pay the price of not being taken too seriously and of being overprotected. If you allow your woman manager to play the role of big sister or mom to you, be aware that her nurturing can turn to jealousy if she begins to see you as a rival for her job.

Snapshot #2: Traditional Masculine and Feminine Strengths

Typical masculine strengths women can develop	Typical feminine strengths women can expand
• Being powerful and forthright.	• Recognizing, accepting, and expressing feelings.
• Becoming entrepreneurial.	• Respecting feelings as an essential part of life, as guides to authenticity and effectiveness, rather than as barriers to achievement.
• Making a direct, visible impact on others rather than just functioning behind the scenes.	
• Stating your own needs and refusing to back down.	• Working for self-fulfillment as well as for money.
• Focusing on a task and regarding it as at least as important as the relationships with the people doing the task.	• Valuing nonwork roles as well as work identity.
• Building support systems with other women and sharing competence with them, rather than competing with them.	• Being able to fail at a task without feeling failure as a person.
• Helping other women succeed; networking.	• Expressing the need to be nurtured at times.
• Intellectualizing and generalizing from experience.	• Touching and being close to both men and women without sexual connotations.
• Behaving impersonally sometimes.	• Listening empathetically, actively experiencing another's reality without feeling responsible for solving others' problems.
• Not turning anger, blame, and pain inward.	
• Moving beyond feelings of suffering and victimization by taking responsibility.	• Sharing feelings as the most meaningful part of one's contact with others, accepting the risk and vulnerability such sharing implies.
• Being invulnerable to destructive feedback.	
• Responding to resentments and anger directly rather than with passive resistance or nagging.	• Building support systems with other women, sharing competencies without competition, and sharing feelings and needs with sincerity.
• Responding directly with *I* statements, rather than with blaming *you* ones.	• Relating to experiences and people on a personal level rather than assuming that the only valid approach to life and interpersonal contact is an abstract, rational, or strictly objective one.
• Becoming an effective problem-solver by being analytical, systematic, and direct.	
• Becoming a risk-taker (calculating probabilities and making appropriate trade-offs).	• Accepting the emotional, spontaneous, and irrational parts of the self.

Sex object. Many men will be interested and will look to you for a little excitement and flirtation, either covert or overt, but you'll pay the price by losing credibility. (There will be men who will try to use you, and if you allow them to go far enough, to later discard you.)

Women's-libber. When some men learn that you refuse to fit into any of the first three categories, they may try to stick you into the women's-lib category. Your insistence on being your own competent self may be interpreted as rebelliousness or hardness. The men may leave you alone, especially when you most need their assistance or cooperation. Therefore, you'll probably want to send clear signals that you're assertive and competent, but that you're also a team player and your own person.

Examine your own beliefs to see if you're holding conflicting stereotypes about your roles. Realize that you can't exhibit opposite kinds of behavior at the same time. For example, you can't be both a *poor little me* helpless kid sister and a credible leader. Focus on the image you want and act accordingly.

Stereotyped Duties

Related to these stereotyped roles are the remnants of old stereotyped thinking about *women's work*. This includes the typing, filing, note-taking, coffee-making, food-ordering, party-planning, donation-gathering tasks typical of wives, mothers, clerks, secretaries, waitresses, hostesses, and volunteer charity workers. If all the men at your level engage in one of these activities, then obviously it's not stereotyped as women's work in this situation. If men and women rotate these chores, they aren't stereotyped. But if you're expected to do them just because you're a woman, suggest rotating them or say you don't have those skills—or find some way out. Above all, don't get trapped in a stereotype.

The going-along trap. This trap involves falling into the stereotyped role rather than being your own person. While it may seem easier at the time, going along will eventually limit your range of behavior, including some of the effective behaviors appropriate to career advancement. It projects a message about you that can hurt your career growth. In order to break out of the stereotype, you'd have to do an about-face on certain issues. It's easier and better for your image to refuse to fall into stereotyped roles from the beginning.

The unnatural trap. This trap involves constantly monitoring your behavior and trying to eliminate actions that might reinforce stereotyping. This leads to unnatural or self-conscious behavior. While monitoring is often necessary in the beginning to establish your professional image, be aware of the importance of being able to relax into a natural businesslike persona. Rise above stereotypes by firmly identifying your own professional image, goals, and priorities, then tie them to organization and team goals, and communicate with others in terms of goal achievement.

Breakout Skill #3: Defuse Stereotypes Held By Your Managers

Women managers say that men at the top still hold stereotypes about women's shortcomings. The most common and devastating of these are:

▶ People won't accept women in top-management roles.

▶ Women aren't committed enough to make it to the top.

▶ Women's decision-making ability is inadequate.

▶ Women are too emotional.

People are becoming more accepting of women in top-management roles. According to *Harvard Business Review* surveys, by 1985, about two-thirds of men and women were saying that it's okay to work for a woman executive, compared with only one-third in 1965. But for those who still resist accepting a woman in a leadership role, you can use the following techniques.

▶ Keep presenting the idea and the image that your leadership is accepted—by your team, your peers, business associates outside the company such as customers and suppliers, and other professional associates.

▶ Discuss your career goals with higher-ups and showcase your commitment. If appropriate, discuss whether and when you'll have children and how you plan to handle that career phase.

▶ Keep records that document your decision-making ability, as well as your ability to facilitate good team decisions. Related to the decision-making myth are myths about your ability to crunch numbers, integrate the computer, and handle financial aspects of your job. Showcase your math-finance-technology savvy as well. Find ways to remind management of your track record.

▶ Manage your emotions in ways that top managers in your company can be comfortable with.

Male Managers Are Diverse Too

You'll deal with a broad range of managers in the workplace. When it comes to stereotyped expectations of working women, male managers tend to fall into three broad types:

1. **The dinosaur** is the traditional patriarchal manager who has always believed that wives and mothers belong at home, that they simply aren't capable of coping as leaders in a *man's world.* This type is easy to recognize.

2. **The two-headed monster** is the manager who tries to play it both ways. One of his heads professes sympathy for women's issues and support for women's career goals. The other head thinks more like the dinosaur manager—either consciously or subconsciously. He's probably the most common type and the most difficult to recognize and deal with.

3. **The enlightened man** is truly free of the traditional, stereotyped expectations of working women. He's rare, but becoming less so, and is great to work with. With him you can move directly to dealing with the issues at hand.

Coping with the stereotyped ideas of managers is especially difficult because they hold so much power over your career progress. The best approach with the first two types is to keep sending the message that you're not their idea of the typical woman. You can do all this while still retaining the best of your feminine strengths, but it may take all the intelligence and intuition you can muster.

Women Managers Create Value

One way to counter old stereotypes is to cite new information. For example, a 2003 study by Catalyst shows that *Fortune* 500 companies with the higher proportions of women executives produced returns about one-third greater than those with the lowest proportions. The research firm examined the 353 companies that held the status of "*Fortune* 500 company" for four of five years from 1996 through 2000. Based on the representation of women in senior management, the companies were divided into four roughly equal quartiles. Catalyst then examined their financial performance on two measures, Return on Equity (ROE) and Total Return to Shareholders (TRS), comparing the highest quartile with the lowest. Two major conclusions are:

1. The group of companies with the highest representation of women on their senior management teams had a 35 percent higher ROE.

2. The same group had a 34 percent higher TRS than companies with the lowest women's representation.

According to Catalyst President Ilene H. Lang, "Business leaders increasingly request hard data to support the link between gender diversity and corporate performance. This study gives business leaders unquestionable evidence that a link does exist. We controlled for industry and company differences, and the conclusion was still the same. Top-performing companies have a higher representation of women on their leadership teams."

Breakout Skill #4: Counter Biases Held by Male Peers

Typical biases held by male peers about women in leadership roles include: she may be a threat, she's not one of the gang, or different rules apply to outsiders (women).

Show that you're not a threat. Male colleagues or peers may feel threatened and resentful of your competence, power, or authority, especially if they're not particularly secure in their own jobs. As a result, you may get no information, help, or suggestions from them, and you may finally realize that your able peers are sitting back and waiting for you to fail. Take the initiative to develop supportive relationships with peers. Capitalize on the I'll-scratch-your-back-if-you'll-scratch-mine approach. Know the language of old school ties and use it. Consistently follow through, send straight messages, pay back favors, and build trusting relationships.

Become accepted as one of the gang. Perhaps a more common problem is merely oversight on the part of male peers, stemming from the fact that women traditionally haven't been included in informal communication channels. For example, you may be excluded from a great deal of useful information that's exchanged in the men's room, in the locker room, on the golf course, and at the corner bar. When possible, make yourself visible and a viable part of these informal gatherings. You'll get information that is available *only* through informal channels.

It's sometimes easy to overlook what amounts to an invitation from a male colleague. If he says, "I'm (we're) going to lunch," that's probably your cue to say, "Good idea. I'll be right with you." Sometimes your only workable solution may be taking the initiative yourself. For example, when you see the men going to lunch, join them, if possible, even without a formal invitation. Your attitude should be casual and confident. When the men head for the corner bar, you can casually ask to join them. This may lead to certain pitfalls, obviously, but there are ways to avoid them. Depending on your capacity, drink nonalcoholic beverages or have only one or two drinks. Insist quietly on paying for your own drinks or on taking your turn in buying an occasional round. Leave with the group, at least the first few times. Then relax and have a good time. If you're fun to be with, the group is more likely to want to have you around. Your goal is for your male peers to be comfortable with you and to think of you as one of the gang—without giving up your unique feminine identity.

Expect fair treatment. Don't accept the unwritten rule that it's okay to treat women differently. In assessing your position with your male peers, your primary concerns should be whether you're treated fairly, with an equal share of the work, responsibilities, and rewards. Another primary concern is whether you're allowed to participate in the events and decisions that affect your job.

Expect fair treatment, and you're more likely to get it. If you don't get it, express your concern in terms of fairness and the good of the organization.

Breakout Skill #5: Overcome Stereotypes Held by Male Reports

Some men who report to you may have misgivings about working for a woman executive, according to the *Harvard Business Review* attitude surveys. The major reservations men have include:

▸ Men think women lack confidence in the leadership role.

▸ Men fear that a woman boss will lack real power.

▸ Men think women don't know how to play the business game.

▸ Many men think women bosses come on too strong and try too hard.

▸ Men are awkward with a woman boss and don't know how to treat her.

▸ Men feel they lose face when they are subordinate to a woman. This is most predominant in men over 50.

▸ When they perceive that a woman is only a token for affirmative action purposes, men feel they must pay the price by having to function under an unqualified manager.

Men who report to a woman can be very difficult to please. If you take an objective, businesslike approach, you may be labeled as too tough, or even as a castrating female. On the other hand, if you show some warmth and concern for male employees on a personal level, they may label you a pushover, and immediately try to take advantage of your weakness. The line between being too hard and too soft may be a very fine one, but women who make it to the top have found it and walked it. You must find the proper approach for your particular situation.

Breakout Skill #6: Understand Stereotypes Held by Other Women

Other women can be great supporters or detractors depending on where they are coming from. Higher-level women managers and peers tend to fall somewhere along a continuum between the nonsupportive queen bee and the supportive liberated woman. Women employees, on the other hand, tend to view you as somewhere between *she's great* and *she's awful.*

The queen bee probably wants to stereotype you as an airhead who's trying to push forward too fast. She's usually a middle-aged or older manager who scratched and fought her way up in spite of the overwhelming odds against her advancement. She may have sacrificed much of her personal life and some of her femininity, leaving her pretty hard around the edges. She has enjoyed the attention of being a rarity in the organization and doesn't welcome competition for the spotlight from bright, fresh-faced young women. The best way to deal with her is to give her the respect she has earned. Let her know you admire her achievements. Ask for suggestions and information. Do *not* make the mistake of confiding in her. Don't tell her about your past or current problems, your personal life, or anything you wouldn't want broadcast throughout the company. Remember, she's a fighter, and she'll probably not hesitate to use such information against you when the time is ripe. Above all, don't become a queen bee yourself some day.

The liberated woman probably wants to stereotype you as a kindred spirit, so she's automatically biased in your favor. She believes career women should support each other and assumes you feel the same way. You'll have to convince her that you're her enemy in order to alienate her, so all you need to do is return the support she offers you and be a good colleague. More and more career women are adopting this stance.

Women employees who work for you may feel very strongly about you. They tend to think you're either one of the best or one of the worst. What most say they like most about a woman boss is:

▶ She understands what it's like to be a working woman. For example, she knows I must have some warning if I'm going to work late.

▶ She understands my problems. How can a man understand? Most of them have wives at home to worry about details.

▶ She understands better than a man what motivates people.

▶ She takes time to explain what she wants.

▶ She'll tell me when I've done a good job, not just when I've made a mistake.

▶ She makes it clear that she cares about people, not just machine-like performance. She has a way of bringing out the best in people.

On the other hand, what women don't like about their women bosses include:

▶ She's too moody and unprofessional.

▶ She talks about me behind my back, when I can't defend myself. She doesn't level with me and tell me what she's thinking.

▶ She doesn't help other women. You can't please her because in doing a good job you become a potential threat to her.

Your job is to manage your emotions, focus on consistency and fairness, be as sincere and honest as you can, avoid harmful gossip, and provide challenges for women to expand their skills along with support for helping them to achieve.

Breakout Skill #7: Challenge the Unqualified Woman Myth

The body of research concerning women's aptitudes and actual performance in new work roles is growing. This provides a factual basis for repudiating some of the more damaging stereotyped ideas—and for boosting your credibility and that of all women. For example, the Johnson O'Connor Research Foundation has been testing the aptitudes of both men and women since 1922. The test battery includes measures of 16 primary job aptitudes, plus English vocabulary knowledge. To begin with, women show higher aptitude on the vocabulary portion. On 10 of the 16 job aptitudes, there are no significant gender differences. Of the remaining six aptitudes, women do better in five, while men have higher aptitude in only one—structural visualization, picturing solid forms in space from various angles. A foundation analysis indicates that even in this one area, women's lower score may actually indicate their higher aptitude for leadership and management.

In addition, statistics from the Labor Department and the U.S. Census Bureau indicate that women must be better qualified than men in order to land comparable paying jobs. For example, female college graduates earn on average about what male high school graduates earn. And there are currently more women than men earning university degrees.

Strategy #3

Manage Sexual Issues and Harassment

Nowhere is sexual game-playing more rampant than in the corporate world. As you climb the ladder, you'll need to be more watchful and tactful than ever because you'll be an increasingly attractive *catch*. You must recognize the office sex game as a male conquest game in which women are usually the losers. You can avoid most problems by saying *no* consistently, but firmly and gracefully. Learn all you can about sexual harassment so you can prevent and manage it.

Sexual Skill #1: Disempower the Office Sex Game

As a woman, you'll probably be the loser if you get involved in office sex games. Remember that you're operating in a male culture and playing by male rules.

Although nearly all organizations profess to be against office sex, unofficially it's usually condoned for the men as long as they stay in control of the situation and are properly discreet. This liberal view of sexual affairs does not apply to you. *You* represent the target of the conquest and, eventually, the victim if you give in. That's why more than 90 percent of sexual harassment complaints are filed by women.

It's a male conquest and power game. The first thing to understand about the office sex game—and about sexual harassment—is that it's nearly always about power and conquest, and usually about guys impressing other guys.

The second thing to realize is that office affairs are almost never a secret. Because sexual conquests of female employees are male status symbols, they would have no value unless the male made sure he got credit. However, if the man shows any sign of emotion or if there's any indication that the woman began the affair or will decide when it's over, the man loses status among his colleagues. Therefore, if you try to change the rules of the game, you can expect a real battle from him.

Is office sex always so bad? And what's wrong with a little flirtation? Most experts would say *no* and *nothing*—if that's what you want to deal with. Granted, the workplace is where you spend most of your time and it follows that attractions, flirtations, and affairs will take place among people who meet there. And some of these relationships actually lead to marriage or to fulfilling, committed relationships. However, these are the exceptions rather than the rule.

It's based on a two-tier system. Many married executives conduct their lives on two levels, which might be dubbed *top level* and *bottom level*. The top level is designed to preserve the appearance of the good family man, responsible executive, and pillar of the community. The bottom level is designed to enhance the male ego through sexual conquest, to impress other males with his apparent sexual prowess, and to add some fun, variety, and excitement to his life through sexual encounters. Corporate wives are off-limits as targets and kept in the dark at all costs about the sexual conquests of any of the husbands. This also goes for wives of important clients and associates in the same industry. Men cooperate with each other in the balancing act of keeping the two levels properly separated so that the appearances so necessary for the top level remain untarnished.

If you participate in the bottom level, you may be perceived as a threat to the top level once the affair is over. You'll know too much about the bottom-level life of your former partner and perhaps about the lives of some of his colleagues as well. The safest way for men to handle this problem is to remove you from the scene. As a result, you may lose your job. Even if you get through this phase with your job intact, you may be automatically excluded from further promotions because you'll probably be branded *inferior*. Ways to become a part of the top level include being a professional friend of the men and befriending their wives—if wives are part of the business social scene. In the beginning, your major focus and the message you want to convey is that you're a professional with a satisfying personal life. The implication is that you'll never be a competitor for their husbands' affection.

To summarize, the objective of the office sex game is to increase the man's status with other men. This is one of the ways he becomes *one of the boys* who make decisions about promotions and salaries. You may therefore increase the status of every man you have sex with and, at the same time, decrease your own status. Clients and suppliers are, generally speaking, included in the sex game. Your best strategy is to keep your sexual relationships completely separate from your business relationships.

Sexual Skill #2: Say No Gracefully, but Firmly

Given the fact that sex in the office is a losing game for you, how can you keep from playing? Here are some suggestions:

Say *No* to overly familiar labels. Think twice about allowing men to use endearing terms without tactfully objecting. These terms indicate possessiveness and can imply a personal relationship beyond normal business dealings. They can also imply that you are childlike or a sex object. You can privately inform men who use them that terms such as *Doll, Dear, Darling, Honey,* and *Babe* have negative connotations for you and you're sure they don't intend to continue making you uncomfortable by addressing you in that manner.

Know when to be oblivious. It's not that you want to play dumb; it's just that you have your mind set on taking care of business. To convey this message, there are times when it makes the most sense to ignore subtle sexual overtures. If the overtures become not so subtle, you can change the subject to a job-related topic and become more businesslike than ever.

Say *No* with *I* messages. If he persists or asks you out, focus on tactful *I* messages, such as, *I want us to be friends*, and *I want to do business with you*, and *That's the only* *kind of relationship I'm comfortable with.* Be firm, but avoid hurting his ego. The person with a hurt ego tends to lash back sooner or later. Your goal is to win as much professional respect and support from him as possible and still say no. You can find literally hundreds of ways of saying, *I like you and I won't have sex with you.* Keep in mind that you always have many more choices than to either give in or insult him. Here are some responses you can use:

▶ *I like you, but I never accept social invitations from business friends.*

▶ *I'd like to join you, but my husband would be hurt if he couldn't share the occasion.*

Say *No* firmly with clear, unmixed messages. The underlying message you want to get across is that you like him, but the answer to sexual involvement is *no* and will *always be no*. Have basically the same response for every man in the office: *No*. If a man in a higher position starts asking about your personal life, tell him about your career aspirations and plans. Give the impression that your career (or career plus husband) is your entire life. Remember, the oldest and most common male defense when they're accused of sexually accosting or harassing women is, *She asked for it.* So be sure that all aspects of your verbal and nonverbal messages communicate clearly that the answer is *no*. You can be friendly and still not get sexual. The best way to send clear, unmixed messages is to be clear in your own mind—from day one—of the professional image you want to project and the reputation you want to build in the workplace. If you consistently project this image in the way you dress, act, and speak, you'll have few, if any, sexual problems.

Sexual Skill #3: Manage Sexual Harassment

Unfortunately, women in our culture have not been raised to be assertive in dealing with men, nor to anticipate the ways men may sexually harass them on the job. Sexual harassment is a commonplace problem, and both men and women need training on how to manage it.

Identify the Legal Issues

When does the office sex game legally become sexual harassment?

▶ When the behavior is unwanted, unsolicited, and nonreciprocal.

▶ When it asserts a person's sex role over her or his function as a worker.

▶ When there is a significant power differential between the two persons. Remember, it's primarily about power rather than attraction, respect, or even sex.

The power differential is especially important because 95 percent of top managers are male, and they set the tone for the organization. We could say that men still hold 95 percent of the power in organizations, which puts women at a decided disadvantage in the sexual power game. Courts have identified two types of sexual harassment: 1) the overt *put out or get out* proposition, and 2) behavior that creates a hostile work environment. Sexual harassment can include:

▶ Physical contact such as patting, stroking, hugging, kissing.

▶ Comments on your clothing, body, or appearance.

▶ Swearing based on sexual images, graphic sexual jokes, pinups, pictures, graffiti, and other visual depictions that are embarrassing or degrading to most women.

▶ Indirect harassment caused by being subjected to an environment where sexual harassment occurs even though you are not a target.

▶ Favoritism that constitutes a hostile environment for other employees.

An example of favoritism is when a manager has a sexual relationship with an employee and rewards that employee with raises, promotions, or perks. Other employees, who are denied comparable rewards, experience a hostile environment based on the manager's sexual relationship with their coworker.

The Supreme Court has further ruled that:

▶ Sexual harassment can exist even if an employee voluntarily engages in sexual activity with a manager. The test is whether the manager has coercive power and the advances are *unwelcome*. In other words, the employee doesn't have to be raped in order for the coercion to be ruled sexual harassment.

▶ An employee's sexually provocative activity, dress, speech, manner, and so on, can be used by an employer as evidence that sexual advances were not unwelcome.

▶ Harassment must be sufficiently severe or pervasive to alter an employee's condition of employment and to create an abusive work environment.

▶ Sexual harassment can consist of nothing more than a hostile environment; no monetary loss is necessary.

▶ The standards of a reasonable woman—not the traditional standards of the *reasonable man*—must be used to determine sexually offensive conduct toward women.

Employees now have the right to jury trials and to punitive damages for sexual harassment—in addition to the reinstatement and back pay formerly provided.

Sexual harassment is pervasive in our society. A poll conducted by the National Association of Female Executives found that 53 percent of its 1,300 members have been victims. According to a 1991 study by Catherine MacKinnon, in about 99 percent of the reported cases, the people accused of harassment are males.

Recognize Differing Male-Female Viewpoints

Men and women view sexual harassment in widely different ways. For one thing, men are more likely to suspect that a woman's claims are false. Yet research indicates that only 1 percent of claims turn out to be questionable. Still, some men try to stereotype women who complain into one of these categories:

▶ **She-devil:** Watch that woman. She's trouble. She's trying to demonize him.

▶ **Seductress:** She asked for it. She led him on. (This is the most common stereotype of women who complain about male sexual violations.)

▶ **Bimbo:** She used him. She can't make it on her own merits. She has to get promotions, attention, or money some other way.

▶ **Woman scorned:** She had a crush on him and he wasn't interested, or he lost interest.

▶ **Fantasizer:** She dreams of male attention and pretends it's there.

▶ **Frustrated wallflower:** She can't get male attention and desperately wants it.

▶ **Martyr:** She loves playing the role of victim or martyr.

In all these stereotypes it's the problem of the woman, not the man who has violated her. And in all of them, the man is the desired and dominant person as well as the innocent victim. Snapshot #3 summarizes some difference in the ways men and women view a workplace flirtation.

Snapshot #3: Male and Female Reactions to a Male Manager Flirting With a Female Employee

Male Observer	Female Observer
It's just a sexual dalliance.	It's a power issue.
It's okay to step out of the manager role to flirt a little.	A manager can't really step out of that role with an employee.
Harassment is rare; it's just when a guy goes over the line of acceptable flirting.	Harassment is pervasive and shows a difference in how men and women see power.
Men often exercise power without noticing it.	Power must be earned; women often don't get power.
What's the big deal?	I feel intimidated and threatened; this touches a nerve.

Most women have some sense of the wide disparity between how men and women view sexual harassment and the stereotyped labels that may be pinned on them if they file a complaint. Understandably, most women have refused to file claims, believing that doing so would only make a bad situation worse. Actually, complaining could eliminate the problem, but you must take the right steps.

Know the Steps to Take

You can't afford to allow any man to persist in actions that constitute sexual harassment. To do so would signal to other men that such behavior may be tolerated by you and would set a poor example for the entire work team. Don't accept such a victim role. If you—or one of your team members—are being harassed, here are some specific steps to take.

Be friendly, but professional. Do as much as you can to project an image of a professional person who does not invite sexual harassment and who won't put up with it. Give clear, unmixed messages that you will not now, or ever, engage in sexual relations with business associates.

Confront your harasser. If he doesn't get your message the first time, escalate your assertion. Tell him that this behavior must stop immediately. Follow up with a memo documenting what you said and hand it to him in the presence of a witness.

Document sexual harassment incidents. Keep notes of what is said and done by your harasser, of what you say and do in response, and the date and place where the incident occurred. Note who, if anyone, witnessed the incident. Discuss it with these witnesses to make it clear in their minds. Ask them to keep notes about what happened, the date, and the place—which will serve to verify your record of the case when you file a complaint.

Confide in trusted associates. If you wish to keep the matter officially confidential while you try to put a stop to his behavior, tell only trusted associates. Ask them to keep notes about what you tell them. These people can later testify that you were concerned about the incident(s).

Look for a behavior pattern. Chances are very good that he has harassed other women. Seek out women who have worked with him. Engage in discreet, probing conversations to learn if they've been harassed. If you can establish that he has a consistent pattern of harassment, your case is greatly strengthened. In fact, the most successful results have occurred when the women got together and built a joint case. When it's your word against his, it's tough, especially if he has more power. When several women get together, he's in trouble.

Report it. Some harassment incidents are so blatant and so offensive that they should be reported at once. Most are more subtle and tentative. In those cases, it's usually best to tell him clearly that you do not welcome his advances, and give him a chance to back off. If the harassment continues, learn company procedures for handling it. Report it to the designated person, often someone in Human Resources. If you need further emotional support or advice, look for a local women's organization that may provide such services.

Weigh the Consequences of Further Action

If you're not satisfied with the way your organization handles your complaint, you can carry it further—to the Equal Employment Opportunity Commission (EEOC) or to court. Consider consulting an attorney who specializes in such cases. Local women's organizations and bar associations may recommend someone. Carefully weigh the pros and cons. Unfortunately, taking legal action against a company usually results in being informally blackballed within the industry, even though this is illegal. As a result, you could experience a career setback of as much as seven years. Your best bet is to team up with other women who have been harassed by this man and to win your case internally, within the company.

Be timely. If you decide to take action outside the company, determine the statute of limitations for reporting sexual harassment in your state. In most states, you must file a claim within six months of the last occurrence.

Take the lead in eliminating harassment. Organizations that ignore sexual harassment may pay dearly. Multimillion-dollar fines have been slapped on such organizations in recent years. One law firm ignored the blatant sexual harassment of an attorney who brought in about a million dollars worth of business per year. The newcomer secretary he harassed had no power in the situation—until she quit and won $3 million in a lawsuit.

You may have more influence than you realize within your organization to make sure it has policies designed to prevent and cope with sexual harassment. As a woman leader, you can play a role in preventing, minimizing, and eliminating harassment in your firm.

Here are some steps that managers in your organization can take:

- ▶ Establish and publicize a strong policy that specifically describes the kinds of actions that constitute sexual harassment and sets out the consequences for offenders.
- ▶ Consistently signal that the organization is committed to fighting harassment.
- ▶ Provide training seminars designed to sensitize all employees to the issue.
- ▶ Set up grievance mechanisms to encourage private complaints of harassment and to bypass immediate supervisors, who are often the offenders.

Training and guidelines that management provides for resolving sexual harassment complaints should include the following:

- ▶ Take sexual harassment complaints as seriously as other grievances; investigate them as thoroughly.
- ▶ Realize that only about 99 percent of complaints are valid.
- ▶ Find out what the complainant wants, try to accommodate her, and be sure to keep the matter entirely confidential.
- ▶ Investigate carefully. Appoint an investigative team (one man, one woman; preferably objective outsiders). Look for documentation, witnesses, confidants, observers.
- ▶ If the team cannot substantiate that sexual harassment has occurred (she says it did; he says it didn't), tell the complainant that the firm cannot take definitive action and to report any further occurrences or any instances of retaliation. Tell the accused. Let him know that the organization had a duty to investigate and that he is cleared, but if another complaint is filed, it will have serious implications.
- ▶ If the team substantiates that sexual harassment has occurred, use disciplinary procedures that are similar to those used in cases of nonperformance of job duties. Normally, the first offense calls for a warning and some sensitivity training. The second offense calls for some form of punishment: no bonus, no promotion, a demotion, docked pay, temporary suspension. The third offense calls for dismissal.
- ▶ Ensure that no one retaliates against the complainant, no matter what the outcome.

Strategy #4 _____

Overcome Organizational Barriers

In addition to building on your strengths and your innate psychological and cultural advantages as a woman, you must also be aware of external and internal barriers to success that you may encounter along your career path. Three major external barriers that women have always faced are the glass ceiling, the pay gap, and corporate cultures and policies that don't support family needs. What you can do is search for companies that are more aware of women's needs and are willing to provide for them.

Career Skill #1: Avoid Firms With Glass Ceilings

The glass ceiling is what we call the barrier to women's advancement in organizations. This barrier is invisible but solid, like glass. Few women see it before they hit it because the organization's leaders don't admit it's there. Although the United States leads the world in percentage of women managers, at 40 percent of all managers, this percentage is somewhat deceptive. A look at the following information will provide a more accurate picture of women's management roles.

▶ Women managers tend to be clustered in the lower-paying, entry levels of management, such as working supervisor and first-line supervisor.

▶ Most are managers of small businesses, with only 17 percent in large firms.

▶ Only 5 percent are in top management because most women hit a glass ceiling to top-level, and even middle-level, positions, according to the Labor Department's Glass Ceiling Commission.

Many women are getting the education they need to move into the well-paying, power positions, but there is still a position gap as well as a pay gap compared to men.

Education

Although there has traditionally been a male-female education gap, with more men getting degrees, the gap closed for 2000 graduates, with women baccalaureates slightly outnumbering men by 28 to 25 percent. Among younger persons, ages 25 to 29, women are now better educated than men, as follows:

▶ High school diplomas are held by 88 percent of young women, 85 percent of young men.

▶ Bachelor's degrees are held by 32 percent of these women, 27 percent of the men.

The fields where women graduates have increased the most dramatically are business and science, as shown in Snapshot #4 on page 61.

Occupations

Women are 52 percent of the U.S. population and 46 percent of the workforce, but they are only 40 percent of all managers and less than 5 percent of top managers in large firms. While most managers, precision production workers, machine operators, and laborers are men, most clerical and service workers are women. Professionals, which include teachers and nurses as well as doctors, lawyers, and accountants, are nearly half-and-half, as are technical and sales workers. Snapshot #4 shows some specific comparisons. Euro-American men are 35 percent of the population and 39 percent of the workforce; yet they are:

▶ 95 percent of top-earning corporate officers in *Fortune* 500 companies.

▶ 80 percent of corporate officers in the 500 largest U.S. companies.
(Of the remaining 20 percent, 16 percent are women and 4 percent are minority men.)

▶ 92 percent of senior managers in mid- to large-sized corporations.
(Of the remaining 8 percent, 5 percent are women and 3 percent are men of all other ethnic groups.)

▸ 82 percent of the *Forbes* 400 persons worth at least 265 million dollars.

▸ 80 percent of Congress (90 percent of the Senate; 78 percent of the House).

▸ 92 percent of state governors.

▸ 70 percent of tenured college faculty.

▸ 90 percent of daily newspaper editors.

▸ 77 percent of TV news directors.

Snapshot #4: Men and Women—Occupations and Education

Relative proportions of men and women:	Male	Female
In total population (2000)	48%	52%
In the workforce	54	46
Managers	58	43
Professionals	46	53
Technical	46	64
Sales	51	50
Clerical	23	80
Service	37	63
Production, craft (electrician, plumber, etc.)	90	9
Machine operators	60	24
Laborers	80	20
Received bachelor's degrees (2000)	28%	25%
Psychology	29	71
Life sciences	49	51
Business degree	53	47
Social sciences	56	44
Physical sciences	69	31
Engineering	86	14
Working on advanced professional degrees (2002)	51%	49%
Law	51	49
Medicine	55	45

Source: Bureau of Labor Statistics, 2002

According to the Glass Ceiling Commission, they "dominate just about everything but NOW and the NAACP." It is clear that they hold the most powerful positions in the economic and political arenas. Still, women's numbers are increasing in the better-paying occupations. For example, in 2000, 19 percent of dentists were women, compared to 9 percent in 1990, and they were 30 percent of lawyers and judges, compared to 21 percent in 1990.

Women managers who were surveyed said the glass ceiling is the most important issue facing ambitious women in the corporate world. Virtually all women who were not CEOs said women were underrepresented at the top in their firms. They said the major reason was the reluctance of the men at the top to include women. They cited the following barriers, in the order listed, as the most important ones for women to overcome:

▸ Top management harbors stereotypes about women, especially regarding their ability to gain acceptance in a top role, their level of career commitment, and their decision-making ability.

- ▶ Women are often excluded from key informal gatherings where information and opinions are exchanged and deals are made.
- ▶ Women's contributions and abilities are not taken as seriously as men's.
- ▶ Women have more difficulty finding mentors.
- ▶ Women don't get equal opportunities to serve on important committees and project teams.

What many women do when they hit the glass ceiling is start their own businesses.

Career Skill #2: Bargain Away the Pay Gap

In 2001, women's median earnings were 74 percent of men's (for full-time, year-round employees), with men making $39,000 compared to women's $28,800. All ethnic groups experience some pay gap, and Euro-Americans have the greatest gender gap (U.S. Census Bureau 2002).

- ▶ Euro-American men earned $42,200, compared to women's $30,800.
- ▶ African American men earned $31,000, compared to women's $25,700.
- ▶ Latino American men earned $25,000, compared to women's $21,000.

The fact that certain occupations are considered "women's work" is the largest contributor to the gender wage gap, according to the Bureau of Labor Statistics. The pay gap was more or less 60 to 65 percent from the 1950s to 1980. The 10 percent improvement since 1980 probably reflects men's lower pay, women's higher educational achievement, their choice of formerly male-dominated fields that pay more, and the tendency to delay having children and to take fewer years off from careers once children arrive. The pay gap is especially tough for single mothers. More families than ever are being headed by single women—28 percent in 1999, compared to 17 percent in 1990 and 11 percent in 1970. Among "minority" households, the proportion of single mothers is even higher: for African Americans the figure is 44 percent and for Latino Americans it is 32 percent, versus 12 percent for Asian American and Euro-American households

On average, these women had to survive on about one-third the median income of married-couple families. Therefore, they were nearly six times as likely to live in poverty. In fact, at all ages, more women than men live in poverty. For example, women over age 65 are twice as likely as older men to live in poverty. And they live longer—by about 7 years on average.

Women still make 26 percent less than men in most occupations, at every level from new worker to executive vice president, regardless of education and experience. The pay gap is smaller if you're in engineering or computers, and larger if you're in human resources, because of demand. When women move into an occupation in significant numbers, the occupation loses status and decreases in pay, and men tend to move out of it. Conversely, if an occupation loses status and pay for other reasons, women are more likely to be hired into it.

So what can you do? First, be aware of the typical pay range for your field, your geographic area, and, if possible, the companies you interview. See such sources as John Wright's *The American Almanac of Jobs and Salaries*. Sharpen your negotiation skills and go for the top of the range or even a little beyond.

Career Skill #3: Negotiate for Flexible Working Arrangements

If you want a satisfying career, rather than just a job, look for:

▶ A corporate culture that values diversity, including women's ways of leading.

▶ Adequate paid maternity leave.

▶ Cooperation in managing affordable, quality childcare and eldercare.

▶ Flexible job structures such as flextime, job sharing, part-time arrangements at certain stages, and home office arrangements.

In the past couple of decades, more women have been delaying marriage and more couples are delaying the time when they have their first child. Most couples think that they have until their late 30s to get started, maybe even their early 40s. That's understandable because it's been only recently that doctors discovered how dramatically a woman's fertility can decline after age 27. While at age 20, her risk of miscarriage is about 9 percent, it doubles by 35, then doubles again by 40. In fact, 90 percent of a woman's eggs are likely to be abnormal by age 42, and she has less than an 8 percent chance of having a normal baby using her own eggs. [See Sylvia Ann Hewlett's book *Creating a Life: Professional Women and the Quest for Children* (Miramax, 2002).]

Many couples are shocked by this news. Some spend tens of thousands of dollars at fertility clinics before they have their first child. Some adopt, and others simply give up the idea of having children. Organizations must become aware of these facts and provide the flexible working arrangements necessary for couples to start families at optimal times.

Rather than lose competent women who choose to start their families and want more time for their small children, some companies are giving them whatever they need in order to do their work (home computers, faxes, cell phones), and letting them do most of their work at home, sometimes packing it into three days instead of five. When young mothers can be near their children and eliminate long, stressful commutes to the office every day, they reap more energy to devote to their careers.

Strategy #5 _____

Learn the Organizational Basics

To access power in the organizational culture, you must understand what organizational structure and culture are all about.

Org Skill #1: Identify Old and New, Rigid and Flexible Structures

You'll be in a better position to understand what's going on in a company and how to gain power within it if you understand some basics of corporate structure. You need to know how to distinguish the whole range of corporate structures—from the old rigid pyramids, to the new flexible webs, to virtual corporations.

The traditional organization. If you draw an organization chart of most traditional organizations, it will resemble a pyramid with a chain of command running from top management down through middle management and first-line management, to the mass of workers below.

Very large organizations may have a dozen or more levels of management, but they can usually be further categorized into one of the three basic levels. However, the number of levels has been shrinking rapidly due to reengineering and downsizing to meet global competition.

The flexible organization. If you make an organization chart of one of the new, flexible organizations, it's likely to resemble a spider's web or ameba, and the connections inside are sometimes called a net or network, as indicated in Snapshot #5. The flexible corporation is evolving from the demands of a diverse, post-industrial, technological, and global economy.

Some of these new structures are so different from traditional organizations that they're called virtual organizations. We know that virtual reality is a computerized experience that seems real, but takes place more in cyberspace than in the physical world.

A virtual organization may carry out the same functions as traditional organizations, but have far fewer physical facilities. The people of the organization may be scattered far and wide, and relate more by phone, fax, e-mail, and the Internet than face to face. In fact, much of the work gets done on computer screens, fax machines, car phones, voice mail, and video conferences.

Work teams may include company specialists, independent contractors, suppliers, customers, and investors. Some of them may be scattered around the globe, change from month to month, and never meet the other members of the team face to face. Or they may be self-managing teams that meet every day. They may work together to scan the environment, locate profit niches, envision new projects, develop action plans, set product and service standards, identify and solve all types of problems, make decisions, and provide the products and services. At every step, their degree of success or failure depends heavily on team member's relationships with one another.

Snapshot #5: Flexible and Traditional Corporate Structures

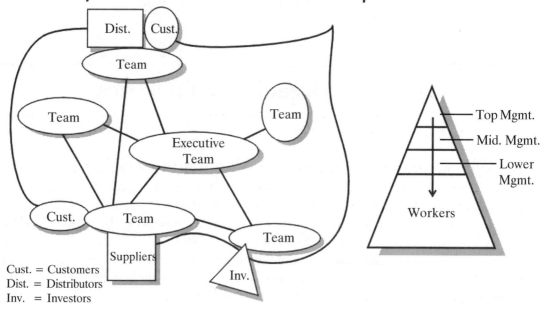

Flexible Corporation   **Traditional Corporation**

Of course, this format affects organizational structure. Old, rigid bureaucratic hierarchies are melting into fluid, shifting networks of relationships among employees, customers, suppliers, and allied competitors, as visually depicted in Snapshot #5 on page 64. These new flexible organizations are built upon trust, collaboration, cooperation, and teamwork, but they also rely on individual achievement and the ability to be entrepreneurial; therefore, they are competitive in outlook. In such organizations, it's more obvious than ever that people are the most valuable resource, that how they work together creates energy and innovation or decay and demoralization, and that their interactions spark the knowledge and information that fuel organizational growth and success. And the kinds of people moving into these new jobs are more diverse each year.

Org Skill #2: Understand Organizational Cultures

You need to understand the key parts of organizational cultures as well as what makes a strong or weak corporate culture.

The Components

Understanding the key parts of organizational cultures can help you identify them in your company and to analyze any corporate culture. Key components include beliefs and values, rules, rituals, symbols, stars, stories, and networks.

Beliefs and values. Our beliefs form the basis of how we view reality and the reality we continually create. Values are the beliefs we hold most dear. Beliefs and values, therefore, form the foundation of the corporate culture. Mottoes often express these beliefs. For example: *Service is our most important product, Better living with (our brand), Things go better with (our brand),* or *People come first.*

Rules. Based on their core beliefs, leaders of a company establish rules of the game for everything, including getting hired, getting perks and raises, getting promotions, getting recognized, and filing expense reports.

Rituals. The customary day-to-day actions people take, their expected actions and responses, are all corporate rituals. *The way we do things around here* expresses the idea of rituals and can include how people say hello, how they do a particular task, and how they conduct team meetings. The way people habitually celebrate, recognize achievement, and play together are also rituals. They reflect key beliefs, rules, symbols, and other cultural components—the unwritten rules about what's okay.

Symbols. Symbols serve an important function in all cultures. Examples of a symbol include a logo, picture, brand name, nickname, motto, song, figure of speech, treasured ritual, legendary hero, mascot, banner, or flag. Symbols may represent the essence of common values, norms, and experiences that bind people together in a common cause and may touch them deeply. A symbol can serve to trigger these communal thoughts and feelings.

Stars. The heroes, heroines, champions, stars, and other leaders in the company are the role models who personify the core values and the strength of the organization. They become symbolic figures whose deeds are out of the ordinary, but not too far out. People can identify with them. They become great motivators—the people everyone will count on when things get tough. They tend to be intuitive, to envision the future, to experiment, and to appreciate the value of celebrations and ceremonies.

Heroes and heroines are most often those top executives or founders who are seen as fearless leaders or courageous adventurers. They also may be top sales representatives, computer geniuses, maverick researchers, or anyone who becomes legendary in a key area. Heroes and heroines reinforce the basic values of the culture by:

- ▶ Showing that success is attainable and human.
- ▶ Providing inspiration.
- ▶ Symbolizing the company to the outside world.
- ▶ Preserving what makes the company special.
- ▶ Setting a standard of performance.
- ▶ Motivating employees.

Stories, myths, and legends. Stars are usually the focus of a company's stories, myths, and legends, which symbolize some basic belief or value the company is built upon. Ask how the company got started or made it big, and you'll often discover an important corporate legend. These stories, in turn, form the basis for various rituals, for unless a ritual is connected to a myth, it's just a habit that does nothing but give people a false sense of security. For example, the founder of the company may believe that his success stems from really listening to people, and now all managers have listening rituals, or times set aside for employees to speak their piece. Myths provide the script by which people act out the beliefs that give meaning to corporate life and bring order to the chaos.

Networks. Stories and new information travel along the informal communication channels. The grapevine is the primary means of communication within an organization because it ties together all parts of the company without respect to the organization chart. It not only transmits information, it also interprets its significance. In most organizations, only about 10 percent of business takes place in formal meetings and events. The real process of developing opinions, gathering support, and making decisions happens before or after meetings. Of course, formal networks are important too. They include the formal organization chart, task forces, work teams, professional and trade associations, and similar groupings.

Strong and Weak Cultures

Some corporate cultures are strong; others are weak. Even weak cultures influence almost everything in the organization, from who gets promoted to what decisions are made, from how people dress to what they do in their time away from work.

Weak cultures. In weak corporate cultures, people adhere primarily to their own group's viewpoints, norms, and values. People have more freedom to determine how to act. However, the extreme of weak culture is organizational chaos. Some essential values must be shared by members if an organization is to be able to achieve its goals. To survive and thrive over time, organizations need strong cultures. Some telltale signs of a weak-culture firm include the following:

- ▶ No set of beliefs about how to succeed is delineated by the leaders.
- ▶ No rank-ordered priority of values is communicated by the leaders.
- ▶ No overriding common values are held by the different subcultures in various parts of the company.

▶ Role models don't serve the culture well. They may be disruptive, even destructive, or don't reinforce key values and beliefs.

▶ Rituals of everyday work life are disorganized or contradictory. People do their own thing or work at cross-purposes, undermining each other.

Strong cultures. In strong corporate cultures, leaders clearly define and enforce values and norms, giving more direction to how people should act, more reinforcement about what they should do, and perhaps higher penalties for not conforming. The result is that people are more likely to view a situation in the same way, to respond similarly, and to expect similar results. In some strong cultures, management expects people to conform to values and norms that encompass most of their activities. In other equally strong cultures, management insists on conformity to only a few core values and norms, but not on less important ones. This type is more suitable for diverse groups because it allows for a greater variety of behaviors.

Strategy #6

Gain Power in New Corporate Cultures

Learn to identify the power lines and which career paths and specific jobs have the greatest power potential. This means you must recognize the power differences between line and staff positions, which is one of the keys to identifying jobs that are likely to lead to career advancement. This skill will enable you to avoid getting stuck in dead-end jobs. If you find yourself stuck, there are techniques for breaking out.

Power Skill #1: Identify a Job's Power Potential

When you're assessing organizations and positions, learn to recognize which positions are powerful, and which are marginal. Use the tips given in Snapshot #6 on page 68.

Power Skill #2: Distinguish Between Line and Staff Jobs

Learn to distinguish between line and staff positions, so you can identify where certain jobs and career paths are likely to take you. Line jobs carry more authority to make important decisions that may affect the entire company, while staff jobs imply you can advise line managers regarding such decisions, but not make them yourself. Because line jobs are considered crucial to company profit and survival, they have greater power potential and are much more likely to be in a career path that can lead to the top.

Traditionally, staff departments have been outside the line chain of command. Think of them as little pyramids, each with its own short chain of command. Their function is supportive, taking care of departments that provide a service, perhaps an essential service, but not one actually providing the product or service the business is in existence to do. Staff departments, because their services are seen as less essential than those of line departments, usually find their budgets are the first ones cut when the company is in trouble. Typical staff departments are human resources, accounting, data processing, advertising, public relations, research, billing, medical, legal, and such technical specialties as

Snapshot #6: How Much Power in a Position?

High-Power Positions	Low-Power Positions
Few rules.	Many rules.
New position or few predecessors.	Many predecessors.
Few established routines.	Many established routines.
Wide variety of tasks.	Narrow range of tasks.
Unusual performance highly rewarded.	Unusual performance brings small or no rewards.
Great flexibility in use of resources.	Little flexibility in use of resources.
Nonroutine decisions require minimal approval.	Nonroutine decisions require an approval process.
At or near company headquarters.	Far from company headquarters.
Much publicity about job activities.	Little visibility of job activities.
Tasks central to current problem areas.	Tasks peripheral to current problem areas.
Focus of tasks is outside department.	Focus of tasks inside department.
Much contact with top management.	Little contact with top management.
Many opportunities to participate in programs, conferences, meetings, task forces, committees.	Few opportunities to participate in programs, conferences, meetings, task forces, committees.
Team members have good career opportunities.	Team members have very limited career opportunities.
High probability of advancement.	Low promotion rates.
Short time span between moves.	Long time span between moves.
Chance for increasing challenges.	Relatively static tasks, static level of skill and mastery.
Eventual access to the most rewarding jobs.	No pathway into rewarded positions.

engineering, sciences, and architecture—if they're not providing the main service the organization is in business to provide. For example, a lawyer holds a line job in a law firm, but a staff job in any other type of firm.

Line jobs are those directly involved in making the products or providing the services, and selling the products or services that the company is in business to make or sell. Line departments may be viewed as profit centers or entrepreneurial units, responsible for generating a portion of the company's profits. For example, some work teams function as business development teams, acting almost as a small business within the business. Managers in these jobs find it relatively easy to pinpoint their contributions to company profits. In nonprofit or government organizations, line jobs are those directly involved with getting the funds the organization needs and providing the service it's set up to provide.

Power Skill #3: Focus on Jobs That Lead to Advancement

Locate the jobs most likely to lead to advancement by asking questions about the career paths of people holding positions you might like to work yourself into. The following types of jobs are most likely to lead to advancement.

Line jobs in corporations. Focus especially on line jobs that most directly affect company profits. Depending on what the company is in business to do, such jobs may involve buying something, making something, bringing something in, selling something, or servicing something for a profit.

Line jobs in nonprofit organizations. Look for jobs that are most directly connected with providing the major service of the organization. For example:

▶ In healthcare organizations—overseeing direct patient services.

▶ In education—overseeing programs of study.

▶ In government agencies—overseeing the service the agency is set up to provide.

▶ In general—attracting users, clients, and customers and getting funding.

Jobs that address current problems. Try to get or create a job where you can help the company move into a new opportunity or solve a critical problem, such as:

▶ Identifying new products or services that put the company back in the running.

▶ Finding ways to make the company competitive.

▶ Finding trade opportunities in other markets or countries.

▶ Leading crisis management during a company crisis.

▶ Establishing new computer applications.

▶ Putting together a crucial merger or acquisition.

▶ Defending the company in a lawsuit with potentially huge punitive awards.

Power Skill #4: Avoid or Break Out of Dead-End Jobs

It's obvious that most clerical, secretarial, and menial jobs in staff departments are dead-end jobs. In addition, certain management jobs tend to be dead-ends.

Working supervisors. In this position, you must continue to do the work of the unit while taking on the responsibility of supervising the other workers. Many companies have moved women into such jobs in order to beef up their statistics on the number of women managers they employ.

First-line supervisors of routine jobs. This includes clerical, word processing, or reproduction work. Here you must make a special effort to move into another functional area, or you'll be stuck.

Most staff jobs. These have limited advancement potential. The top job is head of the staff department, and that may be your ultimate goal. If you want to go further, be aware that if you spend some time in a staff department, you probably must move into the line in order to move up.

Follow these suggestions for breaking out of dead-end positions:

▶ Talk about your career goals with decision-makers; gain their support.

▶ Find out about alternate career paths that are more likely to fit your goals.

▶ Understand the difference between high-power and low-power positions and ask questions that will help you determine which type of job you're being offered.

▶ If a better position is not available, try to expand your job responsibilities and get the title changed; later ask for a pay raise commensurate with your increased responsibilities.

▶ Expand your job by finding ways to take on new responsibilities (for example, volunteering for tasks and then making them visible by sending progress reports to key people or getting other people involved by making them part of a task force).

▶ Ask for a lateral transfer if it would provide necessary experience and put you in a better position for promotion later.

▶ Look for ways to become more visible to decision-makers and to impress them favorably with your abilities and potential.

▶ Ask if there are some seminars, courses, or training programs that will prepare you for promotion; see if the company will provide funds.

▶ Create a demand for your services—make contacts with other companies, departments, people who might be interested in hiring you. Update your resume at least twice a year.

▶ If you can't get a commitment from your boss for a promotion by a certain date, apply for a better job with other companies.

▶ Before you accept another job, find out about its power potential. (See Snapshot #6 on page 68.)

▶ After you take another job, keep evaluating your progress; two or three years is usually long enough in one position.

Power Skill #5: Identify People on Their Way Up

One aspect of identifying power lines in an organization is recognizing how people act when they feel they're on their way up (powerful), as compared to those who feel stuck in dead-end positions (powerless).

Employees who feel powerful. Recognize that upwardly mobile employees are likely to display these traits:

▶ They're turned on, motivated.

▶ They're more willing to invest themselves heavily in their work.

▶ They concern themselves with learning the things that will be useful to them in the future.

▶ They want to know about the power lines inside and outside the organization.

▶ They find out how to use positive politics to get things done.

Opportunity is seductive to most people, and once they sense that the doors of opportunity are open to them, people's aspirations tend to soar.

Employees who feel powerless. According to the research of Harvard professor Rosabeth Moss Kanter, men and women employees who feel marginal or left out—stuck in dead-end positions—tend to respond in similar ways to the realization that their jobs offer them little hope of advancement. So what has been stereotyped as *women workers' attitudes* is actually the powerless employee's attitude. The key traits are:

▸ Low commitment to the company and the job.

▸ Lack of initiative and withdrawal from responsibility.

▸ Focus on their peer group—often with cliques engaging in open rejection and criticism of managers up the ladder, sometimes using passive-aggressive tactics, such as gossip, jokes, and ridicule.

▸ Preoccupation with social recognition—for nonjob skills and achievements.

▸ Resistance to change and innovation.

And what has been called the *secretarial syndrome* is actually the powerless employees' syndrome, as follows:

▸ Narrow specialization and orientation to one boss and one job.

▸ Timidity and self-effacement.

▸ Praise-addiction—overdependence on praise from the boss.

▸ Using emotionality—assuming helplessness and emotional manipulation to get what is wanted, taking advantage of men's discomfort with emotional displays, such as anxiety or tears.

▸ Gossip—using privileged access to information to gain status with others through gossip.

When women who work full-time are less motivated or committed to business careers, it's usually because they're stuck in dead-end jobs. When women perceive they have the same opportunities as men, they tend to become more ambitious, task-oriented, and involved with work.

Managers who feel powerless. Male and female managers who feel powerless tend to focus on exercising what little power they have and holding on to it. This means they're likely to supervise you more closely, try to control your behavior, be a stickler for details and rules, and avidly protect what they see as their territory.

Such managers are likely to select employees who wait for orders, even if such employees are mediocre, because bright, creative employees threaten them. They may resort to discipline or threats to gain cooperation. They tend to:

▸ Make most or all of the decisions.

▸ Do an excessive amount of the routine work.

▸ Refuse to let subordinates represent them at meetings.

▸ Try to control all communications coming in and out of their unit.

▸ Take all the credit themselves for what is accomplished by the team or unit.

Because technical mastery of job content is one of the few areas where they do feel powerful, managers who feel powerless are likely to take over tasks of employees or supervise them too closely by:

▶ Exerting excessive control over employees.

▶ Jumping in too quickly to solve problems for them.

▶ Nit-picking over small things they do differently.

▶ Overdoing demands for strict conformity to procedures, which keeps employees from learning or developing their own styles.

Getting everything *right* according to the rules may be one of the few ways such managers have to impress their boss or to secure their positions. Control of the rules gives them some added power. They may bend the rules for employees who are compliant, rewarding them with a lighter application of the rules—just to exercise power. Powerless managers, especially staff managers, tend to narrow their interests to their particular small territory or piece of the system.

It doesn't take much imagination to realize that you want to avoid powerless managers and find yourself a job in which you'll report to a powerful manager.

Power Skill #6: Access Your Power Resources

If you become comfortable with exercising various kinds of power, you're more likely to be at home in a leadership role. In any organization, the powerful are the ones who have access to tools for action, so you must figure out what tools you need and how to go about getting them. To do this most effectively, you must see yourself as a person who knows how to wield power. The following are sources from which you can derive power:

▶ **Position**—your position or role that gives you authority to get things done.

▶ **Connections**—whom you know and the relationships you build and maintain.

▶ **Resources**—what you can get and give to people—to help them or reward them.

▶ **Information**—what people need and want to get the job done.

▶ **Skills**—your personal skill and expertise to get the job done.

▶ **Your inner resources**—self-esteem, empathy, charisma—that connect with people and energize them.

Become Comfortable Using Direct Power

How do you normally use the power you have? Do you use it in a direct or an indirect way? Women have traditionally relied on indirect uses of power: first influencing their parents to get what they want, then marrying well and influencing their husband's career and achievements, and finally getting what they want through their husbands.

When you rely on indirect power, you tend to live vicariously through your husband and later through your children, basking in the reflected glory of their achievements. If you do this, you invariably fail to fully develop your own sources of direct power and achievement. This syndrome often leads to the *empty-nest syndrome* when the children leave home. The problem can become a tragedy if the husband solves his midlife identity crisis by finding another (usually younger) mate, leaving the wife who sacrificed her own personal and career growth with little in the way of personal resources—little direct power.

Direct power is based on your own power sources rather than on those of a go-between. Instead of influencing a go-between to use his power in ways you think are desirable, develop and use your own power to achieve your goals—or mutually agreed-upon goals in business or personal relationships. Today more and more women are using direct power. To succeed in a leadership role, you must become comfortable with using direct power. Keep in mind that in any organization, some people are needed to lead. And if you believe you would use power in a fair and constructive way, one of those leaders should be you.

Learn How to Gain Credibility and Power

Credibility is power plus competence—the known ability to get results. Ways of gaining it include learning how to:

Work for a supportive manager. Find someone who will serve as a good role model, encourage your growth, and help you achieve your career goals. In order for you to retain any credibility and power, your decisions and actions must be supported by your manager—at least as far as others know.

Build a power base. Develop a support network that includes senior managers, mentors, colleagues, employees—as well as people outside the company, such as contractors, suppliers, customers, and professional association members.

Get needed resources and information. Learn how to get what you and your team need in order to be successful, and *insist* on getting it. Focus on key resources and information you can bring from outside into the group that will help team members, and the team as a whole, to succeed.

Empower people to become more independent. Focus on empowering people, helping them to become more independent by bringing more certainty to their lives, helping them to solve current problems.

Get on the inside track. Become someone who's moving onward and upward. To attract followers, people must perceive you as a leader with power. People want to ally themselves with powerful leaders for several reasons:

▶ Powerful leaders can provide followers with resources and opportunities.
▶ Such leaders can back up their commitments, bring about needed changes, and bring followers into lucrative projects.
▶ They're likely to have an empowering leadership style in which they share information, provide training, and delegate more authority and autonomy.

Handle changes and crises effectively. This will demonstrate your leadership capabilities and make you more visible, especially when you incorporate a problem-solving innovation.

Take calculated risks. Learn to view risk-taking as a welcome challenge. Assess the probabilities and the implications of both failure and success, and overcome any tendency you may have to focus only on the possibility of failure. Successful risk-takers show the company they can perform in the most difficult of circumstances, and they develop charisma in the eyes of others.

Take on high-visibility tasks. Know how to work with other departments or organizations. Be willing to serve on task forces and committees. Make sure your activities are seen as relevant to meeting company needs.

Act as if you have credibility and power. Notice how powerful people look and act and emulate what works. Acting as if you have power is frequently half the battle! Many of the powerful got that way by surrounding themselves with the *aura* of power.

Finally, think about these questions.

▶ What are your major sources of direct power? Review the power sources described on page 72.

▶ What type of power do you need to build?

▶ How will you go about increasing your power?

Answer Key

Self-Awareness Activity #2: Do You Have Self-Limiting Beliefs?

If you score is between 45 and 75, you're burdened with most of the self-limiting beliefs our culture imposes on women, but you can adopt new beliefs, step-by-step.

A score between 30 and 45 means you have a little work to do.

If your score is below 30, you've managed to escape most of these beliefs.

3

Connect Across the Gender Gap

Call it a clan, call it a network, call it a tribe, call it a family.
Whatever you call it, whoever you are, you need one.

—Jane Howard, writer

As a woman, you probably have an advantage over your male peers when it comes to listening and speaking effectively. This, then, is a strength you can capitalize on. What you probably need to focus on is how well you're bridging the gap between male and female worldviews and communication styles. Instrumental to this bridging is the ability to translate your verbal skills into business talk that men understand. Just as crucial is understanding how to build a supportive power base by networking throughout your organization and industry or field. First, think about your current beliefs regarding male-female communications and networking by answering the following questions. Then meet Meg Whitman, eBay CEO, whose leadership style includes connecting across all types of gaps, including the gender gap.

How do men and women relate and connect?

1. Do women focus more on reporting information, while men focus more on making connections with others? Or vice versa?
2. Do men typically understand that women tend to play down their expertise—especially when they're very competent?
3. Is top management the most important group to network with?
4. Is being personable and waiting for someone to adopt you the best way to get a mentor?

Women must understand the competitive nature of men and of the corporate cultures they dominate. To bridge the gap, you must first understand and respect men's personal concerns regarding their status and competitive image. Understand also that men are more likely than women to allow competitive actions to become aggressive. You may be able to help them set some boundaries between assertion and aggression. Remind them that in the new workplace, cooperative alliances are as important as beating out competitors. You may be able to help male peers and employees build their cooperative skills—to gain status by facilitating others' success rather than by dominating and controlling others.

Meg Whitman, CEO of eBay

eBay is "the world's largest personal online trading company," and more. It's one of the few dot-com companies that consistently shows a profit. Meg Whitman joined eBay in 1998. Three years later, her stock was worth $600 million, making her the richest woman CEO in America.

During her high school years, Meg wanted to be a doctor. After graduating, she entered the premed program at Princeton University. A summer job selling advertising for a campus publication triggered a change of majors. In 1977, she got her bachelor's degree in economics, and in 1979 received an MBA from Harvard Business School.

Meg started her career in brand management at Procter & Gamble, followed by stints with consulting firm Bain & Co., Walt Disney, Stride Rite, and Florists' Transworld Delivery (FTD). In 1998, she was head of Hasbro's Playskool division with 600 employees.

Meanwhile, in 1995, a Frenchman, Pierre Omidyar, founded a flea-market-like site called Auction Web. By 1998 it had 20 employees and about $6 million a year in revenues. Pierre had started the site as more of a sideline than a serious business venture. Realizing the Website needed a savvy business leader, he hired a headhunter, who asked Meg to take over at eBay headquarters in California. But she was living in Boston with her two sons and husband, Griffith Harsh, head of neurosurgery at Massachusetts General Hospital. She couldn't imagine uprooting her family and transplanting them on the West Coast.

Eventually, Meg agreed to meet with Pierre. She saw at once that eBay had the makings of a great brand. Naturally curious, Meg was also interested in the dot-com phenomenon. She took the decision home, and her husband soon found he would be welcomed at Stanford University Medical Center. The boys agreed that the move would be cool.

So Meg took over as CEO and helped eBay go public. By 2003, revenues were $1 billion—in sales of everything from BMWs, to real estate, to industrial equipment. The goal for 2005 was $3 billion in sales from the Website as well as brick-and-mortar sites in 53 U.S. cities and five countries. The former online flea market had become a virtual, self-regulating global economy.

All this did not come easily. Competitive firms constantly nip at her heels, technology breaks down, and people try to auction some really weird stuff. Meg managed all these challenges while also making eBay more corporate by asking stores and companies to sell on eBay. Now corporations such as Sun Microsystems sell millions of dollars worth of products on the site. She also installed a program that offers insurance for buyers. In making the Website more corporate, she made it more professional.

What's the secret of Meg Whitman's success? For starters, she focused on eBay's core competencies and expanded the firm gradually in auction-related directions. She sees eBay as providing a marketplace for users, who in turn build the company. They bring the product to the site, merchandise the product, and distribute it once it's sold. When eBay charms customers by informing them of site changes and asking for their votes and feedback, that's Meg's influence at work. Colleagues say she has a strong intuitive sense of how to establish a brand and appeal to consumers. She's consistently upbeat and open to opportunities. For example, customers gravitated toward the fixed-price sales of Half.com, so Meg championed fixed-price sales on eBay, which may one day put it before Amazon as the Web's biggest retailer.

Strategy #1

Bridge the Gender Gap in Worldviews and Communication Styles

Do you sometimes feel that the men in your workplace are speaking a *different language*? If so, you're right. Even though the boys you grew up with *seemed* to be in your world, researchers say a better description is: *Men and women grow up and live in parallel but separate worlds—with some overlap.*

Our ways of relating to each other, and the ways we communicate, often reflect our separate, but parallel, worlds.

Girls and women focus on:	Boys and men focus on:
• Connection.	• Status.
• Talk that establishes rapport.	• Talk that reports information.
• Cooperating.	• Competing.
• Playing down expertise.	• Playing up expertise.
• Agreeing.	• Disagreeing.
• Tentative approaches to topics.	• Assertive approaches to topics.

Skill #1: Bridge the Gap Between Connection and Status

Women live in the world of intimacy, and men live in the world of status concerns. In their world, women focus on connecting with others via networks of supportive friends, according to Georgetown University linguistics professor Deborah Tannen. Much of their communication is aimed at minimizing differences and building on commonalties and agreements. Their ultimate goal is to attain maximum consensus and to function in relationships where people are interdependent. Men certainly have their old-boy networks, but their world of status places higher priority on independence, where the focus of much communication is on giving or taking orders. Men's ultimate goal is to attain more personal freedom through increasing others' perceptions of their knowledge, expertise, power, authority, and status. As a woman, you can show that you can win respect and status as well as the men. At the same time, you can help men see the value of building connections, cooperation, and consensus.

As boys grow into men, their time and activities gain respect and tend to be viewed as important, whereas girls' time and activities are seen as less important. This tendency is tied to the fact that beginning with the Industrial Revolution, men went off to work and got paid, while women stayed home and did not get paid. In a society where income is seen as an indicator of a person's importance and value, women are often expected to be respectful of men's more important responsibilities. As little boys become men, they take on the parent role with women, serving as their protectors. On the other hand, as little girls become women, they retain much of their child role, needing to be protected and indulged, and thus seem less competent than men. Some social scientists are speculating that the recent increase in violent acts against women and girls (rape, child or wife abuse, assault and battery) may be an acting-out of men's confusion, resentment, and fear of women's increasing independence and power. Whatever the ramifications, you must claim your personal power, respect your own activities as being just as important as men's, and expect that same respect from others.

You'll probably need to prove your competence with each new group of people you deal with—simply because you're a woman. Many studies have shown that males are considered more competent than females, at least outside the home. For example, Jerry Eisen, author of *Powertalk!*, reports on a study asking people to evaluate an article, some copies with a woman's byline and identical copies with a man's byline. The article with the male byline was rated as better by 98 percent of the evaluators.

You'll need to be assertive in holding the floor and getting people to give your ideas serious consideration. In a study of mixed-group conversations, 97 percent of interruptions were made by men. There were few interruptions when women were speaking with women or when men were speaking with men. In mixed-group studies of who does most of the talking, men talk from 58 percent to 92 percent of the time. Most women are unaware of this type of domination, perceiving that they did a fair share of the talking in 75 percent of the situations.

Men use humor to take the lead. They tend to remember and repeat jokes, using the opportunity to take center stage and gain control. Most women tend to forget jokes, rarely attempt to repeat them, and serve as a supportive audience, laughing at the jokes men tell. Try your hand at mastering the use of humor to gain rapport, release tension, or hit the right casual tone.

Use information about male-female differences to understand why men do the things they do. Most men feel pressure, from mild to intense, to gain, maintain, and increase their status in the eyes of other men—and women. Because business is still essentially a male culture, you must understand the rules of the status game. Once you prove that you can play that game, and you've gained adequate power within the organization, you'll have some freedom to move beyond it to focus more attention on building mutually supportive relationships.

Skill #2: Bridge the Gap Between Rapport Talk and Report Talk

Woman tend to engage most often in *rapport talk*, the kind meant to establish or maintain connection with someone. In rapport talk, you focus on feelings, personal thoughts, reactions to the day's events, and the details of your life. Men tend to focus more on *report talk*, factual information they think the other person needs to know, information about what's going on in the world.

If you're like most women, you have a high level of verbal skills that are expressed primarily in rapport talk. What you may need is ideas on how to translate these skills into business speak that incorporates report talk. See Snapshot #1 for some ideas on how to do this without going overboard.

Snapshot #1: Translate Women's Verbal Skills Into Business Speak

	Typical barriers for women: speech patterns/ stereotypes	Facilitators in male business culture: alternate patterns	Barriers created by overcorrection of female speech patterns
Gossip	Always ready to participate; indulges in idle or malicious gossip.	Well-informed; alert; listens but rarely participates.	Ignores all gossip.
Content	Focuses on trivia and chitchat.	Focuses on relevant topics (business, politics, etc.).	Business talk only.
Quantity	Babbles on too much, or keeps silent rather than *create conflict*.	Usually speaks with a purpose or keeps her counsel; takes a stand on relevant issues.	Every word carefully monitored; lacks spontaneity.
Quality	Emotion-charged words (*just love it, so sweet, too gross*).	Objective, operational words (*appreciate, thoughtful, effective*).	Never expresses feelings.
Reactions	Chip on shoulder, *women's lib*, angry reactions; or gives in easily to avoid conflict.	Assertive, problem-solving responses.	Swings from rebellion to submission or vice versa.
Clarity	Vague (*the nicest meeting, a super group*).	Clear, specific descriptions (*well-organized meeting, top-performing team*).	Overdoes details and explanations; tedious, boring.
Logic	Illogical, disconnected conclusions, idea hopping.	Coherent, connected, provides closure.	Computer-like logic.
Credibility	Tentative, overpolite, uncertain, indecisive. (*We'll be able to do this? This is a sales problem—isn't it? I sort of think we should....*)	Confident, assertive, decisive. (*We can do it! This appears to be a sales problem. I suggest we wait till the progress report comes in.*)	Arrogant, overbearing.
Interrupting	Avoids; thinks it's impolite; men may assume she has nothing to say.	Competitive turn-taking; holds ground if peer overdoes it.	Constantly interrupts; never gives ground.
Profanity	Responds with shock, embarrassment, giving men a reason to feel uncomfortable having women in their domain.	Communicates normally.	Out-swears the men.
Jargon (military, business)	Unclear on meanings of many words; rarely uses.	Selectively uses jargon to create a sort of fraternity.	Relies on jargon to intimidate and impress *outsiders* who don't understand it.

Skill #3: Bridge the Gap Between Cooperation and Competition

Women's communication often revolves around giving understanding, while men's is more likely to revolve around giving advice. These tendencies are probably based on the different ways men and women measure power. Women view helping, nurturing, and supporting as measures of their power. The related activities they engage in include giving praise, speaking one-on-one, and having private conversations.

Men perceive different measures of their power, such as having information, expertise, and skills. The related activities they engage in include giving information, speaking more and longer, and speaking to groups.

Women tend to:	Men tend to:
• Measure power by how much support they're able to give others.	• Measure power by the information, expertise, and skill they can offer.
• Think work decisions should be shared.	• Think they must make their own decisions.
• Focus on mastering job, increasing skills, and involving others.	• Focus on competition, power, hierarchy, and status.
• Avoid conflict to keep the peace.	• Confront conflict to clear the air.
• Be seen as more approachable.	• Be seen as more intimidating.
• Be more accommodating and self-sacrificing.	• Be more assertive.
• Be better able to use intuition and empathy to deal with difficult situations.	• Be less comfortable with unclear situations and mixed feelings.

To overcome problems arising from these tendencies, you can develop assertiveness skills and habits, and use them in ways that men understand and respect. You can understand that men need clear facts in the communication process and provide them with the facts and figures they need. You can also provide logical, rational reasons for your recommendations and proposals, as well as your sense of the situation and the human relations factors that are involved. When men experience difficulty in coping with unclear situations or in expressing mixed feelings, you may be able to coach them through the emotional processing you've learned to use. You may even inspire your male colleagues to get in touch with their emotions and develop their intuitive abilities. When men understand the power of dealing with ambiguity and using intuition for making complex, high-level decisions, they tend to feel comfortable with developing such skills.

Skill #4: Bridge the Gap Between Showing Off Expertise and Playing It Down

A major source of power for managers, professionals, and other leaders is expertise. Men and women differ in the ways they handle their own expertise and in how they respond to others' expertise.

As a woman, you're most likely to downplay your expertise, act as if you know less than you really do, and operate as one of the group or audience. The men in your workplace are more likely to display their expertise and act as if they know more about their area than others in the group know—they're more comfortable taking center stage. Their main goal is to persuade and, therefore, to firmly state their opinions as facts.

When your male peers are in the expert mode, they're more likely to dominate, do more of the talking, interrupt more, and control the discussion, whether they're speaking to men or women. They want to emphasize their superiority and display their expertise. Their main concerns are likely to be: *Have I won? Do you respect me?*

When you're the expert, and you're talking with the men, your approach is probably to agree, go along, support, and say *yes.* You probably want to emphasize similarities between you and the people with whom you're talking, and so you don't want to *show off.* Your main concerns are likely to be: *Have I been helpful? Do you like me?* Other women are likely to understand this and to accept you as an expert in the topic area. Most men won't understand this approach and are likely to challenge your credibility. To summarize, here are the ways men and women differ in handling the expert role.

Women tend to:
- Play down expertise.
- Avoid showing they know more than others.
- Act as one of the group.
- Focus on not offending.

Men tend to:
- Display expertise.
- Show that they know more than others.
- Act as the central speaker.
- Focus on persuading.

Responding to others' expertise. When men listen to you in your expert mode, they usually don't understand that your main concern is to not offend, so they often conclude that you're either indecisive, incompetent, insecure, or all of the above. They respond by giving you their own opinions and information, and by setting the agenda themselves: That is, they incorrectly perceive a power vacuum and try to take over. This contrasts with women's typical responses to male expertise, which is either to agree or disagree, but not to question their credibility or try to take over.

Style misunderstanding. Gina, a Human Resource specialist, was given full authority by the vice president of Human Resources to establish an employee training center. She had the power to decide what seminars would be offered, to bring in trainers from within the company, or to contract with outside trainers, and to approve seminar content and evaluation methods. Gina's style was to include all the inside trainers in planning the types of seminars that would be offered, as well as their content. She felt that this participative approach would generate better ideas and would motivate people to become committed to the success of the Center.

Several of the male trainers mistook Gina's participative style for weakness and incompetence. If *they* were given the power and authority to make all the decisions on their own, they would have done so. They assumed Gina needed their input and approval in order for the project to fly. This clique of men began holding their own informal meetings to make the decisions and ramrod them through the formal meetings that Gina chaired. They saw a power vacuum and moved in to fill it.

How could Gina have prevented this power takeover? First, she could have clearly explained that she had full authority from the vice president to make these decisions on her own—and that she had very clear, specific ideas about what decisions she would make. Then, she could explain precisely why she chose instead to include the trainers in the decision-making process—and exactly how she intended that process to unfold.

Observing the status ritual. Keep in mind that you must prove your expertise when dealing with most of the men in a male culture. You must demonstrate your power, status, and authority in a way that is clear to them. Once men have accepted your status and you've gained their respect, you may be able to forego some of these status rituals. By understanding how the men in the organization are likely to view your actions, you can communicate with them in their terms and still use your own leadership style.

Skill #5: Bridge the Perceptions of Agreeing and Disagreeing

As a woman, what you say when you're listening to someone, and when you're giving them feedback, tends to be quite different from the responses your male peers give. You probably say a lot more than most men would, and what you say is more positive. You frequently say *mmm, uh huh, yes, yeah*, and similar mutterings that show you're listening or that you agree—a sort of running feedback loop. You probably ask questions, take turns, give your full attention—and want full attention when you're speaking. You probably agree most of the time, and laugh at humorous comments. You're likely to focus on the metamessage—what's indicated between the lines, and the overall picture—even more than the actual words.

When the men you know are listening, they probably say and do less than you. They're more silent and listen less. When they do speak, they're more likely to challenge the speaker's statements and to focus on the literal message—the words.

Because you listen so attentively yourself, you may think a man's silence when you talk implies concentration on your entire message—words, feelings, the situation, the context—when in fact he may not be listening at all.

As a woman, you probably keep your counsel when you hear others making statements with which you disagree. You don't want to start an argument or be disagreeable. If a man doesn't agree with a statement, he'll usually say so—especially if the statement can affect his work, and if speaking up won't offend the boss. If you don't speak up and do the same, men will probably interpret your silence as consent or agreement. When they find out it wasn't, they're likely to see you as weak, indecisive, or flaky. That insight is worth turning into a motto: *Silence is consent—in a man's world.*

Be aware of how your actions, and inactions, are likely to be perceived by the men in your organization. Your assertiveness skills will help you know when to speak up and how to do it in ways that respect your own rights as well as the rights of others. Assertive communication is likely to win respect in male circles and, therefore, to build better long-term relationships. Also, when a man is silent while you talk, learn to ask the right questions to determine whether he has heard and understood your message.

Skill #6: Bridge the Gap Between Tentative and Assertive Talk

Because most people in the business world are accustomed to an assertive male approach to communication, women's credibility is undermined by a tentative, overly polite, uncertain, or indecisive approach, as indicated in Snapshot #1 on page 79. Several studies indicate that women perpetuate the lower-credibility stereotype with the following types of behavior:

▶ **Women ask more questions**—about three times as many on average.

▶ **Women make more statements in a questioning tone**—with a rising inflection at the end of a statement. *Here's a way to do it!* becomes *Here's a way to do it?*

▶ **Women use more tag questions**—adding a brief question at the end of a sentence, such as: *...don't you think? ...okay? ...you know?*

▶ **Women lead off with a question**—more frequently than men do. *You know what? Would you believe this?* Researchers note this and other striking similarities between the conversations of men/women and the conversations of adults/children.

▶ **Women use more qualifiers and intensifiers**—such qualifiers or hedges as *kind of, sort of, a little bit, maybe,* or *could be.* They soften an assertive statement, but also undermine its assertiveness. Intensifiers include *really, very, incredible, fantastic, amazing,* especially when these words are emphasized. The metamessage tends to be: *Because what I say, by itself, is not likely to convince you, I must use double force to make sure you see what I mean.*

All of this means that women tend to express their thoughts more tentatively and work harder to get someone's attention, which may in turn reflect basic power differences, or at least perceptions of power differences.

Your most effective conversational style as a leader usually conveys your sensitivity *and* your commitment to your beliefs and statements. Become aware of your talk patterns and weed out over-tentativeness. Try tape-recording your telephone conversations in order to identify patterns that need modification.

Strategy #2

Build a Power Base

You probably have an advantage in building relationship skills and social skills, simply because you've been socialized as a woman. Make use of this advantage by applying it to building a support network that serves as your power base. A good network is invaluable for connecting, positioning, managing crises, and moving up the ladder. By networking, you bring into play all your internal and external resources in order to succeed. Don't leave networking to chance. Instead, plan ahead to make the most of opportunities. Network with employees, peers, higher managers, mentors, and people in your occupation, field, and industry.

Power Skill #1: Use Internal and External Resources

Most women who venture into formerly male roles find they must prove themselves over and over again. These women say they're more affected than the men are by the need for self-repression and the need to refrain from certain kinds of expressiveness and self-disclosure. Many of these women find it difficult to comfortably participate in the customary ways of relaxing and easing tension, such as various forms of business socializing and joking.

This means you'll probably need to use all the resources you can find in order to build your self-confidence and your personal and organizational power. Two techniques that can be especially valuable are:

1. Develop strong *outside* support groups with whom you can relax and be yourself.
2. Command your *inner* resources. Use the process of relaxing, visualizing, and letting go (described in Chapter 7) to keep in touch with *who you are* and to be your own person.

You need a network of associates, a power base. This is an essential source of power for you and for everyone who creates a successful career. Here's an example of how old-boys' power networks operate: When a job opens, a contract goes out for bids, a stock splits, a story breaks, or a rumor spreads, the old boys meet and business gets done. They'll cut through all the resistance and red tape with ease, simply because they know each other well enough to get in touch informally.

Your power network consists of the relationships you make at every level of the organization—as well as outside the firm. The connections are based on mutual good-will, trust, and willingness to help each other. They're business friendships that are mutually supportive.

Do you tend to concentrate on proving yourself to your manager and pay little attention to proving yourself to others? As a leader, the *best* way to prove yourself is to support your manager while, at the same time, building your own power and your own power base. Start with your work team, branch out to colleagues, mentors, customers, people in your trade or professional associations, and others.

Power Skill #2: Take Five Steps To Create a Network

Networking must be more than socializing and small talk—if you and your contacts are to gain mutual power through the process. Five keys to networking power include planning ahead, creating impact, being direct, picking up on opportunities, and following up.

Plan ahead. Before you go to an event, ask yourself two questions: *What do I have to give? What do I want to receive?* On your *receive* list, put problems you want to solve and opportunities you want to discover—things you want to learn about, understand, connect with, or find. On your *give* list, put ideas, referrals, expertise, enthusiasm—opportunities and solutions you want to share. Planning also includes selecting people to include in your ever-expanding support network. Before and after each event, identify at least two or three people to target for making connections and following up.

Create impact. Introduce yourself with a memorable one-liner and follow up with supporting information. Create a one-liner that captures the essence of what you have to offer. Some examples are: *I create events that people remember; I position people as niche experts; I bring the woman's angle to commercial banking.*

Be direct. Don't be afraid to talk about what you really want. For example, when you realize you want to collaborate with someone, say *I have an idea. Are you interested?*

Pick up on opportunities. When someone asks, *What's new?* or *How are you?* the small-talk answer is some variation of *Not much* or *Just fine.* Instead, be ready to answer with something from your *receive* or *give* list: *I'm looking for an experienced journalist to coauthor an article on networking. Do you know anyone?* or *I'm fine, and I'll be even better when I find a computer consultant. Do you know of a good one?*

Set up your follow-up. End conversations in a way that opens up future possibilities. This may be as simple as telling the person what was valuable or what you enjoyed about meeting her. For instance, *I especially enjoyed hearing about your new project.* It may include making plans for the next step in your relationship; for example, *I'll call you next Wednesday to get that information.*

Power Skill #3: Network With People Outside Your Organization

Your support networks outside the organization may be just as important as the ones inside it—or more so in some job situations. Outside contacts may include customers, suppliers, investors, creditors, regulators, trade or professional association members, members of virtually any organization you may visit or join, and personal friends and acquaintances.

Why network outside the firm? You can gain innumerable benefits from building good relationships with people outside your firm.

▸ To keep up with what's going on in the marketplace.

▸ To cultivate resources, such as people you can hire, people who might hire you, products and services you might buy or sell, and people who can help you when you need information.

▸ To develop contacts to turn to for support in times of trouble or crisis.

▸ To cultivate people who can serve as references when you need to document your experience, achievements, and skills.

▸ To create a demand for your skills package by cultivating people who would like to hire you or work with you.

Of course, good relationships are based on giving and receiving, which means you should be willing to give your business associates and friends the same kind of support they give you.

Make people want to hire you. Let's discuss the last-mentioned reason for networking—cultivating people who'd like to hire you. A major strategy for creating career power is to continually update and expand your marketable skills package. Another strategy is to continually create a demand for your skills package. Set a goal of making people want to hire you—people you're already working for in your department, people in other departments, and people in organizations you've never worked for. As you network with people in all of these areas, be aware of projecting the image of someone who would be a valuable asset to their department or firm. You don't need to brag, but you do need to let people know about your skills and achievements. Communicate your enthusiasm for your work. Try these suggestions:

▶ Celebrate your successes, and ask about and celebrate their successes.

▶ Selectively ask for advice or resources for solving your work problems.

▶ Convey confidence in your ability to succeed in solving the problems.

▶ Offer to share your expertise to help them solve their work problems.

When you create a demand for your skills package, you increase your credibility, your career options, and your personal power. You move beyond dependence on your current job, manager, and company. You create a power aura that makes it easier for you to negotiate lucrative assignments, raises, and promotions.

Power Skill #4: Network With Your Employees

Leaders can lead only if they have the consent of those who are to be led—except in prison-like situations. The most immediate and important area where you must build a support network is among your group of workers. Here are some suggestions:

You become your coworkers' manager: Manage relationship issues. Establishing professional relationships requires special tact when some of your coworkers suddenly become your team members. You can avoid the worst aspects of this situation by not becoming close buddies with them as coworkers. Even so, it can be touchy. One way to prevent potential problems is to discuss your changed role with them in a friendly, sincere way. You can tell them how much you value their friendships. Although you haven't changed as a person, your role has changed. Therefore, your relationships will need to change somewhat. Point out that the other members of the department can make life difficult for them as well as for you if they sense you are playing favorites. Stress the need for teamwork, fairness, and good working relationships.

You're the new manager: Scope out the culture first. When you become manager, you naturally want to use your savvy and skills to improve the situation. But first, you need to fully understand the corporate culture—as it's expressed by your workers. So in addition to keeping your ears open, try the following actions:

▶ Determine who's aligned with whom, who belongs to what clique, who the leaders are, who can be depended upon, and other similar people issues.

▶ Find out what's most important to people. Don't change what may seem to you like minor procedures until you fully understand their importance. Then give everyone a chance to be involved in any decisions.

▶ Build a support base of leaders and dependable types before discussing any major changes.

Manage gossip: Keep lines open, but put it in perspective. Getting information about a work group that's new to you is crucial, so listen to gossip, but never dish the dirt. Also, always evaluate what your workers tell you. Whether Jane is complaining about Jim's nasty attitude or singing the praises of Carol, ask probing questions of both Jane and others before making verbal or action commitments. Always ask yourself, *Why is he or she telling me this?* Follow up by getting other opinions or information—tactfully and discreetly, of course.

Be fair. Don't play favorites; give everyone a chance to shine. Apply policies and procedures in an evenhanded way, but treat people as individuals. Express empathy and concern for their issues and problems, but center most of your conversations around business-related topics. Avoid close, emotional involvement. Keep it friendly but professional. Your goal is for all to feel that they got a fair shake.

Be dependable. Be as honest, sincere, and candid as you can while remaining sensitive to each person's feelings and concerns. Be clear and consistent about your vision for the group and your expectations for individuals. Let all know where you stand—and where they stand with you.

Provide challenge and support for growth. Help each person to achieve, learn, and grow by providing challenging assignments and encouraging challenging job goals. Be patient and professional in working out job problems—even those that seem trivial to you but may be important to the employee. Take a problem-solving approach to performance problems. Focus on making them right and learning how to prevent such problems, not on placing blame. Give workers respect and autonomy by asking them to come up with potential problem solutions for you to confer on. Then give them all the support they need to complete their assignments and achieve job goals. Share information freely and generously in order to increase their savvy, motivation, self-esteem, and performance. Finally, give employees generous credit for achievements. Express appreciation.

Show respect. Little things do mean a lot here. For example, respond promptly to workers' requests, memos, and phone calls. Be prompt and respect workers' time. Don't keep them waiting outside your office or in meetings. Accompany unusual requests with an explanation.

Power Skill #5: Network With Peers

In most organizations you must be generally accepted by your colleagues in order to develop an effective power base and to keep growing. As you gain organizational power, you'll find it increasingly important to get peer cooperation in order to achieve your job goals. If you can form strong peer alliances, others are likely to begin thinking of you as a leader. Signal that you're a team player. All this will enable you to build a power network among your peers. Here are some suggestions:

▶ Share the credit for your achievements with peers who have helped.
▶ Look for opportunities to offer information and constructive opinions, and to touch base with your peers.
▶ Look for opportunities to compliment them.
▶ When you give praise, focus on concrete accomplishments.
▶ Individualize your compliments.
▶ Pass on another person's praise.
▶ Ask for advice in their areas of expertise.

▶ Avoid devious political tactics and, in general, appear more interested in the welfare of the firm than in feathering your own nest.

▶ Know how to trade favors as the basis for constructive cooperation.

▶ Figure out how you can help a peer meet his or her needs and wants.

Trade favors. In the world of male leaders, one way to operate, survive, and get ahead is to trade favors with peers. In this system, managers keep mental track of the IOUs they hold for favors granted as well as those they owe to other managers. They try to cash them in wisely to achieve their highest-priority goals.

Here's an example of turning a negative situation into a positive one by establishing peer solidarity: Giorgio, a credit manager, is refusing to cooperate with sales manager Marsha. She needs for him to expedite certain shipments for one of her important customers. If he won't do it, she's in danger of losing the customer's business. If Marsha goes to the vice president of sales to complain, she can probably force Giorgio to cooperate, but she'll probably make an enemy. Giorgio will feel he *owes her one* in a negative sense and will wait for her to stumble so he can cause trouble for her. Instead, Marsha goes to Giorgio and works through the problem, promising him that once they work it out, the matter will go no further. Marsha keeps her promise and later has only positive things to say to others about Giorgio's cooperation. In this way, she makes an ally of Giorgio instead of an enemy. Now Giorgio owes her one in a positive rather than a negative sense—and he'll probably be much more cooperative with Marsha in the future than he would have been if his boss had called him and instructed him to cooperate.

Help meet their needs and wants. Take the initiative and find out what your colleagues' most pressing needs and wants are, and what problems they're having in achieving their goals. This extra step beyond merely trading favors can be a sign of leadership on your part. But how do you know what a peer really needs or wants?

▶ Be friendly and regularly available to chat.

▶ Gain your peers' trust through showing supportiveness, solving problems, and keeping confidences.

▶ Listen well and ask probing but tactful questions.

▶ Do what you can to help your peers meet their most important needs.

Is a peer having trouble relating well with his boss? Perhaps you can put in a good word for him at an opportune moment. If he is present when you do this, so much the better. If not, casually and tactfully let him know what you did.

Does another peer really want to find a job with a different type of firm? Help her make the right connections, and she'll become part of your external support network.

Support women. Although virtually all successful women managers gain the cooperation of their male colleagues, nearly all say they also need a support network of women. So build this network within your company, outside the company within your particular field, and with other women who bring other types of interests and ideas into your life. Every major city now has a number of women's organizations that serve the function of providing a support network outside the company. In addition, there are many national women's organizations and networks. For more details, check your telephone directory, do an online search, watch for newspaper articles that give information about such organizations, and check issues of magazines directed toward business and professional women that frequently include information on networks.

Power Skill #6: Network With Higher Managers

Obviously, if you want to gain power in the organization, you must network with your immediate manager as well as with other managers, including mentors and top management.

Your Immediate Manager

Your immediate manager is normally the most important manager in your work life, so it's crucial to establish and maintain a positive relationship. If you have a problem with your manager, try to work it out between the two of you. If you can't, you'll need to go to your manager's manager, but do this only as a last resort.

Build trust. Be dependable. Act and speak in a way that assures your manager that she can always depend on you. Be a problem-solver. On the other hand, learn when to stop and consult with your manager. It's crucial to recognize those situations where you need to get your manager's input before blasting ahead on your own. If in doubt, ask, but present your take on the situation and your best ideas for a solution.

If you think you can improve your manager's policies, procedures, or methods of operating, first gain his or her trust by focusing on what's good about departmental operations. Communicate your admiration and approval. Gain your manager's trust by showing you're a loyal team player. Once you're accepted as one of the in-group, you can suggest a way to make *a good operation even better*, one step at a time. If the change is successful, give your manager credit, but be sure to file away memos documenting your role for use in promotion or raise negotiations. By giving your manager credit for successes, you lay the groundwork for acceptance of your future recommendations for change.

Make you manager look good. Be alert to opportunities to boost your manager's image, especially to his or her manager. For example, look for ways to help your manager reach his or her goals. You may have to probe tactfully to get a clear picture of what your manager is trying to accomplish. All too frequently, managers don't have clear, specific goals. It's worth your while to find out, though, because supporting your manager in achieving goals is one of the best ways of winning support in return.

Give generous support and praise. Document your manager's successes as well as your own. Pass on copies of documents or accumulate them to produce at an opportune time. Look for opportunities to sincerely compliment, support, and touch base with your manager in positive ways.

Higher-Level Managers

A major aspect of moving up your career ladder is becoming visible and making connections with higher-level managers. It helps if you can create contact opportunities, be comfortable with key people, project the right image to them, and make the most of conversational opportunities.

Create contact opportunities. Getting to know the top people requires taking initiative and being assertive in a positive way. Look for opportunities to express sincere approval, admiration, and support of their programs and policies. If you can't sincerely support something, then stay quiet about it. If you have unique knowledge or information about why the program is headed for problems, relay it through proper channels in a manner that focuses on the benefits to management and the organization.

Take advantage of opportunities to become visible to top management. Join business and social clubs that provide contacts. Send copies of articles mentioning the executive's achievements or items of interest to him or her. Send notes of congratulation. Keep appropriate people informed of your activities and progress by sending copies of memos or articles.

Become associated with special projects and task forces, especially those that will include meetings with top managers. Then make the most of those meetings by being thoroughly prepared, asking intelligent questions (but not questions that will put a top manager on the spot), volunteering crucial information at opportune moments, and sharing credit with others. Be objective, manage your emotions, stay cool under pressure, and let your leadership qualities shine through.

Become comfortable with power. When your efforts pay off in actually making contact with higher managers, you must be able to relate comfortably to them. Are you so in awe of successful, powerful people that you avoid them or become tongue-tied in their presence? If so, work with the processes of stepping into your own power and with the relaxation, visualization, and letting-go processes given in Chapter 7. Use these processes to become comfortable with powerful people, first through visualizing yourself interacting comfortably, and then in actual practice. Becoming visible to top management can open up all sorts of opportunities and may attract a mentor to your cause.

Project the right image. Show that you would fit into top management through your dress, manners, and habits. Display the right reading material and other items in your office, using top managers as role models. When you have a chance to interact with higher managers, remember that the most effective approach involves sensitivity, judgment, and balance. The impression you want to convey is that you're committed, deeply involved, and competent at your job, as well as friendly and good-natured in your dealings with higher managers and others. What you want to avoid is appearing pushy, being an automatic "yes person," or using manipulative flattery.

Go beyond trivia talk. Your opportunities to initiate conversations may be brief, perhaps in the elevator or hallway. A little small talk may be necessary to get started, but quickly shift to larger issues that involve or affect the company. Stay prepared for these brief opportunities. Formulate your ideas on current issues as they come up and practice verbalizing them to friends. Think ahead and be prepared with interesting one-liners that express your thinking about company issues or current events that could affect the company.

Power Skill #7: Network With Mentors

In most organizations, entrance to middle- and top-management positions is not determined by mere competence. It depends on acceptance by those who are most powerful and influential. This is one reason virtually all people who make it to the top have at least one mentor or sponsor from this powerful, influential group. This fact is consistently reported by researchers who have investigated how men and women make it to the top. Here are some typical questions that arise:

What Is a Mentor?

A mentor is a more experienced person at a higher level in your organization who takes a promising younger person under his or her wing as a protégé. The mentor takes a *personal*, somewhat parental interest in the protégé, to some degree above and beyond the usual professional relationship.

What Does a Mentor Do?

Most mentors are especially helpful in the areas of self-presentation, positioning, and connecting—the essential aspects of promotability that are above and beyond technical competence. In helping you, a mentor can:

▶ Teach, advise, counsel, coach, guide, and sponsor, giving insights into the business.

▶ Serve as a sounding board for decision-making, being a constructive critic, and helping you to achieve by cutting through bureaucratic red tape.

▶ Provide necessary information for career advancement, showing you how to move effectively through the system, teaching you the *political ropes,* and introducing you to the right people.

▶ Increase your visibility, suggesting you as a likely candidate when appropriate opportunities come along, singling you out from the crowd of competitors surrounding you, and arguing for your virtues against theirs.

▶ Stand up for yourself in meetings or discussions with his or her peers, and in case of controversy, fight for *you.*

▶ Provide an important signal to other people that you have his or her backing, helping provide you with an aura of power and upward mobility.

Regardless of the appraisal system an organization uses and its formal attempts at objectively rewarding and promoting people, mentors still make a difference.

How Do I Get a Mentor?

If you can get a mentor to do for you even some of the things just listed, your chances of career success are drastically improved. If mentors are necessary to the success of men in a large organization—as researchers say they are—then they're even more indispensable to your success. After all, women have more barriers to overcome, less access to inside information, and less training from childhood in areas essential for business success.

Becoming the protégé of an appropriate mentor can be more difficult for a woman than for a man. Mentors tend to identify with their protégés and see something of themselves in them. This means males tend to adopt males. Most women tend to adopt women protégés, too, but women at the top are few and far between.

Like any friendship, the mentor-protégé relationship cannot be forced. Either the chemistry is right or it's not. However, you can certainly take some intiative in becoming a likely protégé. And remember, the more mentors you have, the better—assuming you manage the situation so they don't become jealous of one another and that they aren't political enemies. You can get a mentor by projecting a leadership image, taking the initiative in contacting likely mentors and seeking their advice, and if the chemistry seems right, asking directly for support.

Project a leadership image. Put your career commitment up front to offset the stereotype that women are not really career-committed. Let potential mentors see that you know where you want to go and are fully committed to getting there. Good mentors want to feel their efforts will not be wasted. Do everything you can to look like and become an effective leader. Show that you're eager and able to learn and consider yourself a lifelong learner.

Take initiative. Be constantly alert to potential mentors. Identify the most powerful, secure, and upwardly mobile people in your organization. Who are the most likely candidates for mentors? Be sure they're respected and have influence. Aim for multiple mentors who can advise you in various areas of your professional growth. Find ways to become visible to your candidates and to become acquainted with them so that you can see if a sense of rapport develops.

Seek the advice of potential mentors. Ask intelligent, thoughtful questions. Avoid acting helpless. Instead of saying, *I don't know what to do about this*, try, *I'd appreciate your reactions to these two ideas I'm considering.* Give the impression of a competent professional searching for input in order to make intelligent decisions.

Be selective. Try to team up with a winner. It may be better to have no mentor than a weak or highly controversial one. If your mentor falls from power, you may fall also. Try to get a sense of their motivation for giving you advice and be sure you're comfortable with the relationship.

Ask for support. If the relationship goes well, pick the right time and ask for further support. Use a direct approach at this point. Tell your potential mentor that you'd appreciate his or her help in learning the ropes, developing your potential, contributing to the organization, or reaching certain goals.

How Do I Build Powerful Mentor Relationships?

Once you've found a mentor, you're ready to build a powerful, mutually beneficial relationship. Here are some suggestions:

Give as well as receive. Be sure your mentor receives rewards from the relationship. What does she or he want from it? The satisfaction of watching you grow? The knowledge that another key position is being filled by a competent person? A vocal supporter for his or her team? A sincere and simple *Thank you* now and then? The mentor/protégé relationship should be a give-and-receive one. Are you ready and able to give your mentor what he or she is looking for?

Be discreet. If your mentor's position is higher than your own manager's, you have to be careful how you use the reflected power. Avoid alienating your immediate manager or *cashing in your chips* too soon.

Be professional. Send clear messages from the beginning to a male mentor that sexual attraction is not the basis of your interest in him. Tell him in a fairly direct way that you're interested in being a business friend and learning about the company and the job from him. If you were to become sexually involved with your mentor, you'd open the door to a whole set of potential problems. For example, if you're under his direct chain of command, the two of you would be creating an unfair situation for your peers, which violates sexual harassment laws.

Some excellent potential mentors would be reluctant to adopt you as a protégé if they felt that sexual innuendo might be a result. This is another good reason for you to establish a reputation in the organization as an above-board professional who keeps her sex life out of the workplace.

Maintain autonomy. Unless your mentor is your manager, you want advice—not orders. Tactfully discuss advice your mentor gives; use it as a takeoff to discussion of a problem. But leave yourself free to make your own decisions.

Know when to move beyond mentor/protégé. There are times when the mentor/protégé relationship needs to be changed or ended. Such circumstances can include:

▸ Your mentor isn't helping you to grow and move along as you think you should. It's time to look for one who will.

▸ You've chosen unwisely and your mentor is insecure in his or her job or is threatened by you. You must look for another one.

▸ You've chosen wisely and found a good mentor, but you're outgrowing your dependency and becoming more autonomous—as you should. If that doesn't happen, the relationship is stunting your growth. After you've learned the ropes, you must move toward a peer relationship with your mentor.

If you've developed several mentor relationships as you learn and grow, a transition in one of these relationships will be easier. Throughout the relationship, asking for advice rather than for decisions helps you maintain autonomy, and you can gradually shift the balance from mostly asking to mostly sharing and reporting. Also, at this point, you're ready to become a mentor yourself. Find a promising young woman and return the favor.

Power Skill #8: Put a Little Distance in Work Relationships

While you want to be known as a people-oriented, approachable person, if you aim for a leadership role, you must also be known as a credible professional person. Unless you're leading a completely self-directed work team, you'll occasionally be forced to make decisions that don't please everyone. Developing close-chum or best-pal friendships and striving for popularity at all costs are not compatible with your leadership role.

The tendency to become too personal in work relationships is a success barrier that affects women more often than men. Making personal connections and building close relationships have probably been your first impulses since childhood, and one way you did this was by sharing your thoughts and feelings. This can be fraught with hazards in your organizational role, so think in terms of appropriate levels of intimacy as described below and shown in Shapshot #2 on page 94.

Core level: closest intimates. It's appropriate to reveal your inner thoughts, personal problems, deepest feelings, controversial beliefs, and other deeply personal aspects of yourself to your intimates (your most trusted family members and friends). These mutually supportive relationships are the sign of a well-balanced person and provide a safe place for expressing and sorting out your feelings and beliefs. Such relationships are probably essential to managing stress effectively.

Second level: close friends. You probably have some friends whom you feel very close to, but wouldn't feel free to express any and all your deepest feelings and problems with. You trust them with most issues, but not all.

Snapshot #2: Emotional Distances

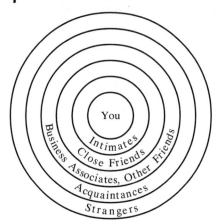

Third level: business associates and casual friends. With these people, you discuss current events and activities of mutual interest. The focus is on events and activities—not necessarily on your personal feelings about them, your evaluations of the people involved, personal problems they create for you, how they affect your intimate relationships at home, and other private matters. Nor is it wise to delve into your deep personal beliefs about the religious or political aspects of situations with business associates.

Why the distance in business or professional relationships? For one thing, you avoid needlessly stepping on toes and alienating people. For another, you avoid providing possible ammunition for future battles to people who haven't yet proven their trustworthiness. While you don't want to become paranoid, it *is* realistic to recognize that most organizations provide fertile ground for frequent power skirmishes, occasional battles, and even a rare all-out war. So why blab unnecessarily, especially about controversial personal beliefs or about anything that might come back to haunt you? Finally, if you keep your distance at work from the very beginning, you avoid the problems inherent in becoming the manager of former buddies. As you can see, by reserving your close, intimate relationships for people outside the workplace (those in the first two levels of intimacy), you'll avoid a number of political pitfalls.

Fourth level: acquaintances. At a more distant level of closeness, of course, are acquaintances: people you recognize, speak to, and perhaps conduct brief exchanges with, but about whom you know little or nothing.

Fifth level: strangers. If you have a burning desire to blab and can't reach an intimate, it's usually better to tell all to a stranger you'll probably never see again than to confide in a business associate. Bartenders and passengers on public transportation can attest to this phenomenon.

If you establish appropriate distances in your relationships, you probably won't alienate people. Instead, you'll merely provide a framework for establishing the support network you need to be effective in your job and to advance in your career. Your support network is your power base, and its inner core is you. This means you must be your own best supporter by continually giving yourself credit, acknowledging your own value, and taking care of your needs.

4

Negotiate Strategic Results

There's nothing so dangerous for manipulators as people
who think for themselves.

—Meg Greenfield, writer

When you negotiate, you interact with another person in order to reach an agreement. You may negotiate something as simple as the purchase of a trinket at a flea market or as complex as a trade treaty with other nations, where you're part of a delegation that deals with teams of negotiators from many other countries. Most of your negotiations may be with employees over work schedules, with suppliers over purchasing terms or delivery dates, with colleagues over getting information from their divisions or teams, or with managers over getting better working conditions or a raise.

Some of these negotiations become quite complex, so to simplify the explanations in this chapter, simple salary and promotion negotiations will be used as examples—but the principles are the same. As you take in these concepts and examples, use your imagination in applying them to current situations in your life.

As a woman, you probably have many strong negotiating skills already, such as the verbal and intuitive abilities that are essential for framing offers or proposals, figuring out how far the other side is willing to go toward making a deal, and deciding when to move to the next step of the process. Before you delve into these steps, think about your current beliefs about negotiating by answering the following questions. Then, meet a master negotiator and stockbroker, Muriel Siebert

How should women negotiate?

1. What's the best way to conduct a negotiation—by resolving one issue at a time or by getting all the issues on the table first?
2. You want to sell something. What's the most crucial information you need? The highest price a potential buyer is willing to pay? Or the least amount you're willing to take?
3. Should you explore differences during a negotiation? Or just stick with what you both agree on?

Muriel Siebert, Stockbroker

When Muriel (Mickie) Siebert arrived in New York City in the mid-1950s, she had $500 in her pocket and drove a used Studebaker. Fifty years later she was known as the "First Woman of Finance," the only woman to head a publicly traded national brokerage firm.

Mickie has been a pioneer in so many ways. In the 1950s, she became one of Wall Street's first female stock analysts. In 1967, she became the first woman to buy a seat on the New York Stock Exchange. In 1977, she ran one of the first discount brokerages and also became New York State's superintendent of banks. In the 1990s, her firm, Muriel Siebert & Co., became one of the first brokerages to go online.

Mickie forged her amazing success in the chaotic and cutthroat world of Wall Street. She survived more than one bear market and worked with many legendary characters. One was Captain Eddie Rickenbacker, the World War I flying ace who ran Eastern Airlines. Another was Robert Brimberg, the mold-breaking "Scarsdale Fats" whose investing savvy was the envy of the Street. During her five years as Superintendent of Banking for New York State, she helped to prevent a national fiscal crisis during the Iran hostage situation. She dared to run as a Republican candidate for Senate even though she is pro-choice. Her reputation for rocking the boat is legendary,

Mickie says that the secret to her success is contained in three four-letter words:

Work—she learns everything there is to know about a company before recommending its stock.

Luck—as an analyst in training, she had the good fortune to follow a fledgling industry that nobody else wanted. (The "dog" industry was airlines.)

Risk—she knows how to assess liability and make a decision.

She remembers to give back to the world that has allowed her such success. She donates substantial time and money to charitable, educational, and women's programs.

Strategy #1

Survey the Situation and Prepare

To become a masterful negotiator, you must learn to take a broad view of the entire situation, determine what you want, estimate what the other party wants, and assess your chances of reaching a win-win agreement. Then you must figure out your best alternative to making a deal (what you'll do if you can't make a deal you like) and the other person's best alternative. You're then in a position to predict the probable bargaining zone—the range of prices or conditions within which you and the other person can agree to make a deal, and to look for possible trade-offs.

Prep Skill #1: Survey the Situation

The first step in preparing for a negotiation is to survey the situation. You must decide what you want from the negotiation, what you think the other person wants, what factors might facilitate a win-win deal, and what factors might block it. Here are the types of questions you can ask yourself:

▶ What do I want? What's the most I'm willing to give or the least I'm willing to take? My goal (in a brief one-liner) is....

▶ What concessions would I be willing to make in order to reach an agreement?

▶ What does the other person want? Goals of the other side are....

▶ What other goals might they have?

▶ What concessions/trade-offs is the other person willing to make?

▶ Do others who must cooperate have the same goals I have? Do they have conflicting or overlapping goals?

▶ Do we view the situation in the same way? Are our key beliefs and viewpoints that affect this issue similar or conflicting?

▶ If we can agree on a goal, would we agree on how to achieve the goal?

▶ What questions may they ask during negotiations? Answers I'll give include....

▶ What surprises may occur during the negotiation? I'll handle them by....

▶ What's the other person's personality type/negotiating style? I'll respond by....

▶ What misunderstandings are likely to create barriers? I'll prevent them by....

▶ What are major barriers to getting the deal I want? I'll overcome them by....

▶ Whose decision is it to make? I'll approach them by....

▶ Who has the power in this situation? Is there an imbalance of power?

Know the other side. For an important negotiation, take time to assess the beliefs, general viewpoint, values, attitudes, personality and style, fears, goals, desires, needs, etc., of the key person(s) on the other side. Gear your strategy accordingly.

Fine-tune your image. What is the most important message about yourself that you want to communicate to the other side? For example:

▶ I'm a very serious and reliable person whom you can trust.

▶ I'm generous and fun to be with.

▶ I'm practical, but I can also be innovative.

Let the way you dress and act showcase your message. Make it uppermost in your mind as you prepare for the negotiation and as you begin it. This will be your major self-image. Before you leave home, look in the mirror one more time and ask, *If I were the other side, what would I see?* Let defining adjectives come to mind, such as friendly, organized, competent, or high-spirited. Is this the right image?

Prep Skill #2: Assess What You Want to Give and Get

We'll define your asset as what you have to offer. What your asset is worth is, in the final analysis, the best price you can get for it given your time frame and other constraints.

The initial value you place on your asset will determine your initial position in the negotiation. In turn, the initial positions of each side act as anchors throughout the negotiation and affect each side's perception of what outcomes are possible. The impact of a prior offer from some source is powerful and can cause you to overvalue or undervalue your asset. People start with some initial value and adjust from there when they estimate the value of their asset.

For example, Jake, who is about to receive his bachelor's degree in psychology, applied for a job in account advertising, in effect offering to sell his services (his asset) to a company. He bases his asking price on reports of the median salary for advertising account executives. He's puzzled when he gets no job offers. The fact is, his asking price is too far above the price such firms are willing to pay a graduate with no business experience and no marketing or advertising courses. Interviewers figure that any reasonable counteroffer they could make would be too low for Jake to consider, so they don't try. The gap, or bargaining zone, is just too huge.

Janet is about to receive her degree in marketing, and she's had two years of internship experience at a top advertising firm. She based her asking price on reports of entry-level salaries for marketing majors. During her first interview, she was offered a job on the spot and accepted the offer. If she had done her homework, had more confidence, and used good negotiating skills, she could have started with a package worth 30 percent more.

Enid did her homework. She consulted John Wright's *The American Almanac of Jobs and Salaries* and personal contacts in the field to find out the salary range for the type of position she wanted—given the type of experience and credentials she has. She set her specific goals for all aspects of the compensation package and job conditions—salary, benefits, perks, challenges, opportunities, empowerment, title, connections, training, equipment, technology. She asked about commissions, bonuses, healthcare, life insurance, company car and expenses, parking, expense account, travel, sick leave, childcare, vacation, sabbaticals, memberships, flextime, and other flexible arrangements. She asked for a figure near the top of the range, indicating that the entire package was more important to her than salary alone.

The base points you use when setting a job asking price might include:

- ▶ Your current (or most recent) salary.
- ▶ The company's initial offer.
- ▶ The least you are willing to accept.
- ▶ Your estimate of the most the company is willing to pay.
- ▶ Your initial salary request.

Research indicates that negotiators will make fewer concessions if they see an offer from a negatively framed base point, such as how much it costs the company to get you. Those who have more positive frames—such as how much value you can contribute to the company or how much salary you're willing to concede—are more likely to perceive the negotiated outcomes as fair.

Final agreements in any negotiation are more strongly influenced by initial offers than by the later concessions the other side makes, especially when people are not sure about the value of the issues or assets. If the other side snaps up your initial offer immediately, you may have valued it too low. If the other side responds to your initial offer by proposing some adjustments, that gives your initial offer some credibility as a base price. If your initial offer is too extreme, the other side can only reestablish the process by walking away or threatening to walk away.

Making an offer. If you want to make the initial offer, decide what offer will attract the attention of the other party. Don't make it too low, nor so high that the other side won't even consider it. Make it attractive enough to serve as a base price for subsequent counteroffers.

Making a response. When you think you'll be responding to an initial offer, prepare before the negotiation and remain flexible throughout. Know enough about the asset or disputed issues to recognize an unrealistic base price. Don't give too much weight to the other party's initial offer too early in the negotiation, and don't legitimize an unacceptable initial offer by making a counteroffer. On the other hand, don't let a low initial base price limit the amount of information and depth of thinking you use to evaluate the situation.

Prep Skill #3: Base Job Negotiations on Specific Achievements

Whether you're applying for a position in a new company or a promotion or raise in your present company, base your asking price on your specific achievements. If management is clear that you're contributing great things and that you're willing and able to provide what the company needs, they'll pay to get you and to keep you. Tactfully let the other party know how you add value to the company, as well as the job goals and standards you've met, how you've specifically contributed to company profit or reduced company expenses, or how your job duties have expanded.

Focus on how you add value. Rather than thinking in terms of how much additional money you need, focus on how much you're worth in the current job market and on what you can produce. Think in terms of your value to the organization, your accomplishments, your dependability, and your commitment. As you prepare for the negotiation meeting:

▶ Refer to your to-do lists and planning calendars to refresh your memory about your achievements.

▶ Stress both performance and learning. Make a two-columned list that shows what you accomplished on one side and what you learned on the other.

▶ Make some charts or graphs that offer a quick visual grasp of your progress.

▶ Make a list of your strengths and growth areas—how you're using your strengths on the job and your program for working on growth areas.

▶ Review your *I Love Me* file where you keep appreciative notes from coworkers, clients, and anyone else connected with your organization.

▶ Put together some figures that show what you've done to bring in money or to save on costs or time since you took the job.

Note goals and standards you've met. Management's response to your request will be based on your performance evaluations. But what if your company doesn't have a management-by-objectives program or effective performance evaluations? To help ensure that you get a fair performance evaluation, develop a plan, including times when you will report your results to your manager. Set deadlines for accomplishment of each goal.

Then make an appointment for a discussion with your manager in a relaxed atmosphere. During the meeting, get your manager to talk about what she or he thinks is important in your job. Get clarification on how your role fits into the overall scheme of the business. This information will help you pinpoint attributes you possess that are important to the company and know what points to stress later when you ask for a promotion.

If your manager gives you a lead in an area you handle well, follow it. Agree with the idea that this is truly a vital function and you'll do your best to achieve more than has ever been accomplished before. Reach an agreement on goals and standards you know you can meet. Try to phrase them in words that will either give a great deal of credit to your manager or will help him or her report your achievements in glowing terms when justifying your promotion at some future time. Send your manager a follow-up memo confirming the goals and standards. Such records will serve you well when you prepare your case for getting a promotion or raise.

Showcase your contribution to profits. Compute the value of your achievements, your productivity, your contributions. To do this, learn the arithmetic of your business and how it affects you. First, be sure you understand financial statements. Study them and talk about them.

If your job involves producing or selling something—a line position—figuring your contribution is fairly simple. If you work in a staff position, one that supports line functions, your department will probably be viewed as an expense rather than as a profit source. Don't let that intimidate you. The services of your department must be contributing to the overall profit of the company or they would soon be eliminated. Your services at least indirectly affect profits. What would happen if these services were not provided by you or your department? Would the company pay freelance people to provide them or farm them out to another firm that specializes in such services? How much would that cost? What advantages does your company enjoy by securing these services through you or your department instead? The answers to these questions can help you figure the dollar value of your contributions.

Perhaps your services have resulted in a decrease in company costs or expenses that, in turn, caused an increase in profits. Have you reorganized the work flow, restructured job descriptions, developed new procedures, or formulated better controls that resulted in a saving of time, money, or both? Time saved represents money saved. Convert the time you've saved the company into the hourly wages of the workers, who can now use that time to accomplish other tasks and, therefore, to achieve a higher level of productivity.

If you work in a government or nonprofit organization, you and your department are contributing a valuable service to the public; otherwise it wouldn't be in existence for long. With a little thought and ingenuity, you can place a value on your services. What would they cost if they were provided by a profit-making organization? How much do they add to the lives of the people who receive them? What would happen if these services weren't provided at all? What resulting costs would society have to pay? Analyze also the increases in productivity and reductions in expenses for which you've been responsible, and translate them into dollars.

Show how your job has expanded. One way to qualify for a raise and to position yourself for a promotion is to expand your present job—either by taking on new responsibilities or by getting your manager to attach to your job an unfilled job that's currently shown on the organization chart. Here are some suggestions:

▶ Volunteer for jobs no one is doing anything about. Look for things you can tackle.

▶ If your manager asks you to look into a project or problem, even very informally, accept the assignment happily and begin to formalize the request through the reports you write and by your attitude.

▶ Make yourself visible as someone who is interested in company progress and problems and ferrets out opportunities.

▶ Send your manager some progress reports with copies to others who might be interested. Talk to appropriate department heads and other executives.

▶ See whether you can get some colleagues to work with you on the project. Their reasons for working on it may be similar to yours. Now you have a task force.

▶ Try to get your new responsibilities or positions formalized on the organization chart. Whether you are able to do so or not, you can provide your boss with justification for giving you a raise outside the salary range for your position.

Prep Skill #4: Assess What They Want to Give and Get

Realistically assess the other party's bargaining position and their true interests—what they really want and why. Sometimes focusing on underlying interests—all the real issues—can help you to identify more useful solutions. What desires underlie the other person's stated position? Asking *why* may reveal this. For example, the interviewer at Company A says he needs you on board by May 1, but you won't be ready to take the job until August 1. If you explore why May 1 is important to him, you may discover that he needs a particular short-term project completed during May. A new set of options emerges.

Try to prioritize the relative importance of each of your own interests and those of the other party. Effective trade-offs can be made by giving up an item that represents a low-priority interest for you but a high-priority interest for the other person, and vice versa. For example, you may be able to do that short-term project for the company on a contract basis, and actually begin full-time work on August 1.

You may not have enough information to assess the other person's true preferences and priorities, but it's important to recognize this deficiency: It helps clarify what you need to learn during the negotiation. Use the negotiation as an opportunity to improve the quality and quantity of information you have about the other party. Knowing what information you're missing keeps you from making certain errors. It's far better to realize that the other party has some valuable information that you don't have than to make uninformed assumptions.

Assess your own underlying interest. For example, make sure the job or promotion you're negotiating fits your career goals. Ask yourself some general questions:

▶ Does the position fit my short-term and long-term career goals?

▶ How does it mesh with my personal life, and personal development goals?

▶ Will the position lead directly to a higher position?

- ▶ Will the job offer the kind of experience that makes me more valuable to the company?
- ▶ Will it give me an opportunity to make more or bigger decisions?
- ▶ Will it provide valuable contacts or opportunities to learn crucial skills?

Prep Skill #5: Assess the Best Alternatives to Making a Deal

What will you do if you can't make a deal that meets your requirements? Before you begin preparing for the negotiation, think about this and determine your best alternative to a negotiated agreement. As a seller, your best alternative determines the lowest price, conditions, or value that you're willing to accept as the outcome of the negotiation. If you can't reach an agreement, you'll have to settle for your best alternative. Therefore, any agreement that is of higher value than your best alternative is better than no agreement.

Consider the other person's circumstances and likely alternatives to making a deal, and you can get a wealth of information about how far they'll move before actually walking away from the negotiation. For example, try to determine the demand-and-supply ratio of people with your type of experience and skills to jobs available in that category. Learn how crucial your skills package is to the company at this moment in time and what alternate job candidates may be available to the firm. Of course, it can be difficult to assess the other party's (the firm's) alternatives, but you should always know your *own* best alternative and then estimate the other's best alternative.

Prep Skill #6: Predict the Bargaining Zone

Think of all the things you could offer the firm and that the firm could offer you as the *plate of goodies*. The negotiation is all about how to divide that plate of goodies—who gets what. When both parties adopt a tough strategy and assume that the other will cave in, confident that only the tough survive, the result is usually *no deal*. Rather than being tough or soft, it's better to be rational overall—tough at times and soft at other times. Evaluate each negotiation and create a strategy that fits. There's not a one-size-fits-all success strategy. Think about your best alternative and the other party's best alternative and make your assessment of the bargaining zone, the range of settlements within which it's better for both of you to agree than not to agree.

For example, you're waging a job campaign and are about to interview at Sybex Co. In figuring an exact asking price, keep in mind that you should always ask for more than you expect to get—as close to the top of the firm's bargaining zone as possible—and you should phrase your price in thousands of dollars per year. Here are some other factors to consider.

- ▶ What you have contributed to this or other firms and can contribute in the future.
- ▶ What the *men* who perform similar functions in the company or industry are making.
- ▶ How the rate of inflation has affected the buying power of your current salary dollars.
- ▶ What competing firms are willing to pay you.
- ▶ The top figure management is probably willing to give you.
- ▶ The bottom figure you're willing to take.

In your search for a job, a package worth $120,000 is your dream package and you'd take it in a minute (see Snapshot #1). However, as you prepare to negotiate with Sybex, you figure that there's a line of job candidates with qualifications similar to yours who would take the job at $100,000, or maybe a little less. So at that price, the firm is relatively indifferent about whether to give you the job or try for someone else. (Their best alternative would cost close to $100,000 so that's their price limit).

Ace Co. has offered you $80,000, but you'd like to get more, so if Sybex offers you $80,000, you're relatively indifferent about whether you accept their offer or Ace's. (Ace is your best alternative, so $80,000 is the lowest offer you'd accept.) You figure that Sybex probably wouldn't pay more than $100,000, but that you can make a deal with them in the bargaining zone of $80,000 to $100,000. Your goal is to get as close to $100,000 as possible, and their goal is to pay as close to $80,000 as possible. It may well be that you'll close the deal at $90,000.

Because you're thinking of this as a package, not just cash salary, be sure to identify perks, benefits, stock options, and other rewards you'd be willing to accept in lieu of cash and consider all tax implications. Say you initially ask for $100,000 and management counters with $80,000. You have a good chance of convincing management that you're worth $90,000. Each side will have made a $10,000 concession, and 50-50 splits are generally considered fair; people like them. How can you manage to negotiate for $100,000? One way is to create a demand for your services and to generate at least one offer of $100,000. That way you can pick and choose among offers, using the alternate offers as leverage. For example, you can say, *I really prefer to work at Sybex, but Ace has made me an offer that's hard to refuse.* People, including executives, tend to want what other people are trying to get.

The bargaining zone is the overlap between the price range a buyer is willing to pay and the price range a seller is willing to accept. If there is an overlap, a deal can be made. The endpoints are worse than indifferent for one person or the other, so no deal can be made in this price range. The overlap (bargaining zone), represents the set of agreements that both parties prefer over no deal. When the price limits of two parties overlap, both parties can benefit by reaching an agreement. If not, then for both parties *no deal* would be considered better than a deal.

Snapshot #1: The Bargaining Zone in a Negotiation

Seller's dream price	Buyer's price limit	Bargaining zone	Seller's price limit	Buyer's dream price
Applicant's Yes zone	Firm's indifferent zone	Overlap	Applicant's indifferent zone	Firm's Yes Zone
$120,000	$100,000	$80,000 to $100,000	$80,000	$70,000
Applicant's target price	Firm's price limit		Applicant's price limit	Firm's target price

When you sell. When you're the seller, say waging a job campaign, think about what your target companies would be willing to pay. Say you decide most would feel that $120,000 is out of their price range and that it would be a waste of their time to try to negotiate. The next question for you to consider is, *What asking price would attract target companies and get me the best possible compensation package?* You may decide it's $100,000, or even $80,000. Suppose a target company offered you $70,000. You'd probably be willing to negotiate with the hope of getting more than $80,000 or $90,000. The offer is close enough to your bargaining zone to interest you. But if the offer was $60,000, you'd probably feel that negotiating would be a waste of time. You might be offended at such a low offer.

When you buy. If you're a buyer, a manager who is hiring for your firm, for example, you want to get good employees at the lowest possible price. Unfortunately, getting something you want at the lowest possible price often requires running the risk of losing it to another buyer. In fact, any strategy other than accepting the other person's offer means some risk of no deal. Good advice is to *fall in love with three, not with one.* To make a well-informed decision as a buyer, you must first think about what would happen if you didn't buy the asset. How attractive is the next best option? To the extent that you love only the one asset and must have it, any bargaining position is weakened. *Falling in love* with the idea of one particular candidate prevents you from thinking clearly and rationally about the best alternative, and it compromises your competitive edge in the negotiation. If you have an alternative, you're better able to risk losing your favored candidate by waiting for her or him to make a concession. An alternative strengthens your position.

The bottom line. As a seller, your goal is to set an asking price that's close enough to potential buyers' bargaining zones (low enough) to encourage them to make offers. As a buyer, you want to make an offer that's just high enough to start a negotiation. One of the critical pieces of information in a negotiation is the other party's price limit (the point at which they become indifferent). If one side can discover the other's price limit without revealing their own, they can push for a resolution that's only marginally acceptable to the other, but greatly acceptable to themselves. In order to stand firm in a negotiation and still retain the chance to make a deal, you must first know the bargaining zone.

Knowing the other person's best alternative—and therefore that person's indifferent zone and price limit—allows you to determine whether an offer would be viewed as unreasonable, conservative, or generous. Focus on the price limits and the bargaining zone instead of your target price. For making deals, the maximum price others might be willing to pay is more crucial than the target price you'd like to get.

If the negotiation is a business deal, you may want to draft a tentative agreement to pass out for study at the appropriate time, usually when you're getting ready to close. You may want to leave blank the major issues to be negotiated, such as prices or fees, locations, times, and so on.

Create a demand for your services. When it comes to job campaigns and moving up the corporate ladder, you can increase your perceived value by continually creating a demand for your services. Never miss an opportunity to make contacts with other companies, departments, or executives who might be interested in hiring you—without neglecting or jeopardizing your current job, of course. Showcase your skills, interests, and achievements in a tactful way. Create your self-image as a desirable professional asset. At least once a year, apply for another job just to keep in touch with the job market and to stay on your toes. The advantages include:

▶ Your confidence and self-esteem are enhanced when you get job offers.

▶ Word may get around to management, without your saying anything, that other firms or departments are pursuing you. You'll appear more valuable while incurring no risk.

▶ During salary or position negotiations, you may be able to use other offers to reinforce your case. (Don't threaten to leave your current job unless you're ready to do so.)

▶ If you're turned down for a promotion, you can always come back with the news that you have a firm offer that's better than your present one.

Psychologically, you gain much personal power if you're always prepared to pack up and go. Always generate some options for your next move, both within the company and outside it. Always be planning and negotiating for your future. If you get a tempting offer, give your company a chance to match it, but don't be surprised if they can't. If you decide to leave, don't burn your bridges behind you. The company may want you back when you get your new experience, and they may be able to pay you more in the future.

Prep Skill #7: Look for Trade-off Possibilities

Alternatives, interests, and their relative importance are the building blocks for trade-offs, for creating unique package deals that work well for both parties. Assess this information before you enter the negotiation. Then you're prepared to analyze the two primary tasks of negotiation: 1) expanding the collection of available resources (issues, elements, preferences, and ideas), and 2) dividing up this plate of goodies. You must think about both of these tasks at the same time.

Expand the plate of goodies. Think in terms of integrating into the deal what each of you wants. Integrative agreements have a number of important benefits. They create better agreements than purely goodie-dividing deals. In some cases, no agreement is possible without finding more issues or goodies to put on the table. What you want, of course, includes money to be exchanged, and products or services to be provided. But it also may include timing of performance or delivery, how and when work is to be done and payment is to be made, method of delivery, and other side issues.

Look for concessions. Consider also what concessions you might be willing to make—and in what order of priority. Concessions are crucial bargaining tools. What would you be willing to give up? What would you be willing to add? For each concession, decide how far you would go. The first concessions you make should be those you can best afford to give, the ones you make to show goodwill and the desire to reach agreement. The more important concessions you should save in case the negotiation seems stalled. Try to keep one or two big concessions in the wings. Then consider possible concessions the other side might make—the things you most want as a sweetener or bonus.

Plan to look for multiple issues in a negotiation so that, when they surface, you can recognize them as trade-off opportunities that expand the plate of available resources, along with concessions either side might make. Key questions are: 1) What is my price limit? 2) What are my interests? 3) How important is each issue to me? 4) What are my priorities? Ask the same questions about the other party's position.

Job/salary trade-offs. For example, in a job negotiation, the job conditions may be more important to your career—or your career-personal life balance, at times, than promotions or raises. Consider alternate job conditions that you need or want as part of the trade-offs that might go into the plate of goodies. Here are some typical issues to consider:

- ▶ Career issues, such as a plateau, dead-end, or lack of challenge.
- ▶ Management issues, such as executives who won't share information, are temperamental, or don't support you.
- ▶ Peer issues, such as employees who are uncooperative or incompetent.
- ▶ Work team issues, such as a member whose performance is inadequate but whom you can't remove.
- ▶ Customer or supplier issues, such as people you can't trust but must deal with.
- ▶ Physical workplace issues, such as lack of space, obsolete equipment, or inconvenient location.
- ▶ System or culture issues, such as unreasonable expectations, workaholic culture, too much travel, or lack of team spirit.
- ▶ Benefits, perks, training opportunities, and job flexibility.

Consider putting your concerns and desired solutions in writing, starting with a summary of the issues and ending with a summary of desired outcomes. With an aggressive person, present this after a verbal discussion. With a detail person, you may want to offer the written memo first for them to study, with a meeting to follow.

Strategy #2

Get Off to a Good Start

You've prepared yourself to conduct a win-win negotiation. At the actual negotiation session, you want to get things off to a good start by preparing some good openers, building trust, sharing information, and asking questions to fill in your information gaps. You'll want to get all the issues on the table, frame options in ways that appeal to the other party, and focus on all relevant information rather than just what's available. Most important, you'll want to think in terms of a win-win deal.

Starter Skill #1: Prepare Good Openers

As you prepare good openers, keep in mind that win-win negotiation is a way of finding out each side's perceived needs and exploring ways of meeting those needs. It's a process of mutual education; an adventure in how to get to *yes*. It's *not* confession time, it's not a sparring match, and it's not an arm-twisting session.

Have several openings ready. Remember, *your first few sentences are usually throwaways* because nobody remembers them. Therefore, make them merely a warm, agreeable greeting. Focus on the sentences that follow for giving introductory information. Address the person with power, looking directly at this person. Use the key words that will appeal to that person's personality type. For example, use:

- ▸ *What* for an aggressive type: This is *what* I propose to do for you.
- ▸ *How* for a detail person: This is *how* I'm going to get it done.
- ▸ *Who* for a social type: Here's *who* will benefit from this.
- ▸ *Why* for an analytical or nice-guy·type: Here's *why* this needs to happen.

Focus first and foremost on the category that the person with power is most interested in, while also touching on the other categories. If you don't know the types of people you're dealing with, or if you're dealing with a team, quickly address each category and watch for responses. One way to begin is to review the basics of why everyone is there.

Starter Skill #2: Build Trust and Share Information

Often both sides end up with a better deal if you find some good trade-offs. But you must build trust and share information in order to get there, which also builds ongoing relationships. You and the other party may discuss a divide-the-plate rule before sharing information. One strategy is to set a rule for sharing any surplus benefits before exchanging confidential information. If you distrust each other, you could also agree to an independent review of all the financial assessments.

Speaking of distrust, you're aware that con artists exist, but how do you spot them when they show up for a negotiation? Ask yourself the follow questions:

- ▸ Do I feel uncomfortable or do I doubt the other person?
- ▸ Is the deal too good to be true?
- ▸ Does the other person's behavior seem congruent with his or her position?
- ▸ Does what I'm told fit with what I know about the situation? If not, ask questions you already know the answers to and see if you get correct information.

You need to be able to recognize con-artist tactics so you can devise an effective response. You also need to monitor your own actions to be sure you don't naively project a bit of a con-artist image. Some examples are:

- ▸ Repetition: Saying the same things over and over in order to break down your resistance.
- ▸ "Good-guy/bad-guy" routine: One person plays the good guy who starts off the negotiation and establishes a bond with you. Another person plays the bad guy who comes in and makes demands or refuses to concede. Then the good guy appeals to you to reach an agreement on the bad guy's terms.
- ▸ Righteous indignation intended to make you feel guilty for doubting their integrity.
- ▸ Victim routine: Acting nervous, fearful, sad, or dumb in order to catch you off guard, appeal to your protective side, play to your guilt, and thus get their way.
- ▸ Flattery, flirting, and other insincere seductive behavior.
- ▸ Playing a nurturing role designed to lull you into a false sense of security that your interests will be protected.
- ▸ Verbal assaults intended to rattle you into agreeing.

Break up these games by refusing to play your role. Find a way to suggest that both parties deal with each other as adults in a straightforward manner. Consider whether you really want to reach an agreement with the people who are playing these win-lose games.

Remember, in win-win negotiation, both sides are seen as basically equal, even if one has some advantage. If *both* parties are committed to meeting the basic needs of both sides and there is mutual trust, you normally can work out an agreement.

Starter Skill #3: Ask Questions to Fill Information Gaps

You know that the more information you have, the greater your negotiating power. So use the negotiation itself to fill in gaps in your information base. If the other person is not answering your questions in a useful way, consider giving away some information, which may break the information deadlock. You may not want to specify your best alternative, but you could offer information concerning the relative importance of the issues to your side. Exchanging this kind of information can help you and the other party find side benefits, use them to make some trade-offs, and end up with a deal.

In our job application example, you may want more information about the power potential of a job, how it fits into your career development plans, and whether you'll have the resources and environment to succeed in this position. Consider these questions:

Will I have adequate authority? Find out what the job or position requires. Whose cooperation must you have? What resources will it take? What kind of latitude will you have as the project moves in different directions?

Will I have to move in on someone's territory? Must part of the assignment be carried out in someone else's domain? Figure out what others have to lose or gain because of your work on this new assignment. How much resistance are you likely to meet from others? Ask to meet such people before you accept the assignment.

How much moral support can I count on? Who can you count on to help you? How supportive will your immediate manager be? Your manager's manager? If inadequate support may be a problem, try to determine why.

Is there a hidden agenda? This is the toughest question to answer. The interviewer(s) may not know of a hidden agenda coming from or through other management levels. Interviewers may have their own agenda, or may not want to level with you until you're committed to the job.

Are the money resources there? Analyze the position carefully and try to determine the budget and other resources you'll need for accomplishing your job goals. What are management's budgetary priorities? Identify a money trail to the source in the company that makes funds available. Try to estimate whether and how soon you can get the money you'll need. Is something lurking in the background to drag you down? If target dates are impossible on your budget, can more money be made available?

Are the time resources there? Unrealistic schedules and deadlines can complicate or even doom your projects. Ask how much time you'll have for projects, and assess whether it's realistic. Find out who set the schedule and why it's set up that way. Ask whether the staff will be willing to work overtime.

Are qualified people on line? Does the staff or team have the skills necessary to do the job? Ask to meet them. If they come up lacking, make sure you have the budget and the authority to hire people with the necessary skills.

How's the team spirit? Have there been attitude problems? Difficult people? Are they likely to be suspicious of you? Will they be taking cuts that are likely to make them dissatisfied or angry? Are they committed to old habits that need changing? Are they receptive to new ideas?

Is technology up-to-date? Can you be competitive with the current technology? Examine the technology used in products, production facilities, research and development, and administration. Is the technology in each current? Is it so new, it's risky?

What's the turnover history of the position? How long have others stayed in this position? Why did they leave? Excessive turnover can signal a problem. In large companies, the normal term in a position is two or three years. If possible, talk with your predecessors about their experiences in the position.

Starter Skill #4: Get All the Issues on the Table First

Most negotiations end in some sort of trade-off, where each side gives up something of lesser value to them in return for something of greater value. Thinking in win-lose terms, you overlook strategies that could work to the advantage of both sides. There may be many side benefits that you could bring to the bargaining table. Once they are there, you have many possibilities for trade-offs that could benefit both sides, but you don't bother to look for them because of your self-limiting belief in a fixed plate. For example, some of these new pieces might benefit only their side, but would cost your side little or nothing, and now you have a chip to trade for something you want.

Another self-limiting belief is, *What's good for them must be bad for us.* Studies indicate that most people would reject a proposal presented by the other side and would accept the identical proposal if presented by someone from their own side. To overcome this, pretend their proposal came from a neutral third party. Examine it first to see how it could benefit you or the advantages it offers. Then look to see what it might cost you or the disadvantages it would impose.

Avoid early agreements. If you focus on one issue or resource at a time, wrapping it up before going to the next issue, you're not discovering side benefits. Once you resolve an issue, it's rare that both sides want to go back and start over on it.

For example, the main issues in a job interview might be job position and title, tasks and responsibilities, base salary, benefits such as healthcare and retirement plan, perks such as company car and expense account, and other compensation such as stock options and bonuses. Your tendency may be to first discuss job position and title and come to an agreement about that, then discuss base salary and agree to that, and so forth. This is a rational, organized, step-by-step way of working through each of the issues or elements of the negotiation. However, this approach will limit your chances of reaching the agreement likely to be most satisfactory to both you and the firm. That's because you are not working with the full plate of issues, so you can't move them around and play with them as a way to make trade-offs and create a unique package of items.

Work with a full plate. Try to get all the issues, ideas, and preferences on the table. Your goal is to jointly generate alternative packages of issues. Don't reach agreement on any of them until you have discussed all of them.

For example, you should discuss your preferences regarding each job element, and the interviewer should discuss company preferences and possibilities in each area. As you discuss the whole range of issues, you increase the chances of discovering new side benefits to put on the table. For example, a flexible schedule may be very important to you and costs the firm nothing. On the other hand, it may be very important to the firm that you be able to handle certain technical aspects of the job, and this is easy for you to do. These are the elements of trade-offs.

Most important, this all-on-the-table approach increases the number of trade-offs that are possible. While resolving one issue at a time seems rational, clean, and methodical, it's not the most effective approach. A messy, even chaotic, approach is better suited to deal-making—and to deals that both sides will like to live with.

Starter Skill #5: Put Offers in an Attractive Frame

How you present the options that are available strongly affects the other side's willingness to make a deal. Frames include what the other person stands to gain, what they must give up, what you stand to gain, what you will give up, or what you'll both gain and give up. The what-you'll-gain focus is obviously very attractive, but the you-may-miss-out can also work. Framing can have a large impact on a side's willingness to take a risk, especially when they're uncertain about future events or outcomes. The base point the other side uses to evaluate an alternative as either a gain or a loss determines the positive or negative frame through which they view their options—and their later willingness to accept or reject those options—so you must play to the right base point.

Play to the Right Base Point

The status quo is one of the most common base points. Most people evaluate their options in terms of whether they represent a gain or loss from where they stand now. It's surprisingly easy to modify what people include as part of their status quo.

Role of attachment. Sellers often price items to include not only the market value, but also the value of the emotional attachment the seller has to the item. Simply owning something often increases the value people place on an asset because they view giving it up as something of a loss. For example, you're interested in selling your expertise by doing some part-time freelance work. But you do like the status quo of having evenings and weekends free from professional work. You may say, *If I can't average at least $100 an hour, I won't take a contract*. That becomes your base point. However, the buyers of your services have no emotional attachment to your time. Their base point is what they must pay for comparable services somewhere else.

Role of risk. Suppose your bottom-line base point is $100, and someone offers you $90. The risk-averse choice is to accept an offered settlement, while the risk-seeking choice is to wait for potential future concessions or better offers.

Obviously, which base point you choose determines whether you frame your decision as negative or positive. With a risk-averse frame, you think, *The $90 is close to the amount*

I thought I'd get and I have a contract nailed down; I'm happy. With a risk-seeking frame, you think, *I took the $90, but I probably should have held out because someone could have come along who would have been willing to give me $100 an hour.*

Role of perspective. Putting things in perspective is an important part of framing—for example, proposing a relatively small add-on *after* a large contract has been agreed upon. Suppose you're offering to complete a project for $900 (base price), one you think will take about 10 hours. After you agree on the $900 contract, you can frame a $100 add-on as a reimbursement of certain expenses. The $100 would loom larger if you presented it earlier—or if you were making only $10 an hour, and the contract (base price) totaled $90. This is how base price affects people's perspective. Why do you suppose nearly half of new car buyers purchase extended warranties averaging $800, when they're mostly pure profit for the dealerships? Only $130 on average goes to cover actual repairs, $110 goes to the auto manufacturer for administrative costs, and $560 is left for dealership profit. The reason is probably that the base price in the negotiation is the total price of the car, so the cost of the warranty seems small in comparison.

Play to the Belief in Fairness and Equity

How you frame a problem will affect how others judge the fairness of the solution. For example, employees will see a change in salary framed as a *wage cut* as unfair, but they may see a small wage increase that won't even cover inflation as more acceptable. That's because people think wages should go up, not down. They think of money as an arbitrary unit in dollar terms rather than in terms of money's real buying power—real dollars adjusted for inflation.

Research indicates that people prefer equal over unequal outcomes, regardless of the reason or situation. People tend to view 50-50 splits as fair. Actually, the fairness of a 50-50 split depends on the comparative fairness of each side's original offer. People who are aware of the appeal of the very term *50-50 split* realize that a variety of 50-50 splits using various original offers can be pulled out of a hat. For example, as seller you can set your asking price a little higher than normal, prompting a higher counteroffer by the buyer, and then agree to split the difference. People also use social comparison; for example, an employee compares her raise to the raise her male colleague got.

Use small gifts. As a negotiator, your generosity and helpfulness tend to generate positive emotions from the other party. This causes people to feel more positive toward you and toward human nature in general at the time, admire your problem-solving ability, and feel less aggressive and hostile. In some studies, when one negotiator gave the other a small gift, it induced a good mood. They were able to reach more creative and plate-expanding agreements than negotiators who didn't give a small gift. The other party was less likely to use highly competitive or contentious tactics.

Promote positive emotions. How do you avoid becoming angry and walking out, or having the other party do so? When we become angry, we may focus more on getting back at the other side than on creating a good deal for ourselves. Studies show that people in positive relationships care far more about how their outcome *compares* with what the other side got than the actual *value* of what they got. But if there are different options to choose from, the comparisons become less important than the person's own outcome value. Fairness and emotional considerations affect negotiations profoundly. When you choose your negotiation strategies, keep in mind the real emotions and concerns for fairness that everyone has. Focus on thoughts that lead to positive emotions—your own and the other person's. Also, to frame your proposals in ways that appeal to the other party, tune in to what *they* might be thinking and feeling. Negotiators who take into account the other party's perspective are most successful in negotiation simulations. They can better predict the other's behavior.

Focus on Potential Gains

When you focus on what you can gain, you're more likely to be concessionary about expenses or other side benefits to the other person—and to make more deals—than when you focus on minimizing your expenses. It's true that minimizing expenses on average will result in a higher average profit per deal. On the other hand, people who focus on the gains from making a deal tend to make more deals and their overall profitability is significantly greater.

For example, you and Joe both sell computers. Joe focuses on minimizing his own expenses, so he refuses to pay for shipping, financing, or installation. He gets his full price and makes buyers pay all expenses, but he closes fewer deals than you. You focus on the profit to be made from each deal, so you're willing to absorb some of those expenses in order to get your price and make a deal. Your flexibility helps you close more deals than Joe, but on average you make less profit per deal than Joe. By the end of the year, you've made more money than Joe.

Frame in gain terms. If you frame your proposal in terms of the other party's potential gain, you're more likely to induce them to assume a positive frame of reference—what they have to gain—and they're more likely to make concessions in order to make a deal, and thus take advantage of that gain. You can also emphasize the inherent risk in the negotiation situation for them—risks of waiting, of someone else getting the item, or the terms being withdrawn and less attractive terms being left—and contrast that with the opportunity for a sure gain that you're offering.

For mediators, framing may be best used when meeting with each party separately. What you frame as positive for one is usually seen as negative by the other.

Understand buyer and seller frames. Being a buyer or seller creates a natural frame. Sellers think about (frame) the transaction in terms of the dollars exchanged and see the process as gaining resources (dollars I get by selling). Buyers may frame the deal in terms of the loss of dollars (dollars I must give up). When you're the buyer (employer, for example), you want to frame your offer in terms of dollars the seller (applicant or employee) will get. When you're the seller (employee), you'll frame your offer in terms of what a great asset the buyer will get and the many great benefits he or she will gain.

Strategy #3 _____

Move the Negotiation to Closure

After getting the negotiation session off to a good start, keep it moving to closure. You need a crucial set of negotiation skills in order to move beyond stalemates, manage surprise moves, and overcome barriers that emerge during the meeting. You need to avoid typical pitfalls by getting adequate information, negotiating around stalemates and barriers, being cooperative but not a doormat, knowing when to cut your losses, and knowing when and how to close a deal.

Negotiation Skill #1: Ask Yourself Key Questions

Here are some self-questions that will help you avoid common mistakes that block negotiations and prevent successful closure:

1. Am I pursuing a negotiated course of action only to justify an earlier decision?
2. Am I assuming that what's good for me is bad for the other party, or vice versa?
3. Am I irrationally affected by an initial offer or base price?
4. Is there another frame that would put a different perspective on the negotiation?
5. Am I too affected by available information and ignoring other valid, but less available, information?
6. Have I fully thought about the decision of the other party?
7. Am I placing too much confidence in my own judgment?

Ask the same seven questions about the other party's behavior.

Negotiation Skill #2: Create Package Deals

You've already prepared yourself to negotiate a package deal by identifying trade-off possibilities. And you know the importance of getting all the issues, ideas, and preferences on the table before agreeing to any one of them. Now, everything is on the table. Be sure you have identified all possible side benefits that could expand the plate of goodies and all possible concessions. You're looking for flexibility so you can make some trade-offs.

Next, put together several package offers that are acceptable to you, and present them all at the same time. By making multiple offers at the same time, you can collect valuable information about what's important to the other party. At the same time, you appear to be more flexible. For example, you can put together several job packages with varying combinations of job responsibilities and conditions, salaries, benefits, and perks.

Negotiation Skill #3: Explore Differences and Options

Learn to think of differences as opportunities rather than barriers. Typical areas of difference are expectations about what's likely to happen, risk preferences, time preferences, and cost-cutting possibilities. Look also at possibilities for adding more resources and finding new, creative options.

Look at differences in expectations. If you have different expectations about what's likely to happen, maybe you can bet on your expectation and the other party can bet on theirs. For example, in a joint venture you think the greatest profit will be in the first year and the other party thinks it will be in the second year. You can agree to split the profit 80-20 the first year and 20-80 the second year. Such contingent contracts are bets that allow the parties to agree, even when they have different perceptions or opinions of the future. These differences can enhance the flexibility of the negotiation, increasing the chances of making a deal.

Look at differences in risk preferences. Rather than seeing one party's relative risk aversion as an obstacle to negotiation, you can use it as an opportunity to trade. One side gets a guarantee in return for increasing the expected value to the other. For example, *I'll guarantee you a 10 percent profit up to $10,000 if I can have 70 percent of any profit more than $10,000*. Different risk-sharing strategies allow for trades that might not otherwise occur.

Look at differences in time preferences. When the other party feels strongly about some time issue, such as receiving earlier payment or delivery, it's an opportunity for a trade.

Look at cost-cutting possibilities. What would make it less costly for the other party to compromise on the primary issue? Cost-cutting calls for one party to get something they especially want while the other has the costs associated with giving that concession reduced or eliminated. For example, you're willing to pay half the costs of shipping if the other party will use the shipping line you prefer, one that brings it to your door. The result is a high level of joint benefit—not because one party wins, but because the other party suffers less. Cost-cutting means the party who makes the major concession receives something to meet the specific goals they gave up. It's similar to a trade-off, but it focuses on reducing or eliminating costs for the party that makes a concession.

Look at adding more resources. If added resources exist, this can work, but only in areas where the parties' interests are not mutually exclusive. For example, *I'll share a customer mailing list with you. It has some value to you and it won't cost me anything to provide it.*

Look for new options. Finding creative options often hinges on redefining the conflict for each side, identifying each side's underlying interests, and brainstorming for a wide variety of potential solutions.

Explore post-settlement options. After you reach an initial agreement, you can propose looking for a better one for both parties, but agree to be bound by the initial agreement if a better one isn't found. Agree that if you do find a better agreement, both of you will share the surplus benefits. This offers both of you a last chance to find the best deal with limited risk to either party.

Negotiation Skill #4: Avoid Typical Pitfalls by Getting Information

Pitfalls include conceding to demands when you should cut your losses, not predicting the results of winning (the winner's curse), focusing on the wrong information, and not getting adequate counsel and advice. You can minimize all these potential problems.

Know When to Cut Your Losses

Realize that the time and money you've already invested are sunk costs. You can't get them back and you should forget them when deciding what to do next. What you do next depends on the current situation and what you project for the future. Generate all the possible alternatives. Then evaluate your best estimate of the *future* costs and benefits of each alternative, forgetting past investments except for lessons you've learned from them.

Misdirected persistence occurs primarily due to misdirected ego. You commit your-self to getting something, the commitment biases your perception and judgment and causes you to make irrational decisions to manage what others think of you, which leads to an upward spiral of competition to get the thing you want.

Avoid the Winner's Curse

What will happen if you win and get the deal you want? Will it really be a good deal for you? In order to make a good deal, you need enough information to know what you're getting into and how the assets you're acquiring are likely to perform or work out. If you cannot get adequate information, you can reduce your risks by assuming the information you're missing would be bad news that uncovers flaws in the asset. If you assume all is as it seems and pay accordingly, you win the asset, but you must deal with what's commonly known as the winner's curse: You got what you wanted, but it's not such a good deal.

Problem: Imbalance of information. The key lesson of the winner's curse for negotia-tors is that one side, usually the seller, often has much better information than the other. Though everyone is familiar with the adage *buyer beware*, it's difficult to put this idea into practice when the other side knows more than you. Against a better-informed party, usu-ally the seller, your expected return from making a deal decreases dramatically.

Example: House buyer. Say you take a job in a city you don't know well. The real-estate market is favorable to buyers and you want to avoid moving twice, so you decide to buy a house. You know very little about real estate in the new city, so you find an agent. After looking at 12 houses in three days, you make an offer on a house. It is immediately accepted. Did you make a good purchase? You had limited information and accepted advice from an agent who stands to gain by closing the sale. The seller is most likely to immediately accept an offer if it's higher than the true value of the house.

Example: Business buyer. You (or your company) find a business you want to buy. It's certainly possible to make money by making an offer on a going operation, but you're twice as likely to lose money as you are to make money on the deal. Actually, the odds are five to two against your making a good deal. The source of this paradox lies in the high likelihood that the seller will accept your offer when the seller's firm is least valuable to you; that is, when it's a lemon. There can be valid reasons for selling a profitable business that has a bright future, but the chances are much greater that the owners won't sell such a business. Consider this fact: Only one-third of corporate acquisitions are as successful as expected, while one-third prove to be failures and one-third fail to live up to expectations.

Research suggests that while stockholders of target firms make significant profits when their firms are purchased, there is usually no gain for the acquirers. The bottom line is: *Only buy a going firm if it's a steal; otherwise, start your firm from scratch.*

Buyer beware. When you're the buyer, especially when buying used goods, remember that the sellers have selectively chosen to sell these goods, and you have an information disadvantage. So, how can you avoid the winner's curse?

▶ Consider the seller's reputation—is it positive and reliable?

▶ Try to get warranties or guarantees that have a reliable track record.

▶ Ask yourself if you can rely on an ongoing relationship that the seller wants to maintain.

▶ Get advice from trusted experts.

▶ Reduce the amount you're willing to pay.

When you can't get adequate information to make a good decision about a deal, consider the odds of winning or losing, assume that what you don't know is bad news, reduce the price you're willing to pay accordingly, and walk away if the seller won't meet your upper price limit.

Focus on Relevant Information

People tend to focus on the information that's up front in their minds, what's readily available to them, and what's most visible or memorable. Unfortunately such information may be totally irrelevant to negotiating a good deal.

Readily-available-information illusion. Things or events you've experienced most frequently are usually the easiest to remember. They're more readily available in your memory. However, the more vivid the event, the more likely you are to remember it too. Something easy to recall seems more numerous than something more difficult to recall. But such easy information may not be the most relevant information, so it can cause you to overestimate or underestimate the value of the other side's offer.

Vivid-information illusion. If you're like most people, you tend to over-estimate the probability of an unlikely event occurring if the memories you associate with the event are especially vivid and easy to recall. For example, if you actually see a house burn, you're more likely to believe that your house could burn than if you just read in the newspaper that a house burned.

Carry this idea into your negotiation. On the one hand, if you present information in colorful or emotionally vivid ways, you're more likely to influence the decisions of the other party—compared to making an equally informative presentation in a dull, matter-of-fact way. Both the amount of information and the way you present it can provide you with power and influence over the negotiation outcome. On the other hand, when you make your own negotiation decisions, identify and use truly relevant and reliable information.

Get Good Counsel and Advice

You're in the process of becoming a skilled negotiator, but you can never know it all. What can you do to increase your chances of making a good deal?

▶ Remind yourself that you're most likely to be overconfident when your knowledge is limited—that's when you could use some expert advice.

▶ Ask yourself why your decision might be wrong, or not quite right, and write down the reasons. This will help you see obvious problems in your judgment.

▶ Seek objective opinions about your position from a neutral party.

▶ Focus on how the other party probably views the situation and the rightness of their position as well as your own.

▶ Ask yourself whether you or others are operating from need-based illusions.

It's common for people to distort their perceptions of situations to make themselves feel more competent and secure, resulting in need-based illusions that motivate them. Such illusions make a situation seem more palatable, while influencing decision-making and negotiation abilities.

Illusion of superiority. You give yourself more responsibility for your own successes and take less responsibility for your own failures, but you hold other people responsible when they fail and don't give them credit when they succeed. Negotiators are especially likely to believe that they're more flexible, purposeful, competent, fair, honest, and cooperative than their opponents.

Illusion of optimism. You underestimate your chances of experiencing *bad* future events and overestimate the likelihood that you'll experience *good* future events.

Illusion of control. You believe that you have more control over outcomes than you really do, even in such obviously random events as throwing dice.

Illusion that contradictory information is irrelevant. When you hold certain beliefs or expectations, you tend to ignore information that contradicts them. You don't seek to disprove an initial belief, and you are more likely to take at face value information you agree with and scrutinize more carefully information you don't agree with. A more useful role is to play devil's advocate. Realize that your initial strategy may not work, and seek to disconfirm it by searching for new information. If you aren't open to disconfirming information, you'll have a harder time adapting when confronted by unexpected circumstances in a negotiation.

Negotiation Skill #5: Negotiate Around Barriers and Stalemates

Constantly reassess the situation as the negotiation unfolds. If you're open and flexible, ready to modify your plan in ways that will help you make a good deal, you increase your chances of making that deal.

Break Through Barriers

You need to know how to recognize a stalemate, reassess during breaks, take the lead in problem-solving, and use various tactics to break through barriers.

Recognize a stalemate. How will you know when the negotiation stalls? Look for such signs as the following:

▸ The process is heading backward.

▸ The other side switches negotiation styles.

▸ The other side becomes extreme or makes unreasonable demands.

What can you do? Your major options include calling for a brief break, scheduling another meeting, or ending the effort, although normally it's best not to walk away first.

Reassess during a break. Your best bet is usually to call for a break to give you time to reassess, incorporate new information, and reformulate your strategy. Ask yourself such questions as:

▸ What's causing the blockage? What is the root problem here? Is it the apparent problem or an underlying one we haven't recognized? Is it a side problem? Is it something that happened earlier, such as a concession or statement made that someone now regrets or resents?

▸ What's happened so far? (Review verbal and nonverbal messages and the sequence of events up to this point.)

▸ Are there any critical messages, verbal or nonverbal, that you're failing to send?

▶ Are you pushing too hard, hanging on too tightly to your bottom-line goals? Do you need to lighten up?

▶ Did you learn anything in the recent interaction that changes your assessment of the other party's price limit or interests, or the importance of issues?

▶ What's your updated assessment of the bargaining zone?

▶ Where should you now look for trades?

▶ Do you need to press for closure in order to move things forward?

▶ Do you need to improve your decision processes?

▶ What are the decision processes of the other party?

▶ Do you need to hold a caucus with your negotiation team to decide what to do next?

▶ Do you need to make some phone calls to get information or advice?

Try a problem-solving mode. When you resume the negotiation, consider using a problem-solving mode to identify problems that either side perceives. Is there a problem that could fatally block reaching an agreement? Why? Deal with that problem now, or determine whether dealing with other issues first could lead to a solution of that problem farther down the road. Next, work on problems you feel you can solve. List issues in a workable sequence for resolving. This will give both sides a sense of forward movement.

Use persuasion. Perhaps you see an approach to resolving the blockage, but you need to influence the other side that this is the best approach. Consider this sequence of persuasion:

▶ Begin with an easy-to-resolve issue.

▶ Send the most attractive or acceptable message first.

▶ Present both sides of the issues.

▶ Be open and flexible about possible solutions.

▶ Repeat the benefits of reaching an agreement.

Try other tactics. Consider these tactics for breaking a stalemate.

Suggest brainstorming possible problems and solutions and ways to move forward.

▶ Ask several questions that you're sure will bring a *yes* response from the other side, shifting the process to a positive mode.

▶ Send up at least three or four trial balloons, what-ifs—never just one. The responses can give you clues about what the other side is thinking and feeling, and can help lead to a solution. Ask them for suggestions and think creatively together.

▶ Present four alternative solutions to the problem, placing the alternative you prefer as third in the sequence. Aggressive people tend to want to say *no*, and doing so a couple of times gives them satisfaction, but if they want to reach an agreement, they're likely to say *yes* the third time around.

▶ Make a concession or two, dramatizing them to stress their magnitude for you.

▶ Can you write up and sign what you've agreed to up to this point and even act on this agreement, saving the remaining problems to be resolved later?

Go deeper to identify tough barriers. If you're still blocked, consider what's going on in the following areas:

- ▶ What's the level of trust?
- ▶ Are both sides really listening?
- ▶ What are the needs of both sides at this point?
- ▶ Does one side seem to be winning and the other side losing?
- ▶ What new alternatives might meet the needs of both sides?

What if both sides conclude that an agreement is not possible at this time? Now is the time to be philosophical and to avoid showing anger, bitterness, or other stressful emotions. Remember that you may be able to work together at a future date. See if you can get the other side to say why they can't agree or negotiate further. What do each of you want to say about the negotiation process? By discussing the problem, each side may learn something, so at least mutual education will result from the time and effort spent.

Handle surprise moves. What if the other side makes a surprise move? Surprises may range from learning new information about the history of the current situation, to where you'll meet or what time you'll start or finish. See if you can turn the surprise into an opportunity. This requires quick thinking on your feet and looking for options. Remain polite and cooperative. Becoming angry or irritable is likely to block your ability to later turn the change to your advantage.

Deal with frustration. What if the other people become frustrated, bored, or tired? Clues that this is occurring include interrupting often, drumming fingers on the table, kicking the floor, studying the wallpaper or pictures, darting eye movements, and packing up their papers. When this occurs, try the following:

- ▶ Summarize what's been agreed upon.
- ▶ Repeat the concessions you've already made.
- ▶ Ask them to be more specific about what they want.
- ▶ Offer new concessions or favors.
- ▶ Ask for a brief break or suggest continuing the meeting on another day.

Tune in to the other people's need for pacing the negotiation and be considerate. Always keep in mind the timing and try to intuit when the time is right to push for closure and agreement. Remember, it usually pays to avoid unnecessary conflict by cooperating as long as the other side does.

AS A GENERAL RULE, DON'T BE THE FIRST TO WALK AWAY.

Handle Barriers in Job Promotion Requests

In negotiating for a job promotion or raise, be prepared to overcome stalemates by anticipating typical objections managers give.

Weak performance area. What if management criticizes an area where your performance has been weak? What can you do to offset this attack? First, prepare yourself by finding some evidence—no matter how small—of progress in your weak area. Don't reveal it until you're in the interview so you can use a slight element of surprise to strengthen your case and move management along to an agreement.

If management brings up the weak area, don't deny that it is a problem. Instead, encourage them to focus on this problem. Try to get them to verbalize it as the main or only obstacle to granting your request. Avoid giving any solutions or progress reports until they've done this. If they're making a strong case you can't refute, they're more likely to concentrate on the weak area to the exclusion of any other.

Next, get management to express support for your work in other areas. They'll be more comfortable supporting you if they think your request can reasonably be denied because of your poor showing in the weak area. Try to get them to state that they'll take a supportive position toward your request when you show improvement in the weak area.

Now produce evidence of improvement or reason for hope. This can be some minor result, some form of solution, a plan of action, or anything that shows promise. State clearly how you intend to take advantage of this improvement and what your plan of action is. Remind management that you can do your best work once your request has been granted and your mind is free to concentrate fully on the job. Mention the job goals you've agreed to in the past and stress how well you've met most of them. Go over your strengths and this one weak area, stressing that your evidence indicates that this weakness is in the process of becoming a strength. Keep stressing your strong points and achievements during the meeting.

If management argues that your evidence is weak, counter with the fact that their objections were based on *incomplete* information about the weak area. Appeal to their sense of fairness in giving you credit. Ask whether they *really* demand perfect performance in every area before giving promotions or raises. Mention how monetary recognition of your achievements provides a strong stimulus to your becoming more effective and productive. Ask for advice and support in making improvements. Stress how you value their leadership and guidance in achieving these improvements. Be patient and firm in maintaining that management was prepared to accept a slight show of progress and that you've given them that as well as a strong showing in other areas.

Botched assignment. If management gives a recent botched assignment as a reason for turning you down, counter in a calm, rational way, focusing on your value. Avoid defensiveness, anger, blame, or accusation. Don't cry. If your emotions go out of control, find an excuse to break for a few moments to work them out in private. The best way to overcome a mistake is to show by your discussion of it and by your actions that this is not typical of you, that you've learned from it, and that you're taking positive action to correct it and prevent similar botches from recurring. If management still carps, you can say calmly, *That's not how I see it*, and briefly explain how you see it.

Tight budget. Prepare for the possibility of management giving the tight budget excuse. Try to determine whether your peers are getting raises. Look for company statements and comments of executives that refute a no-money argument. What percentage of increase did the top executives receive last year, including stock options and other perks? Can you show that your part of the operation has been functioning properly and at a profit, regardless of overall company performance?

Maybe later. If management won't make a commitment, try the following:

▶ Appeal to management's self-image as decision-makers who quickly and easily make on-the-spot decisions.

▸ Tactfully hint at the unfortunate results of delaying or giving a negative answer.

▸ Reassure them that they won't regret a decision in your favor. Indicate that you'll be appreciative and will do everything in your power to make them glad they said *yes*.

▸ When you've said everything you can say, stop talking. Use one more powerful tool: silence, no matter how long it gets.

Negotiation Skill #6: Be Cooperative but Don't Be a Doormat

You cooperate as long as the other side cooperates. But what if the other side walks away? Should you retaliate in some way? Don't think in terms of retaliation, but rather in terms of assertiveness and mutual respect. Remember, if the other person perceives your assertive response as aggressive, as getting back at them for more than their one defection, the negotiation becomes even more adversarial. Still, if you don't stand up in some way to their defection, you risk being exploited—and feeling abused. A generous level of forgiveness is far better than risking unending mutual retaliation. But if your generosity makes you an easy target for exploitation, you must take a stand.

You benefit from the other side's cooperation. Your goal is to encourage that cooperation. A good way to do so is by making it clear that you will reciprocate any cooperation and any defection. Words are important in getting that message across, but actions can speak louder than words, so follow through and be clear about what you're doing and why.

Negotiation Skill #7: Know When and How to Close a Deal

Your goal is to make a good deal or to reach a resolution of some kind. How do you know when you're nearing that goal? Ask such questions as:

▸ Are both sides coming to an understanding?

▸ Can I see what we both need in order to do business together?

▸ Are we starting to work out an agreement that will settle some conflict between us?

Intuition and timing are crucial to recognizing when it's time to go for an agreement and close the negotiation.

When both sides say they're in agreement, refer to your notes to finalize the terms of the agreement. Your notes should show the concessions, compromises, and other points that have been agreed to during the negotiation process. As part of the agreement, is it necessary to designate how future disagreements will be handled? If so, do you need to discuss this now?

If the deal calls for a written agreement, consider having both parties sign a contract or a preliminary document, perhaps a draft you've brought with you. You may add key information or mark out or change certain clauses. Even a handwritten agreement done on the spot is usually legal. The purpose is to nail down the major points of agreement in writing while they're fresh in everyone's mind. If appropriate, a final version of the document can be signed later.

Follow-up. In order to continue building trust and laying the foundation for further business or good relationships, follow through on your part of the agreement.

▶ Do everything you agreed to do.

▶ If you have problems following through, contact the other side and work through the problems.

▶ Be available when they need you.

▶ Maintain a positive relationship by such actions as mentioning the benefits of the agreement and touching base even when you don't need to discuss the agreement.

Closing job negotiations. When you feel it's time to bring a job position negotiation to a close, take the initiative and move on. Base your statements on the assumption that all questions have been answered and that the promotion or raise will be granted. Summarize the main arguments for the promotion or raise and ask for it.

If management balks, smoke out the main objection. Focus on *it* as the main obstacle to granting your request, answer the objection, and then restate your request. Imply the negative results that may result from delay or from a *no*, and reassure management that they'll be making the right move by saying *yes*. If necessary, make one concession and then wait for the answer.

Negotiation Skill #8: Manage Gender Discrimination

In a job negotiation, if you were unable to negotiate the job, promotion, or raise you wanted, ask yourself whether your employer is unfairly discriminating against you because you are a woman. If you think the answer is *yes*, here are some actions to consider.

Talk the problem over with your manager. This is a necessary policy step and legal step, even if you're sure it won't do any good. Remember, your manager may resent your stand and seek revenge. On the other hand, he or she may respect your assertiveness and bend over backward to prevent accusations of discrimination. Either way, it's best to decide whether you're prepared to take the matter further before you talk it over with your manager. Keep these suggestions in mind:

▶ Talk about unfairness rather than discrimination so management won't overreact to what appears to be a threat of legal action.

▶ Give specific examples of unfairness.

▶ Be clear about your exact purpose—what you want from this meeting. Prepare before you go in.

▶ Make a list of your specific concerns and of specific results that show what you've been producing. Practice what you're going to say.

▶ Talk about the facts of the situation without blaming or accusing. Use *I* messages. For example, *My performance went beyond most of the goals we agreed upon. I believe this more than justifies the raise I requested.*

▶ Take an effective, problem-solving approach, not an emotional one or one that reflects *just a gripe.*

Carefully consider more drastic steps. If you aren't satisfied with what your manager says or does, you must decide whether to risk your manager's wrath by going to the next level of management or to the Human Resources department. If you feel that you cannot be satisfied with the status quo, go to the next level and do all you can to resolve the matter within the company. If you still don't get results, you have three basic choices:

1. Stay and cope with the discrimination.
2. Find a company that treats women better.
3. Go outside the company to the Equal Employment Opportunity Commission (EEOC) to file a complaint and, perhaps later, a lawsuit.

Your best bet is probably finding another company. First, consider consulting a lawyer who can coach you in getting the best severance package possible. Before negotiating this package, try to line up your new job.

Filing EEOC complaints or lawsuits can be major trouble, so do it only if fighting the equality fight is more important to you than your career. Women who fight are typically verbally blackballed in the industry, must change fields, and are in relative limbo for about seven years. This is why affirmative action—which operates behind the scenes in terms of overall fair treatment of all the company's employees—is so much more effective than equal opportunity laws. A woman who chooses the latter route must usually file an individual complaint and make huge career sacrifices. She must first complain to the company, and then to the EEOC. Completing this second step may take years because the EEOC is often understaffed. Only then can she file a lawsuit, which nearly always costs far more than she can afford. That means she can't get a lawyer unless she finds one who believes she has a great case and is willing to get paid only when and if the case is won. Even women who join others in class action lawsuits are typically blackballed and suffer severe financial and career setbacks.

On the brighter side, if you show management in a savvy, positive way that you're aware of gender discrimination laws and really want to avoid legal action—but still expect to be treated fairly—you may get results. This approach often encourages management to shape up and treat you with the respect you so richly deserve, while helping you avoid the repercussions of taking legal action.

Strategy #4

Negotiate Conflict Resolution

Negotiating a win-win resolution to a conflict situation calls for many of the negotiating skills and procedures you're learning to use in the basic negotiation situations we've discussed so far. As a leader, you'll find many opportunities to resolve conflicts among employees, groups, and perhaps even organizations. Without the right skills and expertise, conflicts are a headache—even a nightmare. With them, conflicts become opportunities to contribute, to lead, and to build career success.

Your basic skill lies in using women's ways of leading to prevent and handle conflict as a healthy learning process. Other skills are: thinking in terms of win-win outcomes, letting both sides air their views, helping people find the root cause of the problem, identifying the resolution strategies of the parties, creating proposals for solution, and reaching a resolution that all can live with.

Resolution Skill #1: Manage Conflict as a Learning Process

As leader of your group, you have the greatest influence on how conflict is handled. If you're watchful for signs of differences of opinion and see that they are considered and respected, you'll teach your people by your actions that conflict can be constructive. Women's ways are inclusive, information-sharing, and esteem-building. Bring in also your tendency to intuit how people are feeling, to draw people out in order for all to understand what's happening, to listen between the lines, to support honest expression, to verbalize what you sense is going on, and to help people connect and find common ground.

Women tend to understand that bottled-up feelings of resentment, frustration, and other stressful feelings, can poison relationships and work environments. Conflict offers all parties an opportunity to learn about what's really going on with the other side, as well as numerous other learning opportunities. Conflict may also add force, energy, and more intense interest in the idea or situation in question. When conflict is handled constructively, opposing opinions and ideas are discussed openly. This airing of ideas can lead to creative, innovative approaches—and conflict buildup is prevented.

When you view conflict as a natural and healthy aspect of group effort, the people you lead or influence are more likely to be open about their opinions and ideas. Conflicts among your people will surface, and it will be possible to discuss problem situations at a stage when candid discussion is most helpful—before resentments fester and positions harden. As a leader, therefore, your key to avoiding *ongoing* conflict lies in accepting *initial* conflict among workers and airing it as openly as possible. Any conflict or stressful feelings an employee is harboring about an issue or event is worth exploring and resolving.

Resolution Skill #2: Set the Stage for a Win-Win Outcome

Before you set up a meeting to negotiate a conflict resolution, think about how you'll provide a supportive atmosphere for airing differences and reaching solutions. How will you set the stage so the parties will have the best chance of finding a win-win resolution? Consider timing, ground rules, evaluative criteria for proposals, process, and positive tone.

Be sure the time is right. Establish that the parties to the conflict are ready to sit down and try to resolve it. Until they are, everyone will be wasting time.

Establish some ground rules. Make sure that each side has equal time to present its views. Take steps to see that the most powerful or aggressive people don't dominate the situation unfairly. Insist on no interruptions while each side is presenting its view. If the other side refuses to respect the basics of common courtesy, the situation will probably only worsen. Consider suggesting an end to this meeting with rescheduling to occur only when the rules of courtesy are agreed upon.

Aim for the rule of consensus. If the conflict involves groups, they must set a ground rule about how each group will decide on proposals and resolutions. Majority rule is the most common ground rule for making group decisions, but consensus rule is increasingly used. In consensus rule, all group members must agree to a decision. The stance most often taken is that all members need not be enthusiastic about the decision, but they must feel that they can live with it and agree to cooperate in implementing it. Whatever decision rules the group chooses can affect both the complexity of the interaction and the divvying up of outcomes.

Why consensus groups make more agreements. People in a group tend to have varying motives for the outcome of the conflict, so most groups are mixed-motive groups. In a purely competitive group, majority rule is the most efficient, and perhaps the best, way to avoid an impasse. In a mixed-motive group, however, majority rule is not so effective. It doesn't reveal how strongly people feel about their preferences, so members don't have much chance to learn the values others place on the issues. People may not say *why* they're voting one way or another, how they feel about a particular issue, or the relative importance they place on the outcome. Without getting this information into the open, it's much harder to find side benefits to trade off and to find expanded-plate agreements that are based on differing preferences.

Studies have found that mixed-motive groups negotiating under a consensus rule reach more valuable outcomes. To reach a unanimous agreement, each party has to make trade-offs that lead to an expanded-plate outcome. Group members must learn other members' preferences and find ways to expand the plate of resources to accommodate them. It's time-consuming, but it forces group members to consider creative alternatives to increase the plate and satisfy the interests of all group members.

Understand how consensus works. A consensus rule has three phases:

1. Considering the proposal for decision.
2. Stating and resolving members' concerns about the proposal.
3. Resorting to alternative options if consensus can't be reached.

When a proposal to be decided on is presented, members ask questions and state legitimate concerns. The presenter clarifies and responds to the concerns. The leader then calls for consensus, asking if there's any objection to the decision. If there's none, consensus is reached.

If there are one or more concerns that members can't live with, then the entire group addresses these concerns and tries to resolve them. Sometimes the proposal is changed; sometimes the member who objects agrees to stand aside, meaning he or she will live with the decision and support it. If not, then the group may need to reevaluate its purpose and values as well as individual motives in an effort to resolve the concern. As a last resort, the group may try one of these alternatives:

- ▶ Postpone the decision.
- ▶ Withdraw the proposal.
- ▶ Ask for a nonbinding show of hands to gain a sense of support for the proposal.
- ▶ Send the proposal to a subgroup.
- ▶ Ask concerned members to retreat together until they work out their differences.
- ▶ Create team-building where underlying problems come to light.

Finally, if all else fails, the group can decide that a two-thirds majority vote, a 90-percent majority vote, or some other agreed-upon figure will approximate consensus.

Go for a high-quality agreement. To evaluate the quality of a group-negotiated agreement in a mixed-motive situation, ask the following questions:

In reaching this agreement, did the group:

▶ Expand its focus to include all important negotiation issues in the discussion?

▶ Discuss priorities and preferences among issues?

▶ Focus its efforts on problem-solving?

▶ Consider unique and innovative solutions?

▶ Consider trading off issues of high-priority interest?

Recognize the problem of coalitions. The major difference between two-person and group negotiations is the potential for two or more persons within a group to form an informal coalition in order to pool their resources and have a greater influence on outcomes. Coalitions, or factions, involve fewer people than the entire group and are, therefore, easier to manage. They reduce coordination problems, the interests and goals of members are more consistent, and motivating members to act is easier. This gives the coalition an edge over the other group members. Members in a powerful coalition can get what they want using majority rule. However, people often focus on the interests of their particular coalition or their own personal interests rather than what's best for the group.

Research indicates that when group members have equal power, the group achieves more expanded-plate agreements and uses resources more effectively than groups where coalitions are formed and power is distributed unevenly. In groups already suffering from power imbalances, group members are much more likely to form coalitions to take advantage of that imbalance. The bottom line is that you need to recognize that coalitions are inherently unstable, and they often lead to agreements that are not in the best interests of the organization.

Establish an atmosphere that supports openness. Allow for expression of feelings without attack. Accept the feelings that are expressed. Encourage open communication. Be noncritical and nonevaluative. Focus on the problem or situation itself and avoid making people wrong. Focus on the pronouns *we, us, our*, which include both sides and imply a partnership in resolving the issue.

Propose a three-step negotiation process. Cooperative or competitive groups typically function best when operating under agendas that keep them focused on finding the most effective decision in an orderly and efficient manner. In mixed-motive negotiation, however, groups using an issue-by-issue agenda usually reach less expansive agreements than groups that use a process for getting all issues on the table first. If the group can consider all the issues as part of the plate that's on the table, then they can recognize the possibilities for expanding the plate. Mixed-motive groups should use agendas that structure the following three-step process:

1. Identify and prioritize all the issues and benefits.

2. Reveal group members' individual needs and wants for the outcome.

3. Suggest creative approaches to solving the problems—generate package deals.

Focus on benefits from resolving the conflict. Prepare a list of benefits to be gained by cooperation and losses to be suffered by ongoing conflict. Each side must understand that more is to be gained by resolving the conflict than by continuing it.

Resolution Skill #3: Air Opposing Views

Begin the negotiation meeting by setting the tone through your opening remarks, which are optimistic, nonjudgmental, and designed to generate expansive emotions. Present a brief summary overview of the meeting's purpose. Get agreement on ground rules and the process for reaching agreement. Consider getting agreement on criteria for evaluating any proposed resolution—unless that would become a conflict itself.

Each side states its views. Listen carefully with the purpose of finding a clue to possible solutions—and for identifying each side's resolution strategy. Here are suggestions for all parties:

- ▶ Describe the others' actions and why you think this behavior is a problem.
- ▶ Share your perceptions and feelings; avoid judging and blaming.
- ▶ See the conflict as a mutual problem to be resolved in a win-win way; avoid viewing it as a win-lose battle.
- ▶ Share your needs, feelings, and goals; avoid taking rigid positions.
- ▶ Put yourself in the other side's shoes.
- ▶ Listen in order to learn more about the other side's needs, interests, and feelings; show how your proposals address these.
- ▶ Focus on making accurate assessments of the others' feelings and motives.
- ▶ Focus on similarities of goals, needs, wants, and methods.
- ▶ Clearly communicate that you understand the needs, goals, and desires of the others.
- ▶ Ask questions to clarify any aspects you don't understand, with the goal of thoroughly understanding the views of the other side.
- ▶ Take a step-by-step approach to discovering all the issues in the conflict and any resources that can be divided, but aim to get them all on the table before you start bargaining for who will do what and who will get what.
- ▶ After both sides have presented their views, each side might want to summarize what they've heard, but others may have missed. Start building up the *we* toward *our common purpose and goal*.

Leader summarizes views. As the leader of the negotiation, your role is to listen, clarify, summarize, and give feedback. Encourage and support people on both sides. Try to find mutual feeling and common ground. Look for opportunities to reduce tensions. Your goal should be to strengthen the personal relationships between the parties, or at least to avoid their deterioration. Remember, the person who listens has more control. Make this your listening goal: *I need to hear what they're really concerned about.* Take notes regarding what you specifically agree or disagree with. Stay interested, calm, and rational. Don't let angry emotions rob you of self-control. Stay on top of things. Always consider the purpose of what you say: Does it support the negotiation?

Resolution Skill #4: Isolate the Cause of the Problem

Once conflicting opinions and ideas have been adequately discussed, your function is to guide the parties to a satisfactory resolution of the conflict. To do so, you must be aware of the immediate or superficial *reasons* for the conflict. Often you must dig deeper to the root causes underlying the problem actions. Look at four main areas: faulty communication, resentment of another's past behavior, conflicting goals, and conflicting choice of solution.

Faulty communication. The conflict may be more imagined than real because it resulted from faulty communication. First look for signs of faulty perception, misunderstanding, or oversensitivity. The best way to reduce imagined conflicts is to encourage frequent discussion of problems.

Resentment of past behavior. Constructive discussion of a problem may be jeopardized because one of the parties is harboring resentment of another member's past behavior. See whether such resentment can be brought into the open. Try to get the person who resents the behavior to state the objection and describe the behavior specifically. Frequently, the first objections brought up do not get to the heart of the problem. Conflicts based on unvoiced resentment need to be explored in an atmosphere in which feelings are respected so that true feelings can come to the surface.

Conflicting goals. Problems that arise because of conflicting goals are often the most difficult to resolve. Try to get both sides to pinpoint the specific goals they have for the outcome of the situation. Then see whether they can agree on some common goals, such as increased productivity, or even the survival of the company.

Conflicting ways to achieve goals. Sometimes everyone agrees on the major goal to be achieved in a situation, but they can't agree on the best way to achieve that goal. When this happens, be sure everyone thoroughly discusses and understands the conflicting approaches. If conflict persists, search for alternate courses of action that incorporate the best aspects of the conflicting solutions.

Resolution Skill #5: Identify the Resolution Strategy of Each Party

It's important to know how each party to the conflict is trying to resolve the problem. An awareness of strategies for conflict resolution can help you make sure that individuals' concerns or feelings are not squelched, ignored, or avoided. It can also help you equalize power in the situation. Here are five basic strategies for resolving conflict:

1. **Competitive:** A win-lose approach in which one side attempts to dominate the other and to win sympathy for their concerns at the expense of the other.

2. **Avoidant:** A head-in-the-sand approach characterized by an indifference to the concerns of other parties and to the conflict itself. Behaviors include withdrawal, isolation, evasion, flight, and apathy.

3. **Accommodating:** A nonassertive approach characterized by appeasement. One side gives up taking care of its own concerns in order to make peace by giving in to the other's concerns.

4. **Give-and-Take:** A compromise approach that seeks to find a solution somewhere in between the desires of all parties, giving each party moderate but incomplete satisfaction.

5. **Collaborative:** A cooperative approach in which all parties try to integrate their concerns so that all are fully satisfied.

If both sides use a collaborative strategy, your job as leader is much easier. Your goal is to show the benefits to both sides of a collaborative approach, and to promote a negotiation that's fair and a resolution that both sides will carry out in good spirits. You must therefore see that the side with a competitive strategy doesn't unfairly dominate the side with an accommodating strategy. You must build trust with the avoidant side and find ways to bring their hidden issues to the negotiation table. Once you identify the negotiation strategy of each party, you're in a better position to move toward integrating their concerns and proposals, and creating options for solution.

Resolution Skill #6: Integrate Proposals and Create Options

Through open discussion, you've been moving toward a shared understanding of the conflict. As you begin to integrate each other's viewpoints, you can start creating various options for resolving the conflict. Consider the following suggestions:

▶ If you haven't already established the criteria that any proposal must meet, consider doing that now.

▶ Remember that incompatible positions and proposals don't necessarily mean that basic goals and interests are in conflict.

▶ Keep in mind that when a resolution meets the needs of both parties, both are then committed to making the resolution work.

▶ Remember, in ongoing relationships there is rarely a *fixed-plate*, in which the more one side gets, the less the other gets. Instead, reaching a satisfactory resolution has unforeseeable future payoffs for both sides.

▶ Welcome brainstorming and creating as many alternatives as possible, before evaluating them.

▶ At least consider each alternate proposal and look for creative new combinations of options. Avoid thinking in terms of *either my plan or their plan*.

▶ Identify those issues or parts of proposals that both sides agree to.

▶ Consider bundling ideas together and proposing package deals, perhaps with a settlement of one issue being linked to a settlement of another.

▶ Explore differences as a way to create trade-offs.

You already understand how exploring the differences in what people need and want can generate side benefits that expand the plate of goodies on the negotiation table, which in turn leads to trade-offs. You know that differences can boost your chances of making a good deal. When you're working with groups of people or with two or more organizations, the same principle applies, but the negotiation is usually more complex.

Resolution Skill #7: Reach a Resolution and Learn

The last step in the conflict resolution process is to not only reach a resolution, but to consider what all parties have learned from this process.

Reach a resolution. Now is the time to seriously consider all proposals—and to keep repackaging or restructuring them until you find one that both sides can live with. If you've been able to get agreement on the criteria for evaluating proposals, now is the time to measure how well each proposal meets mutual needs and reconciles opposing interests. Determine what each party sees as a possible solution and whether there *can* be a solution that will satisfy all parties. Explore possible alternatives that the parties have not considered. Help the sides find the solution that meets these general criteria:

▶ It's best for the organization.

▶ It's best for *all* parties.

▶ It provides the best foundation for future harmony and cooperation.

Your role is to guide people in selecting the solution that best meets these criteria and any other specific criteria they've set, and to negotiate differences in reaching an agreement that all can live with.

The agreement should indicate that the conflict will end, describe how people will behave differently in the future, describe what will happen if people fail to abide by the agreement, and set future dates to discuss the resolution to see how well it's working. If resources, such as money or equipment, are involved, the agreement should state how they'll be divided or used. Be sure the resolution can be implemented and sustained by both sides. When the agreement is done, suggest some sort of celebration that establishes new, positive bonds.

Learn from the process. Help both sides recognize how learning to manage conflict together creates cooperative bonds. Make the conflict a learning process by getting both sides together to review what they've learned about the relationship and their approach to conflict. They can give each other tactful feedback. Ask people to address such self-questions as:

▶ What ideas and actions were dysfunctional?

▶ What ideas and actions were effective?

▶ How have my negotiation skills improved?

▶ How have my sensitivities deepened?

▶ How could I have improved the process?

Acknowledge the courage, patience, and fortitude it takes to admit that a conflict is occurring, to deal with it in depth, and to work through it together to resolution.

Skill Builders

Skill Builder #1—Case: Erica Negotiates to Buy a Business

Erica is ready to make a career change. She has been working as a sales rep for Wilhaven Wholesale Spice and Preservative Co., for 10 years. She currently sells about $1.5 million of product per year, and her annual income, including salary, commission, and perks, is about $75,000.

Erica believes she has the expertise and customer loyalty to start her own wholesale business, selling additives to food processing companies and large food preparation outlets. She has an opportunity to buy Norris Suppliers, a smaller firm that competes with Wilhaven. Norris financial statements indicate they have $100,000 in assets, and last year they had $3 million in gross sales with a net profit of $150,000.

Erica is interested in buying this business because it's a going concern, so it would free her from the hassles of starting a business from scratch. She makes an appointment to negotiate the terms of possibly buying Norris Suppliers.

➡ What are the potential advantages and disadvantages of buying this business?

➡ What goals should Erica set for the outcome of the negotiation?

➡ What key points should she keep in mind for the negotiation?

Follow-up: Compare your response with the discussion in the answer key on page 132.

Skill Builder #2—Case: Conflict Resolution for Andy and Barbara

You are team leader at a CostLess Pharmacy, one in a chain of pharmacies. Andy and Barbara have a recurring scheduling conflict. Barbara requested schedule changes four times during the past month. Each time she asks to come in later than scheduled, which means Andy must work until she gets there, which is inconvenient for him.

Barbara is a university student who attends classes on Tuesday and Thursday from 8 a.m. to 12:30 p.m. You agreed when she came to work at CostLess that her schedule could be somewhat flexible to allow her to meet course requirements at the university. This past month has been hectic because it's the end of the semester and she must complete various team projects and study for finals with her study group. Her group generally meets for two or three hours after lunch on Tuesday or Thursday, meeting from 1:30 p.m. to 3:30 or 4:30 p.m. That means she can't get to work until 4 or 5 p.m. She's willing to come in earlier the next morning because she doesn't have classes on those days.

Andy is the father of two children, ages 9 and 11. He normally works from 7 a.m. to 3 p.m. But when he was hired, he was told that he could not get a guaranteed schedule, although management policy is to be flexible in helping staff arrange workable schedules. Andy usually needs to leave by 3 p.m. in order to take his children to their various activities. He's been willing to change his schedule a little for Barbara, but he's getting frustrated. He worries about how these schedule changes will affect the commitments he's made to his children and their friends and instructors.

As team leader, you decide a conflict resolution session is in order.

➠ What should you do to prepare for the session?

➠ What should you set as a goal for the outcome of the conflict resolution?

➠ What are some key points to keep in mind as you conduct the session?

Follow-up: Compare your response with the discussion in the answer key below.

Answer Key

Skill Builder #1—Case: Erica Negotiates to Buy a Business

Review the chapter discussion regarding pitfalls, specifically winner's curse and the example of buying an existing business. The seller's advantage of having information about the business' performance that Erica doesn't have means she must assume the missing information is bad news and must set her top price accordingly. Erica should forecast the cost and potential of starting a similar business from scratch in order to clarify her best alternative to making this deal.

Skill Builder #2—Case: Conflict Resolution for Andy and Barbara

Prepare: Review the conflict resolution strategy (pages 123–130), especially Resolution Skill #2 on pages 124–127. Focus on creating an open, supportive environment, agreeing on some ground rules, and following the three-step process.

Goal: To reach a consensus that you, Andy, and Barbara can live with, and to make the conflict resolution a learning process.

Key points: Let Andy and Barbara air their views. Aim to get all the issues on the table. Ask if there might be deeper problems; if so, work on rooting them out. Look for possible trade-offs and creative ways to integrate the needs and wants of all parties.

5

Plan and Prioritize for Success

To succeed you have to believe in something with such a
passion that it becomes a reality.
—Anita Roddick, Body Shop International

"It's so ironic," a career counselor said. "All these adults—some 40 and 50 years old—come in saying they still don't know what they want to be when they grow up." If your definition of success includes doing meaningful, enjoyable work and making a contribution to the planet, then you'd better figure out what you enjoy doing and what you can do well. First, examine your current beliefs about all this by answering these questions. Then meet Carol Bartz, Autodesk CEO, who has succeeded by taking total responsibility for setting her own goals and thereby creating the life she wants.

How should women plan their lives?

1. Does success mean becoming rich? Famous? The head of a company?
2. Is hanging out with successful people just a form of social climbing or a smart career move?
3. Can today's career woman have it all if she's willing to work hard enough, or does she have to sacrifice having a family if she wants to make it to the top?
4. Is it best to keep your goals to yourself, or let the world know about them?

You can create your own success. In fact, deciding what *you* really want, clarifying those goals, setting your priorities, and making life plans and career plans is probably the most important work you'll ever do. Goal-setting can range from deciding what you want to accomplish in a 10-minute meeting to getting in touch with your life's purpose and destiny. Goal-setting skills are the basis for many leadership skills, from personal time management to organizational strategic planning. Gaining such skills marks you as the promotable woman businesses are looking for—someone who knows what she wants and where she's going, who can develop goals and action plans—and who can balance conflicts between work demands, family responsibilities, and personal development needs.

Carol Bartz, CEO of Autodesk, Inc.

Carol Bartz is CEO of Autodesk, Inc., of Sausalito, California—a computer software company with more than 1,600 employees and revenues of $285 million.

Carol believes that she has control of her life and that control is the most powerful thing she could have. She's heard all kinds of excuses from people who say taking control is impossible. They blame company downsizing, a lousy boss, a lousy relationship. She says, "I've worked for lousy management and great management, big companies and small companies, and I've had good relationships and bad relationships, and none of that matters. What matters is that it's my job to manage myself—mentor myself—through these things." Her first guiding strategic principle is: *Observe everything that goes on around you, and from these observations draw conclusions that you can put to practical use.*

She's learned the most from dealing with adversity. For example, when she realized she had a poor manager, she figured out what made this manager so inadequate and what she would do differently if she were the manager. She watched how different people handled situations and learned how and when certain styles work or don't work. As time went on, she practiced these behaviors, and as she became more confident in them, they became her *personal mosaic*. She also found that there's never a situation that's so bad that you can't find some humor in it.

A woman's place is in high technology, according to Carol. She decided early in her career that to succeed she must work outside typical gender stereotypes. She sees sexist attitudes as a challenge. In meeting that challenge, she added another principle to her life-management strategy: *Pick your mountain carefully because there are plenty of them out there that need your energy.*

Carol says that sometimes the best thing to do when you're faced with a mountain is to go around it. You don't have to climb every mountain. And if you do decide to go around it, you don't have to do it quietly. Carol decided to go around one mountain—a boss she had—by changing companies, but first she told him exactly why she was leaving. The move was a risk, but it allowed her to gain a broad base of experience. And while changing firms may mean a cut in pay for a while and that you have to sell yourself all over again, after you've done this a few times, you build a strong base of knowledge and develop the means to master a new skill quickly.

Strategy #1

Stop Self-Sabotage

Before you delve into the goal-setting process, take some time to discover how you might be creating barriers between you and your dreams. See if you're harboring certain fears—of success, of failure, of risk-taking. Look more closely at your self-concept—who you are in your own mind—and define what success would be for *you*.

Self-Awareness Activity #1: What Kinds of Barriers and Payoffs Are You Creating?

Purpose: To identify your personal creativity skills and challenges.

1. *Set goals and strategize before you act.* Do you have any resistance to that suggestion? If so, list your negative or doubting responses.

2. *If only I had....* Does that phrase bring to mind any regrets you've experienced? If so, list the first few that come to mind.

3. Look over the situations you listed in No. 2. Note how the results might have differed if you had clearly identified your top goals and thought about some key activities for reaching them.

4. *I did it! I made it! I got it!* Do these words bring to mind some high points in your life? List the first few that come to mind.

5. Look at the situations you listed in No. 4. Compare them to the situations listed in No. 2. Were you more committed to achieving the results you got in the No. 4 situations? Did you put more thought and planning into them? How many of them were *lucky breaks*? How much of your commitment or desire was subconscious? Conscious? Do you think your subconscious desires and intentions may have helped create any of the lucky breaks? Explain.

6. Are you willing to depend on lucky breaks or subconscious desires to determine the kind of life you have? Or do you want to exercise a higher degree of conscious intention in creating the life you want? Comment.

7. What payoffs can you identify for setting goals, strategizing, and finding focus in your life direction? Refer to the resistant responses you listed in No. 1 and list any rebuttals that come to mind.

If your answers to the questions in Self-Awareness Activity #1 reveal some internal resistance to setting goals and developing a career plan, you are not alone. The first step toward success for many people is getting over the planning barriers they erect for themselves. This activity has hopefully helped you identify your own barriers so that you can move on to a greater awareness of the payoffs for planning. You'll find many Skill Builders at the end of this chapter. Some are designed to help you deal with potential barriers to success; others are designed to guide you in creating action plans that will move you toward the life you want. It's important to identify your own barriers to successful goal-setting and planning, and to overcome them so they don't dominate your thoughts. Learn to focus on what you want, not on your supposed inadequacies. Then you'll be open to the opportunities that come along—you're more likely to see them and grab them. You'll focus on what you *can do*.

Breakthrough Skill #1: Define Your Own Success

Most women who are known for their success have something in common: They've decided what they want in life, and they focus on what they can do rather than what they can't. They define what success is for *them*.

Let go of the *need* to succeed and quit thinking in either-or terms of success or failure. Better yet, realize that learning from *failure* is the path to success. Focus on *intending, risking, creating, observing, problem-solving, celebrating,* and especially *learning.*

Do you feel uncomfortable about exercising power? Are you afraid to set goals because you may fail? Do you fear success even more than failure? How about your self-concept? Who are you? Can you picture yourself in a role that symbolizes success to you? What is success to you?

Three troublesome types of fears that form barriers to success are fear of success itself, fear of failure, and fear of risk-taking.

The first step in overcoming these fears is to bring them into conscious awareness and examine them. The next step is to decide what success is for you. Success means different things to different people. Here's a definition to consider in formulating your own definition.

SUCCESS IS THE ABILITY TO VISUALIZE WHAT YOU WANT IN LIFE—WHAT YOU
WANT TO CONTRIBUTE AND WHAT YOU WANT TO BE, DO, AND HAVE—AND TO
ENJOY THE PROCESS OF TAKING ACTION TOWARD THAT VISION,
LEARNING FROM THE PROCESS, MAKING THE VISION REALITY, AND THEN
CREATING A NEW VISION—AGAIN AND AGAIN.

Related to formulating your own definition of success is honestly answering the question, *Who are you?* What's the first thing that comes to mind? Many people respond to that question in terms of the roles they play or what they do. But you are something more all-encompassing than that. Consider the possibility that you are *not* your feelings, your body, or your mind. *You are a center of consciousness, designed to be self-aware.*

Breakthrough Skill #2: Identify With Successful People

How do you relate to other people's successes? With envy? Resentment? Awe? Appreciation? Enjoyment? Sincere applause? Your responses are clues to your self-concept and to your fears. If your feelings are negative or involve a sense of awe, you are separating yourself from success. Chances are you don't want to be reminded that you are not risking and achieving. On the other hand, when you identify with success and see yourself moving toward your vision of success, your feelings about others' success tend to be positive.

Breakthrough Skill #3: Overcome Fear

Did the Skill Builders in Chapter 1 help you uncover some fear of success, failure, or risk that you've subconsciously been harboring?

Fear of success. If you fear success, you'll need to work out any role conflict that underlies the fear. The best way to root out a fear is to get down to specifics and examine it in detail by exploring questions such as these.

Do you fear that success doesn't fit your self-image? Maybe you need to work on changing it. Deep down, do you picture yourself as an underprivileged type? Slightly inferior in some way? A follower, not a leader? A victim?

Do you fear that success will have some scary consequences? Dig them out and face them. Here are some common ones: *I won't be as attractive to men. I won't be able to catch (or hold) a husband. It will involve too much responsibility. I'll be in the spotlight too much. I'll be blamed when things go wrong. I won't have enough free time for a personal life. People won't like me if I'm the boss—a strong, aggressive woman—and more successful than they are.*

Are you afraid of your parents' reaction to your success—that your mom won't like you if you're more successful than she was? That your parents generally resent successful people? Conversely, are you afraid you will fulfill your parents' wishes? Perhaps you still resent their pushing you. Or maybe you decided as a child that you would *show them* by not giving them what their hearts desired.

Do you merely fear the unknown aspects of success? Moving into new roles, especially leadership roles, is risky. So much of the territory is uncharted.

Do you fear that you don't really deserve success? This ties in with self-image again. If, as a child, you received messages from important people in your life that you interpreted as, *You don't deserve success*, then you may have decided you *aren't* deserving. Or, perhaps, your behavior didn't meet the standards you had internalized, so you decided you were undeserving. Chances are you don't remember making that decision, but it can exert a strong subconscious influence on your actions. In fact, psychological research indicates that we'll do almost anything to prove we are right in these basic life decisions, including sabotaging ourselves.

You can reverse such negative cycles by becoming aware of your subconscious beliefs and changing them. It also helps to take a realistic look at the alternatives to success—in the long run you are much more vulnerable and have far fewer options in life without success!

Fear of failure. The other side of the coin is fear of failure, which involves the fear of revealing yourself as inadequate or wrong. It involves focusing on wrong versus right, instead of moving toward the life you want. When you experience fear of failure, focus on this thought: *All is to my benefit.* The idea is that life is a game in which we are constantly learning, growing, and improving. Situations in which we don't get what we aim for can serve as valuable lessons and signals for future guidance if we choose to use them that way. Ask, *What can I learn from this experience?* Then move on.

Fear of risk. Both the fear of failure and the fear of success are often based on a fear of taking risks. By definition, a risk has a certain probability of success as well as failure. If your informed calculations fall on the side of success, focus on that probability and go for it. It's easy to forget that avoiding a risk can be a risk itself—a risk that you won't grow or be all that you can be.

Handling your fears can help you deal effectively with risk and estimate more objectively the actual probabilities of various outcomes. Taking calculated risks is essential for success in life and is certainly a key to success in business. *Nothing ventured, nothing gained* is one of the rules. What types of risks have you been unwilling to take? How does this unwillingness affect the goals you set for yourself? People often miss opportunities because they won't risk rejection. As one wit has said, *If you haven't experienced rejection at least once this week, you're simply not out there trying.* In other words, playing it safe may make you feel better temporarily, but, in order to experience that heady excitement that comes from a high level of achievement, you must go after challenging goals—goals that involve the risk of rejection or failure.

Breakthrough Skill #4: Use Your Inner Leadership Tools

You create your own reality all the time, only you may do most of it at the subconscious level. Now it's time to bring your reality-creating process up to the conscious level. Begin with envisioning what you want to create. You've been envisioning positive and negative realities that might occur, and you've been creating them, sometimes consciously and sometimes subconsciously. The more consistently you make the process a conscious one, the more consistently your reality will look like your dreams. One way of picturing the reality-creation process is shown in Snapshot #1 on page 139, which reflects a composite of what many anthropologists and psychologists have discovered about reality. The psychological raw materials from which we create reality are aspects of our mind, such as our beliefs, attitudes, feelings, thoughts, decisions, and action choices.

The tools for changing our reality are also aspects of our mind, namely our imagination, desires, and expectancy. Through imagination, we picture, vision, and dream new, and different aspects of reality. Imagination is our tool for creating new ideas and adopting innovative approaches. Our desires fire our motivation and are the basis for our purposes, intentions, and goals. Our expectancy refers to our trust or confidence that we can change aspects of our reality.

Strategy #2

Find Your Passion and Purpose

One of the keys to success is to choose a career doing something you really care about—something that gives purpose and passion to your work and your life. Many adults still don't know what they want to be when they grow up. And most avoid doing the difficult but crucial work of figuring it out. The significance of this self-analysis work is expressed beautifully by author Edith Highman:

> *To each one is given a marble to carve for the wall*
> *A stone that is needed to heighten the beauty of all*
> *And only your soul has the magic to give it grace*
> *And only your hands have the cunning to put it in place.*
> *Yes, the task that is given to each one, no other can do*
> *So the errand is waiting; it has waited through ages for you*
> *And now you appear, and the hushed ones are turning their gaze*
> *To see what you do with your time in the chamber of days.*

To create the most fulfilling life and career, you must first discover what you like and what you do well and how those skills and interests can be packaged into specific types of careers. Then you must get in touch with your life purpose—what you want to accomplish in this world.

Snapshot #1: Elements of Reality—A Mental Map

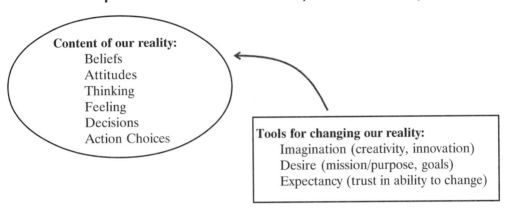

Content of our reality:
  Beliefs
  Attitudes
  Thinking
  Feeling
  Decisions
  Action Choices

Tools for changing our reality:
  Imagination (creativity, innovation)
  Desire (mission/purpose, goals)
  Expectancy (trust in ability to change)

Life Purpose Skill #1: Discover Your Skills and Interests

What you care about and what you enjoy are closely related to what you do well. But many people are not clear about the kinds of things they're good at and really enjoy. They feel there may be many things they could do or would like if they only knew more about them or had a chance to try them—especially in the career area.

The only way to identify your skills and interests is to start with what you know now. Then, as you learn more about various jobs and careers, you have a basis for evaluating how well they fit your skills and interests. At the end of this chapter you'll find Skill Builder #1, which is designed to help you identify your skills and interests. You may get some ideas for repackaging your experience, skills, and interests, and finding the right career field by studying Snapshots #2 and #3.

You may need to learn more about what people in various careers and positions actually *do*, rather than rely on what most outsiders assume they do. Examine John Wright's *The American Almanac of Jobs and Salaries,* which includes job descriptions. Also, each year, usually in July, *Working Woman* magazine describes the 25 hottest careers for women. Ask your librarian for other resources.

Your most valuable resource can be women who are working in the field, industry, company, or position you are considering. Use your networking skills to locate these women and to arrange some informational interviews. Ask such questions as:

▸ Where do you see the industry going in the next few years?

▸ Tell me about your career path.

▸ How did you get your job?

▸ What do you like best and least about your job?

▸ Could you describe a typical day on the job?

▸ What is the average salary for this type of position?

▸ What is the single type of thing I could tell you about myself that would help me get a job?

▸ Is there anyone else I could speak to in a particular job or department? In another company?

Snapshot #2: Repackaging Your Skills

In all instances, these skills can be used in managerial and administrative areas—in sales, marketing, computer, public relations, finance, real estate, insurance, communications, and services.

Your current key skills	Related business needs/applications
Creative/Artistic Writing, editing, graphic arts, announcing.	Communication skills, public relations/media, performing arts, modeling, making/building client relationships, technical supervision.
Business Detail Clerical, bookkeeping, accounting, administrative, computer operations, interviewing, claims, statistical analysis.	Organizing, coordinating, processing, follow-up and control, evaluation, information management, handling administrative procedures.
Humanitarian Childcare, counseling, religious or social work, nursing, therapy, rehabilitation service.	Consensus-style management, service orientation, direct client/customer contact, skills in communicating, motivating, training, supervising.
Accommodating Services Social/recreational services, food services, beauty/barber services, customer services, attendant services, passenger services.	Customer/client orientation, building and maintaining business relationships, skills in communications/public relations.
Selling Retail, real estate and technical sales, advertising and promotion, clerical work related to sales.	Persuasive communication, human relations skills, establishing business relationships, customer/client orientation, results/profit focus.
Physical Performing Coaching and instruction of sports, officiating.	Decision-making, problem-solving, training, coaching, directing workers, setting motivational work climate, setting goals, managing achievement, productivity.
Plants/Animals Farming, forestry, animal services, nursery/groundskeeping, specialty breeding.	Planning, organizing, coordinating, technical applications and supervision, achievement/productivity orientation, problem-solving, decision-making, follow-up, control.
Leading/Influencing Educational/library services, social research, law, politics, public relations, health and safety services, finance, communications.	Managing information, handling authority/accountability, being responsible for results and productivity, dealing with the public/media.
Scientific/Technical Physical/life sciences, laboratory technicians, medical practitioners.	Math skills, technical applications/supervision, design and use of rational procedures, problem-solving, decision-making.

Life Purpose Skill #2: Identify Your Own Life Purpose

Why are you here? Why did you come into this world? If you can get some sense of a life purpose, it can serve as a framework for all your short-term and long-term goals for each major area of your life. When you operate from such a framework, the achievement of your goals is likely to be most rewarding for you. In this mode, the line between work and play becomes fuzzy because those activities that you see as part of your life work you also see as important, satisfying, and even the source of fun and joy in your life. In other words, work that you love to do, you learn to do well, and the work that you do well is most likely to bring in the money you want. Isn't it elegant that the work that brings you joy is most likely to bring you abundance?

Snapshot #3: Finding the Best Field for You

Tolerance for	Keys to power	Individuality	Style	Future
Accounting	Personal influence; building relationships with clients, partners.	Very low.	All-American.	If clients start shopping for brilliance/ originality, will change internal power game.
High-tech	Original ideas in product development, marketing, productivity.	High; innovators who can work within system in great demand.	Consensus-style management pushing out former autocratic styles.	Risk-taker's paradise; high stakes, huge payoffs.
Banking and finance	Profitable ideas; technical analysis; building relationships.	Growing.	Low-key; facts/ numbers focus; serious, fairly trendy, not too ambitious.	Much change, rethinking about mission, services, methods.
Healthcare	Influence with administrators, MDs.	Medium to high.	Analytical; firm, sticking to point; respectful attitude toward MDs.	Booming, but government and insurance companies are setting limits.
Nonprofit	Often on edge of organization, managing special projects; skills: consensus management, public relations, fund raising.	Fairly high.	Project image of idealism; practice rules of political survival.	Change; erratic spurts of growth and decline.
Glamour and media	Ideas supreme; profitability above all; risk-taking, boldness essential.	Highest.	Outgoing; negotiating skills, political savvy.	Always important; some altered forms.

**YOUR LIFE PURPOSE OR MISSION STATEMENT IS A LONG-
RANGE OVERVIEW OF WHAT YOU NOW BELIEVE YOU WANT TO
DO WITH YOUR LIFE—WHY YOU'RE HERE AND WHO YOU ARE
IN THE OVERALL SCHEME OF THINGS.**

▶ We are all here to make contributions to the world and to learn lessons. Do Skill Builder #2 at the end of this chapter to get in touch with this. Verbalize a life purpose even if you're not sure that it's the "right one." Get started and let it evolve. Over a lifetime, this life purpose will undoubtedly grow and shift, but there will be a consistent core. That core is what makes it different from your goals, even long-term goals. When you become consciously aware of your life purpose, you can consciously set goals that are aligned and integrated with that purpose. Your day-to-day activities can lead you in the direction that seems right to you. People who have managed to *get it all together* in this way say their achievements became more meaningful to them. The work itself—and the resulting achievements—began to bring deeper satisfaction and joy.

Snapshot #4: Ashley's Life Purpose, Goals, and Activities

Ashley's Life Purpose:	**Leader/Manager/Teacher**
Career area:	To develop leadership and managerial expertise in the business world. To continually learn about the ways of this world and grow from these experiences.
Family/friends:	To build healthy relationships of many kinds—family, personal, professional.
Personal development:	To continually learn about the philosophical and spiritual aspects of life—what life is all about.
Integration:	To help others learn the types of things I've learned and am learning. To bring together my learning in the business, personal, and philosophical/spiritual areas of my life to enrich all areas.

Ashley's Top Three Goals in March, current year:
1. To complete my MBA degree by December.
2. To negotiate a promotion to sales manager, based on my MBA, by December.
3. To find and join or establish a women's personal growth group by June.

Ashley's Top Three Activities to complete this week:
1. Complete report on workforce diversity for management class.
2. Contact 12 customers in order to meet sales goal for this quarter.
3. Attend evening seminar on women's roles in creating community.

Ashley's life purpose, goals, and activities, shown in Snapshot #4, help illustrate the relationship among these aspects of creating your life. The elements of her life purpose look like goals, and in a sense they are, but they are lifelong goals. Notice the ways in which her life purpose overlaps into all three life areas and leads to an integration of the three areas. You may not see this degree of integration in your life purpose at this point in time, but it's not unusual for the areas to become more integrated over time.

Strategy #3

Develop Clearly Stated Goals

Now that you have dealt with potential barriers to effective goal-setting and have analyzed your unique package of skills and interests and tuned into your life purpose, you should be ready to move into the goal-setting process of allowing for abundance when you brainstorm the things you want in life, refining and ranking your goals, making them clear and specific, and distinguishing them from interchangeable activities.

Goal Skill #1: Allow Abundance in Your Goals

Do you approach goals from a viewpoint of scarcity? Is this your belief? *Because there are not enough resources for everyone to have all they need, then the more I get, the less there will be for someone else.* Think of all the things that are perceived as scarce. Jot them down. If you analyze the world's resources—such as food, fresh water, housing, education, healthcare, money, time, energy, love—you may realize that we have adequate resources, and even abundance, if a critical mass of people were to decide to manage these resources properly. Abundance thinking reflects individual or collective beliefs about the key resources in life.

▶ Take money—our creative energy becomes money; we can think of it as green energy.

▶ Or time—there are always 24 hours in a day; we have abundant time to achieve our top-priority goals once we clarify them and weed out the nonessentials.

▶ Or energy—all that exists in the universe is energy; the only problem is finding and using the best form of energy for each of our purposes.

▶ And love, which exists in our minds and hearts—the more love we give to ourselves and others, the more we tend to receive, and the more we have to give back again. The only limits are our fears that shield us from giving and receiving love.

When you come from an attitude of abundance, you can move more freely toward your goals. Because there's plenty for everyone, your successes don't need to be built on someone else's failures. Your having more doesn't mean that someone else has less. It's a win-win attitude: Everyone can win.

Focus first on setting goals that tie into your life purpose and the contribution you want to make. Then focus with clarity on the type of abundance you want for yourself—abundant material wealth, abundant relationships, abundant health, and abundant joy. When you're *on purpose*, doing what you're here for, the abundance will materialize in the best form for you.

Goal Skill #2: Be Clear About What a Goal Is

The term *goal* as used here is synonymous with *objective* and is quite different from an *activity* in the following ways:

▶ A goal is a specific end result you want by some stated point in time.

▶ Activities are things you *do* in order to achieve your goal.

▶ You may *enjoy* an activity, but that doesn't make it a goal.

▶ There may be a variety of feasible and acceptable activities that can help you reach your goal.

Activities are a means to an end. The end is your goal. That's why it's so important to separate goals from activities—so you'll be clear about what you're really after and feel free to consider alternatives for getting there.

It's also important to have a clear picture of your goals. Write them down. Skill Builder #3 asks you to list your five most important goals. You're much more likely to achieve written goals than mental ones. They're more specific—and they're easier to remember, to update, to revise, and to mark off once they're achieved. And the marking-off increases your sense of satisfaction and your motivation to keep achieving.

Goal Skill #3: Distinguish Between Specific and Vague Goals

Most of us tend to carry around a mixed bag of *wants*. Many of them are vague; some we picture as activities instead of what we hope to gain *from* those activities. We usually wish we had these wants now, and we dreamily hope to have them some day. We must transform such dreamy wants into clear, specific goals in order to achieve them.

How specific? Preferably specific enough so that on the target date you've set for attainment of the goal, you *know* for sure whether you've achieved it or how close you've come to it, and so that anyone knowledgeable on the subject could also tell. You can find examples of vague and specific goals in Snapshot #5.

Snapshot #5: Vague Versus Specific Goals

Vague goals	Specific goals
To make more money.	To earn $30,000 next year.
To move up in the company.	To be general manager of a regional branch by....
To get ahead in life.	To have a net worth of $500,000 by....
To go back to school.	To have an MBA degree by....
To travel more.	To travel to the Far East for three weeks in....

Goal Skill #4: Distinguish Between Goals and Activities

In many cases, only *you* can decide whether a want is a goal or just an activity. Ask yourself, *Why do I want to do this?* If the act or process of doing something is what you desire, then it's probably a goal for you. If the activity is mainly a *means* to having something you desire, then it's not a goal for you.

For example: *Why* do you want more free time? Is it to have more time to pursue a hobby, develop a skill, travel? If so, then those activities are your goals and having more free time is a *means* to that end. On the other hand, you may want freedom to do things on the spur of the moment, to pursue whatever tickles your fancy from time to time. If so, then having more free time is indeed your goal.

Here is another example: *Why* do you want to have a master's degree? Is it to get a better job, make more money, or feel the personal satisfaction of having the degree, regardless of its other advantages? Suppose you find that the major reason you want a degree is to increase your earnings. You might find a number of alternate career paths or ways of becoming qualified for a particular career path that would take less money, time, and energy than getting a degree. When you find it difficult to decide whether a want is a goal or merely an activity you enjoy that is a means to another end, try this:

▶ Get comfortable; relax as fully as possible.

▶ Close your eyes and visualize yourself once you have achieved your goal.

▶ How do you feel? Are you satisfied with that particular end result? Are you satisfied with the *way* you got it? Is anything missing?

▶ What would you have done differently if you could?

Sometimes visualizing the end results and how you feel about them can help you decide what you really want. For example, if you visualize yourself holding a particularly desirable job *without* having gotten the degree, you may determine whether having a degree is your true goal.

After you spontaneously generate a random list of things you want in your life, evaluate the list. Do the Skill Builders at the end of the chapter to help you with this process. Skill Builder #4 is designed to help you develop some specifically stated goals and to reflect on their relative importance. Some of the items are probably variations of the goals you listed in Skill Builder #3. If you have trouble deciding what your goals really are, complete Skill Builder #5.

Strategy #4

Plan for Balance in Your Life

You've set the stage for creating the life you want—an abundant life that spells success for you. Some of those goals you've set have little to do with a career, right? Your next step is to figure out how to create a successful life that *includes* a successful career.

Balancing Skill #1: Learn How to Have It All in Phases

Your goals probably include several kinds of *wants*; few people lead a one-track life where *only* their careers, *only* their personal growth, or *only* their family is important. Women frequently have more difficult choices to make than men when it comes to conflicts between career and private life. In the past, highly trained women have usually given up their career aspirations when they married. Today, some women attempt to be superwoman, setting unrealistically high goals and standards for all areas of their lives. This may lead to what is currently known as *burnout*—frustration, exhaustion, and even depression. Other women are unaware of the implications of the choices they're making until problems begin cropping up.

Women who have managed to *have it all* often say they have a successful marriage because they marry someone who respects their career and both of them put the marriage first; both of them set career goals that will not harm the marriage relationship. Within that context, at times the woman's career goals take priority, but during the small-children phase, family goals take priority. Such couples alternate high-priority phases, so that when the woman is focused on career issues, the man focuses more on family life, and vice versa.

During more mature phases, personal-development goals may take priority as the woman revitalizes and retools for a new career phase, and at a different time, her partner may do the same. The point is that women who have it all don't attempt to make all their life areas a top priority at the same time. They respect their limitations and create their life in phases, with a sense of the flow of life.

Balancing Skill #2: Prioritize Your Life Areas

To have a clear picture of your career goals, you'll need to analyze their importance in relation to the other goals in your life. You have an opportunity to do this in Skill Builder #7, which asks questions concerning the choices you'll make among three areas of your life—career, private life, and personal development. Even if you live alone, you probably have some family or private life considerations and goals. If not, you can concentrate on the other two categories. Base your responses on your *current* life circumstances, not on possible later phases. To decide which life area is most important, picture yourself in a situation where you must make a choice between doing something important for one area that conflicts with priorities in another area. These examples may help you get started.

▶ **Career or personal life?** You have the opportunity to obtain a high-level position that will require you to temporarily relocate to a foreign country where you've always wanted to live, but your husband can't go with you.

▶ **Career or personal development?** You have an opportunity to attend some meetings and seminars that will probably help you prepare for a promotion, but going means you must give up most of your personal reading time or your favorite sport for a while.

▶ **Personal development or private life?** You really want to take the creative writing class at the local college, but it means giving up Saturdays with your family for four months.

After you've analyzed your life areas in Skill Builder #7, go back to the goals you refined in Skill Builder #4 and decide whether each is a career, private life, or personal goal (or some combination of the three). Which are so important that you would like to work on them in more than one area of your life—by taking a course with your partner, for instance? Which aren't leading to achievement or satisfaction for you in one area, but might fit well in another area? For example, getting training in making presentations through company-sponsored seminars versus joining a toastmasters group on your own time. You'll probably find that one broad goal applies more to a specific area rather than to all three areas of your life. For example, you may want increased freedom in your job, but feel no need for it in the areas of private life or personal development.

Balancing Skill #3: Focus on One Area and Nurture the Others

People who create successful careers invariably say they had to pay their dues by putting their careers first during some phase of their lives. This emphasis can have real payoffs: Studies indicate that most millionaires gain their fortunes through their work or profession, not through inheritance. However, if you keep putting your career first throughout your adult life, you may miss out on some of your most cherished goals. For example, most happy couples report that they both put each other first in the scheme of things. So there may be times when you'll place your career second.

Studies to determine what contributes most to women's self-esteem and enjoyment of life indicate that married women with children and careers are the happiest. So the good news is that many women are managing to *have it all*, and they seem to be the happiest women in our society. The bad news is that no matter how hard they work, women still do most of the housework and childcare. A 1995 poll by the Families and Work Institute found that nearly half of married working women provide half or more of their household's income. But while most of their husbands say they do their fair share at home, the women say they don't. Another poll of men and women found that working wives are responsible for 70 to 80 percent of the childcare, grocery shopping, meal preparation, housecleaning, and laundry.

Several studies indicate that while couples are struggling toward equality, many of the traditions that make careers difficult for married women still prevail. Researchers report that husbands with successful wives are happier in their marriages, but most of them don't want the wives to take over the provider role. And there seems to be a point at which most males feel threatened. Wives with the greatest career success had a higher breakup rate unless their husbands achieved a similar level of success.

Dual Career Couples: Ask Questions Before Committing Yourself

All this is a further indication that you need to know what your partner assumes and expects—before you make a long-term commitment. Frank discussions about *who will be responsible for what* may help you avoid impossible situations. Consider the following questions:

▸ Who should manage the money?

▸ Who will take primary responsibility for the cooking? Housecleaning? Laundry? Garbage? Yard work? Home maintenance and repairs?

▸ Who will stay home when a child is sick?

▸ How are we going to handle career opportunities that require travel or relocating? Will it depend on which career phase each of us is in, or will the decision automatically be in favor of his career?

▸ How will we balance career, family, and personal development needs?

▸ What role will friends and a social life play in our relationship?

▸ What kind of commitment does each of us expect to get and give?

▸ What kind of personal freedom does each of us expect to have?

It's important to discuss lifestyle, expectations, priorities, and joint decision-making techniques *before* you become deeply attached and before you have children. Many divorced mothers say they never considered the fact that once they had a child by a man, that man would forever be a part of their lives because of the mutual connection to children—and later to grandchildren.

Discussing life-area priorities with a potential partner can help eliminate unpleasant surprises. Some people have little ambition, work a minimum amount, and live for their leisure time. At the other extreme are people who live for their work. While people who love their careers with a passion are usually happy people, workaholics are not. Career women who marry career men must be especially alert to the potential problems that occur when two workaholics team up.

How do you recognize workaholics? By the fact that they can't really enjoy leisure time that has nothing to do with their careers. They're addicted to work, so they have difficulty enjoying family time, leisure time, and perhaps even personal development time. Their children probably have great difficulty getting some of their basic needs met—needs for parental guidance, support, and affection. Workaholic parents often find it difficult to turn the precious time they spend with their children into *quality time* because they are preoccupied with thoughts of work.

Use Your Managerial and Leadership Skills

Providing for your key life areas requires skills in assertiveness, time management, and delegation—topics that are discussed in later chapters. If you are to avoid the burn-out caused by playing a superwoman role for too long, you must identify your rights within your close relationships, especially where children are involved. Assertiveness on your part will probably be required to reach constructive agreements on how everyone in the household will contribute to its maintenance. You'll need time-management skills to be sure you're taking care of your own top-priority items rather than unwittingly spending too much of your precious time on other people's priorities. And you'll need delegation skills to assign tasks to your children and to paid household helpers.

Strategy #5

Plan Your Activities and Set Priorities

You probably have a sense now of which goals are most important in each area of your life. The next step is to consider which activities will provide the best avenues for reaching these goals by completing Skill Builder #8. To use it, you'll need to check back to Skill Builder #4, then list your three most important goals in each category in Skill Builder #8. Fill in the life area priorities you developed in Skill Builder #7, item 5. You'll then have a summary of what you want in life, right now.

Next, start writing down any and all activities you can think of that might help you achieve your goals, taking one goal at a time. At this point, do not rank the activities. Again, fantasize, brainstorm, let the creative-child part of you take over. Be daring. If you feel blocked or stuck in a career category, review Snapshots #3 and #4, do Skill Builders #9 and #10 as self-starters, and then return to Skill Builder #8.

When you've listed activities for all life areas, summon your critical, practical, reasonable side to help you select the activity that is most feasible and the most likely to contribute to your first goal. Rank that activity #1 on the list in Skill Builder #8. Rank the second most likely activity #2, and so forth, down to the least likely activity. Repeat for each goal.

Does your list of activities boggle your mind? If so, start picking out the activities *you are willing to spend at least five minutes on during the next week.* Now remove from your list all activities you are *not* willing to spend five minutes on. Such activities may be important, but obviously they're not important enough to occupy your time right now, so you'll probably never get to them.

Do some of your goals now have no activities listed for them? Go back and list other activities, then rank them and delete the impractical ones. Keep going until you have for each goal a list of activities that are important to you and are things you are willing to begin acting on right away. Once you've completed all the Skill Builders to this point, you should be close to knowing what you want, what you can do to get it, and what you will do about it in the next week.

Develop Short-Term and Long-Term Action Plans

Skill Builder #11 provides a format for a one-month action plan. Skill Builders #12 and #13 provide for a one-year plan and a five-year plan. Think broadly as you complete the longer-range plans, focusing on goals rather than on activities. Do you need to plan even farther ahead? For 10 years? If so, use a similar format.

To accomplish the most, make a one-month plan *every* month. Use it as the basis for your weekly and daily to-do lists (see Chapter 6). Compare months to see how you're progressing toward long-term goals. Finally, remember to reevaluate your decisions regularly to be sure that your goals reflect what you really want in life and that your activities are the best ones for getting you there.

Tips for Implementing Your Plan

Here are some general suggestions for using your plan.

1. **Envision and focus.** Use relaxed concentration and visualization as a technique to command your inner resources so that all your actions tend to move you toward your goals, which gives you a powerful focus.

2. **Act.** Begin this week, even if you undertake only a five-minute activity for each goal.

3. **Communicate.** Let the important people in your life *know* about the goals they may be able to help you with. For example, let your boss or mentor know about appropriate career goals.

4. **Get support.** Make a list of the people who can help you and give you support as you work toward your goals. Decide the best way to enlist their aid. Include support systems in your plan.

5. **Enjoy.** Make the *process* of achieving your goals as enjoyable as possible. It's important to keep your eye on your desired end result, but it's also important to relax and enjoy yourself along the way. In fact, your enjoyment of an activity should be one of the criteria for selecting it.

6. **Negotiate.** Use your goals to help you achieve specific results on the job that will serve as the basis for negotiating promotions and raises later.

7. **Focus.** Don't get so carried away with the *activities* that you lose sight of the *goal*. Use your action plan to chart activities; mark them off as they are completed and as the goal is achieved. As mentioned earlier, it helps if you keep a list of your top three or four goals handy and refer to it regularly. Some successful women keep their lists (or symbolic pictures of their goals) posted where they'll see them daily in their homes or offices.

8. **Overcome barriers.** Become a problem-solver who can figure out how to overcome barriers to reaching goals. Don't let procrastination, interruptions, and distractions keep you from achieving your goals.

9. **Reevaluate.** If you're having unusual difficulty in achieving a goal, ask yourself whether the goal is right for you. If it is, then reevaluate the activities you have selected and look for new ones if necessary.

10. **Keep goals flexible.** Your goals are not set in concrete. They're just part of a plan that can be changed as *situations* change.

11. **Congratulate yourself.** When you achieve a goal, remember to give yourself credit and reward yourself.

12. **Keep setting goals.** Once you have achieved a major goal, set another one to take its place. You say you've earned a rest? You don't want another major project for a while? Then your new goal might be to have a specific number of additional unstructured hours each week, month, or year to do as you please. The object is to be clear about what you want and what you're doing with your time and your life—so that you're making clear choices rather than drifting.

Skill Builders

Skill Builder #1: What Do You Like to Do? What Do You Do Well?

Purpose: To get to know more about yourself by identifying your key interests and skills, and to organize these into career building blocks.

Instructions: Examine *Ashley's Example* below of favorite activities. Set up a sheet with seven columns for analyzing your own favorite activities—what you enjoy doing. Follow the instructions given in Parts A through D.

Ashley's Example	2	3	4	5	6	7
Favorite activities:	alone – others +	intimacy level	risk factor	last did	need met*	skills-knowledge used**
entertain	+	I+		6/2	S	visualize
go to parties	+	I		5/13	S-P	communicate-intuit
hang out with close friends	+	I+		6/18	S	communicate-intuit
take photographs	–	–	R	6/2	A	visualize-act
travel	+	I	R	1/5-15	S-A-P	visualize-act
write letters, reports, diary	–	–	R+	6/18	A-P	communicate-organize
make presentations	+	–		5/20	A-P	communicate-organize
shop for collectibles	+	I		6/15	A-S	apply information

*A=achievement need   P=power need   S=social/belonging need

**Ashley realizes that her chief skills used in partygoing and hanging out are communication skills with a healthy dose of empathy and intuition. Her skills in writing and making presentations are also primarily communication skills—in these cases allied with the ability to visualize past and future events and to organize her thoughts and feelings about them. She sees the chief skills she uses in photography and travel as being able to visualize what she wants to do and achieve and to follow through. In shopping for collectibles, her chief skill is applying the information she has gained through study and shopping experiences. She can see a strong skill pattern of visualizing, communicating, and organizing—allied with a strong need for social interaction and intimacy, followed by achievement need—in low-risk activities.

She repeats this process in a separate list for what she does well. She finds that most things she does well are also on the favorite list. She identifies those activities that appear on both lists as her core skills—the ones to build a career around.

Part A. Interests—Activities You Like to Do

Step 1: In the first column, randomly list—as they come to mind—20 things you most enjoy doing. Do not attempt to respond to the other columns until you have completed the first column. This should take no more than 20 minutes.

Step 2: Analyze each activity listed in the first column by responding to the other columns.

In column 2, opposite the first activity, place a dash (–) if you most enjoy doing this alone, a plus sign (+) if you enjoy this activity with another, or a slash (/) if either (or no preference).

In column 3, place an I for activities in which you experience intimacy, perhaps I+ for deeper levels of intimacy, or a minus (–) for no intimacy.

In column 4, note activities that carry a risk factor with an R, or R+ for those with a higher risk factor.

In column 5, write the approximate date you last engaged in the activity.

In column 6, identify the primary need filled by engaging in this activity; that is, what motivates you to get involved? A need to achieve (A), to exercise power (P), or to interact socially (S)?

In column 7, identify the types of skills or knowledge that you use when you engage in the activity. See Snapshots #3 and #4 for ideas. Write one word that symbolizes each skill or knowledge area used in this activity.

Step 3: Rank the activities in order of the degree of enjoyment you derive from each.

Part B. Skills and Knowledge—Activities You Do Well

Step 1: If possible, complete this part a day or so after you complete Part A. Complete column 1 by listing, in random order, 10 things you honestly do well; take no more than 20 minutes.

Step 2: Complete columns 2 through 7 as instructed in Part A.

Step 3: Rank the activities in order of their importance to you, also considering your level of expertise in each activity.

Part C. Patterns and Insights

Step 1: What interrelationships do you see among the different factors, such as alone/with another, intimacy, risk, need fulfillment/motivation, and types of skill and knowledge? What patterns seem to emerge concerning what you enjoy (interests) and what you do well (skills/knowledge)? Notice the date column. Are you developing your most likely talents or neglecting them? Are these truly the interests and skills you most enjoy and that seem most important to you? Or do you wish they were, or believe they should be? If so, where do these wishes and beliefs originate? From family? Friends? Teachers? Describe the interrelationships and patterns in writing. From this deep inner source comes your passion for your work and for life.

Step 2: What insights emerged from this exercise? State in writing how these insights affect your image of yourself, what you want in life, and what talents and contributions you have to offer.

Part D. Career Building Blocks

Look over your interests, skills, patterns, and insights. Identify some common building blocks of skills and interests that could form the foundation for a career. Refer to Snapshots #3 and #4, and to your own knowledge of career fields and jobs. Take several sheets of paper; consider each page a block. Give each block a label. Within each one, list the types of interests, skills, and knowledge that apply. Play with your blocks, moving them around in different combinations and configurations to fit various types of jobs and careers.

Skill Builder #2: What Is Your Life Purpose? (Self-Starter)

Purpose: To help you determine your life purpose.

Process: The three steps in this process all center around getting in touch with aspects of your childhood and family situation. First, get in touch with your control strategies, which will block you in achieving your life purpose. Second, identify what you are here to contribute. Third, identify what life lessons you are here to learn. We are all here to contribute and to learn lessons—your life purpose is composed of these two aspects.

Step 1: Identify your control strategies. *Bring your particular control drama and resulting control strategies into full consciousness.* What are you doing to manipulate for attention, for energy, for control? These manipulations and strategies begin in childhood. A control drama is the soap opera episodes you played out. It's the dialogue, the he-said/she-said, the actions and reactions involved in getting attention, energy, and control. The control strategies are specific behaviors you use within this drama.

Identify your childhood family's control dramas. Go back into your past, your early family life, and see how your control habits were formed. Seeing how they began will bring your way of controlling up to the conscious level.

Your family members were no doubt operating in a control drama themselves, trying to pull energy out of you as a child. That's why you had to form a control drama in the first place. You had to have a strategy to win energy back. It is always in relation to our family members that we develop our particular dramas and strategies. But once we recognize the energy dynamics in our families, we can go past these control strategies and see what was really happening.

Examples of control strategies:

➡ Withdrawing, sulking, withholding approval or affection.

➡ Demanding, dominating, taking center stage.

➡ Attacking, accusing, blaming, nagging.

➡ *I did you wrong, but it's okay because I have a conscience and I feel guilty or because I worry about you.*

➡ Lashing out and then withdrawing.

➡ Saying *yes* and going along, but resenting, waiting to get even; saying *yes*, but feeling sorry for yourself or feeling that you sacrifice for others.

➡ Being incompetent, naive, sick, or otherwise weak and needing help.

➡ Demanding perfection of self or others, or both.

➡ Taking charge, doing the work, being the leader—to be sure everyone does it your way.

Key questions:

1. What did your mother do to get attention, to get energy, to control? What was her control drama? How did you react to that?

2. What did your father do? How did you react?

3. What did your sister(s) and/or brother(s) do? How did you react?

Step 2: Identify what you are here to contribute. Reinterpret your family experience from a personal growth viewpoint and discover who you really are. Once you become conscious of your control strategies, then you can focus on the *higher truth* (or contribution) of your family members—the silver lining that lies beyond the energy conflict. This higher truth can energize your life, for it can help you know more about who you are, the path you are on, and what you are doing here. When you discover your life purpose, you can begin to move beyond your subconscious control strategies and more consciously create the life you want.

To discover your real self, consider the belief that the real you began in a position between the higher purposes of your mother and your father. Consider the possibility that you were born to them for this reason: to take a higher perspective on what they stood for. Your path is about discovering a truth that is a higher synthesis of what these two people believed. Your life purpose is about somehow combining the two approaches your parents took.

Example: Ashley was amazed when she first connected her life purpose—to be a management teacher—to the fact that her father was a manager and her mother was a teacher.

Key questions: (Tip: First, write freely about everything that comes to mind. Next, go back and edit, sift, and refine until you get your answers down to a few words.)

1. *Why was I born to this particular family? What might have been the purpose?* (Every person, whether consciously or not, illustrates with her or his life how she or he thinks a human being is supposed to live. Try to discover what each of your parents taught you—the higher truth, or contribution, of each).

2. *Who was my father? What was his message to me? What was his higher truth or contribution?*

3. *What was my mother's underlying message? Her higher truth or contribution?*
4. *When I put the two higher truths together, what do I get? What is my higher truth?*

THIS IS WHAT YOU ARE HERE TO CONTRIBUTE.

Example: Ashley's mother was an advocate of equal rights for all persons, regardless of ethnicity, gender, lifestyle, and other differences. Ashley's father was able to give unconditional love to all his family and friends. Ashley realizes that her contribution as a leader/manager/teacher is to show how unconditional love toward all types of persons represents the type of healing needed in today's world.

Step 3: Discover your life lessons. While your parents were conveying their higher truths, they simultaneously conveyed issues they needed to work through.

Key questions:

1. Looking at your mother's life, what could she have done better? What would you have changed about your mother? (That's one part of what you yourself are working on.)
2. Ask the same about your father's life. (That's the other part you are working on.)
3. Put the two parts together. This is your life lesson.
4. Put this life lesson into the form of a question: *How can I learn to...?*

This is your basic life question. Learn to ask current questions that tie in with this basic life question. The *what next* type of questions are important because their answers keep you on track.

Example: Ashley's mother was an extremely critical person and had an uncontrollable temper. When it flared, she became abusively negative, judgmental, and hostile. Her actions made her family feel she was temporarily insane. Her life lesson was to learn about judgment and anger. Ashley's father had a self-esteem problem. He was very intelligent, powerful, and loving, but he never fully moved into his own power. Ashley realizes that her life lessons are about negative judgment of herself and others and moving into her own power as a woman.

Step 4: On a card, write your life purpose and life lesson.

Skill Builder #3: Initial Statement of Goals

Purpose: To begin the process of identifying those goals that are most important to you.

Step 1: Write your personal mission statement (life purpose) in one sentence (from Skill Builder #2).

Step 2: Keeping in mind that a goal is a specific end result, list your five most important goals. Include goals related to family, career, and personal development.

Skill Builder #4: Refined List of Goals

Purpose: To help you weed out activities from goals, to make your goals as specific as necessary, to identify all the goals that are important to you, and to prioritize them so you become clear about which are the most important to achieve.

Step 1: Distinguish between goals and activities. Look at the list of goals you made in Skill Builder #3. How many are actually activities? Eliminate them.

Step 2: Redefine your goals to make them more specific. Select the following items that reflect your goals and fill in the blanks to make your goals specific. At this point, don't rank or evaluate their practicality or relative importance.

Rank:

_____ To have $_____ in assets by _____(date).

_____ To be_____ (job position) by _____ (date).

_____ To have a relationship with_____ (description of person) in which we
_____ (feel, believe, do...) _____by _____ (date).

_____ To weigh _____ (pounds) by_____ (date).

_____ To have a _____(degree or certificate) by _____ (date).

_____ To retire with $_____ a month income (or equivalent) by _____ (date).

_____ To have_____ days of free time per year by _____ (date).

_____ To learn_____ (specific skills or knowledge) by _____ (date).

_____ To travel to_____ in _____ (date) for _____ (length of time).

_____ To spend_____ hours a _____ (days, week, etc.) in mutually satisfying activities
with_____(description of person(s)).

Other goals:_____

Step 3: Brainstorm. List other goals that don't fit into the preceding categories. Be as outrageous as you like. Use the enthusiastic, creative-child part of your personality to brainstorm. Send that critical, practical part of you *down the hall* till later. Make your goals as fantastic or as simple as you like. Anything goes! (Remember to try Skill Builders #5 and #6 if you're blocked.)

Step 4: Evaluate and rank. After you've freely and wildly listed any goals you can think of, start asking which one of all your goals is the most important (include all goals in Steps #2 and #3). Put the number *1* in the space to the left of that goal. Continue the process for the second most important goal, the third, and so forth, until all are ranked. Do you want to delete any goals? Can any outlandish ones be modified or combined to make them more realistic? Are they all specific?

Skill Builder #5: Clarifying Your Goals (Self-Starter)

Purpose: To help you develop clear, specific goals you are likely to achieve.

Prognosis: Six months. Pretend that you have been given six months to live. Close your eyes and visualize the situation in as much vivid detail as possible. Assume that you'll be in perfect health up to the day you die and that all the necessary arrangements for your death have been taken care of. List the first five things you think of that you would want to achieve in your last six months.

Sudden wealth: In addition to the previous scenario, pretend someone just gave you $5 million tax-free. Close your eyes and visualize the situation in vivid detail. List the first five things you think of that you would want to achieve in the next six months. (Remember, these are your last six months.)

Analysis: Which items on these lists are not connected with pressures of time or money? Which can you achieve now, even without a gift of money? Which can you have in the next six months, even without the pressure of time? Can those items be phrased as goals? How many of them can become obtainable goals with some simple modification to your current situation?

Now go back to Skill Builder #4 and continue refining your goals.

Skill Builder #6: Adding Power to Your Goals (Self-Starter)

Purpose: To help you increase the power and effectiveness of your goals.

Step 1: Visualize end results. During a quiet time, relax deeply and visualize yourself living the end result of each goal. (Refer to Chapter 8 for suggestions.) Focus on what you are doing, having, and most of all *being;* that is, how you feel, how others feel, how relationships are affected. Note any conflicting feelings or thoughts that come up—thoughts about barriers to achieving the goal or about payoffs for not achieving it.

Step 2: Check the source of each goal. Are you sure this is *your* goal? It is very important to establish this. If you are trying to achieve a goal because someone else thinks you should, you can never give it the full level of commitment, passion, and enthusiasm you give to goals that come from deep within you. The achievement of others' goals can never bring you the joy and fulfillment you deserve, and you will never reach the same level or quality of success as you will with your own goals. So analyze each important goal in this light. Have you chosen this goal because it's what you think someone else—a parent figure, spouse, influential friend, teacher—would admire? Or is it truly what *you* want in your life?

Step 3: Apply the energy/emotional level test. If you have difficulty ranking a goal—or if at any point in the goal-setting or goal-implementing process, you are pulled between two alternatives—try the following analysis. First, be sure you have developed an adequate foundation for making the decision, through self-analysis of your life purpose and deepest desires and through gathering the information you need. Then ask yourself the following questions:

- Do I feel energized when I think of a particular choice?
- Do I sense a drop in my energy level when I think of the choice?
- Which option has a special glow around it when I picture it? An emotional attraction?

Then ask yourself, *If the decision were based solely on emotion, which alternative would I choose?* You will probably experience the greatest success when you go for the alternative that energizes you and brings up positive feelings, such as a sense of freedom, well-being, growth/expansion, or enthusiasm.

Step 4: Turn old blocks into new cornerstones. For each major goal, examine your current and past beliefs and attitudes, thoughts and feelings, decisions and choices. Are any of them likely to block your success in achieving the goal? What new beliefs and attitudes could you adopt that would support this goal? How can you change your thoughts, letting go of nonproductive ones and focusing on positive ones that enhance your chances of success? What old decisions—about yourself and others or your place and your roles—might be inappropriate now for what you want to achieve? What actions (based on your beliefs, attitudes, thoughts, feelings, and decisions about you and life) have you made in the past regarding goal achievement? What new action choices might be better?

1. List Goal #1.
2. List current beliefs, attitudes, and so on, that conflict with achieving your goal.
3. Identify new ones that would support it and list them.
4. Repeat the process for each major goal.

Skill Builder #7: What Are Your Most Important Life Areas?

Purpose: To help you decide on prioritizing your goals and activities.

1. If you had to choose between career goals and private-life goals during this phase of your life, what would you choose? (If you have no private-life goals, skip this question.)
2. If you had to choose between pursuing career goals and personal-development goals, which would you choose? (It may be helpful to refer to your list of goals in Skill Builder #4.)
3. If you had to choose between private-life goals and personal-development goals, which would you choose?
4. If you had to choose one life area to work on this month, what would it be?
5. List the three life areas in order of importance to you.
6. Don't worry about the complexity or interrelatedness of the questions. It's obvious that you may be a better daughter, wife, or mother when you're a better person generally. For now, just try to choose among the categories so that you can set priorities and determine the most important area of your life.

Skill Builder #8: Activities for Achieving Your Goals

Purpose: To generate activities leading to achievement of your top goals in each life area.

Step 1: List Career Goal #1. Then list at least four activities that would lead to the achievement of Goal #1.

Step 2: List Career Goals #2 and #3 and their activities, as you did for Goal #1.

Step 3: Repeat the process for personal-development and private-life goals. After you have listed activities for *all* goals, rank the importance of the activities listed for each goal.

Note: See Snapshot #5 for examples of activities that support certain goals.

Skill Builder #9: Becoming a Risk-Taker (Self-Starter)

Purpose: To increase your comfort level with those goals and activities you're attracted to, but that seem too bold and risky. To take the first few steps toward being an effective risk-taker, stepping out beyond the fear to create the life you want.

Step 1: What are some activities you generated that attract you but that you feel are too bold or risky? List them.

Step 2: What other activities can you think of that might be too bold or risky? Add them to the list in Step #1.

Step 3: Pick the least risky activity. Are there ways you could reduce the risk factors? List them beside the activity. Repeat the process for the remaining least risky activity. Repeat for all the activities you've listed, dealing last with the most risky activity. For example:

⇒ The risk of going back to school for a degree could be reduced by starting with one evening course.

⇒ The risk of investing in the stock market could be reduced by investing in a mutual stock fund that has a good 10-year performance record.

⇒ The risk of asking for a raise could be reduced by gathering documentation showing your specific achievements that translate into higher profits for the firm.

Step 4: What goals can you think of that attract you, but that you feel are too bold or risky? Repeat Step #3 for those goals. For example: What is most risky about the goal *to become an executive* (or lawyer, doctor, news anchor, and any other career goal)? Is it *being the target of criticism and political infighting*? If so, what are some good sources of information about handling criticism and office politics? Would getting good information increase your political savvy and reduce the risk factor?

Skill Builder #10: Your Most Productive Career Activities (Self-Starter)

Purpose: To help you identify your most productive career activities.

Part A. Ask Career Questions

By now you should have a specific type of job in mind as your key career goal. You should also be able to describe your ultimate career goal—the top position you're aiming for. To help you identify the activities most likely to help you reach that goal, look at these questions:

1. What type of company do you have in mind? Can you pinpoint a specific company?
2. What type of degree, course(s), or other training will you need?
3. What specific skills and knowledge will be required? At what level of ability?

4. What kinds of people could tell you more about the job, help teach you what you need to know, help you get your foot in the door, help you gain favorable visibility within the company, introduce you to people who can help?

5. What jobs will you need to hold in order to prepare yourself for your *ultimate* career goal? What functions do you need to have experience with? How do these functions link up with each other? (For example, what are the links between production and sales, sales and marketing?) Can you get some actual job descriptions your target company has prepared for these jobs? Which staff positions would give you the best chance of moving into a line job? Which line jobs provide the basic experience you'll need? (See also John Wright's *The American Almanac of Jobs and Salaries*.)

6. Once you have a career plan, who can give you the most helpful evaluation of its effectiveness? Is the plan workable in view of the other top priorities in your life?

Follow-up: Use your answers to help complete Skill Builders #8, #11, #12, and #13.

Part B. Brainstorm With a Friend

Brainstorm with a partner about ways to achieve a particular goal. What types of activities might work? If your goal is to go to Paris, what do you need to get there? How can you get the time, money, and any other resources you'll need? Next, work on your partner's goal.

Part C. Mutual Support With a Friend

Discuss a key goal with a friend. Tell her the specifics of the goal and the actions you plan to take. Verbalizing your commitment, as well as writing it down, tends to strengthen it. Your friend should also share one of her goals with you. Set regular dates to discuss what actions you actually took and how they worked out. Two nationally known authors recently explained how this process worked for them when they were each writing their first books. They agreed to phone each other every Friday to discuss their progress. Each wanted to be able to tell the other that she had moved along in her project. If Thursday arrived, and she hadn't written all week, she was motivated to write something rather than admit on Friday that her project had been neglected.

Part D. Make Your Goals Visible

Find methods of keeping your goals up front, of staying focused, or making them real to you.

1. Pick three top goals: Write them on a business card, along with the target dates. Put the card where you will see it many times a day (tucked in your dresser or bathroom mirror, in the clear-plastic window of your wallet, on your desk calendar, or in another visible place).

2. Draw vivid symbols of your top goals, using colored pens or pencils if possible. Put them on a card and display them as discussed in #1.

Skill Builder #11: One-Month Action Plan

Purpose: To prepare an action plan to help you focus on top-priority goals and activities for the coming month.

Step 1: List your top-priority career goal. Under it, in order of importance, list the major activities, with their target dates, that you plan to complete this month. Put the most important activity on your to-do list for *today* and keep it on the list until you have accomplished it. If you haven't acted on this activity within seven days, go back and re-evaluate your goal and activities.

Step 2: Repeat the process for Career Goals #2 and #3.

Step 3: Repeat the process for any top-priority, personal-development goals, and private-life goals that you want to include.

Skill Builder #12: One-Year Action Plan

Purpose: To develop a one-year plan that will guide you and focus your attention and energy on achieving your top-priority goals.

Step 1: List the top three career goals, with target dates that you plan to accomplish in one year.

Step 2: Repeat the process for your personal-development goals.

Step 3: Repeat the process for your private-life goals.

Skill Builder #13: Five-Year Action Plan

Purpose: To develop a five-year plan that will guide you and focus your attention and energy on achieving your top-priority goals.

Step 1: List the top three career goals, with target dates, that you plan to accomplish in five years, using the same format as Skill Builder #12.

Step 2: Repeat the process for your personal-development goals.

Step 3: Repeat the process for your private-life goals.

6

Balance Priorities: Timing Your Life

One of my rules is: Never try to do anything. Just do it.
—Ani DiFranco, singer-songwriter

As a career woman, you may often feel swamped by the tasks and responsibilities you face—with too many top-priority activities for the time that's available to complete them. The present moment is all you ever really have—moment by moment. All of us in our culture have agreed to measure those moments—those minutes, hours, days, weeks, months, and years—by the same measurement system. Time management is a key tool for managing multiple priorities and achieving your top-priority goals. It's especially important for women who want to have an enriching family life and time for personal development as well as a fulfilling career. In this chapter, you'll master time-management strategies. First, examine a few of your key beliefs about time management. Then see what you can learn from the story "What Are Your Big Rocks?"

How should women manage their time?
1. When you stay busy?
2. When you do what comes up?
3. When you do what other people want you to do?
4. When you do activities that are the most seductive or most fun at the moment?
5. When you're doing more in less time?
6. When you focus on those activities that are most likely to move you toward your highest priority goals?
7. When you plug away at a high-priority activity even though you're not in the mood?

We often speak of managing time, but because we all have the same number of hours in a day, what we really manage is what we *do* within those hours, isn't it? To create the life you want, to bring into actuality those goals you've created for yourself, you must fill your hours with the activities most likely to move you toward those goals.

TIME MANAGEMENT IS ACTUALLY ACTIVITY MANAGEMENT.

What Are Your Big Rocks?

A time-management expert was speaking to a seminar group. He placed a one-gallon glass jar on the table. Then he brought out a dozen fist-sized rocks and carefully placed them, one at a time, into the jar. When the jar was filled to the top, he asked, "Is this jar full?"

Everyone said, "Yes." Then he responded, "Really?" He reached under the table and pulled out a bucket of gravel, dumped it in and shook the jar causing pieces of gravel to work themselves down into the spaces between the big rocks.

He asked the group, "Is the jar full?" By this time they were onto him. "Probably not," one of them answered. "Good!" he replied. He reached under the table and brought out a bucket of sand, dumped it in, and watched it sift into all the spaces left between the rocks and the gravel. Once more he asked, "Is this jar full?"

"No!" the group shouted. Once again he said, "Good!"

Then he grabbed a pitcher of water and poured it in until the jar was filled to the brim. Then he looked up and asked, "What is the point of this illustration?"

One spunky guy said, "The point is, no matter how full your schedule is, if you try really hard, you can always fit some more things into it!"

"No," the leader replied, "that's not the point. The truth this illustration teaches us is this:

If you don't put the big rocks in first, you'll never get them in at all."

Allison, on hearing this, thought about her own situation. She knows that her highest-priority activity right now is getting information for a project report, but she keeps putting it off. Somehow she's just not motivated to dig for information, and dozens of other things capture her attention. For example, instead of working on her project report, she spent 20 minutes this morning on the phone with Doris, catching up on things over at StartOne Company. Then she spent 30 minutes cleaning up her computer files—they *were* getting out of hand. Now she realizes that what she needed was this shot of inspiration to get her attitude in gear—to get fired up about digging for the information she needs. *Time management is also attitude management.*

What are the "big rocks" in your life? A project that you want to accomplish? Time with your loved ones? Your education, your finances, your spiritual growth? A cause? Teaching or mentoring others? Remember each day to put these "big rocks" in first or you'll never get them in at all. Every day ask yourself, *What are the "big rocks" in my life today?* Then, put those in your jar first. It's like a combination Zen rock garden and day planner!

TIME MANAGEMENT IS ALSO

ATTITUDE MANAGEMENT.

We know that ways of doing business are changing by the minute. What are some changes that have affected time-management practices?

Handle each piece of paper only once has become *Coordinate and organize your communication systems*, which include an increasing proportion of voice mail, e-mail, and fax messages, and a decreasing proportion of paper messages. Speed has increased so that most messages—even global ones—are received instantaneously instead of taking days or weeks. Secretaries, receptionists, and clerks are disappearing rapidly as most businesspeople handle their own transactions, communications, and files—using PCs and other electronic equipment. They're being replaced by administrative assistants, assistant managers, and other professionals who have their own PCs and handle many of the administrative, managerial, technical, or professional tasks that support their manager's work. Some of the long, tedious meetings in conference rooms are being replaced by computer networked conferences where a group of people in the same building—or different cities—can work together to create agreements, documents, presentations, reports, and other materials.

To manage multiple priorities, you must know what's important, which means you must focus on your top-priority goals, activities, and time targets. You must know yourself and tailor your time-management style to fit your personal patterns. You must know your people and cooperate with them in managing multiple priorities. You must manage overwhelming projects, often sneaking up on them to overcome procrastination. Finally, you must harness technology in ways that boost your productivity.

Strategy #1

Know What's Important

You know your top-priority goals for creating the life you want and your top-priority activities for achieving those goals. All you need now are some time-management, or TM, skills for directing your energy toward those activities and goals—such skills as setting goals with target dates, using calendars and to-do lists to schedule your day, making the best use of body rhythms, and livening up dead time by multitasking.

TM Skill #1: Set Goals With Target Dates

Remember to include target dates in all your goal statements. When you don't set a target date for completing a task or project, do you put off getting started and then dawdle once you do start? Most people do. Target dates help to keep you on target.

Alternatively, do you keep working to make the task or project perfect, rather than aiming for world-class effectiveness or excellence? A few people are perfectionists, and perfectionism can be extremely costly. It's usually prohibitive over the long term. Successful businesspeople adopt the principle of *sensible approximation*. Ask yourself, *If my life depended on doing this task in half the time I've allocated, what shortcuts would I take? Is there really any reason not to take them?*

For longer projects, do you set many short-term target dates as well as an overall project target date? Doing so helps you to keep working at a steady pace rather than finding yourself swamped near the end.

Consider setting a *special emphasis goal* that lasts from a week to a couple of months. The goal might be to make someone laugh each day, to contribute a creative idea each day, to start each day with an inspirational reading or tape, to listen to a foreign language-learning tape, to find a way to streamline one activity each month. Then, do something every day to squeeze in at least one top-priority activity for that special emphasis goal. This technique is a great morale booster.

TM Skill #2: Schedule Your Day

First, focus on top-priority activities. Then, find the best methods for making your days productive.

Focus on top-priority activities and opportunities. First, clarify which of the day's possible activities are most likely to move you toward your goals. If you don't plan your day, you'll end up doing whatever comes up. This means that other people's actions may determine your priorities instead of your goals defining your actions. Second, keep your mind open to such opportunities as finding new market niches, creating new products or services, doing things in a better way, and making new connections and alliances.

Don't make the fatal mistake of dealing primarily with problems rather than opportunities. If you do, you're likely to be solving other people's problems instead of looking for new things to do and new ways of doing things. Remember, one of the most productive uses of your time is planning ahead. The more effectively you plan a project in advance, the less time it takes to complete it successfully. Don't let busywork crowd out your planning time and creativity time.

Use computerized planning devices. To begin with, an ongoing to-do list plus a planning calendar is a winning combination for scheduling your days. If you don't use a computer every day, you can use traditional planning calendars such as Day Timer or Filofax to help you keep track of priorities, organize and coordinate your long-term projects, keep track of delegated work, and establish goals.

If you're computerized, such programs as ACT! and Schedule+ incorporate all your planning needs, such as a calendar, to-do list, appointment book, and name and address book. You can print out any of these scheduling or contact lists to take with you or to give to others. You can also use such programs to keep track of future actions you want to take, such as starting new projects or contacting customers. You can look up names you've stored by first name, city, or any other key words you want to use. You can keep notes on your calls, meetings, or anything else you want to record, along with a person's vital information. To schedule activities, you can use an activity pop-up box, a pop-up monthly calendar, and a pop-up daily planner. You can assign priority levels to the activities, set an alarm to remind you when it's time to start the activity, and move uncompleted activities forward to another day. With a click of a mouse button, you can see your appointment calendar in a daily, weekly, or monthly format. With another click, you can view the activities on a single task list for any day or you can choose to see a task list of calls, meetings, or to-do's. You can use it to look up numbers of people you want to call and to dial the numbers through your modem and keep a record of all your calls. These are just some of the tasks a computerized scheduler will coordinate for you.

Keep asking, *How can I work smarter?* Any time you sense that you're wasting precious time or not being as productive as you might, ask yourself, *What can I do to work smarter?* Once every month or so, keep a detailed log of how you spend a typical day. Ask yourself as you get ready to begin an activity, *If I weren't already doing this, would I start it now?* If the answer is *no*, why not cut your losses and drop it? If the answer is *yes*, calculate how much time that item deserves and limit your involvement to that much time and no more. Such ongoing assessments keep you aware of good time management. They help you focus on goals that enhance your effectiveness and on activities that get results rather than on merely keeping busy or working hard.

TM Skill #3: Master To-Do Lists

You know how to set goals and prioritize them. You know how to generate activities for reaching those goals and prioritize them. The next step is simple: In the to-do file of your computerized scheduler or on a letter-size sheet of lined paper, list your activities in rank order of importance. That's your to-do list. On your calendar-planner, for each work day select activities from your to-do list that you will work on that day. When you finish an activity, mark it off your to-do list. As you achieve and set new goals, keep adding the related new activities.

Remember that sometimes the activities that are most important for reaching your objectives are not urgent—for example, writing an article, working up a proposal, or working out the details of a new idea. If you find yourself transferring an item from one to-do list to another, time after time, ask yourself: *Is this item really important? Am I procrastinating? Should this go in the follow-up or tickler file?* There's no need to list routine items that you do regularly. List only the items that have high priority today and might not get done unless you give them special attention.

For each item, ask yourself, *What can I delegate?* Then, for each activity, beginning with the one ranked lowest, ask, *What would happen if I didn't do this?* If the answer is *maybe nothing* or *not much*, give the activity an aging period. If there's no follow-up from anyone and no repercussions, you've saved that time to spend on high-priority items.

Schedule and do essential activities. Schedule your important work for first thing in the morning, or for the time of the day when you're most fresh, alert, and energetic. If you give yourself two hours of prime time—no phone calls, meetings, or other interruptions—you can complete twice as much work in half the time, with half the effort. Schedule this block of uninterrupted time on your calendar and think of it as an appointment with your most important client—*you.*

If you have a few minutes between meetings, use it to do quick tasks, such as making a phone call or finding a file.

The key to successful calendar-planners and to-do lists is actually *using* them. Check your list periodically throughout the day, especially:

▸ First thing every morning.

▸ Whenever you wonder if you're making the best use of your time.

▸ Just after an interruption.

- ▶ When you're torn between two activities.
- ▶ When you're running out of energy or interest in your current activity.

It may be tempting to avoid a highly demanding activity, especially one that requires tough decision-making or intense concentration. It helps to frequently ask, *Am I doing the most effective thing right now?*

Stay organized. Keep in mind that the best use of your time is not necessarily doing what comes up. As you go through your e-mail, paper mail, voice mail, and other messages and documents, try the following techniques:

- ▶ Separate the high-priority from the lower-priority messages and documents.
- ▶ Get rid of the lower-priority and organize the higher-priority.
- ▶ File the important items in computer or paper files.
- ▶ If there's work to do, note it on your to-do list.
- ▶ Avoid small pieces of paper, such as Post-it notes. Put most items into your computerized scheduler or on letter-size pieces of lined paper. Use big sheets for to-do lists, notes regarding projects, travel, and other matters—so you'll have room to add information and so you can organize the sheets into file folders to make them easy to find for future reference.

Most people waste at least an hour a day looking for papers that are lost on top of their desks. By staying organized, you can use that time effectively. We all have those times when things pile up—mail, phone messages, paperwork, and computer files. This is especially likely to happen in the final throes of meeting a project deadline or after a business trip. Instead of muddling through, stop. Take minutes you need to get organized again. Your work will go smoother and faster the rest of the day.

Prepare for tomorrow. At the end of the workday, consider taking a few minutes to reorganize and prepare for tomorrow. Check communications that have come in during the day to see if any need to be added to your to-do list and calendar-planner. Clear out papers by filing those that need to be kept and disposing of others. Review tomorrow's calendar and to-do list, and select specific work, tasks, or projects that you think have the highest priority and schedule them for tomorrow.

Preparing in the afternoon gives you a feeling of closure and completion of the workday. But, more important, it gives your subconscious mind time to work on your list during the intervening time, even while you sleep.

After you've made tomorrow's list, clear your desk before leaving the office. Try placing just one important project on your desk and putting everything else in a file drawer or cabinet that's easy to reach. When you come in the next morning, work on that one project as long as you can.

TM Skill #4: Custom-Tailor Your Schedule

As you schedule your time, keep in mind three major considerations: the practical aspects of the situation, your personal energy level, and your preferred-pace patterns. To become more aware of your personal patterns, complete Skill Builder #1 at the end of this chapter.

Practical considerations. Match items that require concentration with times when you're reasonably certain of having an uninterrupted period of peace and quiet. If special equipment or facilities are necessary, are they available only at certain hours? Might there be a waiting time to consider? Do you need to see other people in order to complete the task? When will they be available?

Energy-level considerations. Whenever possible, schedule activities to take advantage of your high-energy times. Schedule routine tasks for times when you're fairly alert but not at your peak. Try to use peak hours for top-priority projects, tasks that require intense concentration or original thinking, or tasks that are stressful or unpleasant, but important. Use your low-energy times for such tasks as catching up on professional reading, proofreading, and signing documents.

Work-pace considerations. Some people require pressure to work at top capacity. If that's your style, use it. However, be sure you plan ahead enough to get the information, approvals, documentation, and other items you need to complete the job so that pressure doesn't turn into panic or disaster. For most people, crash programs are far inferior to well-planned and well-timed programs. Knowing when to stop work on a project is as important as knowing when to start, because overwork leads to diminishing returns, such as increased errors and slowed-down responses. When your muscles are aching or you find yourself reading the same sentence two or three times, it's usually time to quit.

Whenever possible, schedule your time in large blocks so that you won't have to constantly switch back and forth from one type of activity to another. Leave some unscheduled time for visitors, phone calls, unforeseen emergencies, and other unexpected tasks.

Remember to allow for a quiet time for relaxation and meditation. Find a few minutes to back off from the rat race; stand back and gain some perspective on what is going on. This can help you be more objective about trivia and pettiness when you go back to your tasks.

TM Skill #5: Liven Up Dead Time

Dead time is the time we spend waiting for someone or something, sleeping, engaging in early morning activities or inertia, commuting, taking lunch and coffee breaks, and so forth. How much of that time should remain *dead* and how much of it do you want to liven up by making it do double duty?

You don't need to become an overworked time-management nut by frantically packing every moment full of activity. But how about those excruciatingly boring dead times? What about those frustrating dead times when you're just itching to work on a top-priority activity? See how much fun it is to plot and scheme your way to making that dead time work for you. Ideas include multitasking, keeping a quick-task folder, using commute time to prepare or catch up, and regularly asking yourself how you can work smarter.

Multitask. Even if you're a focuser and not a juggler, you can dovetail your work in ways that make the most of the time you have. Start with your time targets and work backward. Establish interim tasks with time targets. Then schedule your days accordingly. For example, you know that you need certain information for a meeting tomorrow. Before you begin work on that major report today, place the phone call that will get the ball rolling on gathering the information. What other quick tasks need to be done before you begin your major task? Multitasking allows you to have several tasks in process at the same time—and still focus on one task at a time.

Keep a quick-task folder. Try keeping a file folder of quick tasks. During the day, drop into it items that can be done during dead time. Take the folder along to meetings and appointments when you may need to wait for someone. Any time you leave the office, drop the folder into your briefcase. Then, when you're faced with dead time, you'll have some quick tasks with you.

Use your commute time. Instead of fretting about traffic, use commute time to prepare for upcoming events or to catch up on certain tasks. For example, during a morning commute you can think about activities for the coming day and mentally rehearse the best ways to handle problems, situations, and tasks. You might carry a small tape recorder and dictate to-do list reminders. If you're not driving, you can even dictate detailed memos and reports. Many women use their car tape decks or CD players for learning new languages, one audio lesson at a time; for catching up with current business information through informational recordings; and for relaxing or boosting creativity through inspirational tapes and CDs.

TM Skill #6: File To-Do Lists and Calendars

Keeping track of what you've accomplished is easy if you put your used-up to-do lists or calendars in special files. For special activities or projects, note the following:

▶ Everything you did well.
▶ What made it successful.
▶ How you went about it.
▶ Everything that went wrong and why.
▶ How to prevent problems from happening again.

Such records are also great additions to your *I Love Me* (ILM) files. Add them to the letters of appreciation, congratulation, and praise you've received. Include special reports, articles, or letters you've written that reflect high-quality work or special achievements. Use these files when you begin planning a similar activity or project. Review them when it's time for a performance appraisal, a raise or promotion request, an update for your resume or biography, or on any other occasion involving your performance. In this way, you can base your comments on specific achievements that you can back up with accurate facts and figures. Also, if your expenses are audited, calendars and to-do lists can help you document the business activities involved.

Strategy #2 —————————————

Tailor Your Day to Fit Your Style

Knowing your workstyle and personal patterns of achievement and procrastination are essential in managing your activities.

Workstyle Skill #1: Locate Time-Wasters and Energy-Drains

The first step in locating typical time-wasters and energy-drains in your life is to track your activities in writing for a couple of weeks. Complete Skill Builder #1 and follow the suggestions for assessing which activities are moving you toward your goals and which are sidetracking you.

Workstyle Skill #2: Adapt Your Focuser or Juggler Style

How you balance your activities is crucial. Some people are focusers. They work best when they focus on one project at a time until it's finished. Other people are jugglers and work best with several projects going at one time. Decide which is your style for taking on projects by completing Self-Awareness Activity #1.

Self-Awareness Activity #1: Are You a Focuser or a Juggler?

Purpose: To become aware of how you work best at the project level.

Instructions: Determine whether each of the statements is true for you, using the following scoring plan.

5 = almost always   4 = usually   3 = sometimes   2 = not usually   1 = almost never

_____ 1. I thrive on multiple projects.

_____ 2. I like to become intensely, exclusively absorbed with one project at a time.

_____ 3. In my mind, I divide a project into several distinct stages of development, such as planning stage, action stage, and follow-up stage, and I like to work on two or more projects that are in various stages.

_____ 4. I tend to eat and breathe a project, day and night, until it's finished.

_____ 5. When I feel blocked, tired, or bored with one project, I can often make progress on a different one.

_____ 6. I feel scattered, distracted, and frustrated when I must deal with more than one project, even though they're in various stages of completion.

_____ 7. I work well when I'm thinking about an upcoming project during the breathing spaces of an active project.

_____ 8. When I'm forced to switch my attention from the action stage of my primary project to the planning stage of another one, I tend to become consumed by the new one.

_____ 9. I like to assign the solution of certain problems on one project to my subconscious mind while I consciously focus on another project.

_____ 10. The only way I can solve problems that arise on a project is to devote myself exclusively to that project.

Follow-up: See the answer key on page 186 to interpret your score.

Are You a Juggler?

If you're a juggler, you're probably easily bored with one major project that goes on and on. You're in your element when you have several irons in the fire. The problem may be your ability to stay focused long enough on one project to make significant headway and to keep plugging away at it until it's completed. You can focus on one task at a time, even while *keeping all your irons hot*. Try these suggestions:

▶ Divide each project into stages and make a step-by-step plan for each stage.

▶ Delegate as many of the tasks as you need to and set a schedule for following up on each task.

▶ As soon as one project is underway, look for another.

If you're an effective juggler, you may be able to get more done during the same time frame than your focuser friends. But remember, we're talking about the project level here. At the task level, almost everyone works best when they focus on one *task* at any one point in time. Other tasks and other projects may be simmering in your subconscious, or other team members may be working on them. But at any one moment, see if you can be totally focused on the task at hand.

Are You a Focuser?

If you're a focuser, you're likely to stick with a major project until it's complete, and you may be comfortable with longer, more intense work sessions on one project than are your juggler colleagues. If your job requires you to juggle more than one major project at a time, you may run into barriers. You probably find it difficult to switch from focusing on tasks for one project to doing tasks for another. You may feel confused, disorganized, and frustrated by juggling. Try these suggestions.

▶ Can you choose the one project that promises to be most fruitful and best suited for you and focus on it? If so, make a plan for completing it, and stick with the project until it's finished. You're in your element!

▶ If other projects must be begun, can you delegate the necessary tasks?

▶ If your job requires you to juggle more than one major project at a time, learn to compartmentalize. It's difficult to tear yourself away from your current project, but once you make the transition, it gets easier. Use your focusing skills to zero in on the new project. When thoughts about the previous project intrude, find techniques for bringing your focus back to the current project. Imagine you're a racehorse wearing blinders so all you can see is the current project. Imagine your mind has compartments for each project and you're staying focused on the current-project compartment.

Are you both? Did your score indicate that you're probably both a juggler and a focuser, depending on the situation? That flexibility is a great asset. Being able to totally focus on a task in the moment is essential for success in most jobs, but so is juggling several projects. Being aware of these two modes and how to use them most effectively will increase your productivity.

Workstyle Skill #3: Identify Your Energy-Level and Work-Pace Patterns

Are you a day person or an evening person? Do you work better with more or less time pressure? Do you work faster at certain times of the day and slow down at other times? Knowing your energy-level and work-pace patterns can help you schedule your day more effectively and to get more done in less time. After you've completed Skill Builder #1 at the end of this chapter, you should have a clear picture of your personal patterns.

Obviously, you'll do better at difficult, complex, creative, or intense tasks when your energy level and work pace are high.

Whether you're a morning person or an evening person is an individual matter. It may be somewhat genetic and hormonal, and it's certainly affected by the schedule you've kept over the years. Research indicates energy patterns tend to vary by age. When you're young, you're likely to be an evening person and as you age, you're likely to become a morning person.

If you find that your peak energy hours simply don't coincide with job demands, it may be possible to change your peaks by changing your sleeping habits. If you're a night person, go to bed early, even though you don't want to. Find ways to lull yourself to sleep—there are many books with suggestions for insomniacs. You'll probably find getting up in the morning easier and easier. After a few weeks or months of the new sleep schedule, you may be surprised to find that you're functioning almost like a morning person.

Workstyle Skill #4: Keep Yourself Motivated

To stay motivated, you may need to identify self-limiting beliefs and payoffs around work and play, and find your own rewards, small and large, as well as ways of rewarding yourself that keep you motivated and productive.

Rework old beliefs and payoffs. Maybe you're holding onto some self-limiting beliefs that keep you from managing your activities most effectively. Maybe you learned as a child to go for payoffs for being a victim because you got sympathy and help when you couldn't get everything done. Or perhaps you're harboring beliefs about keeping your nose to the grindstone, making work a serious, grim business.

In the long run, it pays to take care of that child part of you that wants to run and play and have fun. If you keep the inner child happy, you're better able to avoid burnout. And having some fun along with hard work keeps you coming back for more. Try these suggestions:

▶ Identify old payoffs for not managing your activities well, and focus on new payoffs for managing your own life.

▶ Identify old parent messages that make work grim business, and create new messages that allow you to have fun at work and to reward your inner child.

Use rewards to stay motivated. Are you providing your own inspiration for managing your activities well? Do you regularly reward yourself for work well done? That's how you can keep the energy flowing. It's how you can motivate yourself to stay on track. It's a key to managing your attitude and activities. Give yourself permission to reward yourself many times a day. Find rewards that satisfy you and keep you motivated, but don't block you from completing your high-priority activities. Experiment with how often and what type of rewards you need to optimize your performance and satisfaction. Here are a few ideas:

▶ A brightly colored marker for drawing nice big lines through items on your to-do list as you complete them.

▶ A new decorative item for your office (a figurine, picture, or an artifact you love to look at).

▶ A break when you finish a task (coffee break, chat break, shopping break, outdoor stroll, or trip to another part of the building).

▶ Buying a small (or large) indulgence when you complete a task or project (a little luxury item or an interesting new *toy*, such as the latest software package or electronics gadget, something you want to play with).

▶ A favorite beverage or goodie to sip or munch as you concentrate on an especially tedious project.

▶ A special lunch or dinner, a weekend trip, or vacation days off.

Workstyle Skill #5: Eliminate Aggravating Situations

Your environment can create psychological aggravation and physical distraction, or it can enhance and support your energy level and your motivation to manage your activities and achieve your goals. See if you can eliminate or improve such situations as making a difficult commute, dealing with disrespectful people, or waiting in long lines.

If something in your environment is aggravating, irritating, or distracting you on a regular basis, it reduces your ability to make maximum use of your time and drains your energy. See suggestions in this chapter for using dead time, which refers to time spent in lines and commutes, as well as the chapters on assertiveness and dealing with difficult people. Be creative in finding ways to clean up as much of this *negative junk* as possible.

Workstyle Skill #6: Tailor a Work Environment That Fits

Your physical work space has a strong psychological effect on your attitude and your work habits. Determine what you need in order to feel comfortable with your work space and to enjoy being in it. Set the stage for effective time management by organizing your desk, setting limits on your weekly work hours, and learning to say *no* to nonessential requests.

Nearly everyone finds that a well-ordered desk improves mood and efficiency; it also signals an executive attitude. This is especially important for women who want to avoid a clerical stereotype. In most companies the bigger the person's paycheck, the cleaner the desk. Is that true in your company? If so, can you get papers off your desk and onto someone else's—or into the file cabinet or wastebasket? Avoid in- and out-baskets—keep them on your assistant's desk or use your desk drawers for this purpose. Use the same approach to clearing out e-mail, voice mail, computer files, and other electronic overload.

Workstyle Skill #7: Avoid the Slave or Drudge Syndrome

Women are more likely than men to try to do it all and to say *yes* to demands on their time when they should say *no*. Problems that can occur include workaholism and burnout. Avoid this by focusing on career goals and learning when to say *no* and when to delegate.

Focus on career goals. You'll profit from directing most of your energy toward career-related goals, especially while you're trying to make your mark. Everyone who succeeds pays those kinds of dues. However, don't confuse long hours and hard work with achieving goals. Don't bury yourself in piles of work and neglect opportunities to make important contacts, become professionally involved, and learn important new skills. Except for short periods when you're learning the ropes of a new job or completing a special project, generally avoid working more than 45 hours a week. If you must work overtime, consider doing it early in the morning rather than staying late; this signals that you're on top of things instead of floundering.

Try to get all your work done at the office so you won't need to carry it home. If this is your intention and your goal, you'll rarely need to take work home and you'll probably be more effective. When you get in the habit of thinking, *If I don't finish it today, I can always do it at home tonight*, your *intention* changes and your incentive for managing your time effectively takes a nosedive.

Learn when to delegate and when to say *no*. Are you trying to do too much? You may need to learn when and what tasks to delegate to others. An important benefit of delegating effectively at work is the time it frees up for you to devote to higher-priority items such as planning and organizing or mastering higher-level leadership skills. It may give another employee a chance to learn something new. Delegate tasks at home too—to paid workers, your husband, your children, and others.

If you don't learn to say *no* to tasks, nominations, meetings, and other time-consuming activities in which people ask you to participate, you'll end up managing your time according to other people's priorities rather than your own.

Strategy #3

Cooperate With Others

Your best efforts at managing your time effectively can be sabotaged by your manager, team members, assistant, and peers. It's up to you to use Murphy's Law in order to foresee and circumvent as many obstacles as possible.

Co-op Skill #1: Cooperate With Your Manager

Your manager probably has more impact on your activities than anyone you work with. Typical problems occur when your manager's ideas about what you should be doing conflict with your own, when you manager's not around and you need her, and when your manager doesn't delegate or make decisions in a time-effective manner. Here are some typical time-management problems people encounter with their managers, and suggestions for managing them.

➡ **Manager Problem #1:** Your manager pushes you to complete an item that's low on your priority list.

1. Tactfully discuss your conflict rather than meekly complying.
2. Talk in terms of achieving job goals and team goals and doing what's best for your manager and the organization.
3. Make sure your manager knows what other items are pending on your to-do list, and how they relate to your job goals.

- **Manager Problem #2:** Your manager is difficult to find when you need information, an approval, or a decision.
  1. Plan ahead to avoid delays.
  2. If that doesn't work, discuss the problem with your manager.

- **Manager Problem #3:** Your manager doesn't delegate effectively, or postpones decisions for too long.
  1. Initiate a tactful, open discussion about the impact of your manager's actions on your productivity.
  2. Avoid implying criticism of your manager's actions.
  3. Take a problem-solving approach.
  4. Focus on jointly finding ways your manager can help you improve your performance.

Co-op Skill #2: Cooperate With Your Work Team

Encourage your team to think about time management and to speak up when you ask them to do things they think are ineffective or time-wasters. Work with them on making the best use of your time and theirs. Avoid the following typical problems:

- **Problem:** You communicate instructions poorly or otherwise delegate ineffectively, so they waste time doing the wrong thing or doing it the wrong way.

  Suggestion: Learn how to delegate properly, and practice it frequently.

- **Problem:** You keep team members waiting because you're late for a meeting.

  Suggestion: Be prompt for appointments and meetings. If you see that you're going to be late, let them know so they can use their time constructively until you are ready to see them.

- **Problem:** You interrupt their work unnecessarily.

  Suggestion: Before interrupting, ask yourself: *Is this interruption really necessary, or could it wait? Could I ask this person to drop by when he reaches a stopping point? Could she call me? Could an assistant or receptionist give this person the message during a break?*

Co-op Skill #3: Cooperate With Your Assistant

The most important team member, so far as helping you manage your time is concerned, is your assistant, if you're fortunate enough to have one. The first step is effectively employing this important person's capabilities. The next step is to *treat* your assistant as a teammate. Keep this person fully informed so that he or she knows what you would do in most situations. Some ways of making better use of your assistant's contributions include upgrading his or her duties, keeping his or her workflow in mind, keeping your assistant informed of your goals and priorities, and working out procedures together.

Upgrade your assistant's duties. Work with your assistant to eliminate useless chores and to streamline computer communications and paperwork. In this way, you'll free up some valuable administrative talent. Work together to make the best use of it. Set decision-making guidelines and define areas of authority for your assistant. Inform others of these developments and instruct them to cooperate with your assistant.

Keep your assistant's workflow in mind. Some managers procrastinate all day and then dump their work on their assistants late in the afternoon. That practice can be harmless *unless* you expect to have it all handled before quitting time. Remember that work variety is important, and that assistants can suffer from mental fatigue and boredom. Help your assistant have variety in the course of the day, week, and month. Look for assignments that provide adequate challenge and opportunity for growth. Your assistant will probably respond by working more efficiently and effectively.

Keep your assistant informed about your priorities. Assign priority numbers to tasks you give your assistant, or have him or her rank the items after checking your ranked to-do list. Prioritizing avoids the overwhelming effect of dumping work in a heap on your assistant's desk. It lets your assistant know which tasks to tackle first, even when you assign many tasks at one time.

Work out procedures together. Work with your assistant to devise procedures for managing calls, visitors, and mail. For example, when someone is scheduled to see you in your office, decide how much time you want to allot to the meeting, and tell your assistant to call you when the time is up, giving you a reason to end the meeting. Your assistant can suggest items for your to-do list, help you monitor the progress of projects, and handle the follow-up on actions delegated to other team members at staff meetings. Other suggestions for cooperating with your assistant are:

▸ Be prepared for joint work sessions to avoid delays, searches, and changes.

▸ Every time you leave your office, let your assistant know where you're going and when you'll return.

▸ Ask for suggestions on how you can help your assistant be more effective.

▸ Give your assistant feedback, professional development, support, decision-making autonomy, and recognition.

Co-op Skill #4: Cooperate With Your Peers and Clients

Other team leaders and managers at your level—as well as clients or customers—can smooth the way for your projects to sail to completion. They can also create all sorts of bottlenecks and delays in your plans. It's up to you to foresee and prevent these. Here are some suggestions:

1. Focus on common concerns and goals. When you're discussing the need for action with a peer, stress how the completion of the task in question helps achieve a specific goal. Tie the goal in with an organizational goal you think your colleague is committed to so as to motivate your colleague to cooperate more fully.

2. When you want to end an informal discussion, simply push back your chair, stand up, and start walking slowly toward the door as you end the discussion.

3. When someone drops by your office unannounced and you don't have time for a visit, stand up and remain standing as you talk to prevent a *settling in* for a long session.

4. If you don't have time for a discussion in your office, but you want to at least acknowledge someone, walk out of your office and talk with the person on his or her way down the hall.

5. Set a closing time for all meetings and work to end them on time.

Co-op Skill #5: Cooperate With All to Minimize Interruptions

At the end of the day, do you often feel you haven't made much progress toward high-priority goals because of too many interruptions? Do you often feel that if you only had some blocks of uninterrupted time, you could do wonders?

Research supports your feelings. Nothing is more tiring and frustrating than handling continual interruptions when you're attempting to concentrate on a task. It's especially important to have quiet time when you are faced with a high-priority project that is rather large or complex.

For most of us, it takes 10 minutes to become deeply focused on a task that requires our full attention and intense concentration. We can sustain this concentration for 20 minutes or so. After that, most of us take a break of some kind. Therefore, when you're working on a tough task, you may find yourself actually spending about half your time on getting into it, resting, switching to lower-priority items, and so forth. If you can put in one hour of continuous concentration on a project, you'll typically make more progress than with two hours spent in 10- to 20-minute work sessions. In other words, *you can double your productivity*. To make the best use of your concentration time, have at least one-hour chunks that are interruption-free. Ways you can free up chunks of time include: 1) asking others to honor these times as *in-conference* times and to see you during open-door times, 2) screening your telephone calls, and 3) moving to a secluded place to work—another office or your home, for example.

Strategy #4
Sneak Up on Overwhelming Projects

You know you need to tackle that high-priority project, but you end up making a few phone calls that are much less important. *I'll just get these out of the way.* You move through yesterday's stack of mail *just to see if there's anything important, maybe something I can do quickly*. Next thing you know, it's lunchtime. Even high achievers tend to put off getting to work on overwhelming projects (those daunting jobs that seem overwhelming because of their size, their complexity, their difficulty—or all three).

Get a clear picture of the entire project and prepare a step-by-step plan for completing it. When you think about doing something on the project, don't focus on the whole project, because it's impossible to complete a huge project in one fell swoop. Instead, focus on a quick five-minute task or a doable work session. When you're *not* in the mood to work on the project, do a quick task or two anyway. When you *are* in the mood, plow in and do as much as you can. In this way, you'll keep moving in bits and spurts until, one fine day, that huge, overwhelming, *impossible* project is done.

Sneak-up Skill #1: Organize Projects Into Manageable Segments

Start by making a written project-planning sheet headed by the name of the project. List the major segments of the project. Making a written plan helps you tackle each segment with minimal time loss from building up momentum, retracing steps, reviewing what you've done, and getting your thoughts and materials in order. Avoid having too many large projects going at once. If you accumulate a backlog of partially finished projects, it becomes more and more difficult to finish any of them, and to have a sense of satisfaction and closure.

Sneak-up Skill #2: Break Major Segments Into Task Sessions

After you get some manageable segments, see if you can break each segment into task sessions—things you could probably complete in one work session. Write a description of each task session. At this point ask yourself such questions as:

▸ Should I delegate some of the tasks?

▸ Can some tasks be overlapped or done simultaneously?

Estimate the starting and completion dates for each task session and major segment. Schedule the task sessions on your planning calendar. Do you need to put items on your to-do list? Soon you'll find yourself completing task sessions. If you must leave a task session uncompleted, note the next step so you won't waste time when you come back to it.

Sneak-up Skill #3: Get Started With Quick Tasks

Quick-tasks can be done in five minutes or so. They're seductive because they're so quick and easy, and they can pull you into doing the next thing—and then the next thing—until you're in full swing in a task session. Here are some ideas for quick tasks:

▸ Contact someone to get information that you need.

▸ Spend a few minutes planning some procedures for the project.

▸ Set up a simple filing system for the project.

▸ Do some reading that will be helpful.

▸ Locate a source of information or material.

Try to work on a quick task every day.

Sneak-up Skill #4: Use Other Sneaky Tricks to Keep Going

Is that little girl part of you still procrastinating? Here are a few more strategies for sneaking up on her. Before she knows it, she may actually be enjoying herself!

Do the most unpleasant task first. Get it out of the way so you don't waste energy *doing it in your head over and over*. Congratulate yourself for getting it done. Notice the light, satisfied feeling you get from completing the task, and take time to enjoy that feeling. Reward yourself profusely for getting through this major barrier.

Take advantage of your current mood. Keep returning to the project in your mind. Keep asking yourself, *What am I especially in the mood to do today that could move the project along?*

List the advantages and disadvantages of starting now. You'll usually see that the disadvantages are trivial and the advantages are significant. This can quickly boost you into action.

Ask yourself why you're not progressing. If these direct techniques aren't working, maybe you need to delve deeper. Perhaps fear of failure or fear of success is blocking you. Look deep within. If that's your problem, ask yourself, *What's the worst that can happen?* You'll probably realize either that your fears of the worst are absurd or that you *can* face the worst and handle it comfortably.

Are you afraid of failing at the project if you start it? If so, remind yourself that if you give it a good try, you may succeed. But if you don't, you guarantee failure. If you do your best and it's not good enough, you can at least learn from your mistakes. Studies show that people who work toward success are happier and accomplish more than those who fear failure—and therefore expect it. Virtually all the famous high achievers say they experienced some failure along the way. It's the lessons they learned from those failures that allowed them to keep going and achieve their visions.

Sneak-up Skill #5: Reward Yourself for Making Progress

When you start a task session, make every effort to finish it. When you do, savor the moment by congratulating yourself and taking time to enjoy the satisfaction of completion. Reward yourself in some fitting way. This helps reinforce a sense of closure and satisfaction each time you work on the project. *And* it helps you to keep moving, bit by bit, surge by surge, toward completion.

Strategy #5 _____
Harness Technology to Boost Your Productivity

The average U.S. employee each day must cope with 190 messages every day, according to a 1998 Gallup poll. They include 52 phone calls, 30 e-mail messages, 22 voice mails, 18 interoffice memos, 18 letters, 15 faxes, 11 Post-it notes, 10 phone message slips, 4 pager messages, 4 overnight courier messages, 3 cell phone messages, and 3 postal express letters. Over 40 percent of workers say they're interrupted by incoming messages at least six times an hour.

You can get help by using all the technological assistance you can find to manage this deluge.

Judicious use of the Internet can be a good start. The key word is *judicious*, for it's easy to become lost or addicted, and to waste enormous blocks of time. A good one-day seminar on how to use the Internet is time well spent. Reasons for using the Internet include:

▶ Moving beyond stereotypes about women's lack of technical savvy to gain a most marketable skill.

▶ Enhancing your time-management system.

- Saving time and money in sending and receiving messages, getting and giving out information, paying bills, making travel plans, holding virtual meetings and work sessions, and many other activities.
- Accessing new opportunities to come into contact with potential buyers.
- Accessing all the information you need about products and services you want to buy, along with information about suppliers.
- Accelerating your continuous learning and research efforts by accessing libraries, newsgroups, chat rooms, and other information sites.
- Keeping up with everyone else who is on it—competitors, colleagues, customers, suppliers, the media.

Booster Skill #1: Overcome Myths About Women and Computers

The Internet is all about verbal communication—an area where women excel. It offers incredible opportunities for women to do business without facing stereotypical barriers. If you decide to use your initials as a first name (B.J. instead of Betty, for example), you will be able to function in a gender-neutral environment!

You can also make great networking connections with other women—and use your full name. For example, the FeMiNa.com allows users to search a database of women-oriented Websites. Such sites help create a community of women who are developing sites of their own and help provide inspiration to women on how to make a living with technology. Webgrrls.com gives information about 45 chapters of Webgrrls around the world who meet regularly to talk about employment opportunities, get Internet help, and network. Aliza Sherman, the CEO, says she believes that four basic myths keep women off-line:

- **Myth #1:** It's too hard.
  Reality: If you can type, you can go online.
- **Myth #2:** It's too expensive.
  Reality: It can be expensive, but there are ways to do it inexpensively.
- **Myth #3:** It's too dangerous.
  Reality: Pornography and stalking can take place in any community, including cyberspace communities. Just as you can get information about where you can safely go and what you can safely do in any city you visit, you can get similar information about visiting Websites.
- **Myth #4:** It has nothing for me personally or professionally.
  Reality: Sherman says, "Name what it is that you're interested in, name what it is that you need help with, and I'll tell you that it's available online."

Booster Skill #2: Understand Internet Basics

By merely inserting a little connector into your computer and plugging it into your phone line or cable line, you can access the largest computer system in the world, the Internet. Through this network of networks, you can:

▶ Use electronic mail (e-mail) to contact millions of other Internet subscribers worldwide at minimal cost. It's by far the least expensive way to send messages to people outside your immediate area, and the fastest way to send messages to people anywhere.

▶ Log in to another computer at your company headquarters, local university, or other site and use it to run programs.

▶ Search libraries of information software around the world and transfer it back to your own computer.

Your computer thus becomes an extension of what seems like a single giant computer with branches all over the world. In reality, your computer is talking with one of more than a million other computers. Tens of thousands of networks all over the world connect them, sending information between computers as needed. The resources this makes available to you are tremendous and change daily.

Free Internet links. With an Internet account, you can access all types of libraries housed in universities, corporations, research foundations, and government agencies. Libraries are the most visible and numerous resources on the Internet. There are even virtual libraries of electronic books, and the U.S. Library of Congress has a virtual library catalog. Most libraries will let you browse through their card catalogs and maybe even check their database of newspaper clippings or other special services. Some let you copy electronic books with expired copyrights. You can get scientific information from NASA about science, physics, and aeronautics, and medical information from the National Library of Medicine.

Intranet. Intranet systems are used by most large companies to communicate by e-mail with anyone within the company or to collaborate by groupware on many kinds of projects. Intranet can also be linked seamlessly to the Internet for doing business throughout the world.

The World Wide Web (WWW). The Web is the ever-expanding global collection of hypertext (interconnected and interconnectable documents) available on the Internet. It's the fastest-growing part of the Net. Through the Web, you can access data that includes sounds, pictures, free programs (including Web browsers), and movies. The Web allows you to:

▶ Access the Internet and communicate by e-mail all over the world.

▶ Choose your own path through the Internet or through a book or document.

▶ Jump from resource to resource without knowing which Internet computer you're on.

▶ Put your personal or business *home page* on the Web for others to browse.

Use Browsers and Search Engines. The Internet offers an amazing wealth of information, if you can only find it. Learn to use browsers and search engines that work for you, learn to identify the key words—and the formats for entering those words—that get you the best results. For example, you want to contact the Raffles Hotel Website so you can make a reservation. You enter "Raffles Hotel, Singapore," and you get dozens of travel agencies that will book you a room at the hotel, but with various restrictions and conditions that you don't want. How do you manage to get the hotel's Website so you can contact its staff directly? Try "Raffles Hotel, Singapore + Website."

You can type in a search request, asking your program how to format search requests. You should get information about how and whether to use such designator words as *or, and, not,* and such symbols as plus, minus, quotes, parentheses, and brackets.

Booster Skill #3: Use E-Mail

Electronic mail is the most popular of the traditional Internet applications. It can save big chunks of time in sending messages, but it can eat up chunks of time if you receive a growing pile of e-mail without developing a system for sorting through it.

Unlike Telnet, FTP, and the Web, e-mail is not limited to the Internet. You can send e-mail in the following ways: between two computers connected by modems, across an intranet within your office or company, across the Internet to any commercial network, and to other systems that have gateways to the Internet. You can send e-mail messages to anyone in the world if you know that person's e-mail address and have either your own access to the Internet or access to another system that can send e-mail.

Manage your e-mail. You can manage your e-mail with software programs that run on your computer. Such programs can provide you with:

▸ The ability to write messages off-line before sending them.

▸ Automatic sending and receiving.

▸ Automatic filing of e-mail messages in separate files or folders.

▸ Address book for frequently used e-mail addresses.

▸ Ability to send copies of the same message to a group of people.

Manage your e-mail in the same ways you manage your hard-copy mail. Sort it by urgency and type of action needed, look for software that helps you with this job, and actively work to get your name removed from mailing lists that simply clutter up your in-box.

Send and receive e-mail messages. To communicate by e-mail, type a message, then drop it into an electronic mailbox by clicking the send option. When the recipient checks her or his mailbox and sees the message, that person has several options for handling the message: download it from the host computer, answer you with a few keystrokes, forward it to someone else, file it in his or her computer, or delete it. If you are charged by the amount of time you're connected online, then save online time by writing your messages offline. Remember that fancy formatting will probably be lost, so keep it simple. When writing your messages, consider these tips:

▸ Use a subject line that captures the essence of your message and puts it in a nutshell. If you need a reply, mention it here, perhaps as a question.

▸ In the text, put your most important information first.

▸ Keep the message simple, on one screen, if possible.

▸ Use bulleted or numbered lists that are easy to read.

▸ If your discuss several topics, use all-caps headings to identify each one.

▸ If you must send more information, write a brief description of it and then attach the file of information as an enclosure. Your description might include the purpose of the information, what the receiver should do with it, and when you need a response.

▶ Make your message easy to respond to by asking questions that can be answered *yes* or *no*.

▶ If you'll need to make future reference to an e-mail you're sending or receiving, transfer it to a specific computer file or print it and file the printout.

▶ If your message is very important, controversial, sensitive, confidential, or could easily be misunderstood, use the phone or a face-to-face meeting to communicate.

Use directories. If you belong to a computer group that participates in a Distributed Internet Directory (DID), you have access to a Directory Service Agent (DSA) program that maintains your group's directory. You can also use a Directory Client Agent (DCA) to get e-mail addresses of people in other groups.

Use mailing lists. Computerized mailing lists may save you a great deal of time, giving you access to up-to-date, targeted mailing lists. With a mailing list program, you can keep mailing lists of varied groups of people, such as various types of customers or potential customers, suppliers, interest groups, etc. Any e-mail sent to the mailing list is automatically sent to everyone on the list. A moderated mailing list is one that has been screened by the list administrator, who may weed out duplicate messages or messages inappropriate to the theme of the list. When you use an address list you have compiled, you normally want recipients to see only their own name, so you can send the message to yourself and click your address list into the bcc line (blind carbon copy) .

Join newsgroups and chat rooms. Be selective in the groups you join. You want to make valuable contacts and obtain relevant information, but you can waste as much time in computer interactions as in personal interactions.

Thousands of newsgroups or chat rooms are available to you on the Internet. As the world's largest bulletin board, with topics that cover virtually everything, these servers use e-mail to provide a centralized news service. They gathers messages about a single topic into a central place. You can log on to the server to read these messages, or you can have software on your computer log on and automatically download the latest messages so you can read them at your leisure. Discussions in virtual forums or conferences take place by e-mail, which is sent to a newsgroup's address. A newsgroup, like a mailing list, may be moderated by a person who screens all incoming e-mail for appropriateness before sending it on newsgroup members.

Most newsgroups keep a FAQs file (frequently asked questions) to help new members by answering technical questions about a newsgroup and to give an idea of the range of topics covered by the newsgroup.

Booster Skill #4: Consider Other Internet Applications

World Wide Web and e-mail are the most common applications of the Internet. Other applications that you should know about may include WAIS, talk radio, and virtual reality.

Wide area information server (WAIS) is a research application with a database spread out among many computer sites. Files at each site are indexed. A WAIS search actually looks into files for the terms you're looking for. A WAIS lets you control which databases or sources you look at and keeps track of searches you've made.

Radio and television access is increasingly overlapping and merging with Internet access. Talk radio has been available via Internet for several years. Television is becoming available to those with access to adequate bandwidth and computer capacity to receive it.

Collaboration refers to the ability of people to meet via computer to review and manipulate information simultaneously. For example, an ad executive in Boston could link up with a brand manager in Dallas and, on-screen, review and edit a magazine insert or TV commercial. An architect could show the latest changes in an office blueprint while the client, at another location, could circle a window and ask why it couldn't be bigger. The potential uses in business, education, and medicine are rich.

Virtual reality uses a computer to simulate an interactive environment that appears to you, the observer, to be reality. In a sense, virtual reality systems pick up where watching a realistic movie or reading a good book leave off. *Telepresence* is a method where a video camera is mounted on a robot and sends pictures to you, the operator, at another location. You manipulate the robot by remote control. Telepresence gives you the sense that you are present with the robot. The robot's arms are an extension of your arms, even if the robot is located across the world. Virtual reality permits groups of people to enter the same virtual world, and it is already being used in business, education, medicine, and entertainment.

Booster Skill #5: Use Telecommunications and Software Tools

Other electronic tools that can help you manage time more effectively include telecommunication devices, such as voice mail, beepers, mobile phones, and faxes. Computer software programs can also help you save time. With fax machines, beepers, mobile phones, or laptops with modems, you can make instant contact with people, no matter where you are. Voice mail serves as a virtual receptionist that can accurately take your phone messages and hold them for you. Virtual secretary software goes several steps further in coordinating phone messages that you send and receive.

Voice mail. While some people complain about voice mail—*Either I can't ever find a real person to help me or it takes me 45 steps to get to one*—others bless it because it's so much more dependable and accurate than leaving messages with receptionists, family members, and others. It allows people to leave more detailed messages than could be written down by others, and they can manage more of the nonverbal aspects of the message, such as voice tone. Whether you're leaving a message on someone's voice mail or recording an outgoing message on your own voice mail, follow some good communication strategies.

▸ Speak with energy and enthusiasm.

▸ Smile as you speak, and your voice will reflect a more positive attitude.

▸ If the person doesn't know you, begin by speaking your name slowly and distinctly, then spell it, and give your phone number. If the message is more than a few words, repeat your name and number at the end. Many *cold calls* can't be returned because one number is garbled.

> ▶ Leave specific windows of time when you'll be available for a return call—
> to avoid an ongoing game of *telephone tag*.

Call back if your call isn't returned within a few days. Phone equipment is not infallible. If you leave several messages that aren't returned, try to reach the person's assistant or someone else in the firm. Find out when the person may be available to take your call. Consider sending a fax, e-mail, or letter suggesting when you'll call again or when they can reach you, or asking for a phone appointment.

Virtual secretary. If you send and receive many important phone messages, consider using a virtual secretary program, such as Wildfire. These computerized phone systems include voice recognition and can pick out and deliver the crucially important calls from among the pile of calls your voice mail receives. It can insulate you, your coworkers, and your clients from phone tag and all the other rungs of voice-mail hell—the place where about 75 percent of all business calls end up. It can help you clinch deals by connecting calls you would have otherwise missed. It will call you anywhere in the world, including cars and planes, relay your phone messages, and keep dialing people you want to contact until a connection is made. On plane flights or in a hotel room across the globe, where phone charges can be astronomical, a single call to your system can connect you to several numbers. The system waits in the background when you're on the phone, ready to respond to your every voice command.

Telephone tips. Your telephone can either be a time-saver or a time-waster, depending on how you use it. Analyze the purpose and pattern of your calls. When you need to communicate with someone, take a moment to reflect on the advantages and disadvantages of doing so by telephone, face-to-face meeting, or written message. Ask, *What is my purpose and my goal? Will a phone call now really do any good?* If it will, then have your points and all materials at hand *before* you dial. Here are additional tips:

1. Bunch your telephone calls by making several calls during one time period—
   to free up blocks of time when you can build momentum on important tasks.

2. Consider using special telephone equipment and arrangements, such as a
   speaker phone, shoulder rest, or headset that leaves your hands free to handle
   files and perform other tasks. A headset is essential if you spend hours per day
   conducting business on the phone. Otherwise you're likely to develop painful
   neck and back problems.

3. Decide on a policy about being put on hold. Either avoid it and call back, or
   keep your file of quick tasks handy so that you can put the call on speaker
   phone and keep busy while you're waiting.

4. Use automatic dialing equipment for frequently called numbers.

5. Practice the quick ending: *I'll let you get back to your business...Well, thanks
   so much. I must dash to a meeting now... Fine. If we've covered everything, I'll
   let you go and get back to you later.*

6. Streamline incoming calls by finding out what a caller wants as soon as possible. Ask probing questions such as, *What can I do for you?*

7. Track your calls for a week, then analyze to see which types can be reduced,
   eliminated, shortened, or rerouted.

Computer software that can save you time. Programs that can boost your time-management performance are being upgraded constantly. Some of the best are for writing almost anything—letters, brochures, books; for scheduling your activities; for accounting and other financial recordkeeping; for removing programs from your hard drive or backing up files from hard drive to tape or disk; for printing labels; for transferring files to another computer by modem; for managing computer memory or speeding up your system; for saving printout wait time; and for preventing file damage from viruses.

In summary, you can manage the multiple priorities in your life by focusing on your top-priority goals, tailoring your day's activities to fit your style, cooperating with others on time management, sneaking up on overwhelming projects, and harnessing new technologies. These strategies can help you create the life you want without burning out.

Skill Builders

Skill Builder #1: How Do You Spend Your Time and Energy?

Purpose: To track how you spend your time for two weeks and assess how well you're managing your activities. To track your energy-level patterns and assess whether you're scheduling demanding, important activities during high-energy times of the day.

Step 1. Review your goals. Get in touch with your current goals. What are your current job goals? Project goals? How do they fit in with your overall career goals? With the three or four top-priority goals in your life?

Step 2. Set up a weekly time log. Use a calendar that has enough space to write in your activities, or set up your own weekly time-log sheets.

Step 3. Track your activities, energy levels, and work pace. Pick two weeks that are fairly typical and log all your activities. Include all waking hours and weekends. Note times when your energy level is especially high or low. Also note any variations in the work pace you prefer at various times.

Step 4. Summarize your activities. Calculate some totals for time spent on various types of activities, such as writing reports, reading background material, making routine phone calls, commuting, shopping, and socializing. Calculate the approximate percentage of the total time you spend on each major type of activity.

Step 5. Analyze your patterns (energy level and work pace). Are your highs, midranges, and lows fairly persistent? If not, what factors seem to make a difference? Chart a typical day's energy-level pattern and a typical day's work-pace pattern. How do weekends differ from workdays? Why the variation?

Step 6. Identify time-wasters and energy-drains. Does the amount of time you're spending on each type of task adequately support your top-priority goals? If not, how can you re-prioritize your activities? Are you making best use of your high-energy times? If not, how can you change the timing of your activities? Do some activities or situations regularly waste your time or drain your energy?

Answer Key

Self-Awareness Activity #1: Are You a Focuser or a Juggler?

Add up your total score for the odd-numbered statements, which reflect the juggler style. A score between 18 and 25 means you're a juggler; between 13 and 17, you're both a juggler and a focuser; between 5 and 12, you're not primarily a juggler.

Add up your total score for the even-numbered statements, which reflect the focuser style. A score between 18 and 25 means you're a focuser; between 13 and 17, you're both a focuser and a juggler; between 5 and 12, you're not primarily a focuser.

7

Minimize Stress

*The point is less what we choose than that we have the
power to make a choice.*

—Gloria Steinem

Managing the stress in your life has special importance for you as a career woman. You probably have more stress to cope with than your male colleagues, especially if you're married and if you have children. In addition to typical career-related stress, women have the added issues of home and family responsibilities, workplace stereotypes, harassment, and discrimination. To cope with all this requires a high level of health and well-being, and an ability to access your inner resources in order to empower yourself and others.

The most effective leaders know how to channel their energy toward their goals—including stress-related and emotional energy. Some of the leaders who fall by the way-side simply don't have the stamina or resources to stay in the running. They use up too much emotional energy struggling with stress. Others keep running at high speed until they literally drop dead.

In this chapter, you'll master the strategies for managing stress. First, answer the following questions about your current beliefs regarding stress. Then, meet Eva Chen of Trend Micro, who manages the stress of creating breakthrough innovations.

How should women deal with stress?

1. Is the best approach to managing stress a control strategy (learning to control all aspects of your life) or a go-with-the-flow strategy?

2. Is the major predictor of job stress a lack of control over your job or the fact that you regularly work at least 60 hours a week?

3. Is the most powerful stress strategy to focus on your goals or to relax and let go of the need to achieve?

4. Would the type of event that disrupts your friend's life probably disrupt yours also? Or do people often respond differently to the same type of event?

Eva Chen, Chief Technology Officer of Trend Micro

Eva Chen cofounded Trend Micro with CEO Steve Chang in 1988 to develop software that fights viruses attacking computer networks. Until Eva's breakthrough idea, virus-fighting software went to work *after* a destructive sequence of code was identified. The software could do battle only after the worm had wreaked havoc inside the network's computers. In 13 years of battling, Trend Micro had never stopped a new virus from invading. This bugged Eva, who spent an entire year chewing on the problem. As she met with the 300 engineers she manages around the globe, she asked about better ways to fight this battle.

Her breakthrough idea came while having dinner with her energetic 13-year-old son and 9-year-old daughter at their home in Pasadena, California. That evening her kids got into an argument, and she ordered a time-out to separate them. Suddenly she made a connection: *What if we separate, or segment, the network in order to stop the virus? What if we give questionable data a time-out while we examine it for worms?* She grabbed a piece of paper and started to draw a prototype of her idea.

She called it the Network VirusWall. It would be a box that sits on the edge of a corporate network, scanning data packets and detaining those that might contain worms. Then a program would compare the suspicious data with up-to-the-second information from Trend Micro's virus-tracking command center. If it was a worm, the program would smash it. The only problem: This solution involved hardware, but Trend Micro only made software. When Eva brought the idea to top executives, they were wary of shifting the company's focus to hardware.

Eva decided to build a working prototype. She asked seven of her best engineers to camp out in her home until they came up with a box and a program. For the next two weeks they worked, stopping only to sleep in shifts in the spare bedrooms. They completed the prototype and wrote code to run it. Then Eva invited the top executives to her home for a demonstration of the working model. As the executives and seven tired engineers looked on, she unleashed a worm and the box did the trick. Eva got her approval.

Trend Micro was soon turning out fire-engine red boxes that stand out among an IT department's racks of black and grey servers. Companies quickly snapped up the $6,000 box, pushing Trend Micro's stock to a year-long high.

Strategy #1

Recognize Your Stressors

The first step in converting stress into emotional power is to recognize the typical sources of your stress, how you typically respond, and other options you can choose in dealing with stress. Managing stress is especially important for career women because leadership roles can be quite demanding, especially if you're aiming for visibility and promotion. Some common sources of stress include:

▸ Psychological upsets and anxiety—from your reactions to life events.

▸ Overwork, too many demands and responsibilities, and lack of job control.

▸ Drugs (including medication) and chemicals (including additives and residues in food).

▸ Excessive noise and air pollution.

These are disruptions of a safe, balanced, harmonious environment—or changes in the status quo. We all need *some* change in our lives, of course, to provide interest and challenge. Some people welcome and thrive on change; however, we all have limits to the degree of change we can tolerate within a period of time, without experiencing ill effects. Here are some stress-management skills you can adopt:

Stress Skill #1: Recognize and Cope With Personal Stressors

The number and severity of stressful incidents that occur in your life during a year's time can serve as predictors of the probability that you will become ill within the following year. Of course, if you become aware of stress buildup, you can use strategies described here to reduce stress and heal the damage it has caused.

Do Self-Awareness Activity #1 to visually symbolize your stressors and track their connection to *dis-ease*. Be aware that any type of change can be stressful if you perceive it at any level as a disrupter, including going on vacation, moving to a new home, getting married, or having a child. Become thoroughly aware of the life events and relationships that are likely to create stress for you. Think about the meaning of events for you, and try to identify and process the feelings you experience. In this way, you gain practice in recognizing stress buildup before it gets out of hand.

Self-Awareness Activity #1: Sort Out Your Stressors

Purpose: To raise your awareness of the stressors in your life so you can manage them effectively.

Step 1: Make a drawing that symbolizes the stress in your life as follows:

Draw a picture of yourself—it can be a stick figure, a symbol, or as realistic as you like.

Symbolize in some way all the pressures and demands that you're aware of—using drawings, words, or other symbols.

Show the intensity of each pressure, demand, or anxiety by drawing arrows, bridges, or other connections between the pressure and you. Indicate intensity by the size, thickness, darkness (or similar means) of the connections.

Remember that even positive change can be stressful if it has a disruptive effect.

Step 2: On a separate sheet of paper, make two columns labeled as follows: *External Sources* (other people, situations, cultural factors, physical environment, etc.), and *Internal Sources* (self-doubt, repressed anger, fears, anxieties, etc.). List each stressor from Step #1 in one of these two columns.

Step 3: What personal actions or attitudes tend to feed into or maintain the stress sources you listed in Step #2?

Step 4: For each pressure or demand shown in Step #2, list at least one way you can prevent its occurrence or handle it more effectively to prevent stress.

Step 5: Think of an illness you've had in the past. List the major stressful factors in your life during the year prior to the illness.

Step 6: List payoffs for being ill. (Examples: Getting a vacation from work or class; getting sympathy from a loved one.)

Step 7: How can you take care of yourself and provide reasonable facsimiles of these payoffs without becoming ill? (Example: Allowing yourself to accept more love and attention from others and from yourself when you're well.)

Step 8: What patterns do you see in the ways you respond to stress that may be harmful to your health? List them. (Example: Interpreting a change as a defeat or sign of failure, as proof that life is unfair, or as a trap.)

Step 9: What patterns do you see that are constructive and may prevent illness? List them. (Example: Interpreting a change as an opportunity to move into more appropriate activities, or as a sign that it's time to move on.)

Step 10: Put a small version of your stressor drawing on an index card and place it by your desk calendar, on your mirror, or someplace where you'll be reminded several times a day to manage these stressors.

Stress Skill #2: Identify Home-Career Conflicts

Career women may experience more disruptions than men for many reasons. For one thing, they may have more responsibilities. For example, when they accept the primary responsibility for the children and housework, there are simply more things going on in their lives—things they perceive as crucial. For another, women who have not resolved inner conflicts concerning their career role and their wife or mother role are subject to added stress. In addition, women are likely to experience more stress than men in the process of establishing their credibility and advancing within an organization because of stereotypes and other barriers.

According to Professor Margaret Hennig's surveys, there are now many women in their mid-30s to late-40s who have been deeply involved in their careers for 15 to 20 years, and who have already worked harder in terms of hours and stress anxiety than the traditional 65-year-old man. Most are not willing to sacrifice family relationships in order to move up in their careers. Therefore, when they are faced with the additional stress of children and family in their mid-30s, many drop out. They are the victims of job burnout— too much stress for too long with too little psychological nurturing in return, resulting in a loss of enthusiasm and drive. You have a head start on preventing such burnout because you've gained skills in establishing goals, priorities, and action plans, and, therefore, in balancing your life.

Stress Skill #3: Know How to Predict Job Stress

Female managers report significantly higher stress levels than male managers. When it comes to job-related situations, a significantly greater percentage of female managers report experiencing discrimination and stereotyping, job and role overload, and role conflict.

Middle managers, both male and female, report significantly higher stress levels than senior managers. Also, higher stress levels are correlated with, and can be predicted by:

- ▶ Difficulty picturing oneself comfortably exercising power.
- ▶ Unclear, unrealistic, or conflicting job goals.
- ▶ Heavy job demands.
- ▶ A poor fit between one's job and one's personal needs for development.
- ▶ Lack of participation in decisions affecting one's area of responsibility.

Learn to recognize these stressors in your workplace and to eliminate them or cope effectively with them. Your goal is to anticipate life changes and plan for them well in advance. The more you learn about your psychological and physical reactions to stress, the more adept you can be at managing it. You'll be able to pace yourself when events start building up.

Strategy #2 _____

Recognize Your Response Options

Get to know the typical stress responses of women and of managers in general, and what causes people to burn out on the job. Stay a step ahead of burnout by choosing other options that will convert this energy into a power source for you.

Option Skill #1: Recognize Your Typical Responses

Stress responses include emotional and physical strain symptoms as well as reactive and solution-oriented coping behavior. Each person has a unique pattern of responses. Although men and women experience many of the same responses, women are more likely to experience sadness, nausea and diarrhea, back and neck pain, and skin problems. Men, on the other hand, are more likely to experience high blood pressure.

Managers who report higher stress levels also report more *emotional and physical strain symptoms,* such as anxiety, fear, frustration, back and neck pain, nausea, and diarrhea. They also report a higher frequency of the *coping behaviors* of taking prescription drugs, eating sweets and junk food, engaging in hostile actions, and sleeping longer than normal—all categorized as *reactive behaviors.* Surprisingly, they also seek medical help more often and engage in distracting pastimes more frequently—both categorized as *solution-oriented behaviors.* Seeking medical help may indicate that other solution-oriented behaviors have not been fruitful. It may mean the manager prefers dealing with symptoms, turning responsibility over to a doctor, rather than dealing with the root cause and then using solution-oriented actions appropriate to that root cause. Engaging in distracting pastimes may also deter one from finding a solution.

EXERCISE IS THE SOLUTION-ORIENTED COPING BEHAVIOR THAT HAS THE GREATEST CORRELATION WITH LOW STRESS LEVELS.

The first step in gaining control of stress is to identify those situations in which you are aware of pressure, anxiety, insomnia, or some other strain symptom that you experience when you're stressed. Self-Awareness Activity #1, will guide you.

Option Skill #2: Recognize Burnout Symptoms

People who allow stress to build up tend to experience typical symptoms of burnout. Estimate your burnout status by completing Self-Awareness Activity #2.

Self-Awareness Activity #2: Are You Burning Out?

Purpose: To estimate your job-stress level and burnout status.

Instructions: Rate how often the following stress symptoms are true for you as follows:

1 = never   2 = rarely   3 = sometimes   4 = often   5 = most of the time

Place the appropriate number in the space to the left of each statement. Add the numbers to get your burnout score.

_____ 1. I have trouble concentrating.

_____ 2. I think about quitting.

_____ 3. I'm withdrawn.

_____ 4. When I wake up, I don't want to go to work.

_____ 5. I call in sick to avoid work.

_____ 6. I feel trapped in my job.

_____ 7. I snap easily and get into conflicts with others.

_____ 8. I feel run down.

_____ 9. I'm bored.

_____ 10. I use alcohol, tobacco, prescription drugs, or other escapes to make me feel better.

_____ **Total score**

Follow-up: See the answer key on page 202 to interpret your score.

Option Skill #3: Seek Workable Alternatives

You have many options for thinking about events that disrupt your life—and for processing your emotional reactions to those situations. Ask yourself, *Has focusing on guilt, humiliation, or resentment over what I did in the past, or worrying about what might happen in the future, ever been helpful to me?* An honest evaluation usually reveals that the only positive things we gain from past disasters are lessons for future guidance. Otherwise, they're best forgotten. And the only positive approach to future events is to take action now to prevent them or cope with them and then let the worry go. Mere worry only drags us down now; it causes us to ruin our enjoyment of the present because of a future event that most probably won't happen. Ask, *What can I do now to learn from my past and create the future that I want?* Do it. Then enjoy living in each present moment.

Option Skill #4: Trade Support With Women Friends

A landmark UCLA study suggests that women respond to stress with a cascade of brain chemicals that causes us to make and maintain friendships with other women. The study by S.E. Taylor and others was reported in 2000 in *Psychological Review*.

When the hormone oxytocin is released as part of the stress responses in a woman, it buffers the fight-or-flight response and encourages her to tend children and gather with other women instead. When she actually engages in this tending or befriending, studies suggest that more oxytocin is released, which further counters stress and produces a calming effect. This calming response does not occur in men because testosterone (which men produce in high levels when they're under stress) seems to reduce the effects of oxytocin. Estrogen seems to enhance it.

Nearly 90 percent of the stress research has been done on males. Yet women's "tend and befriend" response is a major key to managing stress. It may explain why women consistently outlive men. Study after study has found that social ties reduce our risk of disease by lowering blood pressure, heart rate, and cholesterol. Several studies indicate that hanging out with friends helps us live longer and better—a more joyful life with fewer physical impairments. In fact, researchers have concluded that not having close friends or confidants is as detrimental to your health as smoking or carrying extra weight! Widows who have a close friend and confidante are more likely than others to survive the loss of a husband without any new physical impairments or permanent loss of vitality.

Schedule enough time to be with women friends. You need some unpressured space for the special kind of talk that women do when they're with other women. It's a very healing experience.

Strategy #3
Take Responsibility for Your Well-Being

You can anticipate the problems (both physical and psychological) that are likely to create disruption and pressure for you. Then you can develop take-charge skills for preventing, reducing, or postponing such problems so that you don't become *swamped*. For example you can take an assertive approach to health and life, exercise regularly, and use your sleep and dream time.

Take-Charge Skill #1: Take an Assertive Approach

Taking total responsibility for your well-being is based on taking an assertive approach to your health and your life. It means managing your own health issues, and using professionals as consultants. It means dealing with people in ways that give you more control over your life and help you avoid becoming the victim of others' manipulations, games, and whims.

The basis for an assertive approach to health is the belief that *I am the cause of my health*. Once we accept that fact, we don't surrender responsibility for our health to the medical system. Instead, we use this system when necessary on a client/customer basis. Only when we become accountable for our own health are we likely to avoid such high-risk behaviors as excessive eating, smoking, and drinking. Because these high-risk behaviors are forms of self-abuse, taking responsibility may involve a consciousness-raising program for building self-esteem and becoming more aware of and responsive to your body and its signals. After all, no one else can know your body and what it needs the way that you can. A basic key to maintaining a healthy, resilient body is good nutrition. To meet your nutritional needs:

▶ Eat a balanced diet—no crash diets—many fresh vegetables and fruits, whole grains, and some high-quality protein, with little or no red meat.

▶ Avoid foods that are refined, processed, enriched, or full of chemicals.

▶ Minimize the use of salt, sugar, coffee, alcohol, colas, and chocolate.

Take-Charge Skill #2: Exercise Regularly

This may be your most powerful preventative. Strangely enough, most people find they have *more* energy when they get some regular form of exercise. Most authorities recommend exercising at least one hour a day; a goal of 20 minutes should be your absolute minimum. Include bending and stretching exercises for flexibility, lifting and pulling exercises for muscle tone, and build up to some cardiovascular-stimulating exercises (aerobic exercise that will make you *huff and puff*, but not get out of breath) for respiratory and circulatory health and to increase your metabolic rate so that you burn off calories faster. Doing 20 minutes of aerobic exercise morning and evening keeps your metabolic rate higher around the clock.

Busy career women often find it difficult to take time for adequate exercise. Often the only way is to give it top priority—*If I don't get anything else done today, I'm going to get some exercise*. It also may help to keep reminding yourself, *If I take care of my body, it will take care of me*. Many experts say you can maintain cardiovascular fitness and weight level with specific aerobic exercises in as little as 20 minutes a day for three days a week. If you spend 20 minutes on three other days doing exercises for flexibility and muscle tone, you'll get all-around results and even a day off! Remember that each time you get a *thorough* workout, you reap many benefits, including:

▶ Using up calories at a faster rate for the next 12 hours.

▶ Slowing the aging process.

▶ Improving your figure.

▶ Keeping bones and muscles healthy and strong.

▶ Preventing stress buildup.

To make exercise an ongoing way of life, find some types you really enjoy, and some that provide social interaction. Above all, don't think of your exercise regimen as a crash program. Move into it one step at a time and make it a permanent way of life. The older you get, the more you need it.

Take-Charge Skill #3: Use Sleep and Dream Time

You can even use your sleep time to move yourself toward your goals. For years we've heard managers say, before making an important or difficult decision, *Let me sleep on it and get back to you tomorrow*—and for a very good reason. Research studies increasingly point to the importance of sleeping, and especially dreaming, to our mental health and ability to function well during waking hours. Your subconscious mind is very powerful, and you can draw on its resources almost effortlessly by using the dream state to help you solve problems, resolve conflicts, and come up with new ideas.

Problem-solve and create. A powerful combination is visualizing results and then *sleeping on it* to help solve problems or create new results. Here are the steps:

1. Just before going to sleep, use a deep relaxation and visualization process to picture a positive solution to your problem or a new situation you want to create.
2. Put your wish into a concise statement, a one-liner.
3. Visualize yourself waking up with the solution or ideas you want. Tell yourself you *will* have them in the morning.
4. Repeat your one-liner as you drift into sleep.

On awakening, lie still and think about your one-liner. Does a response to it come to mind? Do you remember a dream that may give you a clue or idea? Write down any ideas that come to mind. The idea may come to you later in the day. Relax and be open to it. Learn to notice little flashes and glimmers of ideas, pictures, or words.

Expand personal awareness. Once you become accustomed to using your sleep and dream time, consider taking it a step further into pure research. Jungian analysts believe that your dreams can provide you symbolic information about what's going on in your life at the subconscious level. You can expand your awareness and see relationships, events, and problems from a broader perspective by tapping into your dream world. A good dream book can be helpful. Try Betty Bethards' *The Dream Book: Symbols for Self-Understanding.*

Strategy #4

Command Your Inner Resources

Commanding your inner resources is the key to dealing with stress, as well as reaching your goals, becoming an effective leader, and generally creating the life you want for yourself. It is your ultimate source of personal power.

You can learn to turn off stressful thoughts so you can relax, and you can learn to fully experience stressful emotions so they can lift to expansive emotions. When you're in a position of responsibility that calls for risk-taking and decision-making, you may occasionally be hit with an overload of disruption and the resulting pressure, no matter how well you anticipate and prevent problems. The key to managing this stress and the *churning hormones* of the fight-or-flight response is to become skilled at relaxation, visualization, and letting go. A quick technique for staying centered, grounded, and balanced on the job is sometimes essential to regaining your perspective of the situation so that you can handle it effectively. Regular periods of relaxation are also essential for maintaining a level of calmness, serenity, and stability that eliminates the need to overdraw your vital-energy account.

Inner Skill #1: Master Relaxation Processes

The goal of relaxation processes is to cut through tension and mind chatter to reach a deeply relaxed state. As with all the techniques and processes for commanding your inner resources, these may take some time to master in the beginning. With practice, however, you'll be able to use your skills even in the midst of stressful situations, and you'll be able to go into deeper states of relaxation more quickly.

Achieve the alpha-state advantage. The ultimate goal is to be able to move into a state of relaxation so deep that you would be producing alpha brain waves if you were undergoing an EEG. Although biofeedback mechanisms are available for helping you develop this ability quickly, you can learn well enough without them. Research indicates that when you are in such a relaxed state, you can communicate more effectively with your subconscious. You can give it new messages, even messages that override key decisions about life you made long ago—viewpoints that no longer serve you. You can enlist the aid of your subconscious in reaching your goals and solving problems—so that your verbal and nonverbal actions are well integrated and your entire being is moving toward achieving what you decide you want in life.

You get double payoffs for learning to relax deeply. The relaxation alone is an immediate antidote to stress. It enhances your sense of well-being, your health, and potentially, your longevity. In addition, when you combine it with visualization—that is, mental imagery—it helps you create the life you want. (More about that later.)

Set the stage. Four conditions are necessary for mastering the relaxation processes provided here:

1. A quiet, calm place as free from distraction as possible.
2. A comfortable body position.
3. A mental focusing device to help you shut off your mind chatter (internal dialogue) and go deep within yourself. (See Skill Builder #2 for more on focusing devices.)
4. A passive attitude that lets you merely observe distracting thoughts, let them go, and bring your mind back gently to your focusing device.

Keep in mind that you can't *make* relaxation occur; you can only *let* it occur.

Once you've found a quiet place, experiment with comfortable positions. (A favorite of many is sitting in a comfortable, yet firm, chair with back perfectly straight, legs and arms uncrossed, feet flat on the floor, and arms resting on the thighs.) Then experiment with the processes included in Skill Builder #2. Discover the ones that are most relaxing for you.

Be in the present moment. Learning to focus on the present moment and to totally be in the here and now is a powerful way to aid the relaxation process and to turn off mind chatter. Chatter is often associated with guilt, resentment, and worry. Remember, when you're feeling guilty or resentful, you're really living in the past. When you're worrying, you're living in the future. Action in the here and now is the only way to influence events. The key is to focus on the present moment and determine what, if anything, you need to *do*. Skill Builder #1 is designed to bring you into the present moment by helping you focus on the sensations your body is experiencing at a particular time. Practice it frequently when you're *not* under stress, and you'll soon be able to use it quickly, even in stressful situations.

Inner Skill #2: Visualize the Results You Want

Once you're in a deeply relaxed state, you can talk to your subconscious and tell it what you want. Your subconscious is amazingly competent at moving you toward the results you request—if you'll only relax and let it do its work. It tunes in better to pictures and feelings, however, than to words. That's why visualizing results and getting in touch with the feelings you want to experience along with those results is so powerful.

How to visualize. What if you have difficulty "making pictures" when you close your eyes? Don't worry. Everyone differs to some extent in the way they visualize. If you see no picture at all, you're still thinking of it in your "mind's eye," and that's adequate. It may help you to think of what it might be like if you *could* see the picture you're thinking about. Think in terms of *allowing* pictures rather than *making* them.

When to visualize. When should you practice your visualization skills? Shortly before going to sleep each night is a time preferred by many people because it's a quiet time when they're ready to relax fully. To make the most of your personal power, practice deep relaxation and visualization at some time every day so that it becomes a deeply ingrained habit—a way of life that you can put to use almost automatically. If you do this, you'll soon discover that you can use these skills—quickly, with your eyes wide open and with no one the wiser—any time you're dealing with potentially stressful situations. You'll be able to stay centered or to regain your composure quickly, even if you're taken by surprise.

The processes described in Skill Builder #3 are designed to enlist the aid of your subconscious in handling specific types of situations. You can adapt them to any kind of situation; just remember that important final step: letting go.

Inner Skill #3: Learn to Let Go

Have you ever observed someone sabotaging herself because she was trying too hard? You probably thought, *Why doesn't she relax a little?* Can you think of a time when you probably sabotaged yourself by trying too hard or caring too much? Why do people do this? Usually it happens because they're too strongly attached to having the situation turn out just the way they want. They cling—perhaps desperately—to the idea or picture of certain end results. Therefore, they create a tension-producing need to achieve those results, often accompanied by fear that they won't.

Think preferences, not needs. Think of some situations in which you achieved the results you wanted—times when you moved relatively effortlessly toward your goal. Think of top athletes who have done that. Top achievement is usually a result of *relaxed concentration.* You fully intend to achieve certain results, and your mind and body are focused on the process of doing so. You *desire* and *prefer* those results, but you don't desperately *need* them, and you're not focused on fear connected with failure to achieve the results.

Prevent self-sabotage. You prevent the self-sabotage caused by tension-producing needs when you add a letting-go step to the visualization process you use for goal-setting.

Skill Builder #4 offers several techniques for this final step of the personal power process. Remember, when you let go of your goal, you retain a clear picture of having it, but you release the needs and fears related to not having it. This process frees you to work toward your goal in a relaxed, confident way, which in turn makes it easier to gain the cooperation and support of others. But you must truly become comfortable with the idea of *not* achieving your goal. If letting go is accompanied by sadness, regret, or unwillingness, you need to work on your fear of failure.

Allow abundance. You can also adopt a viewpoint that there is abundance in the world. When you let go of your goal pictures, you *put them out into the universe.* The view that there is abundance in the universe implies that everything that happens eventually works toward your benefit. Therefore, if you give a goal situation your best shot, you're confident of achieving it. If it doesn't turn out the way you pictured, then your deep inner self had the wisdom to know that those results were not best for you at this time. That's the time to ask, *What lesson can I learn from this situation? What's my next goal?*

Skill Builders

Skill Builder #1: Get in the Here and Now
Purpose: To learn to stay in the present moment.

Variation 1: Focusing on the Five Senses
Step 1: Breathing. Take a few deep breaths.

Step 2: Seeing. Become internally aware of what you see around you. Look at it in detail as if you've never seen it before. Pretend you just arrived from another planet. Notice colors, patterns, textures.

Step 3: Hearing. If the situation permits, close your eyes. What do you hear? Notice every little sound, identify it, describe it mentally.

Step 4: Touching. Now focus on your sense of touch—the feel of your clothes against your skin, the air on your skin, the floor under your feet, the chair you are sitting on (if you are sitting). Describe the sensations to yourself.

Step 5: Smelling and tasting. If there are noticeable odors around you or tastes in your mouth, become aware of them; identify and describe them.

Did you notice that your focus moved away from your mind and its internal chatter about the past or future and into your body and what it was sensing in the present moment? Here's an alternate technique that may work for you.

Variation 2: Progressive Muscle Relaxation
In this process, you alternately tense and then relax all the muscle groups in your body, beginning with the toes and moving upward. Tense up the toes of your right foot, hold it, then quickly release them all at once. Notice the resulting feeling of relaxation in those muscles. Continue up your right leg, tensing and relaxing the calf muscles and the thigh muscles. Then do the left leg. Next, progress up through the various muscle groups

in the trunk of your body, then the right and left arms, and finally the neck and head. Pay special attention to the muscles of the jawline and between the eyes (both are places where we tend to retain tension).

Skill Builder #2: Deep Relaxation

Purpose: To experiment with various methods of deep relaxation.

Deep relaxation begins with deep breathing. The goal is to slow down your breathing pattern. So start with one of the breathing processes and then move into one of the focusing devices. If you have trouble moving out of a focus on mind chatter and into a passive attitude, do a process for getting in the here and now.

Deep breathing—Variation 1. Breathe in through your nostrils, counting slowly as you do so; hold the breath, starting your counting over again; breathe out through your mouth, lips slightly parted, again counting. The actual process: breathe in 1-2-3-4-5; hold it 1-2-3-4-5; breathe out 1-2-3-4-5. Each time you repeat the process, extend the time you take to breathe in, hold it, and breathe out, counting to 6, then to 7, and so on. See how long you can extend it.

Deep breathing—Variation 2. Visualize yourself stepping onto the top stair of an escalator. As you breathe slowly in and out, watch yourself descending on the escalator into a deeper and deeper state of relaxation and count: 10-9-8-7-6-5-4-3-2-1.

Deep breathing—Variation 3. Close your eyes, take a deep breath, and enjoy the pleasure of feeling yourself breathe. As you breathe in, say quietly to yourself, *I am*. As you breathe out, say to yourself, *relaxed*. Or say, *I am...calm and serene* or *I am...one*.

Deep breathing—Variation 4. Focus all your attention at the tip of your nostrils. Quietly *watch* in your mind's eye the breath flowing in and out past the tip of the nostril. Count from 1 through 10 each time you breathe in and each time you breathe out. Continue counting from 1 through 10 each time you breathe in and out until you're completely relaxed.

Focusing device 1—Candle flame. Place a lighted candle about a foot in front of you and focus all your attention on the flame. As thoughts float by, notice them, let them go, and gently bring your attention back to the flame. This form of relaxed concentration can help you notice how your thoughts and senses keep grabbing at your awareness. The goal is to free your awareness from its identification with thoughts. We cling to our senses and thoughts because we're so attached to them. While focusing on the candle flame, you start becoming aware of that clinging and attachment, and the process of letting go.

Focusing device 2—Centering. Focus all your consciousness into the center of your head. Visualize a point of light about a foot in front of your eyes. Now focus all your attention on the point of light.

Focusing device 3—Grounding. Visualize the center of the Earth as a very dense place of rock or metal. Focus all your attention on the center of the Earth, and picture a huge iron bar there. Next, bring your attention to your spinal cord. Visualize a large cable or cord running from the base of your spine all the way to the center of the Earth. Picture a big hook on the other end of the cord; now hook it in the bar at the center of the Earth. Feel a slight pull toward the center of the Earth and a slight heaviness of the body.

Focusing device 4—Your peaceful place. Think of a place where you usually feel especially serene, relaxed, and happy, such as the beach, the forest, a meadow, or the lake. Picture yourself there. Reexperience in your mind's eye all the sights, sounds, smells, and tastes you experience there. Focus on your sense of touch too—the sun, water, and air on your skin; the sand, earth, or grass under your feet. Bring in as much vivid detail as you can. Get in touch with the positive feelings you experience there—your sense of well-being, confidence, serenity.

Skill Builder #3: Visualize End Results

Purpose: To practice envisioning what your want to create in your life.

Step 1: Focus on the here and now, and move into a deeply relaxed state by using any combination of processes from Skill Builder #2.

Step 2: Select the visualization that applies to your situation from the ones listed here (or adapt one of them to fit your situation).

Step 3: Use one of the letting-go processes from Skill Builder #4.

Basic Visualization

Create a clear, concise, consistent picture. In your mind's eye, develop a clear, concise picture of the desired outcome you want—the end result, the state of being, especially the feeling tone within you and flowing between you and others, in this state of having what you want. Don't get into how the result will come about, but stay focused on the end result you want.

Charge it with passion. Allow your passion, your strong desire, to charge that picture with energy.

Become the essence of that picture. What one word best describes the picture for you? Is it *success*, *abundance*, *joy*, *love*, *peace*, *elegance*, *competence*, or *connectedness*? Become that quality as you focus on your mind's-eye picture.

Persist until it materializes. Bring up the picture as often as possible, each time seeing the same clear picture (not fuzzy, vague, or changing), each time charging it with passion and desire, and each time freely letting it go. The more attention and focus you give it, the greater the likelihood of success.

Visualization variation 1—Problem-resolution. Relax deeply. Get in touch with your problem situation. If thinking of it or picturing it causes you to feel anxious, focus again on a relaxation technique. Repeat until you're able to picture your problem situation without feeling anxious.

What do you want the end results of this situation to be? How do you want it to be resolved? Picture that happening—in vivid detail, bringing all your senses into play: colors, patterns, textures you see; sounds you hear; things you touch, smell, and taste. Picture your interactions with the other person(s) involved, focusing on your specific feelings and those flowing between you and others; for example, understanding, acceptance, warmth, good will. Focus on the pictures and feelings until you feel quite comfortable and secure with them. Now use a letting-go technique to release them.

Visualization variation 2—Goal-achievement. Follow the process described in variation 1, but instead of focusing on a problem situation, focus on a goal you want to achieve. Picture yourself actually achieving the goal. Include all the people involved in helping you reach the goal; focus on the positive feelings flowing between you and them. Now let go.

Visualization variation 3—Evaluating goals. You can carry the process used in variation 2 one step further to help you evaluate possible goals. (For example, if you're not sure whether getting a master's degree should be merely one alternate activity for achieving a career goal or a goal in itself, picture yourself having achieved the career goal without the master's degree.) Picture all the consequences of having achieved the goal. How do you feel about each? Is anything missing? What? Would a different goal have led to better results?

Visualization variation 4—Handling stage fright. Use this process to overcome the jitters that accompany any type of presentation you must make before a group. For best results, practice the visualization several times before your presentation. Just before going to sleep the night before the presentation is an especially good time to visualize positive results. Follow the process described in variation 1, but instead of picturing a problem situation, picture yourself making a successful presentation. See yourself focusing on the major thrust of your message and getting it across in a clear, dynamic, persuasive way. See your audience understanding and accepting it. Get in touch with your positive feelings and theirs. Now let go.

Skill Builder #4: Let Go of End Results

Purpose: To experiment with processes for not clinging to the results you want; to put your purpose out into the universe, trusting that all will work to your benefit.

Step 1: Move into a state of deep relaxation (Skill Builder #2).

Step 2: Visualize the end results you want (Skill Builder #3).

Step 3: Let go of your pictures of end results by one of the following methods (or devise your own method for putting your goals out into the universe).

Variation 1—Hot-air balloon. Picture a beautifully colored hot-air balloon with a lovely passenger basket. It's tied to the ground with velvet ropes. Put the picture of your end results into the basket—and the feelings related to the picture. Untie the ropes and watch the balloon float away up into the sky and away toward the horizon. As it floats out of sight, repeat to yourself, *Let go, let go.*

Variation 2—Space capsule. Follow the process described in variation 1, substituting a sleek space capsule for the hot-air balloon. Picture all the latest technology and equipment for controlling the capsule. Put your end results inside the capsule, lock it, and watch it blast off and disappear into space.

Variation 3—Bottle at sea. Follow the process described in variation 1, substituting a large glass bottle for the hot-air balloon. Put your end results inside it, place the cork in the bottle top, and throw the bottle into the ocean. Watch the tide carry it out to sea, and see it disappear toward the horizon.

Answer Key

Self-Awareness Activity #2: Are You Burning Out?

A score of 10 to 20 means you're doing all right;

21 to 30, think about taking some preventive action;

31 to 40, you're a prime burnout candidate;

over 40, you're burning out.

8

Process Powerful Emotions

*You and only you have control of your life. This is the
most powerful thing you can have.*
—Carol Bartz, CEO, Autodesk, Inc.

One of the most consistent gender stereotypes is that women are so emotional that they can't make rational decisions or handle crises and top-level responsibilities. Obviously, that's also one of the most damaging beliefs for career women to cope with. It's true that you're probably more in touch with your emotions than your male peers. This can be a curse or a blessing depending on how you process and channel that emotional energy. We'll discuss how to use this power source. First, answer the following questions about your current beliefs regarding emotions. Then, meet Colleen Barrett of Southwest Airlines, who uses emotions to enhance her leadership ability.

How should women deal with powerful emotions?

1. What's the best way to manage your feelings? To get a grip and get them under control? To avoid them? Or to fully experience the feelings that come up?

2. Are thinking and feeling two totally separate processes? Or are they linked?

3. Is it unhealthy to feel anger or fear and not act on those feelings?

4. When someone criticizes you, should you let them know at once that you won't let them get away with demeaning you or pushing you around?

To channel your emotional power in the direction you want, you must recognize women's typical emotional patterns and your own emotional profile. You must allow yourself to fully feel your feelings, process and channel stressful feelings, and take conscious control of your actions by assessing your options and choosing wisely.

Strategy #1
Recognize Women's Emotional Patterns

Women and men tend to experience significantly different emotional patterns, and the causes of these differences are probably both innate and cultural. Studies indicate

Colleen Barrett, COO, Southwest Airlines

Managing stress with love—especially tender, loving care of employees, customers, and stockholders. That's a major contribution of Colleen Barrett, President and COO of Southwest Airlines. She leverages the "L-word" to boost morale throughout the corporate culture of Southwest Airlines. LUV is the New York Stock Exchange symbol for Southwest Airlines, and headquarters are at Love Field in Dallas. Colleen says, "We often use LUV when we sign correspondence to each other and to the outside world." She describes the Southwest culture as fun, spirited, zezty, hardworking, and willed with love.

When the airline started in 1978, Colleen was the founder's secretary. She has always been largely responsible for the customer service values that drive Southwest—then and now. She has worked continually to spread the "love" attitude throughout the workforce. By 2003, Southwest was the fourth-largest airline carrier in the United States, with revenues of $5.5 billion.

While the 9/11 crisis decimated larger airlines, Southwest weathered the storm quite well. As soon as planes were allowed to fly again, Southwest concentrated on getting crews to their airplanes and flying planes on normal schedules, knowing full well there might be no passengers on those airplanes. Management gave top priority to showing employees and passengers that Southwest was ready when they were. The goal was to show as much stability as possible.

Colleen believes that front-line supervisors are the key to the future of any firm, so leadership training is especially important for them. She promotes leadership in several ways: 1) bringing in good leaders to talk to managers and directors, 2) scheduling quarterly meetings with briefing by senior management, 3) holding leadership classes that train front-line, first-time supervisors, and 4) offering annual leadership refresher classes. She also holds annual sessions in each region where employees can rap with top management, getting answers to any questions they have. Management uses every opportunity—such as roundtable discussions and brown-bag meetings—to talk about the importance of leadership and the principles they want to see in practice at Southwest. And they hold people accountable for sticking to those leadership principles.

Colleen has learned a great deal about leadership by watching people she admires. She notices how they motivate others, how they excite people, how they handle touchy situations. In turn, she will mentor anyone who seems to have a passion for their work and a desire to learn.

When asked what advice she would give, she talked about several principles:

- Know what you want, and want it with a passion.
- Realize that you have to make choices in life, so really think about your priorities.
- Be true to yourself, and go with your gut feelings.
- Never be afraid to take the initiative.
- Work hard—to show people you're willing to bear more than your fair share.

that women's brains show some differences. For example, women have a stronger link between the right-brain, feeling-intuitive side and the left-brain, rational-linear side. Women, therefore, are better at verbalizing (left-brain activity) what they're feeling (right-brain activity). Cultural expectations, assumptions, and stereotypes about differences between men's and women's emotional experiences and expressions also have a strong impact on how we feel and act.

Awareness Skill #1: Recognize Cultural Stereotypes

You've heard the stereotypes about women and their emotions:

▸ Women are too emotional to be leaders. They go to pieces in a crisis (overlooking the fact that nearly all mothers get their children through the numerous crises growing up entails without *going to pieces*).

▸ You can't afford to put someone in top management who might burst into tears in a crunch.

▸ Women are just too flighty to handle a high-level leadership role.

▸ Women don't roll with the punches like men do.

▸ A man can keep problems in perspective better than a woman.

According to research done by Ed Diener, Professor of Psychology at the Univeristy of Illinois, women do report being in positive moods and in negative moods about twice as often as men, which would indicate that women experience feelings more intensely. However, it does not follow that women are helpless victims of their feelings or must somehow act out all their feelings.

Awareness Skill #2: Consider How Boys and Girls Are Raised

The fact is that boys and girls normally get quite different payoffs and punishments for the same behavior. A key factor that has led to these stereotypes is the different payoffs our culture tends to give to little girls and boys when they express emotions. Girls usually get payoffs of sympathy or approval when they cry, show fear, express sadness or other tender feelings, show sympathy for others, and nurture others. Boys frequently get disapproval or even punishment for such behavior.

In our culture, little boys are trained to be *real men* from an early age through such messages as *Big boys don't cry, big boys are brave and strong,* or *Keep a stiff upper lip.* The result is that men often repress and deny most of their emotions and eventually become numb to them. But most boys usually receive approval, admiration, or at least acceptance when they express dominance and anger in actions ranging from assertion to aggression. Such *masculine* expressions of emotion by girls, however, usually meet with disapproval or rejection.

Awareness Skill #3: Observe Male-Female Emotional Patterns

These different socialization patterns set the stage for adult behavior. As they've grown up, most women have stayed in touch with their feelings and have developed the ability to express their emotions. However, they tend to be significantly less assertive than men. In contrast, most men have a healthy dose of assertiveness and some have an unhealthy dose of aggression. But most men in general are significantly less aware of their feelings. They're therefore less able to verbalize them and act on them.

In the male-dominated business world, therefore, it is generally acceptable to express anger or aggression within certain limits. However, a display of tears or fear signals that you can't handle the game; that is, you can't handle real responsibility on the line where key decisions are made and where the real power is wielded. It's especially important to manage fear, because some political game players can sniff out the nonverbal signs of fear like bloodhounds, and they'll quickly move in for the kill if it suits their purposes.

Openness to feelings is essential to openness to intuitive information. Therefore, women are known to be more emotional and more intuitive than men, on average. Both of these states are normally governed by the right brain, while rational thought and action is governed by the left brain. However, language (verbal ability) is a rational, left-brain activity in which women excel. Women are obviously not lacking in left-brain abilities, but because their traditional roles center on nurturing others, they have focused almost exclusively on the language area, neglecting the strategic, tactical, mechanical, and mathematical areas.

In recent decades, careers using both right-brain and left-brain abilities have opened up to women. Many women have acquired the business and professional skills to move into these fields—and many have excelled in them.

Awareness Skill #4: Use Your Emotional Intelligence

Emotionally intelligent women on average appear to experience deeper, richer, and more expressive emotional lives, according to Daniel Goleman, author of *Emotional Intelligence.* The traits of playfulness, sensuality, and spontaneity correlate with higher intuitive ability. In addition, it's significantly easier to develop rational abilities and intellectual intelligence than to develop emotional intelligence and intuition. Women's advantage in these areas is impressive, but it has been largely ignored, belittled, and neglected. To live up to your potential, honor and respect all your abilities—especially your emotional intelligence. Learn to express it appropriately in business and professional settings. Help others to understand and respect this type of intelligence.

Strategy #2

Feel Your Feelings

Most male managers control their feelings by suppressing them and pretending they don't exist. This practice creates a number of negative side-effects.

Suppressed feelings don't go away. They tend to build up inside until they reach the *explosive stage.* We tend to forget the incident that triggered the feeling and the fact that we suppressed the feeling. Therefore, our outbursts of anger, self-pity, fear, and so forth, come as a surprise to us and are out of our control.

Suppressed feelings can cause illness. Feelings that simmer and fester within us continue to create stress long after the stressful situation has passed. We then become vulnerable to stress-related illnesses, especially ulcers, high blood pressure, migraine headaches, allergies, asthma, and heart disease.

Suppressed feelings block personal growth. If you deny your feelings as a way of coping with life, you'll become more and more out of touch with yourself—how you really feel about things, the way you really are, the true effects of people and events on your life. Such denial will inhibit your personal growth and development as a creative, autonomous person. It will numb you so you can't feel your heart's desire. As a result, you'll find it more and more difficult to be clear about your values and goals, and to evaluate situations and opportunities in light of those goals. This leads to such problems as tunnel vision, workaholism, and burnout.

As a woman, you should hold onto your gender advantage when it comes to feeling your feelings. The fact that you're in touch with your emotions is a major advantage. For one thing, in order to process an emotion, you must be aware of it and be able to feel it. For another, in order to empathize with another person's emotional state, you must be able to feel what they're feeling. People who repress and deny their feelings over the years become numb and have difficulty feeling anything, including what others are feeling.

Emotional savvy gives you a leading edge in the workplace. Business cultures traditionally haven't allowed much space to acknowledge emotions. Most business cultures don't embrace the belief that experiencing and expressing emotions can be beneficial. Nor do they have the tools or methods to access and acknowledge emotional expression. Yet emotions are always with us, always in play. So the business leader who knows how to help individuals and teams channel their emotional power has an obvious edge. The first step in gaining emotional savvy is to become aware of the key stressors in your life, which you've done. The next step is to become aware of the feelings those stressors trigger within you. Self-Awareness Activity #1 will get you started.

Self-Awareness Activity #1: What Feelings Do Your Stressors Trigger?

Purpose: To raise your awareness of the connection between certain stressors and related feelings—so you can process them effectively.

Step 1: Pick the most intense stressor you identified in Self-Awareness Activity #1 in Chapter 7.

Step 2: What feeling(s) do you experience when you focus on that stressor? What feeling(s) have you felt when the stressor was especially active?

Step 3: Process that feeling, using the strategy that follows.

Strategy #3 ───────────────
Process and Channel Stressful Feelings

Once you become aware of stressful feelings, you're in a position to process them, so you can use that emotional energy to achieve what you want to create in your life. You may get some ideas for identifying or labeling your feelings by studying Snapshot #2. Your goals are:

▸ To process contracting, low-energy, stressful feelings before they settle in and build into a mood.

- ▶ If a mood does gain hold, to process the feelings it contains.
- ▶ To allow yourself to spend as much time as possible in the self-empowering, high-energy *expansive* feelings.

Emotional Skill #1: Understand Two Emotional Types

A powerful concept that can help you manage your emotions is the classification of emotions generally into two basic types:

1. The stressful, contracting emotions that are considered fear-based.
2. The self-empowering, expansive emotions that are considered love-based.

Snapshot #1 is a graphic picture of how we look and feel when we're experiencing each of these two emotional categories.

Snapshot #1: Contracting Mood and Expansive Feeling

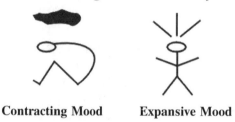

Contracting Mood   **Expansive Mood**

See Snapshot #2 on page 209 for a verbal picture of typical emotions in each category, working from the center of the table, where less intense emotions in each category are listed, to the top and bottom edges of the table, where the more intense root emotions are listed.

Identify Your Contracting, Stressful Feelings

Think about the feelings you associate with the stress in your life. Which emotions come to mind? Many people mention anger, embarrassment, resentment, and frustration—all those feelings listed as contracting emotions in Snapshot #2. When you experience these stressful emotions, do they make you open up and reach out to people? Or do they cause you to focus within yourself on stressful thoughts that lead to more stressful thoughts, and so on? Do these feelings result in your clamming up, closing up, and even withdrawing? Because stressful feelings tend to lead to some type of withdrawal for most people, we'll call them *contracting* emotions. These are low-energy states that act as energy drains and cause other people to avoid you.

Snapshot #2 shows the milder forms of contracting emotions at the top of each column, moving toward generally more intense feelings at the bottom. Key bottom-line contracting emotions are highlighted at the bottom of each column. The underlying, bottom-line emotion is fear, the realm of your negative ego. But how can anger or rage be an expression of fear? You'll address such questions later as you bring root fears out of the shadows. For now, consider the research finding that anger and, in fact, all the contracting emotions involve some type of fear—fear of losing something you value or fear of not getting something you want.

Snapshot #2: Map of Emotions

	compassion	passion	awe, wonder	GOODWILL, LOVE
Expansive Emotions and Moods	empathy	excitement	beauty	ecstasy
	appreciation	enthusiasm	gratitude	joy
	acceptance	eagerness	respect, esteem	happiness
	tolerance	desire	admiration	commitment
	infatuation	determination	imagination	devotion
	admiration	perseverance	curiosity	affection
	relief	optimism	amusement	peace
	satisfaction	openness	interest	certainty
	thoughtfulness	honesty	enjoyment	hope
	surprise	relief	solitude	calmness
	self-acceptance	self-confidence	self-awareness	self-love
Contracting Emotions and Moods	annoyance	ego-pride	envy	boredom
	impatience	judgment	jealousy	distraction
	blame	dislike	hatred	mischievousness
	resentment	pity	hurt	confusion
	frustration	disgust	withdrawal	caution
	hostility	contempt	shock	vulnerability
	stubbornness	revulsion	loss	embarrassment
	anger	condemnation	despair	shyness
	rage, fury	arrogance	humiliation	self-pity
	powerlessness	defensiveness	paranoia	suffering
	bitterness	doubt	hopelessness	remorse
	regret	worry	apathy	victim
	sadness	anxiety	victim	dread
	guilt	resignation	martyr	desperation
	shame	exhaustion	rejection	hysteria
		depression	**loneliness**	terror
				FEAR

When you don't process contracting emotions, they build up within your mind and body. If you hide them away securely enough, they'll stay hidden until they express themselves as illness. If you're lucky, they'll first express themselves as an outburst or a dark mood (which may last for days, weeks, or even years). In your dark mood, you'll walk around with a dark cloud hovering over you and all around you. Your cloud may take the form of self-pity, guilt, blame, resentment, anxiety, or some other dominant stressful emotion. How can this be lucky? Well, if you become aware of your mood, you have the choice of getting at the root emotions and processing them before illness sets in.

Identify Your Expansive Emotions

What happens when you process and release the contracting emotions and moods? You free yourself to move into one or more of the *expansive emotions*. Why do we call them expansive emotions? Well, think about what happens when you feel curiosity, excitement, admiration, empathy, love, happiness, and joy—any of the expansive emotions identified in Snapshot #2. For all of us, these emotions are an *up*, a *high*, and they lead to reaching out to others, as well as sharing and interacting with others. They're high-energy states that act as energy boosts and, therefore, attract people to you.

Expansive emotions feel light and airy, causing you to reach up and out toward life and toward other people. You experience a lot of space within the expansive emotions; therefore, you experience more possibilities. You're more willing to take chances—to do something new and challenging because you're focusing on the bright side of people and situations.

In Snapshot #2, the expansive emotions at the bottom of each column represent the beginning stages of personal expansion, and they usually begin with some type of self-love. They move upward toward the more intensely expansive feelings, with the key expansive emotions highlighted at the top of each column. The root emotion here is goodwill and love—the realm of your higher self.

Overcome the emotional-female stereotypes. A major advantage of processing your contracting emotions is that you can avoid denying the emotion and getting stuck in negative moods. Another power is that you can process your emotions internally. You don't need to share the process, though it usually helps to share your feelings with a trusted confidante. Processing is very active, but you can do it within. This means you can build and maintain a professional image and make better business decisions. Keep in mind these two tips:

1. Process contracting emotions *before* you make a business decision or take action.

2. Make decisions and take action when you're experiencing expansive emotions.

Build on women's intuition. Keep in mind that intuitive insights virtually always have a feeling component. To open up to your intuition, open up to your feelings. This gives you added power in making decisions that are based on both informed thinking and inspired intuition.

But how do you know if a thought-feeling is an intuition coming from your higher self or a trick played by your negative ego? The only way to know for sure is to watch the results. By then it's too late to change that particular decision, but it's not too late to learn about your thinking-feeling process. Intuitive people say they can tell the difference based primarily on whether they're feeling an expansive or contracting emotion when they get the intuitive hit. They trust the expansive side, but they realize also that the human mind is extremely complex and the negative ego can trick us into false expansiveness. Getting in touch with your intuition is based on knowing yourself better and better—getting in touch with the range and depth of your feelings, your inner self, and your higher awareness.

Emotional Skill #2: Process Your Stressful Emotions

Dealing with stressful, painful emotions takes courage. But the investment pays off in mental health and powerful personal growth. Gregg Braden, author of *Awakening to Zero Point*, says it well: "You always have the ability to see beyond the pain, into what the pain is saying to you. Your life is a gift through which you may come to see yourself from many viewpoints, and know yourself as all possibilities."

Step 1: Identify the emotion or mood. Become aware of the mood or emotion you're experiencing. Label the feeling as specifically as possible. Be sure you use a word that indicates something you *feel* and not merely a rational thought or character trait. For example, use *self-confident* or *certain* rather than *ready to make a move* or *decisive*.

Step 2: Locate the emotion in your body. If it's an emotion, locate it in your body by identifying where you feel some tension, some tightness, some pain, some upset, something different, something that doesn't feel normal.

Step 3: Get at root emotions. Ask, *Why do I feel...(anger, sadness, etc.). So what? What difference does that make? Why do I care about that? So what will happen if....* Keep asking these types of questions until you feel a shift, a sense that you've reached the bottom line—the root emotion that's stressful for you. (Learn more about this step in Emotional Skill #3.)

Step 4: Fully experience all emotions that come up. Allow the feeling to be there in your body; fully experience it being there. Be willing to feel the emotion with intensity. Be in the present moment with it—paying attention—with intent to fully feel it, fully believing that you can move on out of the emotion. The crucial attitude is your willingness to feel the feeling, to let it get more intense if it needs to, and to move deeper into another emotion (a root emotion)—or to get less intense. Be willing for it to change locations in your body or to move anywhere on the emotional map that it wants to go. In order to get at root emotions and release them, you may need to use some self-starter Skill Builders, such as Skill Builder #1 and Skill Builder #2.

Step 5: Release the emotion. If you're willing to feel the emotion and any related emotions that want to surface, you will eventually be able to release the feeling or allow it to be lifted. Let it go. Allow it to be lifted.

You may have trouble letting go of certain emotions. Some people say that in those sticky cases, it helps if they picture themselves surrendering to the flow of the universe and asking the universe to lift the emotion. Others say they call on their inner self to lift the emotion. Still others call on a higher power. Look to your belief system and find the greater power that can help you. The important aspect is to realize that you don't have to lift the emotion all by yourself. All you have to do is be *willing* for it to be lifted.

Step 6: Review your options. You have many options about how to view a situation or to think about it. You also have many options about what actions to take when you experience an emotional response to a situation.

Review options for viewing a situation. A dozen people will probably view a single situation in a dozen somewhat different ways. This means you have many options about how to view any particular situation.

For example: A friend betrays a confidence. What options do you have for perceiving this event? What ways of thinking about it? What will you say to yourself? Here are a few options you can try to see what effect they have:

▸ *She's not a true friend, and she doesn't really care about me, and I'm devastated.*

▸ *She was feeling needy when she did that.*

▶ *She meant well.*
▶ *I can handle this.*
▶ *This won't really matter to me in the long run.*

Thinking triggers emotions. Think about a recent situation that triggered an upsetting emotion for you. What other ways could you have chosen to perceive the situation? What emotions might have come up in each of these ways? As you practice different ways of thinking about an event, you'll notice that very different types of thinking patterns lead to very different emotions. By choosing a specific thinking pattern, you can choose a different emotional response.

Review options for acting on emotions. You also have many options about what to do in response to a situation and in response to your emotions. In the situation just described, what are some actions you could have taken? What might be the outcome of each type of action? More about options later, including acting-out options.

Emotional Skill #3: Bring Root Fears Out of the Shadows

Some emotions play around near the surface of your consciousness, while others are rooted much deeper in your being—even at levels below consciousness. Processing an emotion, such as anger, can help you to become aware of deeper-level emotions. Get in touch with root fears. Bring them out of the shadowy subconscious into the light of conscious awareness. Examine them and fully experience them. Then you are more likely to be able to release them. When you move into and through all the emotions brought up by an event and then release them, you move into a lighter space—a space rooted in love and goodwill. The process can begin by asking yourself such questions as:

▶ *Why am I angry?*
▶ *What am I afraid of?*
▶ *What do I fear will happen?*

When you get some answers, you then may need to ask:

▶ *What difference will that make?*
▶ *Why do I care about that?*
▶ *So, what would happen then?*

The answer may be something like:

▶ *I won't get enough attention.*
▶ *I won't have any power.*
▶ *People will think....*

As Snapshot #3 indicates, underneath your anger, sadness, or anxiety, you'll probably uncover a root fear that says one or more of the following:

▶ *I don't really deserve....*
▶ *They'll think I'm not good enough.*
▶ *They'll find out I'm not really good enough.*
▶ *I'm not lovable or likable enough.*
▶ *I'm not capable enough.*

As you continue the process of asking why, you may come to the next root fear:

▶ *I'll be rejected, abandoned, separated, and alone.*

This is the fear that you will be without those human connections so crucial to your well-being. It's the bottom-line fear. You may then say to yourself, *Okay, so I don't want to feel rejected and lonely. Then why don't I reach out to others and connect?* This question may bring you to another root fear: the fear of living fully, of surrendering to the flow of life, of trusting yourself and the universe. It's rooted in the bottom-line fear that if you trust, reach out, live fully, you'll be rejected—either now or later when you become deeply attached—and you'll be abandoned.

The way these root fears express themselves in your life is truly ironic, for when you're holding them, they seem to attract to you the very results you most fear. When you're caught in the root fear of rejection and abandonment, you tend to drive away people who could have mutually supportive relationships with you, and you create situations in which you are bypassed or left in relationships. You may drive people away by being needy and controlling because you fear losing the relationship—choking the relationship by holding on too tightly. You may drive people away because you express your fear as defensiveness and misinterpret well-meaning actions as slights. You're afraid of giving more than you might get. This often results in the decision, *I'll drop him before he drops me.*

When you're caught up in such fears, and people reach out to you in loving ways, you can't fully receive because you feel you don't deserve or you doubt their sincerity. When you fear giving yourself to the process of living life fully, you can't trust life, so you need to control people and situations. It's very difficult to fully feel and express love and goodwill when you're caught up in control issues.

The reason we call these emotions the contracting emotions is that when we experience them, we also experience a withdrawal from others—back into ourselves. This intensifies the feelings of isolation and separation—the most stressful of feelings. In contrast, when we process and let go of these feelings, we're able to reach out, move outside our shell, to trust and to expand. We rise up into the more expansive emotional realms.

Snapshot #3: Typical Root Fears

Root fears:	**How these fears are expressed:**
Not being good enough.	Self-worth issues.
Not lovable enough.	Can't reach expectations for relationships.
Not capable enough.	Can't fully receive.
Not deserving.	
Abandonment	**Driving away relationships**
Rejection.	or always being left in relationships.
Separation.	
Loneliness.	
Fear of living fully	**Inability to love or to express love**
Fear of surrendering to the flow of life.	Need to control people and situations.
Not trusting the process of life—based	
on fear of rejection and abandonment.	

Emotional Skill #4: Lift Your Moods

It's important to remember that you can take charge of your emotional state if you choose to. The following are techniques you can use to elevate your moods.

Understand how moods develop. When you deal with a contracting emotion by denying it (*I'm not angry*) or repressing it (*I simply won't feel angry any more*), you hold onto it. Just as you feel your emotions in a specific part of your body, you also subconsciously store them in a specific part of your body when you don't release them. Denial and repression can become such a habit pattern that they become automatic, below the level of consciousness. You're no longer aware that you're storing your anger. You may also hold onto an emotion through conscious choice (*I have every right to be angry, and I'm not going to forgive or forget*) based on self-justification or self-righteousness.

Understand what a mood is. When you don't process contracting emotions, you hold them in your body and in the space around you as a mood. As indicated in the map of emotions, moods may include such ongoing emotions as irritation, blame, guilt, and self-pity. You know people who stay in long-term moods that make them perpetually irritable, overly sensitive, or defensive. We call those who are frequently moody *difficult* people because such moods cause them to act in aggressive, passive aggressive, or passive ways.

A mood is usually not felt in a specific part of the body. Instead, it is generalized in the body. A mood is like an aura you carry with you. In reality, you're choosing to be there in a mood, so it will last as long as you want. (If you suspect that you're subject to manic-depressive mood swings, you may be unable to manage your moods on your own, but help is available from psychiatrists.) One of the motivations for being in a contracting mood is the need to deny certain emotions.

Have feelings instead of letting feelings have you. When you don't process your contracting emotions, you get in the habit of letting the emotions take charge of you instead of you taking charge of them. Habits become like ruts or paths. A similar event tends to trigger a particular emotional habit pattern, and we find ourselves being caught up without conscious awareness of how we're allowing ourselves to be victimized by our own emotional reactions. By letting yourself fully experience whatever emotion comes up, you not only clear the emotion, you also no longer need to label your feelings as good or bad, right or wrong.

Follow specific mood-lifting steps. How do you lift a mood? Try these steps:

1. Become aware of your moods. Listen to the people who care about you when they give you feedback about your moods.

2. Realize that only you can create a mood and only you can process the emotions beneath the mood. Take full responsibility for your feelings.

3. Be willing to process old, stuffed emotions and to get at root emotions.

4. Once you're able to release contracting, stressful emotions, what's left is your natural state of being—expansive feelings. Allow them, encourage them, groove on them, and think of them as your old friends.

5. Realize that both types of emotions are normal and human.

Let stressful feelings be a learning tool. You'll no doubt continue to create situations that bring up stressful emotions from time to time. This helps you to learn more about yourself and others—to test relationships, your own limits and capacities, and, in general, to continue your personal growth and development.

Don't become discouraged if you're not always able to create *the perfect life*. The key to creating the life you want is to understand your emotional life and to take conscious control of it by dealing constructively with all your feelings as they come up—remembering that your growth path is often unclear and that you must feel your way through in order to learn those lessons you need to master.

Strategy #4

Consciously Manage Emotions

You've figured out by now that you can't directly control your emotions, and trying to do so leads to denying and repressing them. What you can control are the choices you make for how to think about people and situations and how to act in response to them. You can control your choice to process those contracting emotions that do occur. When you process your emotions, you take conscious control of your emotional state. Sometimes emotions feel like a wild horse with you as the rider. You're tossed around, jerked about, powerless and helpless, at the mercy of the horse. Learning to process emotions is like learning to ride the horse—going with its movements, yet in charge of the situation.

Other emotions feel like a whirlpool, sucking you in, pulling you down. When you begin processing the emotions, you can quit fighting, take charge, go down to the depths where the whirlpool ends, then move to one side with a powerful, releasing kick so that you can rise up to calmer waters. After you process an emotion, you feel more free to review all the options and choices you have for viewing situations and acting on them.

Management Skill #1: Review Your Thought-Train Options

You have many options about how to view a situation and, therefore, what emotions may come up as a result of your perception. Your perceptions are formed by your thoughts or, more specifically, a thought that logically leads to another thought that, in turn, logically leads to another—and on and on. We can call this a *thought train*. For example, your roommate growls at you as you enter the kitchen.

▸ You think, *Oh, no, she's in a bad mood this morning and she's going to take it out on me.*

▸ Then you think, *She's done this several times lately.*

▸ Next you think, *I'm getting tired of her moods and being dumped on.*

What kind of feelings does this thought train arouse? What type of action does it lead to? On the other hand, you can choose to think:

▸ *She's having a difficult morning.*

▸ Then you can think, *It has nothing to do with me.*

▸ Next, you're likely to think, *I'm having a good morning.*

▶ This may lead to the thought, *Maybe that will have a positive effect on her, but she's free to feel any way she wants to feel.*

Compare the feelings that this thought train arouses—and the likely actions—with the previous thought train.

When you take charge of the situation, you have available to you the emotional energy you're holding within your body. You can let this *stuck energy* start flowing. You can use it to fuel expansive thought trains. Pay attention to your thought trains. Notice that when you hop onto a thought about the bright side of the picture, the good that's there, and what you want to create in the situation, you board a thought train that can take you up through the expansive emotions. You can even go to the *top of the world*, emotionally speaking—to the heights of awe, wonder, passion, goodwill, love. But when you hop onto a thought about what's wrong, how awful someone is, or what you fear will happen, the thought train takes you down into the contracting emotions, even *down to the dumps*, as symbolized in Snapshot #4.

Snapshot #4: Thought Trains

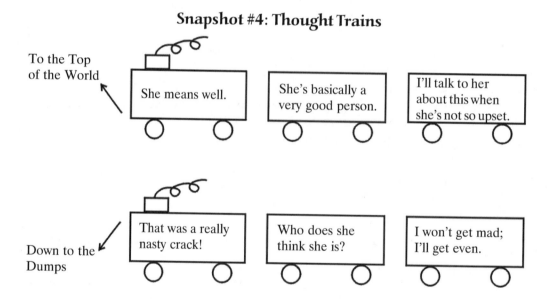

An American Indian folktale can provide insight into the power of choosing our thought trains.

Grandfather: "I feel as if I have two wolves fighting in my heart. One wolf is the vengeful, angry, violent one. The other wolf is the loving, compassionate one."

Grandson: "Which wolf will win the fight in your heart, Grandfather?"

Grandfather: "The one that I feed."

If a stressful emotion keeps coming up, by all means process it. After that, remember that you can become aware of fear-based thoughts moment by moment and break your old contracting thought-train patterns. Try this: As you inhale, pretend you're breathing in love/goodwill through your heart. As you exhale, breathe out blame, judgment, anger—all the contracting emotions. Picture yourself emptying out all the old emotions and filling up with love/goodwill. Next, allow an appreciative or loving thought. Feel your energy expand as you hop onto an expansive thought train. If you make this process a habit, you'll find more and more people attracted to you.

Management Skill #2: Review Your Acting-Out Options

Of course, even when you get on a thought train that takes you to a contracting, stressful emotion, you still have many options about what actions to take. For example, even if you feel irritated or impatient with your roommate's mood, you can choose to fully experience those feelings without saying or doing things that are likely to antagonize her.

Management Skill #3: Channel Anger to Resolve Conflict

We've mentioned that our culture condones anger expressed by men under certain circumstances, such as when people have lied to them, betrayed them, or falsely accused them. Women are permitted to cry and express hurt and upset in such situations, but businesswomen can rarely show anger without paying a price. As one woman said, "Looking back, every time I lost my temper, I lost."

Most people see anger as an antisocial force—something to be avoided. We don't know what to do with it except hold it back or pretend it's not there. Therefore, most of us waste a great deal of energy by holding anger inside. Repressing anger doesn't make it go away. The repressed anger may make us feel irritable or depressed. In turn, we may develop various types of anger-related illnesses. The anger may burst out in an uncontrolled manner at unexpected times, resulting in shouting, cursing, threats, even violence. Anger itself does not cause these problems. Our inability to process and express anger properly is the root problem.

We assume that we get angry because someone did something to us. Actually, we decide when to get angry based on our beliefs and the resulting perceptions of ourselves, others, and the world. Our anger tends to be especially volatile when we believe that the other person's attitude or action belittles us or lowers our self-esteem. This touches on our root fear of being *not good enough*.

People nearly always get angry with other people, not inanimate objects. We most often get angry with people we love or like. People we don't like are the least likely targets of our anger because we tend to ignore or avoid them.

If we learn to manage our anger constructively, it becomes a valuable aspect of cooperative conflict in our relationships. It can help us to confront our problems rather than denying or burying them. It can help us define our position in relation to the issues, the conflict, or the problem that triggers the anger. It can serve as a guide to where we stand and how we feel about situations and relationships. It can help us to understand ourselves. Anger is a feeling to feel, express, move through, and get over with—not to repress or hang onto. Repressing it over the years is linked to the development of cancer.

Follow the Anger Trail

Anger can alert you to problem situations and relationships that need attention and to what's really going on within you.

Dealing with conflict. Anger's specific value in dealing with conflict includes:

▶ Helping you to identify hidden problems that can then be dealt with and resolved to strengthen a relationship.

▶ Getting the other person's attention and motivating him or her to deal with the conflict.

▶ Transforming internal anxiety or frustration into external conflict, moving you to action, and increasing your sense of power to influence situations.

▶ Building your confidence in speaking out and challenging others.

▶ Releasing frustration.

Building relationships. Anger's specific value in building cooperative relationships includes:

▶ Signaling the value you place on another person, and perhaps your dependence or interdependence.

▶ Deepening your awareness and knowledge of others in your life and, as a result, learning more about their values and commitments.

▶ Allowing you to signal that you want to work out problems and improve the relationship, including how you work together to get things done.

Learning about yourself. Anger's specific value in helping you to learn more about yourself includes:

▶ Motivating yourself to analyze the source of your anger and, as a result, learning more about yourself, your values, and your commitments.

▶ Motivating yourself to take vigorous action to deal with problems, achieve your goals, and build your skills.

When you don't express anger, others are often not clear if the problems are important to you and, therefore, whether they merit attention. They may not understand the depth of your concern.

Manage Anger Constructively

The following five steps will guide you in managing your anger constructively.

Step 1: Establish your personal stance.

▶ Express commitment to the relationship and express positive feelings toward the other as a person, even though you're angry about certain behavior.

▶ Use anger to get at the root of the problem and to strengthen the relationship—not to express self-righteousness and moral superiority, which often serve as reasons to hold onto the anger.

▶ Avoid saying things you don't mean or doing things you'd never do under normal circumstances (the old *take some deep breaths and count to 10* adage can work here).

▶ Avoid triggering anger in the other person with belittling remarks or actions. Focus on *I* messages and the problem behavior or situation rather than judging and blaming the other person.

Step 2: State your position.

▸ Describe your feelings, using the energy that anger generates to express yourself, but do not judge or belittle the other person.

▸ Make your expression cathartic—don't repress it.

▸ Specifically identify the exact behavior that bothers you. Knowing the exact action that angered you helps the other person feel less threatened; seeing your feedback as an attack on an action rather than on their personality and self-esteem is a relief.

▸ Take responsibility for your anger; remember that no one can make you feel anything without your permission.

▸ Allow your nonverbal actions to be natural and, therefore, in alignment with your verbal expression of anger.

Step 3: Question and understand the other person's viewpoint.

▸ Don't assume you know what the other person was or is thinking and feeling—ask questions.

▸ Be aware of the other person's feelings, such as defensiveness and anxiety, in the face of your anger.

▸ Ask the other person how she or he feels about your expression of anger.

Step 4: Ask for a resolution to the problem and reach agreement.

▸ Ask what the other person proposes as a resolution.

▸ Express what you need from a resolution.

▸ Explore alternative resolutions and find the one that best meets both your needs, one that you both can live with.

Step 5: Make it a learning process.

▸ Be sure the solution resolves the anger-producing situation.

▸ Put the anger behind you; let it go. Anger is a feeling to move fully into and fully out of—not to hang onto.

▸ Celebrate together your success in expressing and responding to anger and in resolving the problem.

▸ What skills did you both improve upon by successfully dealing with anger?

Management Skill #4: Gain Skill in Exercising Your Options

Feelings become toxic only when you step out of your power and allow yourself to become victimized by them. You can take your power back by recognizing the many options you have for choosing a belief, attitude, worldview, or thought that starts a positive thought train. Learn which thoughts start a chain of thoughts that take you into an expansive emotion (from neutral to joy) rather than a contracting emotion (from irritation to terror). You have the power to choose how you want to perceive a crisis, an insult, or any other event.

Even when you revert to old victim thought patterns—which we all do from time to time—and contracting emotions flood in, you still have options for expressing and processing the feelings. You can choose what you say to yourself, what you learn from the experience, whether you interpret the event as a personal attack, how you interpret someone's criticism of you, and how you express contracting emotions.

Option: Stay Poised in a Crisis

How do you deal with a crisis? Many people hold the stereotype that women fall apart, but you have many options for responding. Here's an effective process for mastering yourself in a crisis:

▶ Slow down your physical and mental processes.

▶ Take a few very deep breaths.

▶ Have the intention of becoming grounded and centered.

▶ Go into slow motion, as if in a slow-motion movie.

▶ See yourself in charge of the situation.

▶ Move very deliberately.

▶ Take action to handle the crisis, one step at a time.

▶ If frantic or harried thoughts come in, repeat the deep breathing.

You can use one or more of the relaxation techniques discussed earlier. The simplest technique is to pause and take a few deep breaths. Don't say, *I must relax.* Instead, start breathing deeply. In fact, avoid telling yourself that you *should, must,* or *need* to do anything. Simply have the intention to follow these strategies.

Become very aware of the present moment. Have the intention to feel centered and grounded in your body and very present mentally. All this helps you to rise above any chaotic mind chatter. Feel your breathing slow down and your entire body slow down, including your thinking process. You must slow down enough to end the frantic rush to action and to take the necessary steps, one step at a time, to deal with the crisis. See yourself moving very slowly, like a slow-motion movie.

Option: Use Self-Talk That Empowers

He made me so mad. It made me so sad. When you talk this way, you tell yourself that you have no choices in how to view an event. You step out of your power, and so give away your power to the person or situation that *made you mad.* This leaves a power vacuum that others can sense from a mile away. You first become a victim in your own mind (*He made me mad*), then you become a victim in someone else's mind.

Does a little self-talk really have that kind of power-draining impact? Yes. Everything you say to yourself programs the subconscious part of your mind about how the world is and how you should respond. If you've said *he made me mad* hundreds or thousands of times during your lifetime, you've programmed your subconscious to respond as if you're a victim. To change the program, stop yourself in mid-sentence or mid-thought and correct yourself: *I chose to see him as a threat and became angry* or *I thought he was belittling me, and that triggered my anger.* Choose your own words, but be sure they reflect your power to choose.

Sometimes thoughts seem obsessive. When certain thoughts just won't go away, let them run their course, much as you process your emotions by letting them run their course.

Don't beat yourself up because you've hopped onto a thought train to the dumps. It takes time to change old thought patterns, and growth is always two steps forward and one step back. The step back usually provides the momentum to take the next two steps forward.

Option: Don't Take It Personally

The tendency to view other people's actions and criticisms as personal put-downs stems from the fear of some sort of personal failure. Why do women seem to take these things more personally than men? Perhaps because men have generally been more single-minded about their career goals. They are more likely to keep focusing on such questions as *What do I have to do? What do I have to learn in order to advance?* That focus makes it easier to keep things in perspective. When the intention to *learn* from our mistakes overcomes our fear of failure, we're less likely to take people's criticisms and actions personally.

It may help to view business as a game. First, what's your major goal in this game? Discovering the limits of your capability? Reaching financial independence? Making a specific kind of contribution to the planet? Once you're clear about your major goal and you let go of any tension-producing *need* to achieve it, you can relax and begin to enjoy the *process* of playing the game in order to achieve the goal. The actions of others become part of the challenge and complexity of the game, and you make your moves with your goals foremost in your mind. Your focus changes from avoiding the risk of failure and protecting yourself from failure, to winning the game. Problem situations merely alert you to the need to take corrective action. You switch from agonizing over the fact that a problem was allowed to develop, to getting on with the job of correcting the problem. Your ego is not on the line.

Option: Keep Criticism in Perspective

Ask yourself about your critic's qualifications on the subject at hand. Suppose you were to take a visitor on a tour of your department and explain major departmental goals, organization, procedures, and controls. He sees some potential problem with the way you're running things and suggests some ways you could improve the setup. The range of possibilities about his qualifications to criticize and advise you is shown on this scale.

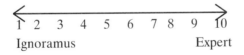

Let's look at the two extreme possibilities. The first possibility is that your critic doesn't know a thing about running the business. In fact, he's so ignorant that he doesn't know the difference between a work schedule and an organization chart. In that case, if you allow yourself to become upset because of the criticism of a business ignoramus, you're acting even more foolishly than the person who criticized you.

At the other extreme, your critic may be a world-renowned expert on business organization. In that case, his observations are probably valid and his suggestions extremely valuable. In fact, if you acted on those suggestions, you might become a top officer of the company in a very short time. To be upset by such criticism, then, would be inappropriate and self-defeating.

Sometimes people will criticize you in such a negative, hostile way that it will be difficult to remain emotionally detached. It may be appropriate to tell such a person that you appreciate the feedback but you *don't* appreciate the manner in which it was given. At the same time, it helps to keep in mind that the hostility is the other person's problem. She or he would react that way to *anyone* who represents to him or her what you do at the moment. It's a part of the individual's own conditioning and working out of his or her own life story, and it really has nothing to do with you personally. And if you *still* feel strong emotions, you don't have to act them out. You can choose one of the substitute acting-out methods that follow.

Option: Look for Lessons and Growth Opportunities

As you grow in your ability to choose thinking or self-talk that results in expansive emotions, you'll sometimes slip into old thought patterns and take yourself straight into a contracting emotion. All is not lost. You not only have options for acting on the feeling, you can also choose to learn from the experience. You have the option of seeing how difficult people and emotionally upsetting events can actually help you learn about yourself and accelerate your personal growth.

When someone betrays you, for example, you'll probably experience a range of contracting emotions. At some point, ask yourself why you attracted such a person into your life? Is it because *you've* betrayed someone recently? If so, you probably need to deal with betrayal issues within yourself. Or is it that you simply hold harsh judgments toward people who betray? Not one of us has completely conquered the tendency to make negative judgments of others, so we all need to work on empathy, compassion, and acceptance of others as they are. Maybe betrayal is coming up in your life at this time because you're ready to develop greater empathy and compassion for betrayers. The bottom line is that instead of hanging onto the contracting emotions of an event (such as betrayal), you can focus on the lessons for growth and self-understanding, which, in turn, will trigger expansive emotions.

Option: Experience Feelings Without Acting Out

As you master the techniques we've been discussing, *problem* emotions will become less and less of a problem. Here's a strategy for constructively handling those *problem* emotions that do occur:

Accept your feelings. Be glad that you're able to experience the whole range of human emotions and that you're aware of being able to do so.

Don't judge your feelings. Tell yourself that a feeling is not right or wrong, good or bad; it just is.

Let yourself fully experience a feeling. Be aware of it in the present moment. Don't begin focusing on guilt (about past experiences associated with a similar feeling) or worry (about what will happen in the future). Stay in the here and now by focusing on your senses: Focus on what you are seeing, hearing, touching, and so forth.

Choose not to act out. Tell yourself that you are choosing *not* to act out your feelings, because to do so would be inappropriate and self-defeating.

Decide whether and when to give feedback. You may decide it's appropriate to *tell* the person who triggered the emotion what you're feeling. If you do this effectively, it's not acting out, and the feedback can be constructive to that person.

If you can't give feedback calmly, postpone it. As a general rule, you don't have to respond immediately to anything. When your feelings are too overpowering for you to *experience them out* quickly, it's more professional to delay responding. You can act out your feelings in privacy, if necessary. Later, when you're ready to deal with the problem situation, you can do so without having to deal with explosive feelings at the same time.

To postpone gracefully, it helps to have some exit lines in mind. Your exit line is what you say before you change the subject or excuse yourself from the scene. Try, *I'd like to check on a few things before I give you my answer (or respond to that, discuss that). May I get back to you at/on...? Let me think about that for a while. I'll get back to you at/ on....* Or try, *I'm glad you brought that up. I must leave for a meeting (or appointment) now, but I want to talk with you about this as soon as I return.*

Use substitute acting out. Tell yourself that you'll enjoy acting out your feelings in an appropriate way later. Sometimes just telling yourself this can defuse the situation enough for you to deal with it effectively at the time it occurs.

You can visualize throwing darts at a picture of the person on a dartboard. (Some people even have dartboards in their office for this purpose.) Here are some substitutes:

▶ Any game that requires hitting a ball: Pretend the ball is the person or thing you resent, and really smash it.

▶ Jogging or walking: Pretend you're stepping on the person you resent *if you need to!*

▶ Karate: Pretend your opponent is the person you resent (but don't get carried away).

▶ Any physical exercise: You can work off the bottled-up energy of unexpressed feelings by reminding yourself while you're exercising that you're working out those feelings. Be aware of the situation and the resulting feelings you're now working out. You'll probably be free to rest peacefully once the tension and energy-drain of unresolved feelings is eliminated.

▶ Hitting a large stuffed doll: Try to knock the stuffing out of a large doll, animal, or dummy, using either your fists or a baseball bat.

▶ A quick mental acting out: Instead of visualizing dart-throwing, you can picture yourself telling off the other person, kicking him or her in the seat of the pants, and so on. You may be able to work out the feeling in a few seconds and go on to deal with the situation calmly.

Option: Express Feelings to a Trusted Friend

Another way of handling your emotions is to talk them out with someone. The more stressful your job, the more essential it is to have at least one trusted friend with whom you can *let your hair down.* It's best if such friends are not connected with your job. Although business friends may understand the problems better than someone outside the company, it's risky to be completely open with them. True friends are rare. Most people are lucky if they have five or six at any one time in their lives. For the relationship to be truly mutually supportive, it should include these aspects:

▶ You can be yourselves with each other.

▶ You are interested in each other's well-being.

▶ You really listen to each other.

▶ You don't make judgments about each other's character, feelings, or behavior. (To avoid making judgments, think in terms of behavior that works or doesn't work, that appears to be constructive or destructive, rather than what is right or wrong, good or bad. Deal more with what *is* rather than with what *should be*.)

▶ You confide in each other about the joyous events in your life as well as the problem situations.

▶ You both feel more lovable and capable as a result of the friendship.

▶ You can trust each other's judgment about revealing shared confidences.

Frequently, you can gain insights into problem situations and learn more about yourself by discussing things with a friend. Such discussions can also be very helpful in *experiencing out* any leftover, bottled-up feelings you may have. This type of friendship can help both parties keep a balanced perspective on life.

You probably have that typical feminine knack of reaching out to close friends when the emotional going gets tough. Women's ability to rally round with a hot cup of tea, a little shopping spree, a heart-to-heart talk, a good cry, and a big hug seems to work wonders in healing those wounds from the slings and arrows of outrageous office politics. Men are often in awe of this power. Researchers note it as a career woman's advantage in managing stress. You can cherish it.

Skill Builders

Skill Builder #1: Worst-Case Scenario

Purpose: To regain a sense of peace and self-confidence during emotional upset.

Step 1: Do the process for getting at root fears discussed in this chapter.

Step 2: As you work through that process, imagine the worst thing that could possibly happen in your current problem situation. For example, if it's a career situation, the worst thing may be losing your job. Imagine that you've lost your job.

Step 3: When you get to a *disastrous* bottom line, ask yourself:

▶ *Is this the end of the world?*

▶ *Will life go on?*

▶ *Can I survive?*

See yourself in that scenario (in this case, without a job). Fully experience the feelings that arise in connection with that picture. Get comfortable with your ability to deal with that scenario.

Step 4: Ask yourself, *What could be worse than this?* For example, you can't find another job that's comparable to the one you now have.

Repeat Step #3 for dealing with this new scenario.

Step 5: Keep going until you get to the worst thing that could reasonably happen.

For example, what type of job could you undoubtedly get? Could you deal with a low-level job, at least for a while until something more appropriate comes along? Become comfortable with this worst-case scenario.

You'll find that imagining the worst-case scenario will bring your fearful shadows and ghosts out of the closet into the realistic light of day. This process will bring you to a sense of competence for coping with whatever comes up. This, in turn, will bring a sense of peace and self-confidence that will serve you well in dealing with the current issue.

Skill Builder #2: Put It in Perspective

Purpose: To help you put an emotional upset into perspective.

A. How bad is it? Think about the current situation that has triggered some contracting emotions for you. Refer to the trauma scale, which shows various levels of damage that could occur to your body, ranked from top to bottom in order of perceived impact, pain, loss, etc. Which item on the trauma scale best corresponds with your current *traumatic* situation?

Trauma scale:

1. Stubbed your toe.
2. Cut your toe; used Band-Aid.
3. Had stitches in your toe.
4. Broke your toe.

5. Lost your toe.
6. Lost your foot.
7. Lost your leg.
8. Paralyzed from neck down.

B. 10 years from now. Picture yourself 10 years from today. Picture any other persons involved in the situation. From that perspective, looking back to this time in your life, ask yourself:

▶ *Ten years from now, how important will this problem be?*

▶ *Ten years from now, what response will I wish I had made?*

Skill Builder #3: Observe Your Stressful Emotions

Purpose: To help you become master of your emotions; to put them in perspective; to allow one part of you to move outside an emotion and observe it while another part of you fully experiences it; to contain raw emotional energy and then transform it into useful forms of self-expression.

Step 1: Create an internal observation room. When you sense the onset of one or more strong, stressful emotions, picture yourself in a mental room. Imagine yourself stepping back from the emotion and sitting down in an observation chair.

Step 2: Stack feelings in the middle of the room. As the first feeling comes up, imagine yourself placing it very carefully on the floor in the middle of the room. If other feelings want to come in, allow them to do so, and carefully stack them one on top of the other.

Step 3: Carefully observe the feelings. Now take one feeling at a time—or the whole stack if that's what seems to be needed. Sit back and watch the feeling—its color, its shape, and the nuances of its emotional tones. Watch the feeling. Don't judge it or put it down. Instead, observe it. Some typical thoughts that might come up are:

1. *Oh, there you are again!*
2. *So, that's what you look like!*
3. *My, you're very dark today.*

Step 4: Experience and let go. Allow yourself to fully feel the feeling in your body while the observer part of you watches it in your mental room. When the force of the feeling has passed, let it go. If you have difficulty letting it go, ask that it be lifted. What you're left with is the energy that was being wrapped around the feeling.

Skill Builder #4: Draw and Redirect Your Stressful Emotions

Purpose: To gain mastery of your stressful emotions so you can channel them into useful forms of self-expression.

Note: *You don't need to have artistic ability to do this exercise. The power of the exercise lies in your ability to imagine and to visualize. Your drawing can be very simple, crude, childlike, or symbolic. In fact, the power lies in the symbolism.*

Step 1: Identify a stressful emotion. Think of a stressful emotion that recurs in your life. It may be an emotion you have difficulty mastering, one that sweeps you up in its force, or one that you act out in destructive ways. It may be an emotion that recurs in your dreams and is troubling to you.

Step 2: Draw the emotion. If you have difficulty seeing it as a symbolic or physical entity, do Skill Builder #3. The emotion might look like a dark cloud, a tornado, a lightning bolt, a solid bunker, a shield, a smoking gun, a raging fire, an icicle, a vise or hand that squeezes—you get the idea. See the emotion as raw energy.

Step 3: Draw the channeling of the emotional energy. Draw a lead-shielded container around this raw energy/emotion. Now draw a small power plant around the container. From this power plant of raw energy, draw power lines and transformers coming out of the container and going to your house, to other houses, to streetlights, to computers—to anything you see as needing this energy.

9

Speak Up

Remove those 'I want you to like me' stickers from your forehead and put
them where they'll do the most good—on your mirror!
—Susan Jeffers, psychologist

What did you learn as a little girl about being nice, doing as you're told, following instructions—and *not* taking over, speaking up, or causing trouble? We'll explore what these kinds of messages from parents, teachers, and others may mean for you today. If you're like most women, you believe in being nice at all costs because you want to please others and avoid problems. Every once in a while you may get fed up with other people walking on you. You might blow your top in an aggressive way and then return to a basically passive, indirect way of dealing with people. Whether you're being walked on, being taken advantage of, or blowing up, you're not in control of yourself. You're not managing how you express your thoughts and feelings. In this chapter, you'll learn strategies and techniques for communicating assertively. But first, answer some questions about your current beliefs regarding assertiveness. Then, meet Cornelia Grunseth, President of Pacific Northwest Painters, Inc., whose assertiveness has helped her grow an innovative business.

What's the best way to stand up for yourself?

1. Does assertion mean taking the dominant role in dealing with people, so you won't be used or pushed around?

2. When you agree to compromise your rights, are you being passive?

3. Someone tries to cut in front of you in a line at the grocery store. You say, *I see that you only have two items to pay for. That doesn't give you the right to go ahead of me, but it's okay this time.* Is that a passive response?

4. A businessperson sells you some faulty merchandise, and you turn her in to the local consumer fraud agency. Is this an aggressive response?

5. Your housemate hasn't cleaned up her messes in the kitchen for two weeks now, and you say, *You're getting pretty sloppy lately.* Is this is an assertive response?

Cornelia Grunseth, President of Pacific Northwest Painters, Inc.

Cornelia Grunseth cofounded Pacific Northwest Painters, Inc., with her husband, Eric, in 1983. In the beginning, Cornelia stayed in the background, running the office and helping clients with color schemes. She was uncomfortable with most types of public relations because it all felt a little too pushy for her taste. By the 1990s, Cornelia's role in the company was expanding. She and Eric realized that she was very good with customers—and her intuitive color sense was blossoming.

She had been studying color psychology and theory as well as feng shui and other ancient wisdoms. When she incorporated all of this into the color selection process, the results were magical. Clients knew that they were getting more than an attractive color scheme. The energy in the rooms and buildings was somehow transformed, taking on a special glow, and it all felt just right to the people using them.

Callers began asking, "Will you come out and just tell me what colors to use?" Cornelia suddenly saw a PR approach that would work for her. Billing herself as "The Color Lady," she offered architectural color consulting services for $100 an hour. Most clients get all the advice they need in a 3-hour service call—a very good deal for them. The added bonus: many clients ask, "Can you just get this paint job done for me?" Enter Pacific Northwest Painters and contracts ranging up to $50,000, and sometimes more.

In 2000, she parlayed a $5,000 color design contract for a 24-building office park into a million-dollar paint contract. Clearly, it was time for Cornelia to head the company. Her growing assertiveness had taken her from backroom office manager to president, whose roles include chief promoter, contract negotiator, and color designer. In 2004 the company won a national competition for its work on historic Jack London Square in Oakland, California. The prize included nationwide publicity for Pacific Northwest Painters, Inc.

Cornelia, who lived for 10 years in Mexico and speaks Spanish fluently, helps Eric direct the work of 15 Latino American painters. Latino machismo normally makes it difficult for men to accept direction from a woman. Cornelia handled this by showing the men that their contributions are crucial to company success. For example, when new workers are going through the probation phase, everyone gets a chance to work with them and then to vote on whether to hire them permanently.

To help these Latino American men express their ideas at staff meetings, Cornelia adapted an American Indian meeting ritual. The tradition says that whoever holds the "talking stick" holds the floor, and it's passed around from member to member. At Pacific Northwest Painters' meetings, the man holding the paintbrush holds the floor until he has his say. Then he passes it to the next man who wants to speak.

Cornelia helps these men to communicate in other ways too. She's often available to translate job tasks for them and to help them understand American ways. The company provides weekly English classes for them.

Cornelia and Eric encourage the men to expand their skills. Pacific Northwest Painters also buys and renovates properties. This gives their painters a chance to cross-train in such areas as bricklaying and tile laying, landscaping, carpentry, plumbing, and other types of restoration They are encouraged to expand and perfect their craft, improving their self-worth as well as their value to the firm.

What do you do when you have a problem with someone at work? Do you drop hints and hope the person gets the message? Do you ask the boss to handle it? Or do you have a friend drop hints? If so, you need to raise your assertion level, for this passive approach creates problems of its own. When you bring others, especially the boss, into the one-on-one picture, the other person may rightfully view this as an act of aggression that violates his or her rights. Effective leaders stick to a tried-and-true motto: *If there's a problem, go directly to the person(s) involved.*

This issue is the tip of the iceberg, and knowing how to ply the waters of assertive action to get the best results takes skill-building. You're going to see the differences between assertiveness, aggressiveness, passiveness, and passive-aggressiveness. You'll see how assertion is based on a clear understanding of your rights, as well as your skill in negotiating a resolution when your rights conflict with those of others. You're going to develop some basic assertive tools (verbal and nonverbal) for handling problem situations.

Strategy #1

Recognize the Action Modes

Consider the idea that you are not an assertive, passive, aggressive, or passive-aggressive person. You take on each of those modes from time to time. You probably spend more time in one of the modes than in the others, and there is probably a mode in which you spend the least time. That still does not make you a *passive person* or an *aggressive person*. You are a center of consciousness. You are not your actions, your traits, or your modes of behavior. These change from time to time; you can try them out, put them on, or take them off at any time.

Snapshot #1: The Range of Assertion

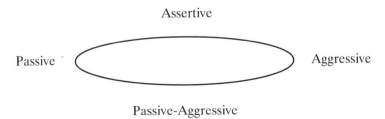

All of us have a range of assertiveness that we use at various times. It may be most helpful to think of the range of assertiveness as a continuum, as shown in Snapshot #1 on page 229. At any one time, you may be somewhere between the passive and assertive range, or the assertive and aggressive range. Within a day, you may move all over the continuum as you initiate actions and respond to others' actions.

Assertive Mode

You're in an assertive mode when you stand up for your personal rights and act in ways that express your thoughts, feelings, and beliefs in direct, honest, and appropriate ways that don't violate another person's rights.

By your actions and your words, you convey to people: *This is what I think. This is what I feel. This is how I see the situation.* You convey this in a way that doesn't dominate, humiliate, or degrade the other person.

Assertion is based on respect for yourself and respect for the other person. You express your preferences and defend your rights in a way that also respects other people's needs and rights. The goal of assertion is:

▶ To get and give respect.

▶ To be fair and ask for fairness.

▶ To create a win-win situation.

▶ To leave space for compromise when your needs and rights conflict with another person's.

Such compromises respect the basic integrity of both people, and both get some of their wishes satisfied. This approach to assertion helps you avoid the temptation of using assertion to manipulate others in order to get what you want. It frequently leads to both people getting what they want, because most people tend to become cooperative when they're approached in a way that respects both parties.

When you're in an assertive mode, you can take these actions:

▶ Ask for what you want—make requests, ask for business, ask for favors.

▶ Give feedback—about problems, about what you admire or enjoy, about what you'd like to see changed.

▶ Say *no* without going into lengthy explanations and apologies.

You're able to take these actions in a way that's kind, friendly, and well-meaning; professional and businesslike; calm and objective—not over-emotional or abusive; and expressive of self-respect and respect for others.

Nonassertive Mode

You're in a passive or nonassertive mode in these kinds of situations:

▶ You let others victimize you by failing to act in ways that express your honest feelings, thoughts, and beliefs.

▶ You express your feelings, thoughts, or beliefs in such an apologetic, unsure, or self-effacing way that others can easily disregard them.

▶ You don't have a strong sense of your rights as a person, a woman, a leader, an employee.

▶ You allow others to violate your basic rights.

By such actions, you communicate nonverbally to others that you don't count for much, that you can be taken advantage of, that your ideas aren't very important, and that your feelings don't count. The message is: *I'm nothing; you're superior.*

Nonassertion reflects a lack of self-respect and a lack of commitment to meeting your own needs and preferences. In an indirect way, it reflects a lack of respect for the other person's ability to handle the disappointment of your saying *no* or speaking up, to assume some responsibility for their actions, or to handle problems caused by their own aggression. The goal of nonassertion is to please others and to avoid conflict at all costs.

Aggressive Mode

You're in an aggressive mode when you stand up for your personal rights and express your thoughts, feelings, and beliefs—but you do it in ways that violate the rights of another person. Such actions and words are often dishonest and usually inappropriate. Such behavior implies the following kinds of messages:

▶ *This is what I think. You're stupid for believing differently.*

▶ *This is what I want. What you want isn't important.*

▶ *This is what I feel. Your feelings don't count.*

The goal is domination and winning—which means the other person loses. Winning is achieved by humiliating, belittling, degrading, intimidating, or overpowering other people so that they become less able to express their preferences and defend their rights.

Passive-Aggressive Mode

You're in a passive-aggressive mode when you're agreeable or assertive in your face-to-face dealings with a person, but the results of your actions are aggressive. Some experts say that all passive behavior has a passive-aggressive component. In other words, nonassertion is always accompanied by some degree of resentment—often at a subconscious level.

Most dirty politics are played from the passive-aggressive mode. And behavior that is passive-aggressive always results in some type of hostile action. For example, you may secretly pout, stew, or fret—all the while being *nice* and giving no clue to your real feelings. If you're unaware of the source of your resentment, you may suddenly explode, surprising even yourself. Aware or not, you may quietly sabotage the other person's efforts or projects.

Why would you resort to such negative behavior? Usually, it's because you fear the consequences of speaking up or taking direct action. You may feel the person is trying to dominate you, and this is your way of resisting. You may think the person has treated you badly, and this is your way of getting back. Such relationships frequently have a persecutor-victim aspect.

When you're in the passive-aggressive mode, you don't feel good about yourself, and you resent the other person. What you really want is to get back at the other person without having to suffer the consequences. You don't have a sense of your own rights or a commitment to honoring them, nor do you respect the other person's rights.

This is a lose-lose mode. When you're in it, you probably feel resentful, vengeful, frustrated, perhaps even hopeless or desperate. If you stay in this mode most of the time, you'll begin to feel like a chronic failure—simply getting through life, resigned to unhappiness, feeling as though nothing matters. You'll set yourself up to get kicked around, demoted, or fired, and then blame others or the world for your own problems, feelings, and actions. People who get deeply stuck in this mode usually become either antisocial or violent or both, and end up deciding that life isn't worth living.

Each Mode in Action

You know how people define assertion, nonassertion, and aggression. Look at some examples of each mode in action to get a sense of how it feels to be in each mode.

➡ **You ask for a long-overdue raise.**

Aggressive: *You've been ignoring the fact that I'm underpaid for what I do. I think you're taking advantage of my good nature.*

Assertive: *I've prepared this analysis, which shows that my job responsibilities and productivity have increased by more than 15 percent since my last raise. I would like a 15 percent raise based on these increases.*

Nonassertive: *Uh...I know things are tight just now, but...uh...do you think you could see your way clear to give me a raise?*

➡ **Your subordinate is habitually late for work.**

Aggressive: *Do you really think you can come dragging in late all the time and keep your job?*

Assertive: *Let's discuss this problem of getting to work on time.*

Nonassertive: You send a memo to all team members regarding the need for punctuality, hoping the late worker will get the message.

➡ **A boss asks you to take on tasks that are not your responsibility and that you don't want to get saddled with.**

Aggressive: *Get someone else to do your dirty work.*

Assertive: *I realize you must find someone to do this, but I don't think it's part of my job responsibilities and I don't want to take on tasks that will prevent me from doing my best with my own responsibilities.*

Nonassertive: *Well, okay, I guess I can handle it.*

➡ **A prospective client suggests having lunch some day.**

Assertive: *Why don't we set a date and time now? When's a good day for you?*

Nonassertive: *Yeah, great, let's do that.*

➡ **A client breaks a lunch date.**

Aggressive: *That really messes up my day!*

Assertive: *Shall we reschedule, then? How about the same time next week?*

Nonassertive: *Well, okay, thanks for calling and letting me know.*

The key in handling each particular situation is knowing what you want to happen. While respecting the other person's rights to get what they want, take the initiative to create what you want.

Strategy #2

Base Assertive Actions on Your Rights

If your assertive actions are to be effective, they must be convincing. You must believe in what you're doing. This means you must be clear about your rights and the rights of others in the situation. Later, we'll discuss what other authorities say about rights. First, get in touch with what you (as your own authority) believe by completing Self-Awareness Activity #1. After you've formulated your own ideas about basic human rights, see how they compare with lists compiled by others.

Self-Awareness Activity #1: What Rights Do You Have?

Purpose: To begin a process of grounding your assertive actions in your rights as a human being, a woman, a leader, and an employee.

Instructions: Think about some basic rights you're entitled to. List them.

A Bill of Assertive Rights

How about this as your prime assertive right: *You have the right to judge your own behavior, thoughts, and emotions, and to take responsibility for their initiation and consequences upon yourself.* If you agree with this, then it follows that you also have the following types of rights:

1. To offer no reasons or excuses for justifying your behavior.
2. To judge if you're responsible for finding solutions to other's problems.
3. To change your mind and to make mistakes—and be responsible for them.
4. To say, *I don't know*, or *I don't understand*, or *I don't care.*
5. To be independent of the goodwill of others before coping with them.
6. To be illogical in making decisions.

Every Woman's Bill of Rights

Women's rights have been denied and violated in many ways. It will probably help your assertive stance to get in touch with those rights that many women are reclaiming. They include the right:

1. To be treated with respect.
2. To have and express your own feelings and opinions.

3. To be listened to and taken seriously.
4. To set your own priorities.
5. To ask for what you want and to get what you pay for.
6. To ask for information from professionals, such as doctors, lawyers, and teachers.
7. To choose to assert yourself—or not.

Strategy #3

To Assert or Not? It's Your Choice

By now you have a feel for what appropriate assertive behavior is like, and you know that you have a right *not* to assert yourself. How are you going to decide when to assert? In making this decision, keep in mind that the choice may involve the rights of others. If so, are you willing to compromise? In deciding when and where to assert, ask yourself the following questions:

Question #1: How will others interpret my nonassertiveness? The men you work with may interpret your behavior in ways you never intended. For example, many women use silence as a way of ignoring a situation, avoiding an embarrassing confrontation, or *rising above* unpleasant circumstances. For men, silence may signal consent, or they may interpret it as weakness—a sign that you'll have trouble in a tough business world.

Question #2: Will assertiveness improve my relationships and my self-respect? Respect is a key factor to consider when you're deciding whether to assert yourself. You've probably been rewarded throughout life for staying in a nonassertive mode. You were probably discouraged or punished when you were in an aggressive mode, so aggressiveness is less likely to be a problem for you than for your male peers. However, you may have decided that you must behave aggressively *to make it in a man's world.* Do you feel you'll become vulnerable and lose control if you don't? You need to know that when you're in the aggressive mode, you cause many people to *go underground* in their reactions to you—and in this passive-aggressive mode, they find indirect ways to undercut your control.

Your most successful relationships are based on assertive behavior. When you begin a relationship with someone who tries to violate your rights early on, it's best to establish your boundaries and assert yourself right away. Otherwise, you're likely to get hooked into playing the other person's games. If you eventually decide to assert yourself and break up the games, your *friend* is likely to react much more negatively at this point than in an initial encounter. And the longer the relationship continues, the more likely you are to have an emotional stake in it. You will therefore experience more turmoil when it runs into trouble.

People like most those people they respect, and you don't gain respect by letting yourself be dominated or manipulated. In fact, people may pity you even while they take advantage of your nonassertion. This pity may eventually become irritation, and even disgust. In the long run, staying in an assertive mode means you fill your life with people you really want to be around—people who like and respect you for who you are. You're more likely to have people in your life who support your growth and autonomy. You'll have a higher level of self-esteem and self-respect. As you feel better about yourself, more self-confident, you'll start getting more of the things you want in life. You'll prevent many of the problems that create stress, including the frustrations and resulting pressures created by nonassertion.

Question #3: Will assertiveness prevent or reduce stress? Stress is another key factor to consider when you're deciding whether to assert yourself in a situation or relationship. You teach people by your actions how you will and will not be treated, and what you think, feel, and believe about certain matters. When people violate your rights and you *don't* say anything, you send the message that it's okay to exploit, dominate, or manipulate you. You must then cope with the results of others' aggression. In addition, you will resent all this, of course, so it creates stress in your life.

Question #4: How much will it cost me to assert myself in this situation? Asserting may cost you the relationship, or it may bring you the great bonus of a relationship based on mutual respect. For example, there's always the chance that you'll upset an aggressive friend in the teaching process—and you may lose the friend. However, if you've shown respect for that person while asserting yourself, then it's fairly safe to say it wasn't much of a friendship to begin with. Asserting yourself always carries a risk, especially in a situation where you've established yourself as a nonassertive person. You must face the fact that it may cost you whatever benefits the relationship seemed to provide.

Question #5: How important is this situation to me? Obviously, some situations and relationships are more important than others. That's why you should practice assertion first in relatively unimportant situations. As you gain mastery, the rule of thumb becomes: *The more important the situation, the more crucial it is to assert.* No need to waste a lot of time and energy asserting yourself in trivial situations. The deciding factor: *How will I feel about it afterward?*

Once you decide you must assert yourself, deal with the worst-case scenario, become comfortable with that, gain confidence that you can handle it, and reestablish that asserting yourself is worth it. Then, formulate your intention and goal for the situation—what you prefer the outcome to be—and focus on that during your assertive interaction. The bottom line is that you strongly intend to have a positive result, but you let go of the *need* for that result.

Question #6: How am I likely to feel afterward about my actions? If you sense that you'll feel resentment if you *don't* assert yourself, that's your cue to assert. Letting resentment build and fester is likely to cause more harm than asserting would cause. On the other hand, each time you successfully assert yourself, you gain some confidence. You develop some skill in creating the life you want. And it can be great fun. Try to make all your assertive encounters happy, fun, and challenging experiences, rather than battlegrounds in which you place your humanity on the line. Have fun seeing how effective you can be. If you succeed in this, but don't invest your entire self-worth in the process, you need never again be a victim. Avoid plowing through with deadpan seriousness or trying hard. Relax and enjoy the challenge.

Strategy #4

Select the Best Assertive Approach

Situations calling for assertiveness can vary widely. Therefore, you need to become familiar with a number of different approaches to asserting yourself so that you can select the most appropriate method or combination of methods for each type of situation. You'll want to assert with empathy in many situations, using *I* messages that don't make others wrong. But at times you must repeat and escalate your assertion to convince people you mean business. Special situations, such as broken agreements or group decision-making, call for special techniques, as does giving feedback in touchy situations.

Approach #1: Basic Assertion

The direct, simple actions involved in standing up for personal likes, opinions, beliefs, or feelings are known as basic assertion. Basic assertion also involves expressing affection and appreciation toward another person. Here are some examples:

▶ You're asked a question for which you have no ready answer. You reply: *I'd like a few minutes to think that over.*

▶ The person in the next room has a radio playing loudly. You say: *Your radio is disturbing me. Would you turn it down?*

▶ Your boss keeps interrupting you while you're trying to make a point. You say: *Excuse me, I'd like to finish making my point.*

▶ A colleague makes a good presentation. You say: *I enjoyed your talk. Your descriptions were very clear.*

Approach #2: Assertion With Empathy

Sometimes you want to express empathy along with your preferences or feelings. You want to show that you recognize the other person's viewpoint or feelings. The empathetic statement is followed by one that stands up for your rights.

Assertion with empathy is often effective because people are more likely to accept your assertion when they feel you have some understanding and respect for their position. It's especially valuable in situations where you tend to overreact in an aggressive way. If you take a moment to try to understand the other person's viewpoint before you react, you're less likely to respond aggressively. On the other hand, your expression of empathy must be sincere to be effective. People can usually spot insincere expressions of empathy, and they resent such attempts to manipulate them. Here are some examples of assertion with empathy.

▶ The boss wants a time-consuming report submitted tomorrow. You say: *I know you need this report as soon as possible, but I have important plans for this evening and won't be able to work overtime.*

▶ A worker is trying to get you, as team leader, to serve as referee in his personality clash with a coworker. You tell him: *I can understand why you want help with this problem, but the two of you will have to work this out together on your own.*

Approach #3: *I* Messages

You're most likely to retain the goodwill of the person you're standing up to if you stick with your own thoughts, feelings, and beliefs, and avoid direct or implied criticism of his or her thoughts, feelings, or beliefs. One way to do that is to think in terms of *I* messages. You need to know the difference between *I* messages and *you* messages. You also need to know various uses of *I* messages, such as preventing problem situations; simply stating your thinking, feeling, or preference; and responding to others' requests or to specific situations.

I messages are statements that describe you. They're expressions of *your* feelings and experiences. They're authentic, honest, and congruent. And because *I* messages express only your inner reality, they don't contain evaluations, judgments, or interpretations of others. Because you're saying what you really feel, your verbal and nonverbal expressions are in harmony. Your messages come through confidently and congruently. A good *I* message is more than words, though. It's a reflection of an attitude: *I'll express what's going on with me without judging what's going on with you.*

You messages are messages that judge, criticize, or blame others. Think about your own reaction to the *you* message, *You talk too loudly* versus the *I* message, *I have sensitive hearing.* Or how about the message, *You made a mess in the mailroom* versus *I like to find the mailroom neat and orderly.*

Preventive *I* Messages

Preventive *I* messages let people know ahead of time what you will need and want. They can prevent many conflicts and misunderstandings. Here are suggestions for sending preventive *I* messages.

1. Know what you want or need in life and in specific situations.
2. Decide to take personal responsibility for meeting your preferences.
3. Express your preferences in an assertive way to the person whose cooperation you need.
4. Be willing to shift gears to listen if the other person becomes defensive.

Here's an example of a preventive *I* message: *I'd like us to figure out what needs to be done before the week is over so we can make sure we have time to get it all done.* (Instead of, *You need to manage your time better.*) The *I* message begins with *I'd like*, to point out that it expresses personal preferences. It may also be phrased as a question: *Could we set a time...?* The important point is to take the initiative to get a result you want, and to do it without blaming or criticizing.

Declarative *I* Messages

Declarative *I* messages help others know more about you. They're self-disclosures that tell people about your beliefs, ideas, likes, dislikes, feelings, reactions, interests, attitudes, and intentions. They let others know what you've experienced, what it feels like to be you. They describe your inner reality. Here are some examples: *I'm worried about completing the project on time*, or *I'm looking forward to more business travel.*

Responsive *I* Messages

Responsive *I* messages clearly communicate *no*, when *no* expresses your authentic feelings. They can also clearly communicate *yes*. In addition to saying *yes* or *no*, you may also want to express how a request will affect you or the reason you're saying *yes* or *no*. Here are some examples: *No, I can't have the report to you on Monday, because I have another project that I want to complete first,* or *Yes, I'll be glad to tackle that project. It will give me a chance to learn more about....*

Approach #4: Repetitive or Escalating Assertion

Usually you can make a simple statement of assertion in a friendly manner, and others will respect it. Occasionally you'll have to deal with people who persist in violating your rights or ignoring your stated preferences. As long as you're convinced you're not violating their rights, it's important to stick with your original assertion by repeating it firmly, perhaps varying the words somewhat, but not wavering. In cases where they're clearly trying to violate your rights, you can state your position with increasing firmness without becoming aggressive. Here is an example:

A worker is repeatedly late in submitting an important periodic report. When you speak with him about it, he argues about the necessity of giving it top priority.

▶ **First response:** *I know it's time consuming to collect all the figures you need for this report, but it has top-priority status. I must receive it on time in order to prepare for the regular staff meetings.*

▶ **Second response:** *You'll have to manage your activities so that this report gets done on time. Make certain you're not late in submitting it again.*

▶ **Third response:** *If you can't manage your work so that the most important jobs are done on time, I'll have no choice but to reassign you to a position with less responsibility.*

In this case, the third response was appropriate because the earlier assertions were ignored. It would have been inappropriate if it had been the initial response.

The third response includes a contract option. The speaker said what her final assertion would be and gave the listener a chance to change his behavior before that occurred. Some people will believe you're serious about standing firm only when you reach the contract-option point. The option should be said not as a threat, but merely as a fact. Therefore, it's important to be calm and rational when you make this type of assertion. Speak in a matter-of-fact tone of voice to show that you're simply giving information about the consequences if the problem is not satisfactorily resolved.

Approach #5: Assertion That Confronts Broken Agreements

When people fail to keep their agreements with you, confrontive assertion is appropriate. Here are four steps you can take:

1. Describe specifically and nonjudgmentally what the other person said he or she would do.
2. State your understanding of what he or she actually did do.

3. Ask for cooperation in resolving this problem. What do they suggest?

4. State what you want to happen in this situation.

Again, it's important to express yourself in a matter-of-fact tone of voice with nonevaluative language. Here is an example: *I agreed that you could use the services of my assistant occasionally, as long as you check with me first. She said you asked her to do some work yesterday, but you didn't mention it to me. I'd like to find out why you did that.*

The confrontive assertion normally involves more two-way interaction than is shown here. You'll usually want to learn more about the circumstances of the broken agreement in order to solve the problem it has created. It's important to avoid a critical, accusing attitude, which usually results in an aggressive confrontation that judges the other person and attempts to make him or her feel guilty. For example: *You broke your promise! Obviously I can't depend on your word and will have to get everything in writing from you from now on.*

Approach #6: Persuasive Assertion in Groups

We've been discussing types of assertion that apply mainly to one-on-one transactions. Now let's look at ways to assert yourself in group situations. To have the greatest impact when expressing honest opinions in task-oriented groups such as staff meetings and committee meetings, you can learn to use timing, clear and concise presentation, congruent body language, and tact.

Tip #1: Timing is crucial. Timing is your most important consideration. It means you must choose the right time to express an opinion, but you must also avoid taking up too much group time by expressing your opinion too frequently. Therefore, you need to decide which of the agenda items being discussed have top priority for you and are worth taking a stand on. Otherwise, you may end up talking far too long about nearly every topic that's brought up. If the other group members decide that you just like to hear yourself talk and that you need to be the center of attention, they'll be likely to ignore your opinions on the issues that are really important to you.

The best time to state your opinion on an issue is probably after a third or a half of the committee members have already expressed their positions. By then, you have a sense of the group's position, and you can respond to the points that have been raised. It's unlikely that the group has made up its mind on the issue, so your position has a good chance of influencing the group's decision.

Tip #2: Clear, concise presentation is important. When you express your opinion on your top-priority item, state it as clearly and concisely as possible without belittling yourself.

▸ **Nonassertive:** *Well, I've been known to be wrong before, but it seems as if maybe we should think of some other ways of doing this.*

▸ **Assertive:** *This approach to marketing the product involves some high-risk factors. I think it would be a good idea to consider some other approaches that could reduce our risks.*

Tip #3: Body language is more important than words. To have the greatest impact, assertive words must be accompanied by assertive body language: look directly at the various members of the group, speak with appropriate loudness and firmness, and use your hands in a relaxed way to make reinforcing gestures. Of course, you must do your homework before the meeting so you know what you're talking about. Present only ideas you believe in wholeheartedly and have strong, positive feelings about.

Tip #4: Tact is essential. Tact is especially important when your viewpoint differs from that of the majority of the group or from that of an influential member. Find something that you honestly think is good about the opposing viewpoint and acknowledge that before stating your viewpoint. For example: *That's a good analysis of our internal budget problem. It's also important to examine the role that our competitors play in the problem.*

Approach #7: Assertion That Gives Feedback

Assertive leaders are able to give feedback that clarifies their thinking, feelings, opinions, and understanding of what others have said and done. As a manager, remember to give regular feedback so that the receiver gets at least as much positive as negative feedback. Give negative feedback early, before a situation builds to the point that strong emotional reactions may be involved. Approach situations in a spirit of helpfulness and willingness to solve any problems.

Use the following four-step feedback process:

Step #1: Give Feedback Specifically and Nonjudgmentally

Most people give feedback about problem behavior in vague, accusatory language. They therefore trigger a defensive reaction from the listener. Keep these tips in mind:

▶ **Paint an observable picture.** Describe the situation so that the listener can see a picture of what you saw, as if he or she were a disinterested observer watching the situation.

▶ **Be specific.** State exactly who did what, when, where, and to whom or what it was done. If appropriate, give a detailed, yet brief, step-by-step replay of exactly what happened. Don't bog down in detail. Keep your purpose clearly in mind.

▶ **Clarify your statements.** Be exact and accurate. Avoid the tendency to exaggerate behavior that bothers you by using all-or-nothing expressions, such as *never, always,* and *every time.* To describe behavior accurately, it's important to be exact by using phrases such as *three times this month, every day this week, sometimes, often.*

▶ **Use nonjudgmental words.** Find words that factually describe the behavior.

Using nonjudgmental words is the most difficult feedback step for most people. When people discuss behavior that offends them, they're prone to use judgmental words such as *sloppy, lazy, inconsiderate,* and *stupid.* These words not only judge a person's behavior, they are frequently used to overgeneralize about a person's character traits. Because they tend to put down a person and imply he or she is wrong, they're aggressive rather than assertive. They usually trigger defensive or guilty feelings. In addition, they give little or no information that can help the listener identify specific behavior that will be acceptable to you, as the following examples reveal:

▸ **Nonspecific, judgmental feedback:** *I would appreciate it if you would at least be considerate and polite in your dealings with me.*

▸ **Specific, descriptive feedback:** *When you came over to my desk yesterday, you spoke in a very loud voice and demanded the Carter Company invoice. When we were unable to furnish it, you called us incompetent....*

Step #2: Describe Concrete Effects

In addition to describing the specific behavior that's creating a problem, it's important to state the specific, concrete effects this behavior has on you or others. Again, it's important to stick with the facts and to express them in nonjudgmental terms. Clarify the situation by separating concrete effects on your life from your feelings about these effects.

▸ **Nonspecific, judgmental feedback:** *We have a problem with your invoicing unit.*

▸ **Specific, descriptive feedback:** *During the last three weeks, your invoicing unit has not informed us of delays in their invoice processing. We have received several telephone calls from angry customers because of these delays....*

Here, the concrete effect is complaints from angry customers.

Step #3: Express Feelings Effectively

Most people have difficulty identifying and expressing their feelings appropriately, but this skill can also be mastered. Even in business situations it can be important to communicate your feelings about another's behavior. Doing so is honest, it's an *I* message that helps to give the other person a clear picture of the situation, and it increases the impact of your feedback message. The listener is more likely to get it and to remember it. To be effective, however, your message must also make clear that you take responsibility for your own feelings. When you're focusing on expressing your feelings, remember to stick with feelings, not thoughts, evaluations, or solutions. And state your feelings directly and clearly—don't expect the other person to be a feelings reader or a mind reader.

Take responsibility for your feelings. In first attempting to communicate your feelings, you're likely to make such statements as: *You make me angry when you accuse me like that.* This *you* message implies that the other person is responsible for your anger and that you're blaming the other person for your feeling and accusing him or her of causing it. This further implies that the other person can control the way you feel, which places you in a weak, helpless role. A more responsible approach would be to use an *I* message: *I felt angry when you called me incompetent.*

State feelings, not evaluations. Let your attitude imply, *I'll tell you very directly what I'm feeling in response to your behavior, but I won't judge your behavior.* This attitude carries quite a different message from one that implies, *I'm going to tell you when you're good or bad, based on your behavior toward me.*

State feelings, not solutions. When you state solutions to the problem instead of expressing your feelings about it, you imply that you're superior to the other person. You're able to figure out the problem and a solution without even discussing it with him or her. This approach also implies a lack of trust—that you don't expect the other person to be able to figure out an acceptable solution to his or her own problem behavior. Also, stating a solution before discussing the problem omits vital problem-solving steps. You haven't agreed on a definition of the problem, much less a solution that is acceptable to both of you. The problem may now become one of enforcing the solution! People may resist your high-handedness even if they agree with your solution.

State feelings directly. Simply say you're pleased, happy, annoyed, frustrated, hurt—or whatever the feeling is. Don't imply your feelings by your tone of voice, emphasis, sarcasm, or other indirect means—and don't expect people to infer them from your cutting remarks, questions, denials, or cloaked messages.

Stating feelings directly is difficult for many people. For example, a direct statement would be, *I really become annoyed when you borrow my directory and don't return it.* But it's tempting to be indirect and say, *If people in this office would be more thoughtful, it would be a nicer place to work.* Such indirect messages usually communicate only a vague, underlying negative feeling. Someone who hears it is likely to interpret it as a generalized rejection of him or her as a person rather than your specific reaction to a specific action. Instead of thinking, *She's upset because I didn't return her directory,* a person is likely to think, *She doesn't like me; I wonder why.*

Step #4: Work Out a Resolution

Once you've expressed your version of the specific behavior that's causing a problem, the concrete effects it has on your life or on others, and how you feel about it, it's time to take the initiative in finding a solution to the problem or resolution of the conflict. Here are some suggestions:

Focus on the other person's viewpoint. Ask the other person how she or he sees this situation, and listen with an open mind, as nonjudgmentally as possible.

Acknowledge what the other person says. You may ask, *You feel that...?* or *You think we should do...?* Avoid the tendency at this point to defend your position by repeating your point and trying to prove it. Instead, focus your energy on understanding the other person's viewpoint, while not losing sight of your own.

Rephrase your position. Once you're sure you clearly understand the other person's viewpoint, you may want to come back to your position, but almost as if you are approaching it from the other person's side. *So the way you see this is that I'm making it difficult for you to cooperate by expecting too much too soon? Is that right?*

Reach an agreement. When both viewpoints are clear, it's time to work toward a solution to the problem or resolution of the conflict. In business situations, you'll normally want to agree on a solution or at least lay the groundwork for moving toward resolution. In personal situations, you may both decide that sharing thoughts and feelings is all that's needed for now. You both may need to think about the situation. You may say, *How are we going to do this from now on?* or *I think it's enough for now if we just understand each other's viewpoints and feelings about this.*

Establish a feeling of closure. Clear closure occurs when you state and restate the exact conditions of the solution the two of you have agreed to. If you decide to think over the situation first, then provide some sense of closure by expressing how you feel *now* at the end of this discussion and asking the other person how she or he feels now. Accept these feelings without trying to change them.

Learn the Four Feedback Steps

Use a four-step feedback process, as follows:

1. **When you...** You nonjudgmentally describe some specific problem behavior of the other person, pinpointing exactly the acts that you see as a problem.

2. **The effects are...** You describe as specifically as possible how the other person's behavior concretely affects your life—the practical problem it creates.

3. **I feel...** You describe the feelings you experience as a result. Take responsibility for your feelings and avoid the expression *You make me....*

4. **I prefer...** First ask what can be done to improve this situation—it works best when the other person volunteers a solution. However, if the answer doesn't quite solve the problem, be sure you describe what you want. Open the door to working together toward a resolution that both of you can support.

Learn to Recognize Effective Feedback

Here's an example of an effective feedback message: *When I don't get the information I need from you about the number of orders your department has processed each day, I'm unable to make appropriate work schedules for the next day. This has happened twice in the last two weeks, and I'm getting frustrated. What procedures can we work out to make sure I get the information I need each day?*

Now test your initial understanding of feedback messages by evaluating this example: *When you don't send me information about the number of orders your department has processed each day, you really frustrate me. I'd like you to be more reliable.*

Do you see anything in this message that doesn't follow the feedback techniques? In the last example, the speaker hasn't stated what effect the problem behavior has on her life. By the way she expresses her feelings, she puts herself in the position of a helpless victim. Instead of asking for a preferred type of behavior that is specific and objective, she makes a vague request that implies a condemnation of the other person's character.

Use Feedback Assertion to Build Authentic Relationships

Now you have the tools to give feedback assertively in problem situations. Even if the feedback doesn't lead to your preferred solution of a problem, it can help you become more open and direct with your thoughts and feelings. As a result, people are more likely to learn they can trust you. They *know where you're at*, for better or worse. They tend to become more open in their dealings with you and with others in the work group.

You can enhance this openness and trust by using feedback assertion about constructive behavior too. Here's an example: *Thank you for getting these reports to me on time every week. That makes it easy for me to be well-prepared for staff meetings. I feel grateful when I get that kind of cooperation. Keep up the good work.*

Feedback assertion helps you build an atmosphere for dealing with all kinds of behavior, while minimizing defensiveness.

Strategy #5

Actions Speak Louder

One reason it's so important to be convinced of your rights is that your true convictions will come through in your nonverbal behavior. It's virtually impossible to consciously control every aspect of your body language, voice tone, and facial expression. And these messages reveal how you really feel about a situation or person. They have far more impact than your words. Here's the relative impact, according to research studies:

Vocal expression	38%
Facial expression	55%
Total nonverbal impact	93%
Impact of words (verbal impact)	7%

If a speaker's facial expression or voice tone conflicts with what he or she is saying, the listener will normally accept and act on the nonverbal message. This makes sense when you consider that feelings have much more influence on actions than rational, logical thoughts do. People are more likely to act on their feelings, so when you get conflicting messages, pay more attention to the nonverbal portion.

Action Skill #1: Align Your Facial Expression and Voice Tone

High-status, assertive males tend to be more impassive than most women are. They are more *poker-faced* in business situations and, thus, express less emotion. They also smile less often and less broadly than women. Monitor your tendency to smile too often. Hold a vision of yourself as a credible professional person.

Most people equate a strong, deep male voice with power and authority. While most women neither want nor could have such a voice, you can almost certainly improve the assertiveness level of your voice. Many women retain the voice pitch and tone of a little girl throughout their lives. Voice pitch can be lowered with practice. Also, some women speak so softly it's difficult to hear them from more than a few feet away. A stronger, louder voice is essential to an assertive image, so practice until you're comfortable speaking so a person 20 feet away can easily hear every word.

You can work to make your voice firm, strong, relaxed, self-confident, and appropriately loud, forceful, low-pitched, and well-modulated. Here are some tips:

▶ Record your normal speaking voice on an audiocassette and play it back.

▶ Record yourself as you practice speaking at a deeper pitch.

▶ As you practice, think of yourself as an extremely powerful leader.

▶ Play it back. Can you detect the difference in the first and second recordings? When you listen to your playbacks, be alert for voice tones that are apologetic, tentative, meek, imploring, whining, prissy, nagging, or schoolmarmish.

▶ Tape your telephone conversations in order to pick up other voice patterns you want to change.

High-status male executives are usually somewhat less expressive in their voice modulation, as well as in their facial expression, than low-status women workers. This is one way they project a more self-possessed, rational image—one of cool moderation, carefully revealing only what they intend another to know. While a highly expressive voice is a real asset in public speaking, it can signal low status if it's overdone. In summary, your mental vision of yourself and your audiotape feedback are powerful tools for developing an assertive voice tone.

Action Skill #2: Project Power in Your Body Language

Your body language is a major part of your image—and it should project both power and approachability. Position your body language so it conveys self-confidence, liking, involvement, and interest in others. Research indicates that people with outgoing body language are more likely to take the lead in all types of situations.

Women's nonverbal behavior tends to convey more liking than that of men, as well as more empathy and connection with others. Women also convey more tenseness and submissiveness. Are you projecting an assertive, powerful image through your body language? Watch the high-status business executives you know. Then observe low-status workers. You may want to consciously practice some of the nonverbal behaviors that signal personal power and strength. Snapshot #2 gives comparisons of male power postures and female weakness postures—and some alternate female responses. Snapshot #3 on page 246 can help you identify other nonverbal behaviors you may want to modify in order to boost your assertive image.

Snapshot #2: Nonverbal Power Postures

Male Power Postures	Female Weakness Postures	Alternative Response
The Power Position: A woman walks into a man's office. He leans back in his chair, puts his hands behind his head, spreads his elbows wide, and straightens his knees. The message is that the woman is inferior.	The woman clasps her hands, leans forward. If seated, she crosses her legs and looks slightly downward.	Assume a relaxed posture. Put your fingertips together, your hands pointed upward, a gesture called *steepling*; or stand over his desk.
The Power Stance: A man approaches a woman's desk where she's seated, and he talks to her from above. *Or,* a man who is much taller than a woman moves close to her during a conversation.	The woman remains seated, straining to look up at the man during the conversation. *Or,* the woman throws her head back in order to look up at the man.	Move casually back and then stand up. Step back. Find an excuse to casually move away so your eyes seems to be level with his; or get him to sit.
The Power Touch: A man puts his arm around a woman to discuss an office procedure (showing power by acting in a more intimate way than she would initiate).	The woman touches her hair, wets her lips, smiles.	If standing or walking, step back and turn toward him in a relaxed way as you continue to talk, listen, and/or walk along, gently forcing him to drop his arm. If you're seated, turn in your chair or get up. If he repeats the touch, fold your arms and move away. If he persists, tell him he's invading your space.

Snapshot #3: Nonverbal Behaviors and the Range of Assertion

Nonassertive Behavior	Assertive Behavior	Aggressive Behavior
Facial: Smiling often, broadly; relatively animated, expressive.	Relatively impassive; less smiling.	Tight with anger; jaw and brow tense; scornful; patronizing; seductive, smiling, manipulative.
Voice tone: Relatively expressive, sometimes apologetic; tentative, meek, prissy.	Relatively impassive; objective, self-confident, firm, decisive.	Angry, sarcastic, sneering, flippant, nagging, scolding, or scornful; extremely loud or menacingly low.
Voice pitch: High, little-girl quality.	Relatively low, forceful.	Menacingly low or yelling.
Hands: Playing with hair; nervous; folded in lap primly.	Still or purposeful, smooth movements; hands at sides.	On one or both hips; pointing or shaking finger.
Eyes: Cast downward, little contact while speaking; watching speaker intently; avoiding direct contact.	Frequent eye contact while talking; steady, firm; casual, relaxed observation while another is talking.	Staring; angry, challenging; cold, expressionless.
Head: Tilted, moving from side to side, up and down; ducked.	Still, straight.	Stiff, erect.
Posture: Slumped, stooped, yet tense; ramrod tense, at attention, nervous.	Almost military, yet relaxed; head and spine straight; feet slightly apart, well-grounded; arms at sides.	Tense—knees locked; feet spread widely apart, firmly planted; fists clenched.
Positions: Hesitantly standing; sitting forward tensely, knees and feet together; arms folded tightly in lap; other balanced, tense positions; vigilant.	Asymmetrical, expansive positions; arms on sides of chair, sometimes leaning to one side in relaxed way; leaning back, clasping hands behind neck; males: turning chair around and straddling it or putting feet on desk; casually turning one's back on another to get something.	Tensely, forcefully leaning forward; pointing fingers; pounding desk.
Movements: Small, controlled, tense; covering face with hand; fiddling with an object; rhythmic shaking of leg/foot.	Expansive, relaxed, free; pressing fingertips together in a steeple; free of nervous mannerisms.	Waving arms angrily; closely towering over another; invading another's personal territory.

Offer an assertive handshake. In our culture the handshake is almost universally obligatory for men when they are introduced and frequently when they meet or say good-bye. Women have traditionally used the handshake selectively and at their own option. Psychologist Albert Mehrabian says that a person's general level of preference for handshakes reflects how positively he or she feels toward others. Here are some suggestions for handling handshakes:

▶ Shake hands to show professionalism, assertiveness, and personal power.

▶ Shake hands when you first meet someone, when you haven't seen them for a while, to offer congratulations, and to seal deals.

▶ Use a firm handshake, which indicates sincerity and self-confidence as well as a greater liking for the person and warmer feelings.

▶ Avoid prolonged handshakes, which are generally considered too intimate.

▶ Avoid a loosely clasped handshake, which is usually interpreted as a sign of aloofness and unwillingness to become involved.

Think tall. The average woman (5 ft. 4 1/2 in. tall) is 4 1/2 inches shorter than the average man (5 ft. 9 in. tall). In the business world, being taller usually means being more respected, more powerful, and more affluent. Several studies have established these relationships. In fact, a 1985 study showed that each additional inch was worth an extra $600 a year to male MBAs. A 4 1/2-inch average difference would have been worth $2,700 that year—and much more in today's dollars.

In business, tall women tend to have the same advantages as tall men. On the other hand, a short man may be even more threatened by a tall woman than by a tall man. He may see the short woman as less threatening than anyone else in the office and therefore let down his guard and confide in her. In addition, being short can be overcome by projecting a competent, self-confident attitude, as exemplified by cabinet member Donna Shalala and author-lecturer Dr. Ruth Westheimer. Attitude can create a taller *image*, which in turn can enhance your career. Here are some specific techniques:

▶ *Think of yourself as tall.* Your self-image can have greater impact than physical size.

▶ *Walk tall.* Pull yourself up to your full height; practice this as often as you can think of it.

▶ *Dress tall.* Find some good books on how to dress for the illusion of greater height, which include some of the same techniques as dressing for an illusion of slenderness. Typical techniques include a one-color effect from head to toe, solid colors or small-scale patterns, softer fabrics that follow body lines, simple lines, vertical or diagonal lines, and uncluttered necklines.

▶ *Project an assertive professional image.* If you begin to feel intimidated or overpowered when someone is towering over you or is stereotyping you as childlike or weak because of your size, focus on your career goals and picture yourself as a confident, assertive professional.

Use power dressing and grooming. Your appearance tells people a great deal about your attitude toward yourself and others, your competence, and your role in the company.

Your clothing and grooming signal how well you fit in with the company image and with others in the company. Find role models who have the kind of power, jobs, and assertiveness you want to have. Dress for where you want to be next, not for where you are now. Decision-makers are more likely to think of you as promotable when you look the part.

Master the power stance and power walk. In our culture, relaxation and tension are very important ways in which status differences are subtly conveyed, according to Mehrabian. His research into the significance of relaxed, as opposed to tense, body positions indicates that males in our culture assume more relaxed postures than females do. This pattern predominates in a variety of circumstances, whether the men are in the presence of women or of other men. Some of these power postures and ways women can respond to them are shown in Snapshot #3 on page 246. It's important for you to respond with a message of strength, because most men know the signs of weakness and look for them (though not necessarily at a conscious level).

The stance and walk of upper-middle-class people is different from that of people from the lower middle class. Upper-middle-class people keep their shoulders straight, head aligned, eyes forward, arms in toward their body, fingers lightly cupped, and walk almost military with even strides of about 12 inches. The most powerful individuals walk with the relaxed power of a panther—unhurried, smooth movements, but ready to spring. Lower-middle-class people walk with their shoulders and body rolling more, hips swinging, arms swinging out, head thrown more forward and downward, and using long or erratic strides.

Hold a mental picture of your power image. How can you be sure your nonverbal messages match your verbal ones? Perhaps most important is being very clear about what you *intend* to communicate. Before you meet with the other person, periodically relax and focus on your intended message. See yourself as a credible, powerful, professional person. Visualize coming across assertively, both verbally and nonverbally, behaving naturally and appropriately, and achieving your intended goals. When the time comes to be assertive, your subconscious mind will take over the nonverbal aspects if you'll let it.

Practice new body language. The good news is that you can change the way people perceive you by consciously changing your nonverbal messages. When you send high-status messages, people peg you at that level whether you're actually there or not. Any time you try out new assertive verbal messages, it's important to practice the nonverbal actions that must accompany your words. New ways of behaving may seem difficult and awkward at first, but they'll become natural with practice.

Remember, you learned your current body language as a woman in a patriarchal culture. Those movements are no more *you* than any other learned behavior. There are many potential *you's*, and you can have fun experimenting with new body language that expresses the *you* that you want to create. As one professional woman said, "Batting my eyelashes and tossing my head are no more *me* than is direct, assertive eye contact. Batting eyelashes just seemed to work in the culture I grew up in. Now it doesn't serve me." Practice the power postures and nonverbal actions given in Snapshots #2 and #3. When you get a chance, record yourself in an assertive mode, using videotape and audiotape. Study your nonverbal language. Videotape is such a powerful tool for change because you step outside yourself and get the picture so vividly. Soon you'll have a new power image.

Action Skill #3: Establish Assertive Eye Contact

The eyes are considered by many to be the most important means of nonverbal communication. Often they're a clue to thoughts and feelings the sender may be trying to hide. In normal conversation, you glance at a person who is speaking for about a second, and then glance away to show the speaker you're listening but not staring. Whether you're speaking or listening, if you avoid eye contact, it will probably be interpreted as a sign of low self-esteem, weakness, or guilty feelings. Research indicates that people tend to maintain a higher degree of eye contact with those they believe will be approving or supportive of them. However, an overly long meeting of the eyes is uncommon and therefore can have special meaning, such as anger, challenge, or sexual attraction.

Action Skill #4: Make Assertive Use of Space and Symbols

The way space is used is also a means of nonverbal communication. Humans, as well as other animals, tend to lay claim to and defend a particular territory. There is a psychological advantage to meeting with someone in your own territory. Lawyers like to hold important meetings with adversaries in their own offices, just as athletic teams prefer to play on their *home* court or field. People with high status tend to:

▶ Control a larger territory (space, subordinates, decision-making authority, and other aspects of power) than people with lower status.

▶ Protect their territory better.

▶ Invade the territory of lower-status employees more readily.

Look at the people in your organization. In most firms, the higher the status, the larger the office and the more private. As executives move up, their territory is better protected by the number of stories in the building, the length of hallways, and the presence of walls, doors, receptionists, and other barriers to immediate access.

Executives usually presume familiarity with subordinates by casually dropping by their desks or offices. They usually feel free to sit down without being asked, implying that they are relaxed and intend to stay awhile. Most employees, on the other hand, would hesitate to invade the territory of their manager in this way. The larger the gap in status between the executive and the employee, the freer the executive tends to feel to invade and the more hesitant the subordinate is to do so.

Your male peers and workers may attempt to subtly dominate you through such territorial moves. Unless you're aware of the significance of such actions, you may unconsciously respond with submissive behavior. Here are some tips for countering subtle territorial moves by the men in your office:

▶ Mentally hold your ground.

▶ Rise and move casually around your office during the conversation.

▶ Excuse yourself on the pretext of keeping an appointment.

▶ Set up a barrier to screen visitors to your office or desk.

▶ Assume the same familiarity with peers by dropping by their offices.

Nonverbal status symbols trigger strong feelings because they can satisfy or frustrate ego needs. People are usually quite sensitive to the messages implied by the ways in which managers handle status symbols such as their names on routing slips, lists, directories, organization charts, office doors, and stationery; the size and location of their offices; their furniture and equipment; their secretarial and clerical support; and their access to other company resources. The more visible these status symbols are to others, the stronger the feelings likely to be attached to them, especially if these symbols are taken away.

Strategy #6

Try Out New Assertive Ways

You've had a chance to become aware of your current attitudes and actions in the area of assertiveness and to see some ways in which assertiveness enhances a leader's effectiveness. Now, it's time to start playing with new ways of thinking, feeling, and acting in your relationships. It's time to identify patterns that are not creating what you want in your life—and to experiment with new patterns that are more likely to bring the results you want.

You developed your current behavior patterns by copying role models, developing beliefs and self-talk habits based on parent messages, and responding to the rewards parents and others gave you. You can learn new, more productive behaviors in exactly the same way you learned the old, now nonproductive behavior—only now you're doing it at a conscious level.

Assertion Skill #1: Rewrite Old Parent Messages

All of us operate at times on *parent messages* that we internalized in childhood. But we're frequently unaware of these messages and their impact on our behavior. When you become aware of the parent messages underlying your nonproductive behavior, the behavior changes you make are likely to be more profound and long lasting than when you remain unaware.

Take shyness, for example. Its root cause is an excessive concern that you'll be evaluated, plus an assumption that the evaluation will be negative and that you'll be rejected in some way. Dreading or fearing rejection, the shy person hangs back, *freezes*, becomes self-conscious, and won't risk taking assertive action. Simply developing and practicing relevant verbal and nonverbal skills can do much to remedy shyness—for example, practicing assertiveness, public speaking, and social skills.

Such behavior change will be longer lasting, however, if you look at underlying causes and make changes at a deeper level. That means becoming aware of parent messages you internalized, such as *You must achieve, you must compete, you must win to be okay.* The implied message is, *If you fail, it's because you're a loser, and you don't try hard enough.* The cure for nonproductive parent messages is to refute them in your own mind now and make new messages to yourself. Then focus on your strengths, keep substituting your new messages, and spend more time being involved with activities and people who enhance your feeling of self-worth.

Snapshot #4 on page 251 and Skill Builder #2 on page 256 list common messages parental figures stress to children through verbal and nonverbal communication.

Snapshot #4: Parent Messages That Limit You

Parent Message	Effect on Rights	Effect on Behavior	Alternate Messages
Think of others first. (Give to others even if you're hurting. Don't be selfish.)	I have no right to place my needs above those of other people.	When I have conflict with someone else, I'll give in and satisfy the other person's needs and forget about my own.	To be selfish is to place your desires before everyone else's, ignoring others' rights and needs. However, you must take responsibility for meeting your own needs and goals. Your needs are as important as other people's. Try a compromise when needs conflict.
Be modest and humble. (Don't act superior to others.)	I have no right to do anything that would imply that I'm better than others.	I'll discontinue my achievements and turn aside any compliments. I'll encourage others' contributions and keep silent about my own. I'll keep my opinions to myself.	It's undesirable to build yourself up at the expense of another person. However, you have as much right as others to show your abilities and take pride in yourself. It's healthy to enjoy your accomplishments.
Be understanding and overlook trivial irritations. (Don't be a nag or shrew and complain.)	I have no right to feel angry or express my anger.	When I'm in a line and someone cuts in front of me, I'll say nothing. I won't tell my girlfriend that I don't like her constant interruptions.	It's undesirable to deliberately nitpick, but life is made up of trivial incidents that are sometimes irritating. You have a right to your angry feelings; if you express them somehow as they occur, they won't build to an explosion.

In parentheses, following the parent messages in Snapshot #4, are explanations of how children frequently interpret them. This is followed by the effect such interpretations can have on their rights and their assertive behavior, and alternate messages that are more realistic and workable. Skill Builder #2 on page 256 lists only the parent messages, not the effects or alternate messages. See whether any of these messages, or similar ones, are affecting your viewpoints and actions.

Assertion Skill #2: Revise Self-Limiting Beliefs

Irrational self-limiting beliefs sabotage your efforts. They create stressful emotions. If you irrationally believe that it would be *awful* and *catastrophic* to fail to accomplish a major goal or to be rejected by a significant person in your life, then you'll feel anxious, depressed, or guilty. Another irrational idea is that it's terrible if others treat you unfairly and those who do so should be blamed and severely punished. This idea leads to intense anger when others behave unfairly toward you.

Self-limiting beliefs often involve *I need* or *I must*, while rational beliefs involve *I want* or *I prefer*. Here are some self-limiting beliefs and alternate beliefs that are especially significant for women:

➡ *If I stand up for my rights, others will get mad at me.*
  ▸ **Alternate belief:** *If I stand up for my rights, people may get mad, they may not care much one way or the other, or they may like and respect me more. When I assert a legitimate right, chances are the results will be at least partially favorable.*

➡ *If people do get mad at me, it will be terrible. I will be shattered.*
  ▸ **Alternate belief 1:** *I can handle other people's anger without feeling devastated.*
  ▸ **Alternate belief 2:** *When I stand up for a legitimate right, I don't have to feel responsible for another person's emotional reaction.*

➡ *If I'm honest and direct with people and say* no, *I'll hurt them.*
  ▸ **Alternate belief 1:** *People may or may not feel hurt if I say* no *directly.*
  ▸ **Alternate belief 2:** *Most people are not so easily shattered that they can't handle another's honest, straightforward message.*

➡ *If the other person does feel hurt when I say* no, *then I'm responsible.*
  ▸ **Alternate belief 1:** *Although they may be surprised and perhaps a little embarrassed when I say* no, *most people are not so vulnerable that they'll be devastated by it.*
  ▸ **Alternate belief 2:** *I can let people know I care for them at the same time that I'm saying* no.
  ▸ **Alternate belief 3:** *The other person's hurt or angry feelings may be his or her own problem.*

➡ *It's selfish and bad for me to turn down others' valid requests. They'll think I'm mean, and they won't like me.*
  ▸ **Alternate belief 1:** *Even valid requests don't necessarily warrant my time and energy.*
  ▸ **Alternate belief 2:** *I can find myself continually doing other people's priorities rather than my own.*
  ▸ **Alternate belief 3:** *It's okay to take care of my own needs before the needs of others.*
  ▸ **Alternate belief 4:** *The more decision-making power and visibility I have, the more critics I'll have. This is true for all managers and leaders.*

➡ *I must be extremely cautious about making statements or asking questions that might appear dumb.*
  ▸ **Alternate belief:** *No one's perfect and no one knows everything—even about his or her area of expertise. Asking seemingly dumb questions at times reflects confidence and competence. (I figure if I don't understand it, there's a reason.)*

➥ *People label women who stand up, speak out, and fight back. They'll call me a nag or a shrew. They'll say I'm grouchy or difficult.*

▸ **Alternate belief:** *When I'm direct, honest, and stand up for my rights appropriately, others are likely to respect me. Those who don't would probably not respect my nonassertiveness either; rather, they would probably use my timidity, fear, or anxiety to manipulate me and take advantage of me.*

Assertion Skill #3: End Negative Self-Talk

What you say to yourself just before, during, and after an incident is based on your parent messages and beliefs. It has a very important influence on your behavior. Examples of nonassertive self-talk include: *They'll think I'm dumb*; *I'll probably blow it.* Examples of assertive self-talk include: *I'll relax and let my best self handle this*; *I can do it.*

Most self-talk that leads to nonassertive or aggressive behavior is typical of the negative thought trains discussed earlier. It has one or more of these characteristics:

▸ Draws a conclusion when evidence is lacking or even contradictory: *He said there was no need to discuss next year's vacation now. I'll bet he's planning to let me go before the first of the year.*

▸ Exaggerates the meaning of the event: *I never expected to get the news that I was a failure in front of the copy machine on a Monday morning.*

▸ Disregards some important aspect of the situation: *The boss has a hangover and is running behind on current projects.*

▸ Oversimplifies events as good or bad, right or wrong: *He's had it in for me ever since we lost the Acme account. He probably thinks it's all my fault.*

▸ Overgeneralizes from a single incident: *It's terrible to be a failure at 35. I'll bet no one will want to hire such a failure.*

Negative self-statements can cause you to cycle down into a state of anxiety or despair. You can begin to break the cycle by staying in the present moment and dealing with current reality. To interrupt negative self-talk and stop it in its tracks, ask yourself the following key questions:

1. *What's my anxiety level (on a scale of 1 to 10)?*
2. *What am I doing (verbally and nonverbally)?*
3. *What am I feeling? What am I thinking?*
4. *What do I want to be thinking, feeling, and doing?*
5. *What thoughts, opinions, desires, or feelings do I want to express in this situation? What do I want the other person to know?*
6. *What thoughts are keeping me from doing what I want?*
7. *What do I think is appropriate to express?*
8. *How can I go ahead and express what I want?*

Now, to assert yourself appropriately, practice new, more constructive self-talk. Also, when your anxiety level is high, remember to use an effective relaxation technique or self-mastery visualization. Excuse yourself as soon as possible and find a private place to relax and get things in perspective. Here are some examples of positive self-talk.

Before the event: *I know how to deal with this even though it's upsetting. Easy does it! Remember to keep your sense of humor. I'm not going to let him get to me. I'll look for the positives and not assume the worst.*

During the event: *Getting upset won't help. My anger (or anxiety) is a signal of what I need to do; it's time to instruct myself. I can keep my cool.*

After the event: *I don't need to take it personally. Can I laugh about it? Is it really so serious? I won't let the bullies (turkeys, mosquitoes, etc.) get me down. I can win this game if I play my cards right. I handled that one pretty well!*

Assertion Skill #4: Go for Positive Payoffs

If you're like most women, you're comfortable with the *security* payoffs that nonassertiveness helps you hold onto. You may be unaware of the high-level payoffs assertiveness brings, or you may be afraid to risk losing what you're sure of. In other words, although you're not satisfied with what your current behavior is getting you, at least you know more or less what to expect. You may fear that you'll lose more than you'll gain if you begin asserting yourself.

Recognize negative and positive payoffs. Research indicates that when women begin realistically to weigh what they gain against what they lose, the risks of assertiveness become more attractive. Here are some typical comments about nonassertiveness:

▶ *I get to be nice and feel everyone's approval, but I'm seeing that I'm not sure who I am, other than what people want me to be. Maybe it's time to give up letting everyone else define me.*

▶ *I avoid rejection, but I give up lots of opportunities to learn and grow.*

▶ *My boss will protect me, but I never develop the confidence of standing on my own two feet.*

▶ *I get to be safe and secure in the short run. But I'm beginning to see that I'm dependent too, and that just invites people to encroach on my rights and my space.*

▶ *I get to avoid putting up a fight or being called a troublemaker. But when I set a low value on myself, in a way I make life hard for all women.*

Let's focus for a moment on those situations in which you've behaved nonassertively, with poor results. Understanding *why* you acted that way—what payoffs you get from such behavior—can help you decide to assert. Remember, you only repeat behavior that brings you some type of reward or payoff. You may even perceive negative attention as a payoff, though probably at a subconscious level. *Some attention is better than nothing, and at least I know what to expect.* Here are some payoffs other women report. See how they compare with yours:

▶ Avoiding risk, playing it safe, and not rocking the boat.

▶ Getting approval (avoiding losing another person's approval).

▶ Avoiding a scene or hassle.

▶ Being able to blame someone else if things don't work out.

▶ Being polite, being helpful.

▶ Avoiding rude or aggressive behavior.

These payoffs obscure the greater rewards assertiveness can bring. If you focus on *safety payoffs*, you forget that standing up for your rights can pay off in increased respect and goodwill from others. Whenever you find yourself *not* taking assertive action because of fear, ask yourself, *What am I getting out of this?*

Focus on positive payoffs. What are the positive payoffs you stand to gain when you spend more time in an assertive mode? Women mention these rewards:

▸ *I like myself better when I speak out and stand up for my rights. It may be more trouble at the time, but it feels so good afterward. I no longer have to deal with conflict over what I should have said and done.*

▸ *I was driving down the street, listening to the car radio. I heard the speaker say, 'If you're not being rejected at least once a week, you're simply not trying.' What a revelation! Most men risk rejection all the time. That's when I started coming out of my protective shell.*

▸ *At first it was scary coming out of my cocoon. But at least my achievements are my own now. There's no way I would go back again.*

▸ *I've decided it's better to be a lion for a day than a sheep for life.*

The final step in the change process is to select the assertive techniques or combination of techniques that you think will work best for you in your problem situation. Think about how you'll apply them and rehearse them with a friend.

Assertion Skill #5: Start With One Low-Risk Situation

You may find many areas in your life where you'd like to get better results. Work on one area at a time. Begin with situations where little is at stake: interactions with strangers and acquaintances who have little impact or significance in your life, such as sales clerks and office bureaucrats. If you blow it, it doesn't really matter.

Don't *condemn* your ineffective behavior or actively try to squelch it. This kind of attention tends to reinforce it so that it becomes more deeply entrenched than ever! Simply notice it and try out new, assertive behavior. Identify your rights. Build on the strengths you already have: You're in the assertive mode in some types of situations already. Spend more time in this mode. Then start using the assertive mode in other kinds of situations. You'll find that a small success in one area of your life will provide incentive to make changes in other areas. You'll gain confidence in asserting yourself in increasingly significant situations where the stakes are higher.

Now you have the strategies and techniques for deciding when and how to assert yourself effectively. The Skill Builders that follow give you a chance to practice new behaviors and rehearse anticipated situations. Build on your successes. Take time to notice your growing sense of strength and self-confidence. And above all, *enjoy* being the director of your own life story.

Skill Builders

Skill Builder #1: Case Study—Giving Assertive Feedback to Jennifer

Purpose: To apply your knowledge of giving feedback.

Step 1: Read the following story. You have a new apartment mate, Jennifer. You have been sharing an apartment for about a month now, and things have been going fairly smoothly. However, two or three times you have come home from the office to the following scene: In the entry hall, Jennifer's coat is thrown over the chair; her shoes are lying in the middle of the floor; and her briefcase is on the floor, leaning against the wall. In the living room, the newspaper is spread all over—part of it on the floor, and the rest of it on the table and the sofa. Various articles of clothing are also scattered around the room. Jennifer, wearing an old robe, is sitting in the easychair, with her feet propped up on the arm of the sofa. She's drinking a can of beer and eating peanuts. Some peanuts and an empty beer can are on the living-room floor. The television is playing loudly.

Now it's Friday. This morning a man you've been interested in getting to know better called you at the office and asked you out to dinner. You agreed and suggested he come by your apartment about 7 p.m. for a before-dinner drink. You rush home from the office and reach your apartment at 5:30. As you enter, you see a repeat of the previously described scenario. You decide that the time has come to give Jennifer some feedback about her behavior. You say, *Jennifer, I want to talk with you....*

Step 2: Finish the statement to Jennifer. On a sheet of paper, write what you would say to Jennifer.

Step 3: Evaluate your statement. Get feedback on your feedback skills. First, compare your statement with the suggestions given in Approach #7, "Assertion That Gives Feedback." (See page 240.) Then, ask a friend to read your statement and evaluate your effectiveness in describing behavior nonjudgmentally, assertively expressing how the behavior affects your feelings and your life, and opening the door to consensus on changing the situation. Revise the statement until you're satisfied with it.

Skill Builder #2: Rewrite Old Parent Messages

Purpose: To change self-limiting parent messages you've internalized.

Step 1: Examine the parent messages that follow. Did you receive any of these messages as a child? Think about what effect they had on your sense of your own rights.

- ➡ Be perfect.
- ➡ Hurry up. (And grow up. And get out of my hair.)
- ➡ Please me. (Act in ways that are important to me at the expense of your own growth or desires.)
- ➡ Try hard. (And make me proud. And never notice that you've made it.)
- ➡ Be nice. (Even if it results in being used or abused.)
- ➡ Be strong. (Don't be afraid. Don't be sad. Don't cry.)
- ➡ List any other parent messages that affected your right to be yourself, to do the things you wanted in your own way.

Step 2: Select the first parent message you want to work on.

Step 3: Identify the effect it had *on your rights*, and write about it. Then write about the effect it had *on your assertive behavior.*

Step 4: What alternate message can you now give yourself? Write a new message that supports your right to assert yourself.

Step 5: Give the new message to the child who is still within you. The child part of you still has a powerful effect on your current life. Try a deep relaxation technique. Go back in memory to your childhood and find the child who received the old parent message. Ask her what she needs and wants. Give her the support, love, and comfort she needs. Then give her the new message that allows her to act assertively, with confidence and security.

Step 6: Repeat Steps 3 through 5 for other parent messages you want to rewrite.

Skill Builder #3: Changing Modes—From Nonproductive to Assertive

Purpose: To practice changing to an assertive mode.

Step 1: Identify a situation that you'd like to improve. Define it clearly and specifically and decide exactly what your goal is. State your current behavior and your desired behavior. Determine how much control you have over these outcomes. (Does the outcome depend mostly on your behavior or on another person's?)

Step 2: Name one or more *role models* who handle similar situations well. Describe what they say and do that's effective. Practice saying and doing those things.

Step 3: Identify any parent messages, self-limiting beliefs, negative self-talk, and stressful feelings about what would happen if you acted assertively.

Step 4: Rewrite and change parent messages, beliefs, and self-talk about your rights and behavior in this situation. Process stressful emotions.

Step 5: Identify the *payoffs* you get from the current mode and payoffs you stand to gain if you use an assertive mode.

Step 6: Identify your *personal rights* in the situation—rights you're willing to stand up for. Identify other's rights that you're willing to respect.

Skill Builder #4: Saying *No* Assertively and Gracefully

Purpose: To develop the ability to say *no* assertively and gracefully.

Step 1: Briefly describe in writing a specific situation in which you avoided saying *no* for reasons such as the following:

➡ You felt obligated to give a lengthy explanation (perhaps untrue) to justify your behavior.

➡ You feared you'd be perceived as hostile or aggressive.

➡ You feared you would handle the situation awkwardly, not as gracefully as you'd like.

➡ You wouldn't be able to stick with your refusal, so you might as well say *yes*.

➡ You feared you would feel guilty if you said *no*.

The following are typical situations calling for assertiveness that might help you think of your own situations:

➡ Ending a telephone conversation with a talkative friend.

➡ Refusing an invitation.

➡ Saying *no* to a request.

➡ Canceling or changing plans.

➡ Returning merchandise and getting a full refund.

➡ Leaving a shop without buying anything after a salesperson has spent a great deal of time and energy trying to make a sale.

Step 2: Briefly describe in writing a *specific* situation in which you *have* said *no*, but you weren't satisfied with either the process or the outcome for one of the reasons mentioned in Step 1.

Step 3: Briefly describe in writing a *general* type of situation in which you normally have the same type of difficulty saying *no*.

Step 4: For each of these situations, move into an assertive mode and practice giving your assertive message without encountering the difficulty you fear. Here are some sample phrases you might use:

➡ *It's been great talking with you. I must go now. See you soon.*

➡ *That sounds wonderful, but I have plans. Maybe next time.*

➡ *I see a real need for that, but I'm not the one to do it.*

➡ *Thanks, but my workload (schedule, etc.) won't permit me to do that.*

➡ *I'll consider your concerns, but I can't make a commitment at this time.*

➡ *I appreciate what you're saying, and I still must decline.*

➡ *I'm unable to use this dress. It doesn't work with my wardrobe. Please credit my account.*

➡ *Thanks for helping me. I must go now. I look forward to shopping here again.*

Step 5: If you still have reservations about saying *no*, review the relevant concepts we've discussed.

The need to over-explain: This stems from holding a powerless position relative to men in our culture. It reflects a child-to-parent belief that others are entitled to a full, detailed explanation of your comings and goings. Professional persons offer such responses as, *I have a previous commitment.* It's understood that professionals keep their commitments.

Perception of aggressiveness: Review the discussion of your rights found in Strategy #2. As long as your *no* reflects a basic right and doesn't violate another's right without consultation, you're not being aggressive. Monitor your attitude to avoid resentment and hostility. Try assertion with empathy.

A feeling of awkwardness: Keep rights and empathy in mind; then practice, practice, practice—grace will come.

Not able to stick with *no*: Review your rights and become firmly committed to your right to say *no*. Review the discussion of assertion with increasing firmness. Try the *broken-record technique*, which consists of repeating your refusal each time the other person repeats the request. Keep saying *no*—politely, firmly, with slightly different phraseology, but still sticking with *no*.

A feeling of guilt: Search for old parent messages that may trigger guilt—as well as self-limiting beliefs, negative payoffs, and negative self-talk. Guilt is often based on a feeling of resentment or anger—*I said no, but they made me feel wrong*. This is a victim viewpoint. Review the discussion of taking responsibility found in Strategy #4.

Skill Builder #5: Define the Motives and Meaning of Your Own Actions

Purpose: To recognize when your actions are misperceived or misinterpreted and when others attribute incorrect motives or meanings to you and your actions; to practice direct and nondefensive ways of responding to such redefinitions.

Step 1: Briefly describe in writing a situation in which someone has redefined the meaning of your actions and you did not respond assertively. Here are some examples to help you get started.

➡ You refused a friend a favor, and he or she defined the refusal as a personal insult or rejection.

➡ You spent time with a friend, and another friend reacted jealously and took it as a personal put-down.

➡ You arrived late, and someone assumed the meeting wasn't important to you.

Step 2: For each incident, write briefly how you could stand up to the other person and make whatever assertive statements you wish to make about your motives or the meaning of your actions.

Step 3: In front of a mirror, practice making your assertive statements until you feel your words and actions convey the tone you want.

10

Handle Difficult People

Everything that irritates us about others can lead us to an understanding of ourselves.

—Carl Jung, psychiatrist

People are fascinating and fun most of the time. They're also perplexing and frustrating to deal with sometimes—an eternal mystery in their complexity. One way to sort out the maze of difficult people situations you encounter is to recognize that most problems stem from people's inability or unwillingness to act assertively. When you recognize the types of situations that stem from aggressive, passive-aggressive, and passive modes of behavior, you've taken the first step in resolving difficult people situations. Before you get into the steps, though, review your current beliefs about dealing with difficult people. Then, meet Cathleen Black, a publisher who has mastered the art of building positive relationships with an honest, direct approach.

How should women deal with difficult people?

1. Should your main goal in a difficult people situation be turning it into a winning situation for you?
2. When political game-playing is involved, should you avoid the situation or dive right in?
3. Is it always best to call game-playing as you see it?
4. Does the power you need to transcend difficult people situations stem primarily from your power network?

Maintaining *good mind* is the key to maintaining your balance in difficult people situations. You need to recognize the difficulty and deal with it, but not be pulled into negative viewpoints or contracting emotions.

Aggressive actions. When someone behaves aggressively, for example, you understand that they're violating your rights. A major strategy, therefore, is to maintain your self-respect by standing up for your rights. At the same time you must maintain respect for the other person's rights, try to get at the root of the problem, and work toward a joint resolution.

Cathleen Black, Publisher

Cathleen Black began her career by selling ads for magazines such as *Holiday* and *Travel & Leisure* before joining *New York* magazine in 1970. In 1972, she helped launch the first feminist magazine, *Ms.*, and rose to associate publisher. Later, she agreed to return to *New York* magazine with the understanding that if she improved business, she would be made publisher. In 1979, she made history, becoming the first woman publisher of a weekly consumer magazine, *New York*.

Cathleen is widely credited for the success of *USA TODAY*, where for eight years (from 1983 to 1991) she first held the title of president, then publisher. She also served as a board member and executive vice president for marketing of Gannett, its parent company.

In 1991, she became president and CEO of the Newspaper Association of America, the industry's largest trade group, where she served for five years before joining Hearst.

Cathleen made history again in 1995, when she was hired to run Hearst Magazines, becoming the first woman to hold the position. The Hearst Corporation is the world's largest publisher of monthly magazines, including *Cosmopolitan*; *Esquire*; *Good Housekeeping*; *Harper's Bazaar*; *Marie Claire*; *O, The Oprah Magazine*; *Popular Mechanics*; *Redbook*; and *Town & Country*—18 magazines in all. Cathleen also oversees 133 international editions of those magazines, in more than 100 countries.

One of her key areas of emphasis is extending the brand names of Hearst's titles beyond magazines, into more than 3,500 products on the world market. She also has promoted growth in licensing and the Internet, and has overseen aggressive international expansion. As electronic media continue to carve into the market for the printed word, her outspoken commitment to magazines will be invaluable to the industry.

Cathleen's style is to meet challenges head-on. She's known to be very direct, and she will not be pushed around. She believes in heading off problems by reviewing them before they become big. The *Financial Times* recently named her "The First Lady of American Magazines" and "one of the leading figures in American publishing over the past two decades." She has consistently been listed among *Fortune* magazine's "Most Powerful Women in American Business." In 2000, she was named "Publishing Executive of the Year" by *Advertising Age*, and in 2002, *Crain's New York Business* named her one of its "100 Most Influential Business Leaders."

Cathleen serves as a member of the boards of IBM, *i*Village, and the Coca-Cola Company. She has recently completed a two-year term as chairman of the Magazine Publishers of America. She is also a board member of the Advertising Council, a trustee of the University of Notre Dame, and a member of the Council on Foreign Relations.

Passive-aggressive actions. When someone behaves in a passive-aggressive way toward you, you know that there's a hidden agenda involved. The person appears passive, agreeable, yet aggression is occurring. To thoroughly resolve the problem, you must discover the underlying problem that's triggering the aggression. Ideally, you can lead the other person to help you discover what's really going on, to discuss it, and work out a joint resolution. If he or she is unwilling or unable to do this, you must work out a resolution that at least deals with the surface problem.

Passive actions. When others behave in a passive way toward you, you know that they're unable or unwilling to express their views or feelings—or to stand up for their rights. You must discover what they're thinking and feeling about the situation before you can reach a joint resolution. Again, if they can't or won't work with you on this exploration, you must do your best to reach a resolution they can agree with.

Difficult people situations provide powerful tools for learning more about yourself and how you deal with the world. Each tough situation provides a potent opportunity to learn a powerful lesson. As you learn the lessons and grow in self-awareness, you develop powerful people skills, which you can use in leading others to deeper levels of self-awareness. In fact, this ability may become your most powerful leadership skill!

We'll discuss difficult situations with your managers, peers, and employees—as well as in business-social situations. In each category, you'll find that most problems stem from people functioning in either an aggressive, passive, or passive-aggressive mode. As you learn to recognize the underlying mode, you gain skill in responding most effectively.

Strategy #1

Manage Difficult Situations With Your Manager

No one person has the power that your manager does to implement or block your immediate career goals. Dealing assertively and tactfully with this important person is essential to your career success.

Do you see your manager as an authority figure? In our patriarchal culture, male managers can be especially intimidating to women. The more levels between you and a particular manager, the higher the level of awe and intimidation tend to be.

Your manager may operate primarily in an assertive mode, which would make life easier for you. Your life becomes more difficult if your manager operates primarily in an aggressive, passive-aggressive, or passive mode. Most likely, your manager will function in each of these modes at varying times. You can learn to respond constructively to your manager's actions regardless of the mode. You can be perceptive and assertive in order to gain his respect and to communicate your needs, wants, and goals. You can learn to assert yourself in every area—from discussing your manager's behavior that's a problem for you, to requesting a promotion and raise.

When Your Manager Is in an Aggressive Mode

One of your greatest challenges may be dealing with your manager when he is in an aggressive mode. At such times your manager may be abusive, arrogant, rude, excluding, or ruthless.

Abusive Manager

Your manager may be abusive in such ways as treating you harshly, criticizing you abusively, or negatively comparing you with others.

➡ **Your manager treats you in a high-handed, harsh, or dictatorial way—or erupts in an angry tantrum.**

The key is to let go of any hurt you experience and focus on what's really important to you: succeeding in your job.

1. Remember, you can't reason with a person who is enraged. As a general rule, wait until the person calms down, then talk it over and try to agree on some goals.

2. If you think he'll become violent, excuse yourself at once, saying you'll talk later.

3. If you must resolve a crisis at once and he's having a tantrum, continue to calmly repeat his name until he stops. When he calms down and you have a chance to discuss the problem—listen, plan your strategy, and think before you speak.

4. Appear firm, strong, completely courteous, and unemotional. Act serene and don't threaten the person's ego or self-image.

5. Use tact to get attention and respect. Ask questions that show that you want to talk—questions that may get at what's really bugging the other person.

6. If you agree with part of what he says, say so while indicating other points that confuse you. If you completely disagree, show respect for the person's opinion and ask him to consider another possibility.

➡ **Your manager harshly criticizes your mistake.**

1. Your immediate goal is to remedy your mistake and regain your manager's goodwill.

2. Admit your error without giving excuses, and discuss how you will correct it and prevent it from occurring in the future.

3. Ask your manager to offer suggestions and then to agree to your plan.

4. If the harshness continues, speak up about its effect on you and how you feel about it. Say you accept the criticism, but you have some difficulty with the way it's delivered.

5. Focus on your goal of maintaining a positive relationship and doing an excellent job.

➡ **Your manager compares you unfavorably with your peers.**

Remember that the comparison has nothing to do with you as a person. The manager would do the same to any person willing to take it.

1. Say, *You're using other people's examples as reasons why I should be a certain way, but I'm not any of those other people.*

2. Use sentences that begin with *you* to indicate that you're not internalizing the boss's efforts to compare you: *You think I should be more like Bob? You think I should do things the same way as Jim?* Be sure to sound incredulous and bewildered.

3. Give an honest evaluation of what you see going on: *You're comparing me with someone else so that I'll stop trying to do what I believe in.*

4. Ask yourself, *What do I want from this encounter?* rather than *Who does he think he is, telling me I should be like someone else?* In this way, you can avoid becoming angry. You can focus on getting what you want rather than on your manager's behavior.

5. Ask yourself, *Does he need to feel powerful, understood, important, effective?* If you can see what your manager needs out of this encounter, you're more likely to see an appropriate way to let him *save face* while you still assert your rights.

6. If your manager later makes comparisons in spite of what you've done, confront the issue again—and again, if necessary. It's important to be persistent and consistent.

Arrogant Manager

When your manager is acting in an aggressively arrogant way, she may take credit for your work, haggle with you, act rudely, or exclude you.

➡ **Your manager takes credit for your work, giving you no credit.**
1. Beat your manager to the punch. Share the credit for your work with your manager before she gets a chance to claim it. Give effusive praise and credit to your manager for her role in approving the project and supporting you in your successful efforts.

2. Send copies of confirming memos, reports, etc., to your manager's manager and other appropriate people.

➡ **Your boss haggles over requests, errors, and similar trivia in a petty, obnoxious manner.**
1. Help your manager see the larger picture. Refuse to get bogged down in trivia.

2. Change the subject by summarizing briefly what's been said and mentioning the bigger issue.

3. Ignore petty insinuations, and stay focused on the big issue.

Rude Manager

When managers act in aggressively rude ways, they may be inconsiderate, ridiculing, or condescending—acting as if they're better than you. Your goal is to get your manager to show you the respect you deserve. You won't get it unless you believe you deserve it.

1. Confront the issue. Be calm and firm, and limit your remarks to the issue.

2. If your manager isn't paying attention while you're speaking, ask if another time would be better for this meeting. If necessary, excuse yourself and leave.

3. If you think your manager is tuned out, ask a question to bring him back.

4. If your manager has insensitively created a problem for you, explain the problem in terms of the trouble it creates for him and the benefits of preventing or solving it.

5. If your manager has been sarcastic, made a teasing yet hurtful remark, or otherwise ridiculed you, ask for a private meeting. Be professional and matter-of-fact in giving feedback assertion. State the exact comment, the effect it had on you, and how you felt. Ask what your manager meant by the remark. If the remark was in fact a legitimate criticism of your performance, say that you appreciate constructive criticism given in private like this.

6. If your manager has acted in a condescending way by ignoring your idea, or attacking or downplaying it, give gentle reminders of your achievements and your contribution to his success. Do this regularly.

7. Focus on how good you really are. Use your manager's rude superiority as a motivator to be even better, not as a drag on your confidence. Build your power network of supporters who help you rise above the hurt of rude managers and move on to bigger and better things.

Manager Who Excludes You

Subtle exclusion is perhaps the most common game directed against women by men in power—both by managers and by peers. Some of the forms it takes are as follows: At meetings your male manager and peers listen politely to your contributions, then continue the conversation as if you had said nothing. Later, one of them may present a similar or identical idea phrased in a slightly different way, and it's accepted and perhaps adopted by the group. You get no credit. Or, your managers may fail to include you in planning and decision-making, meetings, business-related social functions, or business trips. Here are some tactics you can use:

1. If your manager excludes you from a meeting, trip, or other event you think you should attend, talk with your manager in person, or write a memo. Say you understand there will be a meeting (or trip) concerning (the topic) on (the date). Tell him that you have some ideas on this subject or that you think the experience will help your job performance.

2. If the exclusion is ongoing, decide whether it's an oversight, a test of your assertiveness, or the first stage of an all-out war. Then, develop your own strategies accordingly.

3. If it's an oversight or test of your assertiveness, you'll probably have to bring up the unpleasant fact that you're being excluded. You can easily fall into the role of the shrew or nag unless you confront exclusion matter-of-factly without a trace of emotion. Keep your goal in mind (being included *and* accepted), stick to the facts, and assume that the exclusion is an unintentional oversight. Project the image of a cool, rational, professional person, and focus on the business reasons that make it important for you to be included.

4. If it's apparently the beginning of a war, consider setting up your own meetings, merely bypassing your manager or the peers who exclude you. Focus on strengthening your own support group.

Ruthless Manager

Let's take a look at the worst-case scenario. You get an aggressively ruthless manager who wants to see you fail and in fact tries to get rid of you. Let's look first at the games such managers may play.

The setup is probably the most common game played by male managers who resent women in leadership roles. It involves setting you up in an assignment or project you're not ready to handle, then failing to give you the support and resources you need to succeed. If you blow it, your manager will tell others, *Let's face it—a woman just can't hack this job.*

Abolishing the position is an especially devious way of getting rid of you. Instead of firing you, your manager gets the job position eliminated, then *regretfully* lets you go because there's no longer a job for you to do.

Kicking up is a game to get you out of a meaningful job and into a meaningless one by giving you a promotion, a raise, and a fancy title, but little or no power or responsibility. Get full information about any job promotion offer, whether or not you suspect your manager of trying to kick you up.

Threat of a bad reference is a game to force you to resign so that your manager won't have to fire you. You're promised a favorable reference if you resign, and threatened with a negative one if you don't.

Making life miserable may be played when your manager has inadequate grounds for firing you, but wants you out. The tactics range from phrasing all communications to you in a negative tone, to frequently transferring you from place to place, especially places you don't want to go.

Preventing retaliation is a strategy of managers for getting rid of people whom they've wounded in battle so they won't have to worry about past victims getting revenge later. If your manager is setting you up to fail or get fired, consider these tips:

1. Stay out of his or her way, and don't come across as a threat—that's your best protection from ruthlessly aggressive managers and peers.

2. Build a strong support network that includes powerful people in higher management.

3. Insist on specific, measurable goals and standards—for your job and for each major assignment. Make sure they're reasonable and that you achieve them. Propose them, get agreement, and document them in a confirming memo.

4. Confront your manager with the situation and try to work through the causes and possible solutions.

5. Make the best of the situation for a while if you think your manager may be moved soon.

6. If you can't work it out with your manager, fight it within the organization. Go over your manager's head to find a solution or to ask for a transfer. But first build a case, get witnesses, and document it.

7. When you meet with your manager's manager, be clear about why you're asking for the meeting and what you want as a result of it (the action you want). Give a brief overview of the situation, the major problem, and the major concern. Don't get bogged down in details. Let them come out, as needed, in response to the manager's questions. Remain objective and stick with facts. Avoid bad-mouthing your manager, but be frank about the facts. Stress what's *for the good of the company*.

8. If you lose the fight, you can take your battle outside the organization by filing a discrimination complaint with the regional office of the EEOC—and possibly going to court later on. Do this only if you want to play Joan of Arc—because you feel passionately that proving a point about principles and fairness is more important than your career. On average, people who take legal action are verbally blackballed within the industry—even though it's illegal. Many have had to change industries and suffered a seven-year setback in their careers.

When Your Manager Is in a Passive-Aggressive Mode

Your manager may act in a passive-aggressive mode by being deceitful or manipulative, even a con artist. The passive-aggressive mode is the most difficult to deal with because there's always a hidden agenda. Remember, when people are in this mode, they won't or can't be honest about their thoughts, feelings, motives, and actions. You must figure these out for yourself, or get the passive-aggressive person to help you do so. Focus on the ultimate benefits of working together harmoniously and productively: job success, team success, and company success.

Deceitful Manager

Deceit destroys trust, so it's of crucial importance that you resolve the problem. Your manager may act in a passive-aggressive mode by being deceitful in many ways, including not keeping promises, blaming you unfairly, and sending mixed messages. Here are some helpful tips:

1. First, work out your anger so that you can rise above judging and blaming, and so you can focus on your goals. Remember, blaming the system for the problem is better than blaming your manager. The question now is, *What is the real problem and the real message—and how can we communicate clearly in the future about these matters?*

2. See if you can find some goals the two of you can agree on.

3. Ask questions that require direct answers. Your ultimate goal is to find out what's making your manager act in what seems to be a deceitful way. Your immediate goal is to see if you can get a straight answer so you can know where you stand and how to plan.

4. Protect yourself in the future. Don't accept what your manager says at face value, but check and double-check, get it in writing, and take other precautions.

➡ **Your manager fails to keep a promise or blames you unfairly.**

Talk about the problem as the manager's—not yours. Politely state the real facts as you see them. Focus on achieving mutual goals and the benefits to your manager and the firm.

Make it easy for your manager to keep promises by spelling out what needs to be done and by helping in any way you can.

➡ **Your manager sends mixed messages or conflicting messages.**

Focus on nailing down one clear message—as soon as possible. Try to establish some ground rules for clear communication that you both agree on.

Con-Artist Manager

Con-artist managers act in a passive-aggressive mode by exploiting you through overwork, refusing to take responsibility for failures, operating with hidden agendas, and using insincere flattery to manipulate you. Consider the following scenarios and ways to overcome them:

➡ **Your manager exploits you by trying to work you to death.**

1. Is your manager really demanding this much work, or are you being compulsive in trying to meet what you perceive are the expectations? Have a talk.

2. Have you spoken up about the overload? Speak factually and calmly about what's possible and reasonable.

3. Say, *I know there's a lot to be done, but I'm overloaded right now. Let's discuss what my top priorities should be, and I'll work on those first.*

4. Say, *I'll be happy to see that this gets done, but I must have some help in order to get it out on time. Do you want to assign someone to work with me?* If you get help but remain in charge, you might expand your area of responsibility, giving you the basis to later ask for a raise and perhaps a new title.

5. Have you ever said *no*? Be prepared to give a reason why you can't handle the overload, without going into a lengthy explanation. Be professional. Say *I'd like to, but I have a prior commitment.* Practice your refusal mentally when you're calm. Picture yourself being calm when you say it.

6. Negotiate a better deal. Ask why you're getting so much work to do. Find out what your manager's priorities are and work out a deal to handle top priorities first.

7. If others are being worked to death too, get together and approach the boss with suggestions for a more reasonable workload.

➡ **Your manager hides out when action plans fail.**

When you discussed the plan earlier, your manager implied approval. But now that the project has gone wrong, your manager blames you. She wanted to avoid the risk of failure, so she let you be the one to go out on a limb, and now she's leaving you alone out there. She will saw that limb off, if necessary.

Your first goal is to stop feeling like a victim and take charge. Your second goal is to get your manager's support instead of being the guinea pig or fall guy.

1. If your manager has any sense of fairness, appeal to it.
2. Make suggestions about how your manager can look good to higher management and peers in spite of this situation.
3. Gently guide your manager toward accepting challenges, pointing out the benefits of becoming known as a good risk-taker—one who accepts responsibility as well as takes credit.

➡ **Your manager has hidden agendas.**

Your manager tells half-truths and omits important facts, hides true personal goals for specific situations, and pretends to be concerned about your agreed-upon goals. Often you don't know what the hidden agenda is.

1. Your goal is to avoid unreasonable, illegal, or unethical actions your manager may want you to take—and still retain a decent relationship.
2. Forget past broken promises and deals—unless they're in writing. Do what you can reasonably do—because you want to be seen as cooperative, reasonable, dependable.
3. Suggest alternate options.
4. Stay calm, pleasant, and helpful—even though you're not playing the game.
5. The more unprofessional your manager becomes, the more professional you remain.

➡ **Your manager uses a divide-and-conquer strategy.**

This is done in order to maintain control of you and your peers. Your manager sets you up to be suspicious of each other and to fight among yourselves—so you're less likely to form an alliance against her.

1. Good managers encourage teamwork, so be on guard if your manager doesn't.
2. Tactful questioning of peers can unearth this game.
3. Peer solidarity can stymie this game, even without your forming an anti-manager alliance.
4. The greatest challenge is to overcome the suspicion, competitiveness, and self-serving mind-sets among peers in order to work together.

➡ **Your manager flatters you excessively or insincerely.**

1. Try to determine why your manager flatters people. Is it because she feels insecure that her leadership or plans are inadequate? Or perhaps she feels that she must flatter in order to be liked—and intensely needs to be liked?
2. Your first goal is to get ahead without buying into phoniness.

3. Persistent flattery indicates weakness—a power vacuum that you may help fill.
4. Be objective and don't get sucked in to the phony praise.
5. Work on clearly stated goals that you both agree to.
6. Work with an entire team as much as possible in order to get more input and reality checks.

When Your Manager Is in a Passive Mode

Your manager may operate in a passive mode, creating roadblocks to your work, acting stubborn and rigid, or being withdrawn and uncommunicative.

Roadblock Manager

Your manager may act out passive behavior by stalling on your request or project, overcommitting and then not coming through, or blowing with the wind.

➡ **Your manager creates roadblocks to your request or project.**
1. Your goal is to get the action you need by tactfully following through and pushing, but not creating backlash.
2. Make your manager feel that he has a part in the development of your project or proposal. Ask for advice. Get your manager involved so that he has a stake in the project and wants to share in its potential success.
3. Do your homework and be prepared to defend your proposal if it's attacked.
4. If your manager puts off giving you a decision on your proposal, ask when you can expect an answer, and follow up.

➡ **Your manager is stalling**
1. Determine whether and why the manager hopes the project will go away and die if he stalls long enough. Find out why the manager is stalling.
2. Show how completing the action can benefit your manager—and how blocking it also blocks opportunities for him to shine or creates problems for the manager as well as you. Ask what you can do to help.
3. Figure out what you can do without your manager's action. Take whatever initiative you can, but keep your manager informed. Rally peers around your cause—without making your manager wrong. If your manager doesn't like your taking initiative, apologize and don't repeat it.

➡ **Your manager is waffling.**
1. If the problem is the unknown consequences of two or more alternatives, take responsibility for the alternative you're asking him to select. Make the results your problem if this will relieve your manager and remove the block.
2. Talk with your manager in a problem-solving mode, and try to get at the root of the inaction. Perhaps it's a matter of goals and priorities—or of how the action would affect other stakeholders. Once you understand the problem, you can work on solutions.

➡ **Your manager blows with the wind.**

1. Your goal is to get a decision he will stand by.

2. Help your manager focus. Go over the essential background information, analyze the situation, and summarize it with a focus on the big picture and specific goals. Offer specific actions that will solve the problem or lead to the desired results.

3. If your manager's changeability is an ongoing problem, especially with certain types of decisions, see if you can get her or him to delegate these to you—and take full responsibility for their consequences on yourself.

4. Have a regular system of follow-up on needed decisions and actions from your manager. Give yourself enough lead time for delay and change. Keep following up until you get what you need.

Rigid, Stubborn Managers

Your manager may act in a passive or passive-aggressive mode by being stubborn, rigid, and unbending. This may take the form of nit-picking, refusing to listen to information that could change her mind, or making you a scapegoat.

➡ **Your boss nitpicks over your proposal or your performance.**

1. Remember, she may have no imagination, may be fearful that failure will be brought back to her, or may not understand the practical aspects of your job.

2. You need to reassure the nitpicker of your trustworthiness and competence—and perhaps guide this manager into more appropriate uses for her energy.

3. Your goal is to help your manager see the big picture, to understand what's involved, to open up to new ideas, new ways—and to quit micromanaging you.

4. Ask questions about why your manager is so concerned about the issue.

5. Give the facts about what's involved, the benefits to your manager for letting you carry out your proposal or job in your own way. See if you can find documentation that there's a demand for the action you're proposing— to help your manager see the need and benefits and to feel more assured of success.

6. Acknowledge costs and obstacles to carrying out your proposal, and give facts about how you'll overcome them.

7. If necessary, scale down your proposal, making changes one step at a time.

8. See if you can reword or reshape the proposal and present it in a way that doesn't trigger your manager's fears or concerns.

➡ **Your manager refuses to listen to the facts.**

1. If this unreasonableness makes it difficult for you to do your job, your goal is to break through the resistance.

2. Ask your manager why she refuses to consider alternatives. See if you can get at underlying problems, such as the need to limit costs, increase sales, or avoid mistakes.

3. Come up with alternatives that will meet your manager's business needs and add emotional appeal by linking your suggestions with your manager's personal needs for more recognition, security, free time, or other need.

4. Act as if you expect your manager to agree, and attribute to her the traits you think your manager would like to be known for. Focus on supporting this manager, making her look good, and producing results that meet goals. Open up ways for this manager to save face.

5. If your manager still refuses, don't criticize or complain, but follow up with a confirming memo or, better yet, get the manager to do so. Do as you're told, but document your actions to show you were following orders.

➡ **Your manager makes you a scapegoat.**

1. Deal first with your stressful feelings, then deal with the manager's hostility.

2. Use questions to voice your objections and to show you won't play the victim role. *Which order did you want me to follow? Did we get our signals crossed?*

3. Use a problem-solving mode and provide a way for your manager to change and still save face.

Withdrawn, Uncommunicative Managers

Your manager may act in a passive mode by being withdrawn and uncommunicative. In this mode, your manager may seem reserved, unemotional, unresponsive, secretive, or unwilling to discuss issues or have needed confrontations.

➡ **Your manager is withdrawn and uncommunicative.**

1. Your goal is to get your manager's attention to be sure you're on the right track, to get a decision made, or a problem resolved.

2. Don't take your manager's withdrawal personally. Do some tactful investigation and you'll probably find that this behavior is fairly typical of him.

3. Keep giving positive feedback to your manager and use your imagination in keeping morale high—both yours and your manager's.

4. Ask open-ended questions that can't be answered with a *yes* or *no* in order to get the detailed, specific information you need.

➡ **You get a long silence.**

1. Take a few deep breaths and slow down. Avoid becoming flustered and feeling as though you need to fill the void with words, because this may cause you to blurt out more than you really want to.

2. Ask yourself how you can make it easier for your manager to digest important information and give you needed responses—to deal with the problem situations, reach decisions, confront conflict situations.

3. Ask yourself if you could make the decision or take the needed action and then inform your manager—without undermining trust.

➡ **You're not getting needed information from your manager.**
   1. Look for other sources.
   2. Be patient and supportive, and build trust—otherwise, a withdrawing manager will probably become more withdrawn.

➡ **You must get a problem situation resolved.**
   1. Ask for a meeting.
   2. Say you want the two of you to achieve mutual goals.
   3. Be friendly, yet candid, in stating what you sense is going on, the problem it's causing, and the effect it has, and ask for a resolution.
   4. Give your manager a chance to offer solutions. If none seem workable, make your own suggestions, tying them to his where possible.
   5. If you sense hostility, become more calm and friendly.
   6. If you sense fear of taking a risk, provide information about the probability of success.

Other Difficult Situations With Your Manager

Some difficult situations with your manager don't fall precisely into the aggressive, passive-aggressive, or passive modes. Here are some common problems and suggestions for coping:

➡ **Your manager makes a decision you think is disastrous.**
Counter with another suggestion or slant your manager's suggestion differently. Introduce your idea by saying, *That ties in with something I had in mind. What would you think if we did it this way?* or *Perhaps the most professional way to handle it would be....*

➡ **You're uncomfortable using your manager's first name.**
   1. If your manager and your peers use first names, you should too. Bite the bullet and do it. It gets easier each time you do it.
   2. It's important for your assertive stance that you think of yourself as basically equal to your manager as well as to your peers. Being on a first-name basis can help you feel equal and reduce the possibility of being intimidated or dominated.

➡ **You're afraid you aren't pleasing your manager.**
   1. Ask yourself if you're caught in the trying-to-please trap. Many women depend on others, especially authority figures, for approval of their behavior, decisions, or ideas.

2. Remember, people are more likely to respect you if you're clear about what you want in your life and in your career. If you please yourself, you're likely to gain the respect of your manager.

3. Keep cooperation and achievement on an objective level rather than making it personal. Focus on company goals, department goals, your job goals.

4. Find a manager you can honestly admire, respect enough to support, and be reasonably loyal to. Still, focus on goals—not on pleasing your manager.

➡ **You're worried about relating to your new manager.**

It's true that when new managers take over, they frequently bring in some of their own staff. You may suddenly find your job in jeopardy.

1. Consider meeting with your new manager. Before the meeting, review your achievements and update your job goals.

2. If you've heard about possible layoffs, say so, and then tell your new manager what you're contributing to the firm. Briefly go over what you've accomplished in specific, measurable terms, and provide documentation.

3. Lay out future plans for your job and your unit, if you're the leader.

4. Avoid becoming defensive or belittling towards anyone in the company.

➡ **Your manager won't give you adequate autonomy.**

If your manager won't give you adequate autonomy or authority, or is constantly giving you advice and warning you about mistakes, you cannot excel and grow.

1. Before taking any job or project, get clear with your manager what your areas of responsibility and authority are.

2. Make it clear that you're ready to use your authority and to accept responsibility for the consequences of your decisions and actions.

3. Communicate your concern about dependence and independence.

➡ **Your manager often fights your battles or makes your decisions.**

1. Ask her to let you try your wings—to come to you first with issues.

2. Say you prefer asking for her opinions and information, and then making your own decisions.

3. Say you think you're at a point in your professional development where you need to try your wings more, even if this means making some mistakes.

4. Acknowledge how much you appreciate the advice and support—that you still welcome it at the same time that you're developing more autonomy.

5. Your goal is to maintain your manager's support, your peers' and teammates' respect for your autonomy, and your growing self-confidence.

Strategy #2
Manage Difficult Situations With Your Peers

Peers or colleagues can connect you with new opportunities, can help you avoid disasters, and can smooth the way to getting things done. They can also make it difficult to impossible for you to get certain things done. Cooperating, trading favors, and passing along information is the name of the game among peers in your support network. When you can deal assertively and tactfully in difficult situations with your peers, you oil the wheels of business and smooth the road to success.

When a Peer Is in an Aggressive Mode

Your peers may sometimes be in an aggressive mode, acting in a belligerent, dogmatic and arrogant, or rude and inconsiderate manner.

Belligerent Peer

Belligerent peer situations occur when a colleague personally attacks you—especially in front of managers and others; envies you and therefore acts in a resentful and grudging way; or intimidates you in an attempt to gain power.

➡ **A peer attacks you personally when you're at a meeting.**
1. Continue your game plan. Don't fight back. Elevate the discussion by moving the emphasis away from personalities, and back to the issue at hand.
2. Hold a private conversation if it happens more than once. Say you'd like to have a better relationship, and ask how the two of you might resolve your differences.
3. Learn who your peer's supporters are, where you can and can't expect support, and continue to expand your own support network.

➡ **A peer is resentful and envious of you.**
1. Keep your conversation on a high and friendly level. Don't argue.
2. Express the belief that each person's effort is judged on its own merit, and just because one person's performance is good doesn't mean another's is not.
3. Express admiration for what the peer does well, and talk about your peer's interests, perhaps making positive suggestions for building on her talents.

➡ **A peer intimidates, hurts, or embarrasses you.**
Make your goal managing your emotions and actions.
1. Rehearse your replies at home after you've processed any stressful emotions and gotten in touch with your worst fears around the situation.
2. Appear poised and calm.
3. Psych yourself up by pretending to be encased in protective, clear plastic or white light, which their verbal attacks can't penetrate.

4. Use your intuition to figure out when to take a hurtful action lightly and brush it off with a touch of humor.

5. Concentrate on what you want the outcome to be, staying positive. Allow yourself to feel friendly and to smile.

6. Find a good time to talk about why this peer seems upset or annoyed with you.

Dogmatic, Arrogant Peer

Your peers may act in an aggressively dogmatic or arrogant way by trying to force their views on you, bullying you, or intimidating you with their zealousness.

➡ **Your peer forces his views on you, taking a dogmatic, opinionated, even zealous mode.**

1. If the peer tries to bully you, don't allow it. Get your emotions under control, breathe deeply, deliberately slow your movements, and stand up to the peer.

2. Review your position on the issue, all the pros and cons, and develop clear, specific reasons for your position.

3. Ask your peer for details on how his position compares with yours or that of others. Without attacking the position, get the peer to discuss and defend it.

4. Analyze the possible result of actions based on your position, and of actions based on your peer's position. How would these actions affect each of you? Others?

5. If you're convinced your position is right, be as firm in expressing your conviction as your peer is in expressing his.

6. Suggest a problem-solving, professional approach, and work toward a win-win solution.

7. Show how you can help the peer get what he really wants.

8. If you can't work it out and it involves turf problems, consider asking a manager at a higher level to help resolve the overlap of authority.

Rude or Inconsiderate Peer

Your peers may be aggressively rude or inconsiderate by interrupting your sentences or your work, putting you down, or prying. At meetings, peers may exclude you, interrupt you, or ignore you.

➡ **Your peer is rude or inconsiderate.**

1. If your peer interrupts you when you're speaking, be polite but firm in asserting your right to finish what you were saying: *Excuse me, I'd like to finish what I was saying.*

2. If your peer regularly interrupts your work for idle chitchat, stand up and remain standing so your peer doesn't get to settle in. After a few moments, excuse yourself. Say, *I'd like to chat but I have a deadline looming—thanks for dropping by.*

3. If your peer takes up too much of your work time with rambling conversations, offer focused questions and comments that keep the conversation on track and get to the point. Cut to the chase and ask, *What's the bottom line and how can I help?*

4. If your peer insults you or pays you a left-handed compliment, breathe deeply and stay calm. Consider these types of actions: Sort out the praise and put-down parts of the remark. Ask what the remark means. Ask why she says or thinks that. Ask if there's a problem, and say that you'd like to work it out.

5. If a peer pries into your business, first give him the benefit of the doubt and assume he doesn't know he's out of line. Remember that you don't have to give any information you don't care to give. You might ask why he wants to know. If pushed, you might respond with humor: *A person who would tell that would tell anything!*

6. If you discover a peer reading your mail or personal files, say, *What can I do for you?*

➡ **At meetings, your peers exclude you, interrupt you, or ignore you.**

1. Be prepared for meetings by reviewing your facts, then be positive about expressing yourself. Use such phrases as *I think...* or *I believe.....*

2. If negative self-talk starts (*They'll think this is silly, I'm no good at expressing myself at meetings*), stop that train of thought by saying *stop*, then *calm*, and taking a few deep breaths, allowing your muscles to relax. Use positive self-talk instead: *I can say what I think.*

3. Before you speak up, focus totally on the bottom-line message you want to get across. Think of yourself as just a vehicle for bringing the message.

➡ **Your peers ignore you.**
   If certain peers generally exclude you in conversation, try feedback assertiveness.

1. Describe the behavior nonjudgmentally. Say, *I've been listening to this discussion for the past 20 minutes, and three people have spoken, mainly to each other. Prior to that I contributed my opinion a couple of times and received little or no comment. I've had the same experience at other meetings. I'd like to contribute to this group, but I feel frustrated in my efforts to do so.*

2. If they ignore your idea and later adopt an almost identical idea presented by one of the men, tactfully address the issue: *Bob, I like the way we work together and bounce ideas off each other. You took my suggestion of... and gave it a slightly different twist, so we ended up with....*

3. Be prepared to make specific suggestions for increasing your level of participation. For example, you could suggest that the meeting leader stop the discussion before going on to a new item—and ask if anyone has anything to add. If you're stumped for suggestions, at least ask the group what can be worked out to increase participation by all members.

When a Peer Is in a Passive-Aggressive Mode

Peers act in a passive-aggressive mode when they're deceitful, when they scheme like con artists, and when they gripe, overcriticize, or backbite.

Deceitful Peer

Peers may act out their passive-aggressive deceitfulness by stealing your ideas, being two-faced, and undermining you and your work.

➡ **Your peer steals your idea or takes credit for your work.**
  1. Be friendly, but quit sharing such information with this peer.
  2. If you've been working as a twosome and you need to bounce ideas off someone, expand the group by calling in other peers.
  3. Document your work in the future (see suggestions for when your manager takes credit for your work on page 265).

➡ **Your peer supports you to your face, then stabs you behind your back.**
  1. You must decide whether the event demands that you ignore it, settle it because it's a legitimate criticism of you, confront your back-stabbing accuser, or prepare your own offensive against your accuser's assault.
  2. Usually, it's best to confront a back-stabber by reporting what you heard, calmly, without blame or anger. Ask this peer to tell you specifically what the problem is that was discussed behind your back.
  3. If you made a mistake, apologize.
  4. Provide a way out for back-stabbers, if they deny their actions. In the future, they'll probably back off once they know you'll confront them.

➡ **A peer falsely accuses you or gives a false version of events.**
  1. Prepare an outline of the facts, including the actions of the deceitful peer. Make it objective, free of judging and blaming.
  2. If the impact of the deceit is relatively minor, simply send the memo to your manager with a copy to your peer and any others involved.
  3. If the impact is serious, personally meet with key people in your power network, especially your managers and mentors. Give each a copy of the offensive evidence and your outline of the facts. Ask for advice and support.

➡ **Certain peers go beyond back-stabbing to undermine you.**
  Peers could launch a sneak attack that undercuts support for your project or otherwise reduces the impact of your efforts—perhaps by being late with needed information, giving wrong information, or not showing up. Perhaps they agree to go along with a proposal but when they sense little support for it from others, they withdraw and leave you holding the bag.

  Other peers may build case files against people. For example, such peers jot down the dates and circumstances of any suspicious actions, as well as reports, letters, and other documents containing errors or possible gaffes. Such file-builders hope to build a case against all rivals so that they can threaten or discredit them—or at least protect themselves if someone attacks them.

1. To protect yourself against such hostility and paranoia, watch what you say and do. Be scrupulous in your work and in documenting your actions.

2. Build that power network of supporters! They can shift the balance of favorable opinion in your direction.

3. Keep your own files of your achievements, and keep your manager up to date on them.

4. Don't take the actions of hostile peers personally—it's their ongoing problem.

Con-Artist Peer Who Schemes or Imposes

Peers may act out their passive-aggressive con-artist games by imposing, plotting, and manipulating. These people can somehow separate themselves from the emotions normally involved in exploiting and betraying others. This allows them to smoothly play their games while appearing sincere and charming. Maybe they're just great actors whose talents could be channeled more constructively.

➥ **You discover a scheme.**

Don't take action until you're in control of your emotions. Don't show anxiety, anger, or other stressful emotions. See if there's anything you can support in the scheme, and if you can tie it to your own goals.

➥ **The scheme involves an inconsiderate request.**
1. Say *no* without overdoing explanations about why.
2. Don't take responsibility for how they can solve their problem.
3. Think ahead about what you'll do if a peer asks to borrow money, your car, or other possession you don't want to share. What will you do if a peer asks you to do her work or take over some responsibility you don't want to assume? Have a ready answer: *I'd love to loan you the money, but all my cash is invested. I'd like to, but my insurance doesn't cover other drivers. Wish I could help, but I'll barely meet my top-priority goals as it is.*
4. If you're not sure about the scheme or request, ask many probing questions before giving an answer. Your questions could be geared to pointing the peer in a different direction for solving their problems—one that doesn't involve you: *Have you tried the credit union? Rent-a-wreck? Asking your manager?*

➥ **They've done you a minor favor in the past.**
Now they demand a major favor of you—one that's distinctly out of line.
1. Respond that you owe them one, but you can't pay them back at this time.
2. Remember to refuse future favors from con artists.
3. Be courteous, but don't get anxious about hurting their feelings. Most con artists manage to keep their schemes and feelings separate.

➡ **It's a scheme to provoke you to anger or tears.**

Your immediate goal is to avoid getting hooked into a flare-up. Excuse yourself to go to the bathroom or make a phone call, and then regain your composure.

➡ **It's a scheme to give you incomplete or false information.**
1. Keep all lines of communication open, and double-check information until you get to know your players.
2. Be sure you don't get taken in a second time.

➡ **It's a scheme to give you self-serving advice.**

Such advice influences you to do what the peer wants, but it is definitely not in your best interests.
1. Be wary. Consider the sources of all advice.
2. Get advice and information from several sources.
3. Make up your own mind.

Griping, Overcritical, or Backbiting Peer

Peers may act in a passive-aggressive mode by griping about almost everything, criticizing you in front of others, and gossiping viciously.

➡ **Your peer criticizes you before others, perhaps by wisecracking.**
1. Don't let the wisecrack pass as just a little harmless teasing. Don't accept the comeback, *Can't you take a little joke?*
2. Take deep breaths and rise above pettiness.
3. Do a quick mental review of the facts leading up to this situation.
4. Confront the criticism by asking what they mean or why they said what they did. Explain briefly, if necessary.
5. Meet in private later. When you meet in private, give assertive feedback, repeating exactly what the peer said, the effect it had, how you felt.

➡ **Your peers backbite or try to gossip with you.**
1. To them, your silence means consent, so you must speak up, ask probing questions, and say how you disagree.
2. If they swear you to secrecy, don't play the game. Say you can't swear secrecy and still resolve the problem.
3. If you're the target of the gossip, ask questions designed to get the entire issue out in the open.
4. Focus on resolving any underlying issues, as well as any other problems.
5. Determine what can be done to prevent similar problems in the future.
6. Determine if you need to touch base more often with gripers or backbiters to reassure them and to stay tuned in to what they're saying.

When a Peer Is in a Passive Mode

Your peers may act in a passive mode by creating roadblocks to your work or project, such as being rigid and stubborn or withdrawn and uncommunicative.

Roadblock Peers

Your peers may act out passive behavior by causing delays in your work. They may do this by oversocializing, dawdling, being a perfectionist, or failing to adequately organize the work and manage time.

➡ **Your peer creates roadblocks to your work or project.**

Your goal is to remove the roadblock and get the work done, but you have no authority over your peer.

1. Communicate how important the task is, as well as the role the peer plays in getting the work done.
2. Focus on your immediate concern: getting this specific task done.
3. Act friendly, self-assured, and focused.
4. Ask probing questions about what's going on and what can be done to expedite the work.
5. If the blocking behavior continues, do your homework, find factual and experiential support for your position, and bring up the problem in a staff meeting or a meeting with your manager.
6. Keep your eyes on the prize, achieving your goals, and don't let the roadblocks get you down. Remain positive and action-oriented.

➡ **Your peer is a perfectionist.**
1. Realize that this peer is a worrier.
2. Help this peer deal with the reality of limited time and funds.
3. Reassure him that even world-class standards don't mean *perfect*.

➡ **Your peer doesn't organize the work or manage time adequately.**
1. Share how you deal with such problems. Don't act superior. Say, *I had such a problem with that until Ann showed me a good way to handle it.*
2. Show how completing the task in a timely manner can benefit the peer. Say, *I told your manager how I depend on your good work. We'll have a celebration when this is done.*
3. If it's an ongoing or serious problem, ask your manager to review responsibilities, deadlines, and workflow patterns with the entire staff.

Rigid, Stubborn Peer

Your peers may act out passive or passive-aggressive behavior by being stubborn, rigid, and unbending. They usually don't enjoy their work and dampen team spirits. They often focus excessively on rules and procedures. They despise change and make it more difficult for everyone. Get them to relax and loosen up a little.

1. If people shun them, they tend to become even more rigid. Be willing to be a friend and a good listener. Use tactful humor to lighten them up.
2. Lead them to go beyond what *is* to what *might be* if they tried a new tack.
3. If they want to see themselves as the organized, efficient ones—the ones who keep track of all procedures and activities—show appreciation for those contributions.

4. Keep in touch with job goals, team goals, company goals.
5. Don't let peers' rigidity roadblock your creative projects. Promise to put them to work after you work through the basics of your idea.
6. Stick to the issues, and don't get into personal attacks.
7. Let rigid peers save face. Give them a gracious way to change their minds without admitting they were wrong. Phrase your objections in a positive frame, such as, *I think we're not that far apart. Let's look at this one issue where we differ.*

Withdrawn, Uncommunicative Peer

Your peers may act out passive behavior by being withdrawn and uncommunicative. They may do this by acting suspicious, withholding information, or giving you meaningful looks without words.

➡ **Withdrawn peers act suspicious.**
1. Your goal is to convince them of your sincerity and good intentions.
2. Refer to the idea or project as *ours* rather than *mine*. Report useful news they may not have heard. When you can, offer to help them with their problems or work.
3. Be candid and explain obstacles as well as benefits with a reassuring, confident attitude.
4. Build trust by keeping your commitments and aligning your actions with your words.
5. Express appreciation and admiration when you can sincerely do so.
6. Don't push too hard. Be willing to move slowly while you build trust.

➡ **Peers act miffed and withhold information.**
Perhaps you haven't adequately acknowledged their expertise. Your goal is to get them to give you the information they're withholding.
1. Give them the recognition and appreciation they want, and word your request tactfully.
2. Ask them to confirm your conclusions or the limited facts you already have. Admit you need their help, and ask them for it. Ask them how they would go about handling the project or resolving the issue.
3. If withdrawn peers give you angry or hurt looks, you must first win back enough confidence to get them to talk about what's wrong.
4. Ask for a meeting. State how much their goodwill means to you and your desire to maintain a good relationship. Ask probing questions to try to get at the source of the problem. If you get nowhere, be patient and try again. While their behavior may seem childish, rise above it and focus on your goal of maintaining a good working relationship.
5. Once you resolve the problem, discuss how you can avoid creating similar situations in the future.

Strategy #3

Manage Difficult Situations With Your Employees

If you're in a leadership role, your job success depends on your relationships with the employees you lead. Because you're in the role-model position with this group, you have the most potent opportunity to inspire assertive behavior that reflects self-respect and respect for others. But first, you may need to deal with stereotyped assumptions about women in leadership roles. Then, you must gain their acceptance by building trust and handling difficult people situations in a sensitive, assertive manner.

When an Employee Is in an Aggressive Mode

Your employees may act in a rebellious, arrogant, rude, or egocentric manner.

Rebellious Employees

Employees may express an aggressive, rebellious mode by acting angry and argumentative, acting resentful and trying to get back at you for perceived mistreatment, or attacking you, sometimes in a passive-aggressive way with wisecracks and jokes. Consider these suggestions for turning such negative situations around:

1. Review your leadership style and actions to be sure you're treating everyone fairly and showing no favoritism.
2. Discuss the situation in private when the employee is not angry.
3. Take a joint problem-solving approach to get at the root of the problem.
4. Look for misperceptions, and then clear them up.
5. If the resentment is over a higher manager's system or another employee's actions, refuse to play referee. Focus on the employee's responsibility to cooperate and to work out personality clashes in order to achieve goals.
6. Don't be intimidated if an employee threatens to quit unless you meet his demands. Say that you'll do what you can to meet all employees' needs, but that beyond that, career decisions are up to an individual employee.
7. Express any sincere appreciation you can muster—for the employee's performance, traits that enhance team performance, etc.
8. Determine how you can prevent future instances of resentment and anger.
9. If an employee takes a potshot in front of others, don't ignore it, even if it's said as a joke. Think of it as a leaf of poison ivy—it's small, but it must be nipped in the bud. Breathe deeply and slow down your movements so that you can calmly say that you'll be glad to meet later to discuss any legitimate criticism. Then get on with the business at hand. Later, talk with the employee in private.

Arrogant Employees

Employees may act aggressively arrogant by ignoring procedures, trying to gain power through a clique at your expense, or just going their own way.

➡ **Your employee ignores procedures and precedents, and tries to gain power on his own or through a clique.**

Your goals are to get the employee to obtain permission before trying questionable actions and, if possible, to retain enthusiasm and productivity.

1. First ask yourself, *Is the employee looking for something I'm not giving her enough of? Is she voicing what restrained employees are thinking and don't dare say? Does she just want to cause trouble?*

2. Be consistent and evenhanded in applying policies, procedures, and rules; otherwise, you'll have resentment by other employees and future chaos.

3. Meet with the employee who violates rules. Praise good performance and cooperation, and then focus on the specific problem behavior, the importance of all employees marching to the same drumbeat, and what the employee intends to do about it in the future. Show appreciation for future cooperation.

4. Follow up with feedback on how well the employee is doing. Acknowledge any improvement. If appropriate, offer further suggestions.

➡ **The employee is the leader of a clique.**

1. Try to win her over. Ask for help in very specific ways, and express appreciation when you get cooperation.

2. Try to set up a situation in which the employee feels your support.

3. Build good relationships with other members of the clique—offering challenging assignments, support, coaching, praise, etc.

4. Consider tapping into the power of the clique to work together as a team in ways that win support and rewards from you and the company.

5. If a clique continues to be disruptive, break it up without fanfare through work assignments and schedules that give them little or no time together.

➡ **The employee is a loner whom others resent.**

1. Try to channel her energy and enthusiasm into constructive channels. Give the employee a chance to shine, and give recognition that's due.

2. Coach this employee on asserting in ways that respect the rights of others.

3. Hold a staff meeting on the general problem and let others express their opinions without directly attacking the employee, who *will* get the message.

Rude or Inconsiderate Employees

Employees may act in an aggressive manner by being rude or inconsiderate. They may speak in a presumptuous, rebellious, or needling way that takes these forms: being angry and argumentative, being resentful and trying to get back at you for perceived mistreatment, or attacking you, sometimes in a passive-aggressive way with wisecracks and jokes.

➡ **An employee is rude or inconsiderate.**
1. Review your management style. Do you send the message that employees can feel free to talk with you about problems and concerns so that they don't need to complain in a resentful or defensive way? Are you open and fair with all your employees?

2. Put such employees at ease, and let them speak their piece.

3. Ask questions to get at the root of the problem. Problem-solve together and find solutions.

➡ **An employee needles you.**
1. Ask questions, without anger but pointedly: *What do you mean by that remark? Why do you say that?*

2. Talk privately with such needlers. Let them know that their jokes are not the best way to convey concerns or to correct problems.

3. Try to get at the real criticism, the root problem, and work it out.

Egocentric Employees

Your employees may act in an aggressive manner by being egocentric or arrogant. They may try to build their own little empires, hog the spotlight, or exaggerate their own importance.

➡ **Your employee's egocentric actions are disruptive.**

Your goal is to maintain the egocentric's enthusiasm and motivation, while protecting fellow employees and team spirit.

1. Praise the egocentric's ability to create excitement and enthusiasm, while setting a limit on this behavior. Insist that the employee adhere to team rules.

2. Don't fall for the star's line that you or the team can't do without him or her. Help the employee become a better team member. Be friendly but firm in insisting that team procedures be followed. Make the team responsible for keeping all members in line.

3. When employees exaggerate their contributions or problems, remind them of the big picture and of the relative importance of things. Guide them in using some time-management techniques for prioritizing tasks and monitoring the time spent on them. Help them build self-esteem and confidence by giving ample recognition and rewards when they handle top-priority tasks first.

When an Employee Is in a Passive-Aggressive Mode

Employees may act in a passive-aggressive mode by being deceitful or manipulative, or by taking on a victim role.

Deceitful Employees

Employees act in passive-aggressive, deceitful ways by being evasive and shifty, bluffing instead of being candid, and trouble-making.

➡ Employees act evasive, shifty, sneaky, or sly.

Try to figure out why they act in a sneaky way. Are they intimidated by you and by all authority figures? Are they primarily shy and prefer to be clever rather than pushy in trying to meet their needs? Do they feel left out, ignored, not part of the inner circle?

➡ Employees try to get rid of competent rivals.

Coworkers have been known to influence rivals by helping them get hired by other organizations. Because the more competent team members may be removed in this manner, it's important for you to stay on top of what's going on.

1. Try to find out what's going on and nip the treachery in the bud. Your actions and words must send the clear message that such behavior will backfire.

2. Employees who try to outsmart you often feel like outsiders; make them insiders. Make your goal to put shrewdness to work for you rather than against you.

3. Give them a challenging extra assignment, such as analyzing a department work process and finding ways to improve it. Tell them you'll reward successful performance on this assignment.

4. Find ways to give them and others more credit where it's due.

5. If you think the problem is boredom, resentment, or restriction, see the suggestions given next for troublemakers.

➡ Employees create crises in order to be indispensable.

Employees may allow or create a crisis so they can come to the rescue, solve the problem, and be seen as indispensable. Such employees may keep poor records so that no one else can step in and replace them when they're off duty—or they don't allow anyone else to do what they do.

1. Give them greater rewards and more attention for anticipating and preventing problems than for solving them.

2. Require everyone to prepare written procedures for all important recurring tasks that they're responsible for.

3. Begin a process of cross-training.

➡ Employees are troublemakers.

Troublemakers stir up dissatisfaction and urge people to act against you or the firm—distorting or exaggerating the truth to rile up coworkers. Look for one of three major causes: resentment, boredom, or lack of freedom. Meet with troublemakers to try to get at the root of the problem and jointly find solutions.

When you think troublemaking is caused by resentment, look for answers to these questions:

1. Are they trying to break into a clique by becoming visible?

2. Do they have a good point, such as fighting the red tape that stifles initiative?

3. Are they disillusioned by broken promises, phoniness, or compromises of managers?

When you think troublemaking is caused by boredom, look for answers to these questions:

1. How can you add excitement to their work life?
2. Can you find another position that's more suited to their talents and interests?
3. Can you provide training courses, new assignments or projects, job rotation, and similar ways to spice up their lives?

When you think troublemaking is caused by too little freedom, try the following approaches:

1. Giving them more autonomy.
2. Sharing responsibility and information, delegating more, and eliminating unnecessary red tape, procedures, and rules.
3. Letting them design plans and implement them (with your approval).

➡ **Employees bluff instead of being candid.**

Try to determine why employees bluff. Look for three major reasons: 1) they feel threatened, 2) they feel inadequate, 3) they don't want to take responsibility and do what's expected. Try the following ways of handling such situations:

1. Talk to them personally in ways that calm their fears, show support, and lead them to take responsibility so they don't need to bluff their way through.
2. Set joint goals that are clear and specific so they know exactly what you expect.
3. Find a better way to give specific, frequent feedback that's more helpful and less threatening.
4. Link their performance to team spirit. Talk in terms of the value of their work to the whole team or unit.

Manipulative Employees

Employees may act in a passive-aggressive manipulative mode by fawning, asking for special favors, whining, tattling, gossiping viciously, or blaming you for their mistakes.

➡ **Employees fawn, act like "yes-people."**

Ask yourself, *Are they just seeking attention but lack self-confidence?* If so, your goal is to help them gain confidence and security. Try the following tactics:

1. Give assignments, training, coaching, feedback that guides them toward earning the rewards they want.
2. Be courteous but firm in your dealings with fawners. Focus on measurable performance and achievement of goals.
3. Role model appropriate ways of praising by giving specific feedback on performance.
4. Always make criticism constructive, focusing on solving a performance problem.
5. For extreme cases, use feedback assertion and *I* messages: *When you...the effect on me is... I feel... How about....*

➠ **Employees withhold feedback.**

When employees aren't candid about errors, new developments, or other information you need, try these actions:

1. Confront the problem immediately.

2. Take a problem-solving approach and ask for help in getting at the root of the problem. Sometimes the problem is caused by resentment, sometimes by employees who want you to fail, sometimes by employees who are reluctant to give managers unpleasant information and who tell you what they think you want to hear.

3. Ask for and propose solutions, but make it clear that you'll get the needed information one way or another.

➠ **Employees try to manipulate you into granting special favors.**

1. If requests for favors take you by surprise, say you'll get back to them with an answer. Decide if the request is reasonable or would show favoritism.

2. Remember that your employees want a leader who's confident, assertive, and fair. People admire a sense of fairness that includes equal rights for all.

3. If you refuse the favor, assert your rights, the company's rights, and coworker's rights for fair and even treatment of all employees.

4. Point out that the other employees expect fairness and will resent favoritism. If one gets away with breaking the rules or policies, many will try it, leading to chaos.

5. Most employees will agree with the idea that it wouldn't be fair to coworkers for you to approve an unreasonable request.

➠ **Employees whine a lot.**

Your goal is to guide them toward acting in a more mature, responsible way.

1. Sort out the whiner's exaggerated concern from any real concerns. If you think the whiner's complaint reflects other's concerns, ask other employees.

2. Reassure whiners through praise for taking responsibility, give them frequent feedback, and share key information. Focus on achieving work and team goals.

➠ **Employees tattle or gossip viciously.**

Your first goal is to sort out the information you get from them. Your second goal is to keep the disruption under control. The underlying message of your words and actions should be, *Tattling and gossip don't get you ahead here; just the opposite.*

1. If the purpose of the whining, tattling, or gossiping is to make you the referee, refuse this role. Suggest a process they might use for working out the conflict, and make it clear you expect them to handle the problem.

2. If an employee comes to you with idle vicious gossip, respond in a disinterested, noncommittal way, and then change the subject.

3. If the gossip has serious implications regarding the firm, ask probing questions to get at the source and reliability of the information. Then check it out.

4. If you get word that an employee is causing trouble through vicious gossip, meet with that person and, without revealing your source, ask what he or she knows about this problem.

5. Stay tuned in to the grapevine so you'll know what's going on and can decide when to step in before vicious gossip goes too far.

➡ **Employees blame you for their mistakes.**
Your goal is to get such employees to take responsibility for their own actions.

1. Let them voice their feelings, which often include anger or frustration. Be empathetic and listen closely without responding to blame and criticism.

2. Suggest that you meet in private to discuss the issue when things have settled down.

3. When you meet, give sincere praise on specific matters the employee has handled well. In a problem-solving mode, discuss areas that need to be improved. Stay friendly and focused on actions that lead to achievement of goals.

4. Make them responsible for working on a solution and following through. Explain the consequences of meeting the goals and not meeting them. Set a time for reporting back.

Victim Employees

Employees may act out their passive-aggressive manipulations by playing a victim role.

➡ **Employees blame themselves for whatever goes wrong.**
Such employees are probably asking for reassurance, hoping you'll relieve them of blame and responsibility. Your goal is to help them move beyond a victim role and the need for constant reassurance from you. Gently teach them how a victim stance drains their personal power, and then provide some assertiveness training.

1. When they cry for reassurance by taking the blame, give them a job they can handle and the recognition and praise they deserve. Don't be blackmailed into giving phony praise.

2. Get them to express their underlying concerns—why they feel the need to take the blame for events they didn't create.

➡ **Victims complain about overwork.**
Employees may do this even when you haven't asked for their help. You're probably dealing with a workaholic who uses work to avoid resolving personal problems. Workaholic martyrs create resentment within the team because they usually love to gripe about overwork but refuse to accept real help. They usually want you, the team, and the firm to be dependent upon them. Your goal is to ease unnecessary tension by resolving legitimate complaints about an imbalance in the workload.

1. Meet with such victim-martyrs to see if you can get at underlying problems.

2. Work toward a plan that will redistribute the work and limit the amount of work the victim-martyr is allowed to do.

3. If they volunteer for projects, politely refuse by pointing out that their plate is full just now and you don't want them to become overloaded again.

4. Give as much recognition and praise as they deserve. Can you give them higher-level work, more challenging work, but not so much of it?

When an Employee Is in a Passive Mode

Employees operating in a passive mode may create roadblocks to getting the work done. They may be rigid and stubborn to deal with. They may be withdrawn and uncommunicative.

Roadblock Employees

Your employees may act out passive behavior by causing delays in your work. They may do this by getting by with doing as little work as possible, procrastinating, or frequently being late or absent.

➡ **Employees create roadblocks by doing as little as possible and putting things off.**

Your goal is to get goof-offs and delayers to assume responsibility, to make the work and the firm their own. First, be sure that you're doing everything you can to support employees, to eliminate environmental problems, to provide resources, to motivate, coach, and give helpful feedback.

1. Use a problem-solving mode and ask what's wrong. Try to get at root problems. Is it boredom? Incompetence? Poor work habits? Perfectionism? Fear of failure? Hostility and revenge?

2. Work together to find a solution to the work problem and the underlying problem.

3. To boost motivation, consider holding regular idea-exchange meetings and do what you can to increase their sense of belonging. Recognize and reward cooperation and good performance.

4. Be sure they know that you're always there to help solve problems. Help them to feel free to approach you before a roadblock occurs.

5. Follow up with helpful feedback and recognition of improvement.

6. Don't nag. Find out what the problem is. If it's solvable, jointly find a solution. If the employee won't or can't take responsibility, find a way to move him or her out.

7. Be a role model of punctuality, time management, work organization, and similar aspects of taking care of business and getting the work done. Do this without acting superior. Instead, act as a resource and support person—someone who's learned these strategies and techniques and is willing to share them.

➡ **An employee is frequently late or absent.**
1. Describe the specific behavior in nonjudgmental terms. Say, *We agreed to begin our meetings at 8:30, but at the last three meetings, you arrived at 8:40, 8:50, and 8:45. This means that all 10 of us lose 10 or 15 minutes getting started each time.*

2. Ask whether there is an underlying problem. If there is a legitimate problem, let the team member know you'll appreciate being informed of such problems at the time they crop up so you can plan accordingly.

3. Express feelings. Mention the kinds of feelings the lateness triggers, such as frustration and impatience.

4. Describe the effect. You might want to point out that it's unfair for some people to violate an agreement and get away with it, while other team members make sacrifices to keep the agreement.

5. Ask for resolution. Make it clear that the team expects the member to honor this agreement in the future.

Rigid, Stubborn Employees

Your employees may act out passive or passive-aggressive behavior by being stubborn, rigid, too proud to ask for help, unwilling to cooperate, and clinging desperately to unworkable ideas or actions. Your goal is to increase their self-confidence so that they feel secure enough to ask for help as soon as they need it.

1. If such employees refuse to get help, they may fear that revealing they need help will jeopardize their jobs.

2. When they ask for help, be supportive and also start teaching them how to figure it out for themselves. For example, ask them to give you at least one solution to the problem. Then, talk about how it would work and what other solutions are possible. Ask them to choose one and then talk about the likely outcomes.

3. If such employees are sticklers for detail, tense, or boxed in by procedure, your goal is to get them to relax and to ease the tension in the office.

4. Try to find out why they're so attached to detail. What's the underlying problem? Can you work out a solution together?

5. Use tactful humor to put things in perspective and to show the light side of the situation.

6. If they stubbornly cling to a poor procedure or idea, your goal is to get them to see the various outcomes of alternate procedures or ideas. Focus on how they can be more successful. Be supportive.

7. Sometimes employees who stubbornly believe their idea will work need help in learning how to analyze and evaluate a proposal. Maintain their enthusiasm, but keep them from jumping into action too soon.

Withdrawn, Uncommunicative Employees

Your employees may act out passive behavior by being withdrawn and uncommunicative. They may do this because they're just-getting-by while putting on a pleasant face.

They may do it because they're worried. Or they may do it because they have difficulty speaking up. Consider these tips:

➡ **Employees are withdrawn and uncommunicative.**
1. Check your management style. Be sure you're approachable and supportive.
2. Ask open-ended questions that get at what such employees are thinking and feeling. Often, withdrawal signals unexpressed hurt or worry.
3. Be still and wait for them to reply. Don't feel compelled to fill the empty space.
4. Listen between the lines—to what isn't said as well as what is. Watch for nonverbal cues.

➡ **Employees are worried.**
1. Give them information that will help to alleviate their concerns.
2. Can you share more information about future plans?
3. Can you be more specific about how changes are likely to affect them?

➡ **Employees lack confidence or verbal ability to express themselves.**
Your goal is to create a space in which they feel comfortable talking to you and to others.
1. Create a trusting relationship in one-on-one meetings. Suggest ways they can speak up and express themselves—with you and at meetings with peers.
2. Provide for specific communication training, if possible, such as a public speaking course.
3. Ask them direct questions in their area of expertise—questions you know they can easily answer. Do this at first in private meetings, then in meetings with peers.
4. Assign them to work with a small team or committee where they can gain confidence in speaking up.

Other Difficult Situations With Employees

Difficult situations with employees sometimes don't fit precisely in the aggressive, passive-aggressive, or passive modes. These include situations in which employees assume you'll be a pushover, or where you must give performance criticism to a sensitive employee.

➡ **Employees assume you'll be a pushover because you're a woman.**
1. Get to know team members.
2. Think through the personalities and the requirements for optimal team performance.
3. Anticipate the general types of situations you're likely to encounter—situations that call for assertiveness—and various types of action you could take.
4. Decide where you'll draw the line in each type of situation. Stick to it, unless you discover valid reasons for changing your mind. Before changing

your mind, ask yourself if the switch is based on insecurity rather than flexibility.

5. Develop the right degree of firmness.

To be firm, women managers generally must develop a little toughness. This ability to dish it out and take it without complaining is expected of good leaders. Only you can decide the best place on the scale for you in dealing with your particular team members.

1	2	3	4	5	6	7	8	9	10
Soft				Firm, Fair Consistent					Hard

➡ **Employees' performance is not up to par, and they're very sensitive to criticism.**

1. If performance needs improvement, give the feedback in private—unless the team has worked out ways to handle this as a team.

2. Give feedback as soon as possible after the action occurs.

3. Focus on solving the problem and preventing similar problems in the future.

4. Tie desirable behavior to achieving the job goals or team goals the employee has set. Don't compare performances of team members.

5. Focus on the *actions*, not the attitudes or personality traits that led to the actions.

6. Be prepared to make suggestions or give guidance on how to improve performance.

Strategy #4

Manage Angry Customers

When you deal with an angry customer, your major challenge is to stay emotionally detached and positive—no matter what. You don't have to be abused, and you won't experience abuse if you don't take the attacks personally and stay emotionally above it all. The key is to remain professional. Use the following techniques:

1. Listen attentively to what's being said, including the verbal, nonverbal, and between-the-lines information.

2. Never argue. Agree in a mild way—in order to help defuse the customer's anger. *I can understand how you feel... I can imagine how upsetting this could be.*

3. If they exaggerate and distort the situation, simply repeat back what they've said: *You feel they were trying to destroy your home.*

4. Don't judge their feelings. They'll often see how ridiculous they sound, and even start seeing the humor. If so, you can gently laugh with them, not at them, and show empathy: *We all get upset over such things at times.*

Once upset customers have expressed their anger or frustration, they tend to calm down if they feel they've been heard and understood. That's when you can start negotiating a resolution to the problem, because now they can listen to you.

Strategy #5

Don't Forget the Office Party

Ah, yes. The office party. The main thing to remember about office parties—and other social events with a business connection—is that they're first and foremost business events. That means keeping in place most of the strategies you use for handling people situations, building credibility, and gaining personal power. Business socials are a little more festive and informal but not that different in bottom-line purpose.

They are *not* the place to let your hair down, drink until you're feeling no pain, have a ball, or otherwise let it all hang out. Confine those activities to parties with your close friends or other groups. While your work associates may enjoy your performance, you can be sure the decision-makers and their partners are observing all your actions. So whether it's a casual drink after work, the company picnic, or the Christmas party, keep your professional image intact by carefully monitoring your attire and your behavior—as well as that of your partner or escort. This approach will pay off in the long run.

Socializing with business associates from any and all levels—inside and outside the organization—can be extremely helpful for gaining useful information, cementing relationships, and making transactions more effective on the job. It's essential to some jobs and careers.

➡ **At business social functions.**
1. Don't become too personal or intimate.
2. Don't get involved unnecessarily in other people's battles.
3. Avoid engaging in vicious gossip—it often finds its way back to its victim.
4. Do engage in harmless gossip or small talk, which brings important information on the organization and its people.

➡ **With a male business associate, who pays the bill and opens doors?**
1. Focus on the fact that the two of you are friends and associates, not a dating couple.
2. Handle these issues the same way you handle them with women friends— and the same way two male business associates handle them.
3. The person who does the inviting pays the tab, you agree to go halves, or you agree to take turns.
4. The person who gets to the door first opens it for the other.

5. If one of you is struggling to get into or out of a coat or a car, the other helps out.

6. In general, treat each other as equals—with respect and consideration.

Strategy #6

Use 10 Win-Win Techniques

In addition to the many specific strategies and techniques that can help you manage difficult people situations, keep in mind these 10 general techniques that tend to produce win-win results.

1. Be alert and perceptive to political games. Note passive-aggressive tactics—without becoming unduly suspicious or cynical.

2. Read nonverbal messages and behavior patterns. The most astute leaders can pick up and understand people's nonverbal messages. In fact, by merely taking a walk through the office, they can pick up reams of information. This skill is especially valuable in dealing with difficult people situations. Few people are such accomplished actors that they can totally control their nonverbal behavior in order to hide their emotions and hidden agendas. Body language, facial expression, and voice tone will often give them away.

3. Look for the cause. The first step in devising strategies for difficult people situations is to look for the reasons behind a difficult person's actions. What's he or she trying to accomplish or avoid? Is it being done at a conscious or subconscious level? Subconscious games are more difficult to counter because the player probably won't understand a direct confrontation and would probably respond with denial or rationalization. Is it just an oversight or misunderstanding? Is the action a test of your spunk or savvy? Or is it the first skirmish in an all-out war to discredit or remove you?

The longer the game-players can keep you in the dark about their undermining activities, the better their chances of success. This means you must nip any war efforts in the bud without overreacting to mere tests, misunderstandings, or oversights. Figuring all this out is difficult for beginners and is a necessary part of gaining experience. Often you can get some cooperation if you ask the problem person directly to help you identify underlying problems.

4. Focus on win-win solutions. Work toward a solution you both can live with; one that respects everyone's rights. Find mutually agreeable ways to prevent similar problems from occurring in the future. Make your motto, *I respect myself and others.*

5. Be knowledgeable. If you're the target of political game-playing, arm yourself with knowledge and documentation. Begin by learning the basics—everything in the company manual and employee's handbook; company policies, strategies, procedures, goals, and rules; legal aspects of employee relations and company activities. You can limit a game-player's potential moves by knowing the score in these basic areas. Also, learn as much as you can about the unwritten rules, and keep in touch with day-to-day events. Keep lines of communication open with as many people as possible, and keep your antennae up at all times. Never make the mistake of thinking you have it made so you needn't pay attention to difficult people situations and power politics. You're never immune.

6. Stay goal-oriented. Stay focused on job goals, team goals, company goals—to keep from getting sidetracked with overemotional, ego-protecting responses.

7. Document transactions. Follow up all important or questionable transactions with written memos to the appropriate persons, with copies to key people. Keep your own copies on file where you can find them easily if you need them. They can be invaluable in backing up your case when you need to confront a player's game. Document your achievements also.

8. Use your support network. To succeed in derailing you, people operating in difficult modes must usually have your cooperation. You're most vulnerable if you're an isolated victim. Therefore, a key to turning the situation around is to use your power network. To maintain your network, ask for supportive action selectively, where it will do the most good, then look for opportunities to repay the favor.

9. Don't take it personally. This is probably the most difficult, and most important, key to dealing with difficult people situations. With experience and hindsight, you'll find it easier to realize that when people are in a difficult mode, they'll create the same difficulties for anyone in your position. It has nothing to do with you as a person—in fact, when game-playing is involved, the players normally don't really know you. They don't bother to get to know people on an authentic, personal basis, but only on a manipulative basis. Their main motive for learning about you is to discover how to pull your strings. So don't assume there's something wrong with you, become defensive, or rise to their bait. Keep your counsel and decide on your own game plan.

10. Stay in command of your inner resources. This ability goes hand in hand with not taking attacks personally. Together, they furnish the power you need to transcend difficult people situations. Remember the process for commanding your inner resources: relax, envision positive results, and let go. This process allows you:

▶ To maintain a relaxed focus on your goals so that you can intuitively pick up verbal and nonverbal clues to people's intentions.

▶ To put games in perspective and not take threats personally.

▶ To respond in a relaxed but effective manner.

Your key strategy, then, is to maintain your poise and self-confidence by commanding these inner resources.

Skill Builders

Skill Builder #1: Practice Looking Inward in Difficult People Situations

Purpose: To help you turn difficult people situations into tools for your personal awareness and growth.

Instructions: Briefly describe a difficult people situation in which you're not asserting yourself effectively (you're communicating in a passive, passive-aggressive, or aggressive mode).

Phase I. For this situation, complete the five incomplete statements below, using the following five related questions as guidelines:

1. What are all the things you want to happen in this situation? *I want....*
2. What are all the feelings you have about this situation? *I feel....*
3. What are all the things you want the other(s) to do in this situation? *She/he/they should....*
4. What do you need to feel okay? *In order to feel okay in this situation, I need....*
5. What are you not willing to do in this situation? *I'm not willing to....*

Phase II. Complete the same five statements a second time, using the guidelines below. Be open to insights:

1. Look at what you want from another perspective. Is it attainable? Is this what you *really* want? *I want....*
2. Look again at your feelings. Do you only and always feel this way about this type of situation? What are your feelings toward yourself in this situation? *I feel....*
3. What should *you* do in this situation? *I should....*
4. What do *you* need to do in order to feel okay? *I need to....*
5. What are you *willing* to do, at least sometimes? Is there anything you're ever willing to do—sometimes? *I'm willing to....*

Follow-up: See the answer key on page 300 for further insight.

Based on Byron Katie's *The Work*, P.O. Box 2205, Barstow, CA 92312.

Skill Builder #2: Minicases—Difficult People Situations

Minicase A: Manager Ben and Coworker Faye

Faye, your coworker, has been with the company for about five years. You were hired about a year ago. You and Faye have had a good working relationship until recently. Ben, the manager, has been giving you increased responsibilities recently—you're handling many client accounts almost by yourself, just getting his approval on major matters. You sense that this fact might have something to do with the tension you feel between you and Faye. You also sense that Faye has been complaining about you to Ben, although you have no clue as to what the complaints are.

Yesterday afternoon, when Ben's assistant manager, Frank, went into Ben's office, Ben closed the door. Later you heard Ben speaking loudly: *Don't give her any more stuff to do! She's trying to take over!* When Frank came out, you sensed that his attitude toward you was strange and distant. A little later, Ben came out and handed you two large files representing new clients' work to be done. He didn't give you any specific instructions; he just handed them to you, and you took them.

This morning, you woke up puzzled. You're asking yourself, *What's going on here? Why did Ben give me all this added work and responsibility without comment? Is he testing me to see if I'm trying to take over? What does all this mean?* Answer the following questions:

➡ What modes of behavior may be represented here?

➡ What questions should you pursue to learn more about what's going on?

➡ What actions should you take next?

Minicase B: Peer John

At a team meeting you speak up, expressing your concern about adopting a fair process for reaching a team decision. John, a team member, says, *I think the process I have proposed is just fine.* Turning to you, he says, *When you were chair of the hiring committee three years ago, you didn't ask for the team's input at all!*

You're shocked. You feel John is misrepresenting and oversimplifying a very complex situation, one that is past history anyway. Consider the following questions.

➡ What modes of behavior may be represented here?

➡ What actions should you take next?

Minicase C: Employee Beth

At team meetings that you facilitate, Beth rarely contributes. However, she often carries on side conversations with one or another of the team members. She has become very slick and adept at this. By the time you sense a distraction and look her way, she has clammed up. After a recent meeting at the end of a long day, you decide you must speak with Beth first thing tomorrow about this recurring situation. However, the next day she is absent and you get busy with other issues and still don't have that talk. In addition, at the next team meeting, Beth gives her total attention to the process, but still doesn't speak up or contribute. Now you're in the midst of a follow-up team meeting, and Beth's old behavior is back.

➡ What modes of behavior may be represented here?

➡ What questions should you pursue in order to learn more about what's going on?

➡ What actions should you take next?

Follow-up: Compare your responses with those in the answer key on page 301.

Skill Builder #3: Setting Your Own Boundaries and Connections

Purpose: To protect yourself from negative energy and input from others; to establish relationships at varying depths and levels in ways that maintain your personal integrity and individuality; to avoid domination by others, including any and all males in your life.

Creating a boundary. Close your eyes, begin breathing deeply, and relax. Picture yourself surrounded by your energy field: a large oval that radiates out from you. Get in touch with the edge of this oval-shaped field. Create an imaginary boundary around the outside edge, perhaps giving the boundary a color, such as deep blue. Imagine a stream of bright white light coming in through an opening in the crown area of your head, filling up your body, emanating from your body, and filling up your energy field right out to its blue edge. Think of this field as your personal space. This bubble of pure white light provides a buffer from others' contracting thoughts and feelings. You can choose to let in or radiate out expansive thoughts and feelings, but you are protected from the domination, manipulation, and whims of others, whether thoughtless or calculating.

Sensing your energy centers. Imagine seven major energy centers within your body and the issues traditionally connected with each.

1. *Base of the spine*—the center of survival and physical safety issues.
2. *Abdomen area*—sexuality and money issues; power and control in the material world.
3. *Stomach area*—the center of personal power issues and related fears; survival intuition.
4. *Heart area*—center of love; creating from the heart and following your heart's desire.
5. *Throat area*—personal expression, communication, and willpower issues.
6. *Third-eye area*—intuitive/psychic skills, higher reasoning, and use of knowledge.
7. *Crown area at top of head*—life purpose and meaning; spiritual connection.

Establishing connections. Imagine a person you're building a relationship with. See the other's energy field with a boundary similar to yours and the seven energy centers. Don't merge energy fields! Maintain your individuality and the integrity of your personal space. Decide the level of connection you need and want with this person. Is it strictly a survival connection at level one? Or a money connection at level two? Is this person a soul mate and you want to connect at all levels? Imagine a strong silver cord running from your energy center to the matching energy center of the other person. Feel yourself bonded and connected to the other at this level. Repeat for other levels as appropriate. If you get the other person, such as an intimate friend, to participate in this process, you'll dramatically boost the power connection.

Answer Key

Skill Builder #1: Practice Looking Inward in Difficult People Situations
Insights from Phase II.

Question 2: Through the answer, did you realize that you really felt toward yourself the feelings mentioned in Phase I? For example, you're really angry at yourself for putting yourself up to this! If so, that's the *taking responsibility* point for cocreating situations.

Question 4: To be okay, that part of you that's reflected in the statement needs to do what the statement says. Bottom line: Did you get that you're okay, regardless of what situation you're in? Nothing can make you not okay.

Question 5: Does your answer reveal that you're being rigid? Or that you're viewing the situation from a narrow perspective? What would happen if you were a little more flexible?

Any situation that we view as caused by a *difficult person* reflects our own beliefs and attitudes, thoughts and feelings, decisions and choices. It always reflects something about our own rigidity and narrowness in viewing the situation. Such situations are great opportunities to extend your personal growth process.

Skill Builder #2: Minicases—Difficult People Situations

Manager Ben and coworker Faye: Both Ben and Faye are engaging in passive-aggressive behavior that's deceitful, manipulative, blaming, and backbiting. See suggestions in this chapter for dealing with these types of situations. In addition, ask for a meeting with Ben and Faye. Use feedback assertion to describe what you've experienced. Ask them what they believe is going on, what problems they perceive, and possible solutions.

John: His action mode appears to be aggressive, specifically, belligerent, arrogant, and rude. Speak up and express your thinking that John is bringing up an old situation that's irrelevant to the current issue, that you don't wish to get embroiled in rehashing past events, and that you would like to focus on dealing with the current decision-making process.

Beth: Her action mode is passive-aggressive or passive. You need more information to determine whether her goal is to make trouble, manipulate, or simply withhold feedback and participation—and why. Meet with Beth. Ask what she thinks and feels about the team meetings and the team process. Consider using feedback assertion to express what you experience in the meetings, and then ask for resolution.

Index